Dead Letters Sent

Dead Letters Sent

Queer Literary Transmission

Kevin Ohi

University of Minnesota Press

Minneapolis | London

The University of Minnesota Press gratefully acknowledges financial assistance for the publication of this book from Boston College.

Portions of chapter 2 were previously published as "Forgetting *The Tempest*," in *Shakesqueer: A Queer Companion to the Complete Works of Shakespeare*, ed. Madhavi Menon (Durham, N.C.: Duke University Press, 2011), 351–60. Portions of chapter 4 were previously published as "The Queer Atavisms of Hippolytus," *Pater Newsletter* 58 (Spring 2008): 13–22; reprinted courtesy of *Pater Newsletter*. Chapter 6 was previously published as "Erotic Bafflement and the Lesson of Oscar Wilde," *Genre: Forms of Discourse and Culture* 35 (Summer 2002): 309–30. Chapter 8 was previously published as "The Beast's Storied End," *Henry James Review* 33, no. 1 (Winter 2012): 1–16; copyright 2012 The Johns Hopkins University Press. Portions of chapter 9 were previously published as "'My Spirit's Posthumeity' and the Sleeper's Outflung Hand: Queer Transmissions in *Absalom, Absalom!*," in *Queer Times, Queer Belongings*, ed. E. L. McCallum and Mikko Tuhkanen (Buffalo: SUNY Press, 2011), 205–32; copyright 2011 SUNY Press.

Copyright 2015 by the Regents of the University of Minnesota

Published by the University of Minnesota Press
111 Third Avenue South, Suite 290
Minneapolis, MN 55401-2520
http://www.upress.umn.edu

Library of Congress Cataloging-in-Publication Data
Ohi, Kevin.
Dead letters sent : queer literary transmission / Kevin Ohi.
Includes bibliographical references and index.
    ISBN 978-0-8166-9477-8 (hc)
    ISBN 978-0-8166-9478-5 (pb)
1. Homosexuality and literature. 2. English literature—History and criticism. 3. English literature—19th century—History and criticism 4. American literature—19th century—History and criticism. 5. American literature—20th century—History and criticism. 6. Transmission of texts. 7. Influence (Literary, artistic, etc.) 8. Literature—History and criticism—Theory, etc. 9. Queer theory. I. Title.
    PR408.H65O38   2015
    820.9'353—dc23   2015002779

Printed in the United States of America on acid-free paper

The University of Minnesota is an equal-opportunity educator and employer.

20 19 18 17 16 15   10 9 8 7 6 5 4 3 2 1

For my father

I wake and feel the fell of dark, not day.
What hours, O what black hours we have spent
This night! what sights you, heart, saw; ways you went!
And more must, in yet longer light's delay.

With witness I speak this. But where I say
Hours I mean years, mean life. And my lament
Is cries countless, cries like dead letters sent
To dearest him that lives alas! away

—GERARD MANLEY HOPKINS

Contents

Introduction

. . . viersified and piersified may the treeth we tale of live in stoney.
Here line the refrains of.

—James Joyce, *Finnegans Wake*

Dead Letters Sent: Queer Literary Transmission explores the queerness of
"transmission," understood broadly: the conveying of knowledge in pedagogy, the transmission and material preservation of texts, the maintaining
of a tradition of knowledge about those texts, and even the impalpable
communication between text and reader. "Queer transmission," then,
can be understood in at least two ways: First, it can be understood as the
transmission (in all these senses) of a minority queer culture, of the modes
through which queer forms of life and specialized knowledges move from
generation to generation. How is such knowledge passed on in a world that
is, to say the least, inhospitable to queer forms of life? How do texts encode
queer meaning in contexts that often forbid explicit mention of queer concerns (or that cast them as trivial or unworthy of sustained attention), for
example, or, from the other side, what is entailed in "recognizing" one's
desires in a literary text or an often inexplicit or elusive queer "intention"
in the work of art? Second, "queer transmission" can be understood to ask,
more generally, what is queer about the transmission of literary and cultural knowledge, and what conclusions might be drawn about the effects
of that queerness on the literary "objects" conveyed.

Recurrently, literary texts concerned with tradition and the transmission of knowledge turn not to preservation but to loss, to scenarios
of thwarted transmission: writings lost or of equivocal provenance, texts
reduced to fragments or adulterated in translation, historical contexts lost
to posterity, tantalizing details left unrecorded by unobservant contemporaries, critical receptions of seminal texts inalterably shaped by charis-
matic misreadings, and pedagogical relations thwarted by incompetent or
too interested teachers or by dull or otherwise distracted students. *Dead
Letters Sent* begins with the intuition that such scenarios allow texts to

explore the modalities of "queer transmission," thereby addressing, sometimes obliquely, the communication of sexual desire and the secrets of minority sexual cultures, and meditating, often profoundly, on what constitutes literary knowledge. The thwarting of reproduction, not surprisingly, offers a way to figure the transmission of queer knowledge; the opposition between "literal" reproduction (giving birth to babies) and a more impalpable form of it (creating knowledge and texts, idea-babies) goes back at least to Plato's *Symposium,* where idea-babies and the male intergenerational eros that forms them are foundational to both philosophy and the city-state. But to understand imaginings of thwarted transmission as thematizations of queer transmission is perhaps most consequential when the latter is taken in its more general sense; thus, such scenes of interrupted transmission are, for these writers, far from exceptional events in the history of literature and far from mere regrettable accidents to which any artifact of human cognition is subject insofar as its preservation depends on the contingences of its material existence—for without the book, "poor earthly casket of immortal verse,"[1] there can be no immortality for the verse. Rather, such scenes raise the question of what constitutes literary knowledge, and whether it can properly be said to be an "object" to be transmitted, preserved, or, on the contrary, lost. Such texts suggest that imaginings of thwarted transmission figure the literary tradition as such.

The recurrent imaginings of lost knowledge that structure the chapters that follow replay the fate of what is perhaps the origin of the modern idea of tradition in the West: the Library of Alexandria, "an institution," Daniel Heller-Roazen suggests, "in which the conservation and the destruction of tradition can hardly be told apart, an archive that, in a vertiginous movement of self-abolition, threatens to coincide entirely with its own destruction."[2] Noting that it is largely to the Library of Alexandria that we owe the formulation of the "principles and practices of the first textual criticism in the West"—so that "the history of the Alexandrian Museum may well be regarded as the history of the development of classical scholarship as such" (136, 137)—Heller-Roazen examines the persistent myth of the library's destruction, of the famous fire that may have never occurred. That myth of destruction, he suggests, is made necessary by the library's ambition to collect everything, "to constitute an archive in which the totality of literary works would be meticulously ordered and secured" (141). Noting the forms of truncation and dismemberment that of necessity follow from the consigning of a text to a catalog or table, as well as the contingent effects of forgery and falsification to which the overweening ambition of the library gave rise (not only because it provided motivation for forgery, but also because the mechanism of preservation—copying—made falsification or distortion possible), he traces a more fundamental betrayal structural to the imagining of tradition as a totality, a ruin to which texts are consigned from the moment one seeks to preserve them. This paradoxical betrayal is made visible by the legendary fire: "In the history of the Alexandrian Library, every break with the past, every rupture in the transmission of texts, anticipates the final catastrophe of tradition that already in the ancient world invariably accompanied any account of the Ptolemaic institution: the fire that, in one stroke, consumed the monument to classical learning" (147–48). That the event of the fire, too, may be a falsification points to the central place of this myth of destruction in the imagining of tradition:

> One might be tempted to suggest that, had there not been a fire to consume the Library, one would have had to be invented: What fate, after all, could await the universal archive other than its destruction? Real or imagined, the conflagration remains the supreme emblem of the Alexandrian archive itself, which sheltered the works of the past in exposing them to disaster, constituting and conserving its history in threatening it with its own destruction. For the very life of the Library, like that of the fire, was to nourish itself on what it consumed, to allow writing to live in outliving itself, bearing witness, in this way, to the catastrophe of the past in the present, the destruction of a tradition grown as "totally, eternally transient" as nature itself. (150–51)[3]

The chapters that follow all begin with versions of this conflagration, with ostensible failures of transmission that are central to each text's imagining of tradition and of a paradoxical form of preservation: the curious drama of uncertain transmission in Plato's *Symposium* that seems to unsettle the dialogue's philosophical conclusions; forgetting as a recurrent concern in Shakespeare's *The Tempest*, where it shapes the play's paradoxical figuring of enchantment and absorption, and its imagined relation to precursor poets, particularly Ovid and Virgil; the reduction to tantalizing fragments of Sappho's poetic corpus, particularly as it appears in the work of later poets such as Algernon Charles Swinburne and Anne Carson; the disappearance of pre-Attic cultural life and religious forms of observance, irrecoverable (but absorbed, also therefore ineradicable) after the ascendency of Athens, as it is allegorized by Walter Pater's retelling of the story of Hippolytus in a play by Euripides (and, indirectly, in the writing of Ovid, Seneca, and Racine), the surviving play itself a revision of an earlier Euripidean text, now lost, which gives Pater's imaginary portrait its name; the oblivion of the self and its history that paradoxically grounds Pater's understanding of aesthetic *Bildung*; the ostensible failure in Oscar Wilde's "The Portrait of Mr. W.H." to discover the historical referent for the dedicatee of Shakespeare's sonnets; the baffled and baffling pedagogy of Wilde's prison letter, commonly called *De Profundis,* where a lover chastises his beloved for failing to learn an impossible lesson; the recurrent concern with thwarted pedagogy and lost aesthetic objects in Henry James's fiction, which, while often concerned with realization and shifts of consciousness, also resolutely refuses to represent anyone learning anything; the curious falling-short of belated enlightenment in James's *The Beast in the Jungle,* which later comes to mark queer theory with its forms of exorbitant address; the failure to remember the vanished past in William Faulkner's *Absalom, Absalom!,* which becomes the paradoxical index of that past's refusal ever to pass away; and the various forms of thwarted transmission in Faulkner's *Go Down, Moses,* which, leaving lessons unlearned and unlearnable, also thematizes a central illegitimacy (ultimately tied to invasion of personal relations by property in slavery) that disrupts paternal naming and the inheritance of property. Across the wide divergences of style and theme in these texts, in each case, thwarted transmission is both a locus of queer eroticism and a way of rethinking literary and cultural transmission.

Queer Theory and Literary Tradition

Dead Letters Sent seeks to read the structure of moments when "the conservation and the destruction of tradition can hardly be told apart" (Heller-Roazen, "Tradition," 133) in relation to queer tradition: the transmission of queer tradition, I suggested, and the queerness of literary transmission. The question of queer tradition—in its general and specialized senses, and in the relation between the two—has been a central, if not always explicitly remarked, question in queer theory from its inception. In a famous passage in *Epistemology of the Closet,* Eve Kosofsky Sedgwick commented on the anomalous place of homosexuality in 1980s debates about the literary canon.[4] Noting that the ostensible options—adding minority figures to "the" canon (including Mary Shelley, Felicia Hemans, Harriet Jacobs, or Olaudah Equiano in *The Norton Anthology,* for instance) or pluralizing it (teaching a white male canon, a women's canon, a Latino/a canon, a canon of slave narratives)—were incoherent when it came to gay writers, she pointed not only to the notable presence of gay people in "the" Western canon, but also to the different principle of exclusion operating in the case of homosexual desire. Adapting Saul Bellow's inflammatory question challenging multiculturalism (Who is the Tolstoy of the Zulus? The Proust of the Papuans?)[5] to ask it of gay writers—"Has there ever been a gay Socrates? Has there ever been a gay Shakespeare? Has there ever been a gay Proust"—Sedgwick famously retorted, "Does the Pope wear a dress?" (*Epistemology of the Closet,* 52). The "gay canon" is difficult to distinguish from "the" canon, to which there can also be no question of "adding" writers (especially male writers) who experienced same-sex desire (many were never excluded); at issue is less the constitution of the canon than its legibility, and the unstable relation of identity categories to assessments of literary value. Unlike race and gender—both ideologically structured by the presumption (however delusory in reality) of self-evidence—sexuality explicitly raises questions of interpretation: of a deceit that is not the exception but the rule, of the ways that ostensibly neutral onlookers are implicated in the interpretation of desire, of a fundamentally uncertain relation between signs and their meanings, of the obscure relation between desired and desiring bodies and the forms of meaning that animate them.

For Sedgwick, this uncertainty structures homophobia in the nineteenth and twentieth centuries: homophobia is a mode of social control because, in this society in which same-sex bonds (especially between men) are both demanded (for access to male privilege) and forbidden, the opacity of one's own desire (above all to oneself) is both inevitable and intolerable.[6] "Homosexual panic," in her account of it, traffics in the necessity of interpreting sexual signs even as it forbids acknowledging the uncertainty that makes interpretation necessary. "Male entitlement" demands bonds between men that must *seem* but must not *be* gay; homophobia mandates an equivocal signification that it then renders pathological. One must know one's desire, and one cannot know it; homophobia is a fundamentally paranoid structure—such that much of Sedgwick's late work seeks to escape the manifold cognitive rewards of paranoia.[7] On one level, Sedgwick's response to Bellow is deceptively simple: the exclusion of gay (male) desire from "the" canon is a function not of any omission of the contributions to culture by those who experienced same-sex (again, especially male same-sex) desire, but of a failure to perceive the desire. I take her point also to be, however, that to speak of a gay canon may be misguided because it presumes a transparent relation between felt desires (themselves hardly transparent) and literary production. Surely the point is also that the pope does not, of course, wear a dress, and that the snappy rhetorical question (which, like all rhetorical questions, by definition does not wait for an answer) to a certain extent relies on homophobic presumption for the perlocutionary effects of its asserted obviousness. (We accede to the knowingness to the degree that we join in the assumption that nothing could be more ludicrous than a man in a dress, even as the riposte trades on another kind of knowingness: the puncturing of papal authority also reaffirms it insofar as any citation of the phrase assigns to another—valorized, but valorized as more authentic because ignorant—the mistaking of papal vestments for "a dress.") Sedgwick, perhaps more than any other critic, taught us to read such effects in the realm of sexuality, and also taught us to suspect knowingness and claims of transparent meaning around sex. The presumption of homosexual legibility is—as Sedgwick and Lee Edelman, among others, have conclusively shown—structural to homophobia.[8] The question of queer desire's relation to the literary canon raises all the intractable conundrums of the closet itself.

That is also to say that the ostensibly special-interest questions of homosexual desire in considerations of literary tradition raise much larger ones of interpretation "in general," just as general questions of literary transmission and categorization are not separable from ostensibly narrower ones of sexuality and homophobia. Indeed, the two aspects of "transmission" in this book follow a structuring opposition of Sedgwick's *Epistemology of the Closet*: between "minoritizing" and "universalizing" conceptions of sexual identity. It should not be surprising that the analyses here cannot pretend to resolve the contradictions that for Sedgwick made the incoherence of sexual identity central to structures of knowing from the Victorian period on. Sedgwick's discussion of canon formation turns from the pope to Allan Bloom—to Bloom's claims about the power of the closet (or sexual repression more generally) to energize writing, claims that Sedgwick can neither embrace nor fully discount.[9] To embrace them would risk endorsing a romanticized (or at least complacent) view of homophobia, yet what most energizes Sedgwick's own readings is the conflicted, highly ambivalent relation of the texts she addresses to same-sex desire. And—most explicitly in the chapter on James in *Epistemology of the Closet*—she registers the critic's (and in this case, her own) vested interest in the spectacle of the closet as a fund of secrets and as fuel for interpretive acuity. Her discussion of Bloom, notably, turns to pedagogy; she credits Bloom (as she encountered him at Cornell of the late 1960s) with teaching her a practice of reading that highlighted ways that canonical texts are at odds with themselves but that, learned, also made evident the limitations of his animadversions on sexual liberation at this moment in his *Closing of the American Mind*. Sedgwick's own writing is not just concerned—throughout her career— with questions of pedagogy; it is also more or less explicitly pedagogical, and its influence on queer readers (and not just them) has extended far beyond her particular claims (engendering even in those who never studied with her personally recognizable aspects of a style of writing and thinking).[10] I try to address something of that influence in chapter 8, on James's *The Beast in the Jungle*.

Like my previous books, *Dead Letters Sent* invokes the term *queer* in contexts that are often removed from the specificity of gay desire. As I wrote in *Henry James and the Queerness of Style,* the word *queer* appeals to me because it embodies an unresolved tension between sexual specificity and a possibly desexualizing abstraction, "retaining its sexual resonance even at the farthest remove from specific sexual thematics and abstracting specific sexual practices so that they, in turn, resonate with linguistic and conceptual categories (ostensibly) far removed from sex."[11] For this book, *queer* also resonates because it has come to signal—at least for queer theoretical discourse—an anarchic troubling of heteronormative lines of cultural transmission, and because it indicates, paradoxically, a tradition of such troubling. Thus, while the center of gravity in *Dead Letters Sent* is a sometimes abstracted version of queerness—one that tends toward the more generalized version of queer transmission—it is worth registering that the book's arguments also intersect a wide range of work in contemporary queer studies that could be reframed in relation to transmission.[12] Edelman's diagnosis of "reproductive futurism" offers a bracing contemporary polemic against heteronormative transmission; considering how precursor texts imagine alternatives to reproductive futurism is part of what led me to consider queer transmission by making me wonder if one necessarily had to think of literary culture on the model of reproduction.[13] The effort by Heather Love and others to think about "bad affect" in queer texts, to use affect theory to ask about the consequences for queer history and politics of a triumphalist editing out of the pain of queer be-coming and of queer existence, is also a reconsideration of how queer lives are remembered and how sexuality affects the movement of knowledge through history. D. A. Miller's writing about the Broadway musical, which traces, among other things, the survival of unassimilated forms of am-bivalence in personal identities as in wider cultures, explores, often very movingly, both the curious forms of atavism through which contemporary identities harken back to painful eras of personal and social history and the sometimes excruciating asynchronicity of sociohistorical change and personal itineraries of development.[14] As a consideration of the relation of queer identity to particular aesthetic forms, it is also one of the most profound examinations of the difficulties—some specific to the history of homophobia—of making a shared experience of exclusion the basis for affiliation and belonging and the ground for constructing transmissible forms of culture: its consideration of an aesthetic enthusiasm where stig-matizing isolation is inseparable from an exorbitant desire for commu-nity retells the story of mid-twentieth-century gay life while also evok-ing a more generalizable experience of rapture. Riveted to and riven by one's isolation in such moments, one also wants to share it.[15] Leo Bersani's ongoing effort to formulate new forms of relating to the world grounded neither in a reification of difference nor in an anthropomorphic appropria-tion of the world often centers on the constitution of an "aesthetic subject" that is a product of the equivocal commerce between minds and works of art. The argument here also intersects other work in queer studies: the re-cent writing, particularly by lesbian theorists, about "queer time";[16] Lauren Berlant's "cruel optimism" and Judith Halberstam's "queer art of failure";[17] Kathryn Bond Stockton's queer child; the detailed work of critics such as Michael Moon and George Chauncey (among many others) in recovering queer culture and queer history; and the "literary turn" in queer studies, including not just Miller's writing on Jane Austen but also the writing by a number of other critics seeking to think about literary form in the context of queer studies. This book, in other terms, is part of a recent tradition of queer theoretical writing.[18]

For all that this book would scarcely have been possible without queer theory, however, it is one of the luxuries of my belatedness to begin from coordinates that are invested in but in an oblique relation to the assump-tions and procedures of queer theory, and to the current preoccupations of queer studies. In chapter 10, I argue that the queerness of Faulkner's prose consists in part in its unresolved, unhierarchized superimposition of multiple systems of meaning—race, sexuality, class, and ecology, but also history, ideology, narrative, and personal development. That superimposition is enacted by the prose itself, by Faulkner's syntax; and I suggest that it is insofar as they can leave the relations among multiple systems thus unresolved that literary texts—and, therefore, if attentively done, close readings of them—have the potential to exceed "theoretical" texts whose arguments cannot easily afford to leave such relations unarticulated. I further note that the ideal of such literary reading is one I learned from reading queer theory, and Sedgwick's work in particular.[19] The implicit question is again one of transmission: of whether queer theory can comprise its outside, can become literary reading, while remaining queer. For the remainder of the introduction, I will try to indicate the general shape of a genealogy for this book's critical method and its mode of reading. In so doing, I depart in crucial ways from the critical methodologies (and shared canon) of queer theory, but I also hope thereby to spell out something of queer theory's exorbitant potential.

The Mortal Body and the Time of Art

Thus, to return to the question of canon formation, examining the relation of taxonomies of persons to taxonomies of literary works raises another kind of concern, related, even though obliquely, to the traces of homophobia in the determination of literary value and to the particular political effects of such judgments. In pondering the transmission of literary knowledge, the texts addressed here often confront the relation between "life" and "art"—both how the artist's life is registered in his or her work and how the encounter with art comes to mark the life of a reader or viewer. For better or worse, readings of texts focused on gay desire risk bracketing those far from simple questions in the often salutary spelling-out of our culture's cultivated obliviousness to—what Sedgwick called the "active incuriosity" about[20]—homosexual desire. When, year after year, one finds that most of the few students who encountered Shakespeare's sonnets in high school have been led to think that they were uniformly addressed to a woman, merely to draw up a list of gay writers—no matter how reductive such a designation must necessarily be—can seem important. For many of the writers in this study, however, the question of the relation of specific desires to writing is more complicated, posing the question, at once, of the sexual valence of art and of an author's relation to tradition—of what of the creator's life survives in the work of art, of what it means for an author for "writing to live on in outliving itself" (Heller-Roazen, "Tradition's Destruction," 151). For Wilde, Pater, James, Swinburne, Faulkner, and Carson, and for various readings of Sappho, Plato, and Shakespeare, to contemplate the writing of desire is also to contemplate the formation of a literary tradition.

Those questions are perhaps most sharply posed here by Swinburne's reading of Sappho and Wilde's reading of Shakespeare, and I dwell on their complexity for these writers in later chapters. For the moment, I turn briefly to a more unexpected context. One of the more moving meditations on the relation of the individual life to literary and cultural tradition is Samuel Johnson's preface to *A Dictionary of the English Language*.[21] His professed desire to stabilize the changing of language (or as he puts it, to halt or delay its "degeneration") is baffled, he finds, by the mutability of language and by human finitude. Formative of the sublunary imperfection of language as a human invention, that finitude appears not only in the "natural tendency to degeneration" of human tongues—"it remains that we retard what we cannot repel, that we palliate what we cannot cure" (109)—but as if symptomatically in curiously personal remarks, perhaps unexpected from the great neoclassical prose stylist. These come together at the end of the preface in one of the most beautiful paragraphs in the English language:[22]

> In this work, when it shall be found that much is omitted, let it not be forgotten that much likewise is performed; and though no book was ever spared out of tenderness to the author, and the world is little solicitous to know whence proceeded the faults of that which it condemns; yet it may gratify curiosity to inform it, that the *English Dictionary* was written with little assistance of the learned, and without any patronage of the great; not in the soft obscurities of retirement, or under the shelter of academick bowers, but amidst inconvenience and distraction, in sickness and in sorrow. It may repress the triumph of malignant criticism to observe that if our language is not here fully displayed, I have only failed in an attempt which no human powers have hitherto completed. If the lexicons of ancient tongues, now immutably fixed and comprised in a few volumes, are yet, after the toil of successive ages, inadequate and

delusive; if the aggregated knowledge, and co-operating diligence
of the Italian academicians did not secure them from the censure
of Beni; if the embodied criticks of France, when fifty years had
been spent upon their work, were obliged to change its oeconomy
and give their second edition another form, I may surely be con-
tented without the praise of perfection, which, if I could obtain, in
this gloom of solitude, what would it avail me? I have protracted
my work till most of those whom I wished to please, have sunk
into the grave, and success and miscarriage are empty sounds: I
therefore dismiss it with frigid tranquillity, having little to fear or
hope from censure or from praise. (111–13)

Even without registering that his statements preface a dictionary he had
single-handedly composed, it is startling to find the consummately articulate Johnson referring to any words as mere "empty sounds."[23] If this closing paragraph might be read to lament art's failure to console, the failure
of even so monumental an achievement to recompense Johnson for the
human losses of those years, more desolating, perhaps, is the failure of
such losses to register when seen from the *longue durée* of the history of
the language. For "empty sounds" appears once before in the preface to
evoke particular words that defy definition:

Other words there are, of which the sense is too subtle and eva-
nescent to be fixed in a paraphrase; such are all those which are by
grammarians termed *expletives,* and, in dead languages, are suffered to pass for empty sounds, of no other use than to fill a verse,
or to modulate a period, but which are easily perceived in living
tongues to have power and emphasis, though it be sometimes such
as no other form of expression can convey. (89)

"Success and miscarriage" are thus "empty sounds" not because—or not
only because—Johnson's personal losses make him unable to care about
the censure or praise of his contemporaries. His frigid tranquility comes
at the expense of the fading vitality of those cares themselves, the consigning of those personal losses to sounds that, once meaningful, now serve a
purely formal function, and *pain* and *sorrow,* like *joy,* come to signify only
insofar as they, like expressive words in a dead tongue, complete a meter
or affect the emphasis of a cadence. Johnson's complex meditation on the

ways that human finitude marks the structure of human language is also a reflection on the desolations that attend the vanishing of human presence in the immortality of language and art.

An Archeology of Reading and Voice: Erotic Equality, Tradition, and the Impersonal Aesthetic Subject

The equivocal commerce between the human and the art that immortalizes human strivings and desires is legible in the earliest experience of reading in the West, where that commerce is linked, also seemingly from the beginning, to eroticism. In his fascinating "anthropology" of reading in ancient Greece, Jesper Svenbro spells out the literal grounding of some of the tropes of reading that will persist for millennia.[24] Much of his anthropology turns on the fact that before about the middle of the fifth century BC, the Greeks read out loud; most, he suggests, would have been unable to understand written words without sounding them out. (He compares this habit of mind to musical notation as most nonmusicians experience it today: while some have the capacity to "hear" music seen printed, most of us need a realization of the score in order to hear it [18].) As a consequence, what look like figures of reading need to be taken literally; writing, which needs a voice to actualize it, does not figure or represent a prior speech act. It solicits one, and it is not until the advent of silent reading that writing figuratively "speaks."[25] That makes for what might be called (speaking anachronistically) a depersonalization of the first person; more precisely, it makes explicit the belated personalization of the first person. Writing does not express a self; in the beginning, *I* designates not a self but an object. Svenbro's investigation begins with the first written instances of the first person, on funerary inscriptions. Noting that there is no contradiction in the collating (in these inscriptions) of "ego-centric" or first-person pronouns with demonstrative ones (for example, of *I* with *that one*), he suggests that the *I* belongs, in the first place, to objects; the author is "systematically absent" (30), consigned to a third person. (Not until about 550 BC do these inscriptions refer to themselves in the third person, at which point the inscriptions themselves figure—instead of, or in addition to, soliciting—a voice and come to represent a speech act.)

> By denying the *egṓ* any psychological depth, one can understand why, when the earliest inscriptions were produced, the first-person

was chosen to refer to the object bearing the inscription. For as long as the inscription can be read, the object will be there. No one could lay greater claim than the object itself to the Hierheit of the written speech-act. Soon the writer would no longer be there; he became the third person by virtue of the fact that *he wrote.*

Verbs "denoting dedicating, setting up, making, and writing appear in these inscriptions" in the third person, he continues. The writer, on the other hand, is "that one":

> In relation to the object, present because it stands before a passerby (the reader, the addressee), the person who made it or inscribed it finds himself in a kind of "beyond," in an *ekeî* "over there" that stands in contrast to the *entháde* or *têide* "here" of the inscribed object. The way that the earliest inscriptions were devised thus presents us with a speech-act subject that, albeit without voice or inner life, has more claim than any other to the Hierheit of the first-person, that Hierheit that the demonstrative pronoun *tóde* may convey with no less deictic force. (42–43)

The speech act is "here," with the inscription; the writer is "over there," with the dead. The writer, he later notes, is "someone who has already disappeared" (156).

These early inscriptions do not transcribe a prior speech act, and they do not represent a voice. They are a voice, to the precise extent that they are read.[26] For Svenbro, writing becomes linked to questions of eroticism for the Greeks because of the implied power relation between reader and writer that that fact entails. If the inscription needs to be spoken in order to be read, that also means that the writer has the power to co-opt the very breath of the reader. One is led to think that the later tropes—as in Shakespeare's Sonnet 81, "Your monument shall be my gentle verse, / Which eyes not yet created shall o'er-read; / And tongues to be your being shall rehearse, / When all the breathers of this world are dead; / You still shall live, such virtue hath my pen, / Where breath most breathes, even in the mouths of men"[27]—have, at their origins, a literal referent.[28] Reading, in Svenbro's terms, becomes "an exercise of power" (47) as the reader becomes the "instrument" of the writer: "If he lends his voice to these mute signs, the text appropriates it: his voice becomes the voice of the written text. . . . He has lent his voice, relinquished it" (46).[29] Co-opting the reader's breath, the writer takes over his soul—in what Svenbro suggests is a reanimation even more than a reincarnation:

> What is reading? From the Greeks' point of view, it is the act in which the reader's vocal apparatus is controlled not by his own *psukhé* ["breath" or "soul," a term later translated into Latin as *anima*] (except in an intermediary fashion) but by the written inscription that he sees before him, so as to produce a particular sequence of sounds that will be intelligible to the ear. To be read is to take control of somebody else's vocal apparatus, to exercise power over the body of the reader, even from a distance, possibly a great distance both in space and in time. (142)

Svenbro points out that this power dynamic is analogous to Greek conceptualizations of sex—an analogy that the evidence of ancient graffiti suggests did not escape the Greeks themselves.[30] Svenbro writes:

> To put it in schematic terms, to write is to behave as an *erastés*; to read is to behave as an *erómenos,* either *kalós* or *katapúgōn* as the case may be.[31] To write is to be dominant, active, triumphant, as long as one finds a reader prepared to be amenable. To read is to submit to what the writer has written, to be dominated, to occupy the position of the one overcome, to submit to the metaphorical *erastés* in the person of the writer. . . . Although writing is honorable, reading may present problems, for it is perceived as servitude and as "passivity" (the one who submits to the writing is "passive"). . . . [At the same time,] only the metaphorical *erómenos,* who is the reader, can ensure the success of the writing. The ambiguity of the reader, who is at once necessary and inferior (or servile, in relation to the writer who makes use of him), is similar to the ambiguity of the *erómenos.*" (192–93)

Reading is potentially problematic, therefore, just as pederasty was. Pederasty—in Svenbro's (or his translator's) unfortunate phrase, "a 'sore point' for Greek society" (187)—was the mechanism of education and hence was crucial to the functioning of the state;[32] it was, however (or therefore), problematic both for the boys who were the objects of desire and for the state they would someday lead.

Svenbro here takes up Michel Foucault's account of the "antinomy of the boy" in Greek erotics. While the beautiful boy was valorized as an object of pleasure, he could not himself "identify" with his place as an object of pleasure. According to Foucault, what was problematic for the Greeks was not same-sex eroticism but the submission to another's pleasure:

> Sexual relations—always conceived in terms of the model act of penetration, assuming a polarity that opposed activity and passivity—were seen as being of the same type as the relationship between a superior and his subordinate, an individual who dominates and one who is dominated, one who commands and one who complies, one who vanquishes and one who is vanquished. Pleasure practices were conceptualized using the same categories as those in the field of social rivalries and hierarchies: an analogous agonistic structure, analogous oppositions and differentiations, analogous values attributed to the respective roles of the partners. And this suggests that in sexual behavior there was one role that was intrinsically honorable and valorized without question: the one that consisted in being active, in dominating, in penetrating, in asserting one's superiority.[33]

In such a system, Foucault notes, the "position of the (freeborn) boy was difficult" (216). The difficulty for him was being an object of desire who would one day be a free citizen, expected to exercise power rather than submit to it. This difficulty frames for Foucault the startling innovation of Plato's *Phaedrus* and *Symposium*: by recasting the question of the boy's honor as a shared search for truth, these dialogues make conceivable what otherwise would be inconceivable, a sexual relation of reciprocity.[34] For Svenbro, this innovation extends to the relation of reading: the *Phaedrus* turns an erotic relation of domination and objectification into a reciprocal relation between subjects. The palinode of Socrates, in other words, counters two forms of coerced speaking (Phaedrus's recitation of Lysias's speech, and Socrates's first speech, under the compulsion of Phaedrus) to offer, in their place, an instance of free, uncoerced speech. The palinode, Svenbro writes, produces:

[an] extraordinary transformation of the relationship between the
erastés and the *erómenos.* . . . This transformation of the loving relationship into a "Platonic love"—involving no penetration—implies
the possibility of a similar transformation of the relationship
between writer/reader and speaker/listener, in the sense that both
these relationships are, as in the *Phaedrus,* invested by pederastic
values. What the central section of the *Phaedrus* renders possible is
a new way of thinking about writing and rhetoric. (210–11)[35]

"One cannot take part in the search for truth if one is forced into the
role of an object," Svenbro writes; "to reach knowledge and declare the
truth, one must act as a subject" (205). The question therefore arises of
how to understand the subject thus constituted. In his elaboration of Foucault's reading of Plato, Bersani suggests that what makes reciprocal sexual relations possible is an "impersonal narcissism." Reading the Platonic
myth of the celestial chariot, Bersani argues that narcissism can become
a form of object love because it is circuited through a shared relation to a
god: the boy and his lover alike strive to become "more" themselves and
more like the god they once followed. Having charted the various ways
that psychoanalytic accounts of the subject spell out, with incontrovertible
rigor, the incompatibility of human desire with peaceful sociality, Bersani
finds in Plato's *Phaedrus* a nonpsychological individuation[36] (in his terms,
a shared "sameness") that offers a different account of love, beyond the
psychoanalytic subject.[37] (Much of Bersani's writing is, of course, devoted
to the ethical potential of this "aesthetic subject.")[38] In this impersonal narcissism, lover and beloved seek to attain to a potentialization of identity.

Carson's *Eros the Bittersweet* suggests that we might link these various
strands to questions of literary transmission—links that are, albeit sometimes implicitly, likewise addressed by the texts I read in later chapters.
The experience of desire forces us to confront a contradiction between
an atemporal form (desire as a search for truth, for example) and a temporality of human experience—a contradiction between, in other terms,
the time of "life" and the time of the text. In a beautiful reading of a fragment by Sophocles that compares desire to holding ice in one's hands, she
writes, "Time is the condition of delightfulness and of perishing both.
Time brings the nature of ice into fatal conjuncture with human nature,
so that at a critical moment the crystal glamour of ice and the human sus-

ceptibility to novelty intersect. One kind of time (that of aesthetic events) intersects another (the time of physical events) and dislocates it."[39] This is the time of reading—which is both a part of one's life and unassimilable to life or experience. Thus, her reading of the *Phaedrus* emphasizes Socrates's refusal to extract desire from time, his search to remain within the sometimes painful paradoxes of ice-pleasure. She suggests that Lysias, in his speech asserting that the boy should yield to the man who does not truly love him, is trying to short-circuit the time of desire; his proposition is cynical because he seeks to perceive the experience of desire from the perspective of its end (from a moment after the desire has passed). No lover, she says, would tolerate this. Socrates, in contrast, seeks the impossible prolongation of the now—to dwell in that impossibility, which for Carson names the paradox of reading and desire: "As a lover you want ice to be ice and yet not melt in your hands. As a reader you want knowledge to be knowledge and yet lie fixed on the written page. Such wants cannot help but pain you, at least in part, because they place you in a blind point from which you watch the object of your desire disappear into yourself" (145).[40] Beginning from premises very different from Bersani's—*Eros the Bittersweet* explores desire as a function of a lack, exactly what, according to Bersani, Plato's dialogues eschew—Carson perhaps allows one to specify the dislocation of self in the aesthetic subject. What unites reading and desire is a common experience of impossibility, which also links her understanding of lack to the vagaries of historical transmission (of Sappho's fragmented corpus, for instance).[41]

Recurrently, Carson suggests that reading and desire involve a kind of "stereoscopy"—a split in consciousness, an impossible holding in view of two scenes simultaneously.[42] That split is eros. Thus, text and the beloved person alike excite, but also thwart, a desire to merge with them. Conceiving desire in relation to lack (*eros,* she points out, literally means "lack") brings out what is paradoxical about the disappearance of self in impersonal narcissism or aesthetic pleasure: the lover or reader wants to merge with the beloved or with the text—to submerge his personality in the impersonality of reading—but also to know it. The subject of "impersonal narcissism" both does and does not disappear. Carson's description of desire is therefore also a description of the rapture of reading, and it calls to mind for me a similar evocation of the ecstasy of intense perception in Virginia Woolf's *Moments of Being*:

> If life has a base that it stands upon, if it is a bowl that one fills
> and fills and fills—then my bowl without a doubt stands upon this
> memory. It is of lying half asleep, half awake, in bed in the nursery
> at St. Ives. It is of hearing the waves breaking, one, two, one, two,
> and sending a splash of water over the beach; and then breaking,
> one, two, one, two, behind the yellow blind. It is of hearing the
> blind draw its little acorn across the floor as the wind blew the
> blind out. It is of lying and hearing the splash and seeing this light,
> and feeling, it is almost impossible that I should be here; of feeling
> the purest ecstasy I can conceive.[43]

A description of the external occasion for rapture (waves breaking on the shore, and the "acorn" of a curtain being drawn across the floor by the wind) takes the place of any subjective content, any description (beyond "purest ecstasy") of what she felt, even as the external description, too, is conspicuously spare. The ecstasy is evoked rather by the movement between a voiding of self and a positing of a self to experience that voiding: "It is almost impossible that I should be here." The suspended, potential being has as its objective correlative less the event (which is hardly described) than the prose that evokes it. One's own reading does not fill in that experience with one's own personal St. Ives so much as feel, in the rapture of the prose, the paradoxical experience of seeing the world without oneself in it.[44]

Thus, the relatively banal insight that the lover prefers pursuit to the consummation that would end his quest becomes more compelling when considered in relation to the cognition of desire. Carson recurs to the figure of the edge; desire is the space between. Carson's book offers many avenues for exploring reading's relation to desire and joins concrete historical and philological detail with a recurrent structure of desire—for example, in one of the most beautiful chapters of the book, which presents a historical account of the invention of the Greek alphabet. Adapting Phoenician script (whose adoption was driven, philologists suggest, in the first place by poetry, not trade),[45] the Greeks separated vowels from consonants. This remarkable feat of abstraction—a consonant cannot be pronounced without a vowel, she points out, and so the consonant is an abstraction, not a representation of sound—is a phenomenalization of an edge, of the starting and stopping of sound. In eros and in writing, "the mind reaches out from what is present and actual to something else" (Carson, *Eros the Bitter-*

sweet, 61), tries to reach the boundaries of what it can know.[46] In Carson's account, the mind's search for truth ceases to be merely analogous to an experience of desire. Repeatedly, she suggests that what thwarts—and also constitutes—desire is nothing other than the mind's act of cognition. In its thwarted desire to merge—with text or beloved—the mind perceives its edge, paradoxically cognizes its own disappearance. Eros thus also gives one a glimpse of the living subject's bittersweet relation to the *longue durée* of language and art.

Tradition, Impersonality, Queer Pedagogy

From this perspective, historical transmission becomes a special case of a more general structure in the erotics of reading. And the tension that for Carson makes for this erotics is visible in accounts of tradition. One thinks immediately of T. S. Eliot's description of the paradoxical temporality of tradition (an ever-complete whole that nevertheless changes with shifting perspectives on it), which is shaped through a "continual extinction of personality."[47] The living poet must take his place "among the dead" (38); Eliot's description of the "impersonal emotion" (43) of poetry evokes a proleptic assimilation to the tradition that forms the poet (so that the knowledge of the dead that forms what the poet "knows" anticipates his place among them).[48] At the same time, this "impersonal emotion" is premised on the human emotion it consigns to extinction. (In Eliot's aside, "Poetry is not a turning loose of emotion, but an escape from emotion; it is not the expression of personality, but an escape from personality. But, of course, only those who have personality and emotions know what it means to want to escape from these things" [43].)

The possibly awkward join in a term like *queer transmission* between depersonalizing, depsychologizing questions of language or tradition and (at least ostensibly) personal and psychological ones of queer desire might therefore be internal to thinking about tradition itself, in which the living poet sees himself among the dead, or where the emotions of living persons encounter the impersonal emotions of art. ("I therefore dismiss it with frigid tranquillity, having little to fear or hope from censure or from praise"; "I want to make Romeo jealous. I want the dead lovers of the world to hear our laughter, and grow sad. I want a breath of our passion to stir their dust into consciousness, to wake their ashes into pain.")[49] In Carson's recurrent formulation, eros marks "that point where we disappear into ourselves in order to look" (*Eros the Bittersweet,* 72).[50] One disappears, but it is oneself that obscures the vision that one's disappearance also constitutes: it is almost impossible that I should be here. The two sides of queer transmission, in other terms, are, like the equivocal suspension of impersonal narcissism, internal to the rapture of reading.

One might thus take seriously Harold Bloom's repeated assertions (on the face of them, unlikely) that his model of influence is not Oedipal.[51] Against the metaphorics of "strong" and "weak" poets and the somewhat unpleasant celebrations of "virility,"[52] one might counterpose his suggestion that anxiety marks not the state of mind of the poet but a relation between poems—"the poem is not an overcoming of anxiety, but is that anxiety" (*The Anxiety of Influence,* 94). "The meaning of the poem can only be a poem, but *another poem—a poem not itself*" (70; emphasis in original; see also 94). The relation of misreading does not depend on the poet's having read the precursor poem, which might, in any event, be a composite of several poems. Hence he also speaks of influence as a "language":

> The effort of criticism is to teach a language, for what is never
> learned but comes as the gift of a language is a poetry already
> written—an insight I derive from Shelley's remark that every
> language is the relic of an abandoned cyclic poem. I mean that
> criticism teaches not a language of criticism . . . but a language
> in which poetry already is written, the language of influence, of
> the dialectic that governs the relation between poets *as poets.* (25;
> emphasis in original)

Strikingly, however, Bloom renders his theory of poetic tradition in metaphorics that are, whatever he asserts, unmistakably Oedipal, and he describes this dialectic of influence as a drama of preeminence—indicatively, of sons over fathers. In one fascinating moment, Bloom (discussing "tesserae or completion and antithesis") remarks that the young poet needs to defend against being flooded by the creative power of the precursor: "The ephebe who fears his precursors as he might fear a flood is taking a vital part for a whole, the whole being everything that constitutes his creative anxiety, the spectral blocking agent in every poet. Yet this metonymy is hardly to be avoided; every good reader properly *desires* to drown, but if the poet drowns, he will become *only a reader*" (57; emphasis in original). Bloom's account is both Oedipal and something else. Here and elsewhere, what is rendered as an Oedipal drama between "father" and "son" seems to name a struggle internal to expression—"the spectral blocking agent in every poet," which the agonistic relation to the precursor serves to reify or represent (and is misrecognized by the critic as *the* drama?). That spectral blocking Bloom links (by way of Freud) to embodiment, "our universal fear of domination, of our being trapped by nature in our body as a dungeon" (57). Read in these terms, *virility* might name not (only) the struggle to be a man but (also) the doomed effort to escape embodiment, to become a poet who is purely a poet (perhaps, "an artificial man / At a distance, a secondary expositor, / A being of sound").[53] Bloom's agonistic terms, if one downplays the heroics of struggling manhood, strive to forestall a pastoralizing or sentimentalizing account of this struggle of (or within) expression.

In one of the many entertainingly cranky asides in *The Anatomy of Influence,* Bloom remarks,

> My emphasis on agon as a central feature of literary relationships nevertheless encountered considerable resistance. Much seems to depend on the idea of literary influence as a seamless and friendly mode of transmission, a gift graciously bestowed and gratefully received. *The Anxiety of Influence* also inspired certain marginalized groups to assert their moral superiority. For decades, I was informed that women and homosexual writers entered no contest but cooperated in a community of love. Frequently I was assured that black, Hispanic, and Asian literary artists too rose above mere competition. Agon was apparently a pathology confined to white heterosexual males. (7)

In tracing the queerness of literary transmission, I do not want to be found guilty of this particular kind of special pleading. Seeking to reframe the question of transmission outside Bloom's agonistic, Oedipal metaphorics does not, however, necessarily entail a pastoralizing, redemptive model of tradition. Only from within an Oedipal model need possible alternatives register as mirror-image negations of competition, and other writers' models might allow one to sidestep this stark opposition: For instance, Gilles Deleuze's characterization of the works of Herman Melville and American literature more generally as a democratization that seeks to "liberate man from the father function, to give birth to the new man or the man without particularities, to reunite the original and humanity by constituting a society of brothers as a new universality. In a society of brothers, alliance replaces filiation and the blood pact replaces consanguinity."[54] Or, indeed, his "anti-Oedipus." As I have suggested, too, Bersani's work might be read as an effort to imagine alternatives to Oedipal rivalry that do not turn on a redemptive account of sexual relations or culture. The chapters below derive alternatives from readings of particular texts. Thus chapters 9 and 10 about Faulkner (especially) dwell, in different ways, on the stakes of thinking about the utopian potential of anti-Oedipal transmission. Swinburne's appropriation of Sappho also offers an alternative model for "misreading," and Pater and Wilde explicitly articulate other models of literary history. More generally, questions of transmission and canonization are, perhaps inevitably, questions about teaching, and this book often addresses queer pedagogy, most directly in chapters 5 and 6 (on Wilde) and 7 and 8 (on James), but obliquely elsewhere as well. One need hardly be invested in the moral superiority of queer people to think that they might have a different relation to Oedipal rivalry than Bloom's beleaguered "white heterosexual males," and in fact many of the writers here—beginning with Plato— reimagine the analogy between the transmission of knowledge and biological reproduction. As in other contexts, my emphasis might fall more, however, on the queer qualities of pedagogy in general than on the particular pedagogy associated with queer persons.

This is not a book about the contemporary politics of education, but it is not irrelevant to those debates, either. In reactions to the ostensible "crisis" of higher education, and in responses dictated by an austere financial climate, I am struck by the simultaneous devaluation and objectification of knowledge: scant resources lead to the denigration of any inquiry that cannot be immediately translated into monetary value (tending toward an ideal of vocational or business training) even as they also dictate a mania for measurement and assessment (driven ultimately by consumerism: Do students get their money's worth? Is the "product" advertised the one delivered, or, to put the antipedagogical assumption more baldly, is the knowledge promised by a course obvious in advance to everyone? Is knowledge "efficiently" conveyed—do faculty convey as much knowledge as possible to as many students as possible in as short a time as possible?).[55] Knowledge, valued for its use value, is, when it takes any specific form, denigrated; even the rare defense of the humanities that turns to more impalpable kinds of student formation tends to treat specialized knowledge as form of base self-indulgence.[56] (Such defenses, perhaps insofar as they are defenses, cannot avoid accepting the terms of knowledge's objectification, after all.) This is the regime of what Jean-Claude Milner calls "la politique des choses";[57] no doubt a development of biopower, there is everywhere a denigration of the speaking subject in favor of measurable objects that can be turned into data. Detective shows increasingly focus on autopsies, and universities invest in technologies that aspire, it often seems, to have classroom "discussion" bypass altogether the messy business of talking. (It is perhaps not the contradiction that it seems that teaching is also understood in interpersonal terms. The content of knowledge falls away in the mania to measure its transmission. And intersubjective interactions are moved to the register of the imaginary—specular ego-ratification, grading, course evaluations.)[58] All this is a sort of "transmission"—to which I would oppose the "queer transmission" adumbrated in this book. In the context of contemporary debates about education, to examine queer transmission might lead one to consider not just the ways that the value of literary study can be measured (by the remunerative possibilities of "critical thinking skills," or even by their no doubt crucial importance for an informed electorate, for instance), but also what models of transmission and literary texts suggest about conveying knowledge, what conclusions they might lead one to draw about the possibility of objectifying—and measuring—the "contents" of literature.

Reading and Other Minds; Potentiality and Close Reading

One of the most compelling recent models for thinking about literary value is offered by Andrew H. Miller's *The Burdens of Perfection*—perhaps most of all in its mode of reading.[59] To read his book in the context of my argument suggests the possibility of bringing out questions of queer transmission in the Victorian tradition of ethical thinking that Miller elucidates. Arguing that nineteenth-century literature was "inescapably moral in orientation: ethical in its form, its motivation, its aim, its tonality, its diction, its very style, ethical in ways that remain to be adequately assessed" (xi), Miller suggests that this ethics takes the form of "perfectionism"—a striving for self-improvement. (He specifies that the ethical question is in a sense prior to duty or to decisions about actions; it is a question of "what it is to have a life: this one rather than that, only one, one at all" [2].) The trajectory of self-improvement seems to take an intersubjective form (perhaps even when its dynamics are internalized): implicitly pedagogical, it turns on the power of exemplary lives (more than, for instance, on maxims or doctrines) to inspire the self to become more perfectly itself.

The narrative form of perfectionism, Miller suggests, responds to skepticism: most specifically, to "the problem of other minds, the question of whether we can know anything of the inner lives of others," but also more generally to a broad cultural doubt about "one's convictions about oneself and one's relations to others" (xii). This is at once the question of embodiment (to which many of the chapters below will return)—to what extent am I yoked to the particularity of my body, and to this one life that I have been given—and the question of transmission, and therefore of teaching: what can minds convey to other minds, to what extent can knowledge be transmitted?[60] The narrative of perfectionism, he suggests, responds to skepticism by transforming epistemological doubts into social dynamics—into "second-person" forms. (The discussion of skepticism movingly asks, among other things, whether it is possible to think one's way out of isolation.) Hence he is particularly interested in the perlocutionary effects of reading and in how novels' stagings of their own reading implicitly pose ethical questions. For many of the Victorian texts he reads, the ethical burden is carried by absorption, of readers in and of the texts, and their ethical deliberation often takes the form of meditations on what it means to read. As a consequence, too, Miller's argument is made through a series of such readings and through the perlocutionary effects of his own rhetorical performance.

It would certainly be worth dwelling on the consequences for my readings of what he helps us to perceive about Victorian ethics. For instance: Pater and Wilde become, in such a view, much more complex in their responses to the ethical preoccupations of their age. Among other things, the "openness to example" that he describes in perfectionism leads one to reconsider the susceptibility that, for Pater, is the ideal for the aesthetic spectator: the capacity to be changed or remade by one's encounter with the work of art.[61] Likewise, a more strictly Victorianist book than the one I have written might begin with Miller to trace a Victorian genealogy for the effects of impersonal transformation in Bersani—which I will later find in Pater, Wilde, and James (discovering one source, for example, in Cardinal John Henry Newman's use of St. Paul). For my purposes, even more relevant is what Miller suggests—often obliquely—about the possibilities for criticism. For his interest in the perlocutionary effects of texts also extends to the practice of criticism and leads him, at the expense of "conclusive" arguments, to privilege what he calls "implicative" writing: writing that inspires one to "perfect" it or to make it something else.[62] That model I would like to connect to the practice of close reading I pursue here.

Of special interest to me is Miller's discussion of free-indirect discourse, which he ties to these questions of critical practice. For Miller, free-indirect style responds to a particular quandary of the will, expressed narratively by the coordinating of first- and third-person perspectives on action (which is to say the possibility of acting ethically).[63] That question of a possible second-person relation to a text raises questions of embodiment and of the commerce between the insides and outsides of texts; thus, for instance, a moment in George Eliot's *Daniel Deronda* where Deronda offers Gwendolen letters (in place of marriage) "registers the costs that come with the conversion of the body into its signs" (Miller, *The Burdens of Perfection*, 86). More generally, the novel's response to skepticism (which could be phrased in another way: "Am I alone when I read?") is a question not only of how one coordinates an "objective" view of oneself (a view from nowhere) with an embodied perspective (a self who makes commitments in the world), but also of whether the novel's form can serve as a bridge connecting minds—whether we can know other minds, whether we can communicate. The nineteenth-century novel leads Miller to a paradoxical form of connection, which, for him, names a capacity of criticism: an "impersonal intimacy" or, quoting Stanley Cavell's *The World Viewed*, "'a power to accept intimacy without taking it personally'" (89).[64] "Free indirect discourse," Miller writes, "is the voice of that philosophical aspect of the novel which I've been calling perfectionist" (89).

The problematics of skepticism is also a way to phrase the question of whether the transmission of literary knowledge is possible, and Miller's beautiful, subtle book offers one framework for understanding why attempting to think about transmission in terms other than agonistic ones need not involve a redemptive—or delusional—reification of moral superiority. It is perhaps worth recognizing at this point the different kinds of projects that might have emerged from a consideration of queer literary transmission—if only to clarify what, for better or worse, this book does not seek to do: It is not an intellectual history tracing different models of tradition, for instance. Nor is it an archaeology of the modern concept of tradition—neither a book that attempts to do for tradition what Christopher Herbert's *Culture and Anomie* does for the idea of culture,[65] nor an attempt to demystify that concept as a technology of power.[66] (It also does not present a polemic to counter that latter demystification.) I also might have written a study tracing the development of a particular trope or topos as a way of thinking about tradition.[67] A Bloom of different sensibilities might have tried to codify and defend a particular queer canon, but the texts read here attempt to bring out different conceptual strands of queer transmission, not to offer a queer canon. A large part of the book does focus on Victorian texts; given the importance of the period for codifying both the contemporary dispositif of sexuality and, to a large extent, contemporary understandings of literary and cultural tradition—as of formation, pedagogy, and institutions of cultural preservation and transmission—a fascinating book could be written about the intellectual and social history of those intertwined concepts. The inclusion here of two long chapters on Faulkner and of chapters on Plato and Shakespeare are meant to broaden the range of historical resonance while narrowing the ambition that would seek to make specific sociohistorical claims. What links the chapters, ultimately, is a critical practice, and in lieu of such diverse projects, this book presents a series of detailed readings of specific texts.

There are programmatic reasons for structuring the book this way: its central claims about literary transmission will emerge from the readings. Aspiring, in practice, to what Miller calls "implicative" criticism, I will suggest that close reading serves to access the potentiality of the literary—potentiality as it is articulated for contemporary criticism by Giorgio Agamben. In "Bartleby; or, On Contingency," Agamben describes a passage from the *Theodicy* of Leibniz, which, continuing a story told in Lorenzo Valla's *De libero arbitrio,* depicts a "Palace of Destinies, an immense pyramid that shines at its peak, extending infinitely downwards," with "each of the innumerable apartments" displaying "one of Sextus's possible destinies" and a corresponding "possible world that was never realized."[68] "The pyramid of possible worlds," Agamben continues, represents for Leibniz the "divine intellect. . . . God's mind is the Piranesi-like prison or, rather, the Egyptian mausoleum that, until the end of time, guards the image of what was not, but could have been." Against Leibniz's "pharisaic . . . demiurge, who contemplates all uncreated possible worlds to take delight in his own single choice," who "must close his own ears to the incessant lamentation that, throughout the infinite chambers of this Baroque inferno of potentiality, arises from everything that could have been but was not," Agamben counterposes Melville's Bartleby, who says, of course, "I would prefer not to."[69] What Deleuze hears as the "agrammaticality" of Bartleby's formula (Deleuze, "Bartleby," 68) and what for Agamben is an "anaphora absolutized to the point of losing all reference . . . an absolute anaphora, spinning on itself, no longer referring either to a real object or to an anaphorized term: *I would prefer not to prefer not to . . .*" (Agamben, "Bartleby," 255) marks the "interruption of writing" (270)—that is, both Bartleby's interrupting of writing by his giving up of copying and the "interruption" that writing shelters within it to the precise extent that it is actualized: "On the writing tablet of the celestial scribe, the letter, the act of writing, marks the passage from potentiality to actuality, the occurrence of a contingency. But precisely for this reason, every letter also marks the nonoccurrence of something" (269).

"Precisely for this reason": this nonoccurrence is a consequence, in Agamben's account, of Aristotle's definition of potentiality. "A thing," writes Aristotle, "is said to be potential if, when the act of which it is said to be potential is realized, there will be nothing impotential."[70] These "last three words," Agamben asserts, do not mean, as they are sometimes understood, "there will be nothing impossible"; "they specify, rather, the condition in which potentiality—which can both be and not be—can realize itself. . . . What is potential can pass over into actuality only at the point at which it sets aside its own potential not to be, . . . when nothing in it is potential not to be and . . . when it can, therefore, not not-be" (Agamben, "Bartleby," 264). Actuality, as Daniel Heller-Roazen writes, is thus "nothing other than the self-suspension of potentiality, the mode in which Being can *not* not be."[71] Heller-Roazen links this structure of potentiality to a fundamental aspect of language: the impossibility of its signifying itself as language.[72] (Potentiality is perhaps another way to render an effect of the stereoscopy of eros, of that impossible recursion whereby I disappear into myself in order to look.) "The linguistic element," he writes,

> cannot be said as such, Agamben explains, for the simple reason that what is at issue in it—the making manifest of something in language—is always presupposed in everything said; the intention to signify always exceeds the possibility of itself being signified precisely because it always already anticipates and renders possible signification in general. Only because they always presuppose the fact that there is language are statements necessarily incapable of saying the event of language, of naming the word's power to name;

> only because language, as actual discourse, always presupposes itself as having taken place can language not say itself. Preceding and exceeding every proposition is not something unsayable and ineffable but, rather, an event presupposed in every utterance, a *factum linguae* to which all actual speech incessantly, necessarily bears witness. (4)

Beginning with Plato's "thing itself," he traces this problem through the history of philosophy, concluding, "in every case, the 'thing itself' exists in the mode of possibility, and the problem of the existence of language necessarily leads to the problem of the existence of potentiality. Agamben's recent work takes precisely this implication as its point of departure in formulating its most original philosophical project: *to conceive of the existence of language as the existence of potentiality*" (13; emphasis in original). If, therefore, "actuality is itself nothing other than the full realization of the potential not to be (or do)" (17),

> The same must be said of the potentiality constitutive of language: like all potentiality, it is not effaced but rather fulfilled and completed in the passage to actuality. Actual, accomplished reference is therefore not the elimination of the purely expressible dimension of language; instead, it is the form in which the potentiality of language, capable of *not* not referring, passes wholly into actuality in referring to something as such. Every utterance, every word is, in this sense, a mode in which the thing itself exists; every enunciation, of any kind, is simply a manner in which the potentiality of language resolves itself, as such, into actuality. . . . Every utterance is in essence nothing other than the irreparable exposition of the "thing itself," the very taking place of language as the potentiality for expression. (21)[73]

Thus does Bartleby bring out the "interruption" of writing; precisely insofar as it is actualized, "every letter also marks the nonoccurrence of something." Making manifest that "every letter is always in this sense a 'dead letter'" that carries, within the actualization that sets it aside (that can thus *not* not be), a potentiality that thereby consigns every utterance to a reflection on its own taking place, Bartleby's formula, Agamben writes, "calls the past into question, re-calling it—not simply to redeem what was, to make it exist again but, more precisely, to consign it once again to potentiality, to the indifferent truth of the tautology. 'I would prefer not to' is the *restitutio in integrum* of possibility, which keeps possibility suspended between occurrence and nonoccurrence, between the capacity to be and the capacity not to be" (Agamben, "Bartleby," 267).[74] The scrivener who would prefer not to thus contests "the retroactive unrealizability of potentiality" (266), the inevitability, as one might phrase it, of history; in the terms Agamben takes from Walter Benjamin, Bartleby brings out the capacity of "remembrance" to "redeem" the past: "Remembrance is neither what happened nor what did not happen but, rather, their potentialization, their becoming possible once again" (267).[75]

In Heller-Roazen's words (taken, likewise, from Benjamin—who quotes Hugo von Hofmannsthal), such a redemption is "to read what was never written";[76] to understand close reading as a redemption of the past is to understand it as a mode of recovering the potentiality sheltered within actualization, and such reading must therefore be structured by something other than the fantasy of an accuracy that could, at last, be true to the text. Close reading therefore offers a way to access the potentiality of the literary work—not to settle it, once and for all, in a meaning that masters it, but to rewrite it, perpetually. Close reading is thus closer to what Bloom calls "misreading," or to the "betrayal" that, in his account of Alexandria, Heller-Roazen suggests is the founding gesture of philology (Bloom, *The Anxiety of Influence*, throughout; Heller-Roazen, "Tradition's Destruction," 151–52). Read in terms of potentiality, the ostensibly failed transmission imagined by the texts in this book becomes difficult to distinguish from transmission itself.

If not always marked explicitly as such, potentiality is a recurrent topos in queer writing, where it is a mode of sexual and political critique and where imaginings of utopian sexual possibilities take shape in readings and rewritings of precursor texts. Among the works of more-literary contemporary writers, one thinks, for instance, of Mark Merliss's *An Arrow's Flight* and its bravura rewriting of *The Iliad*; or of the importance of the palinode, as a form perhaps invented by Stesichorus, in Carson's *Autobiography of Red*; or of that novel's rewriting of Stesichorus, Gertrude Stein, and Emily Dickinson, to name only the most important figures there; or of Neil Bartlett's loving address to Oscar Wilde in *Who Was That Man? A Present for Mr. Oscar Wilde*. Bartlett's *Ready to Catch Him Should He Fall* could be read in similar terms, as could Marguerite Yourcenar's *Memoirs of Hadrian* or the exploration of gay history in Alan Hollinghurst's *The Swimming-Pool Library* (or in Merliss's *American Studies*) or the focus on sexuality and war trauma in Pat Barker's *Regeneration* trilogy. The allegory of the ravages of AIDS in Hollinghurst's *Line of Beauty* often turns on a reading of Henry James, among others; his *The Folding Star* might be read as a retelling of James's "The Pupil." One might think, likewise, of Matthew Stadler's novel about Gertrude Stein's nephew, *Allan Stein,* or of the invocation of Flann O'Brien, James Joyce, and William Butler Yeats (among others) in Jaimie O'Neill's *At Swim, Two Boys.* Colm Tóibín's *The Master* might be read as attempting to do something similar with Henry James, not to recover the "real" experience "behind" James's texts but to return us to the moment when they might be written yet again. Djuna Barnes's *Nightwood* or Gertrude Stein's *Autobiography of Alice B. Toklas* or Virginia Woolf's *Orlando* (or, for that matter, her *Room of One's Own* or *To the Lighthouse,* in addition to the explicitly autobiographical writing collected in *Moments of Being*) might be read as performing similar operations on their own lives, like, of course, Marcel Proust's *À la recherche du temps perdu* or James's late autobiographical writing (*A Small Boy and Others, Notes of a Son and Brother,* and *The Middle Years*). As will become clear, I read Pater's "The Child in the House" and Wilde's *De Profundis* in similar ways. Reading as a mode of rewriting in contemporary queer fiction harkens back to modernist and protomodernist experiments. While this book does not offer explicit readings of any of these contemporary texts, it attempts to formulate some queer strands in thinking about literary transmission—strands that might help specify the interest of such writing, as well as its indebtedness to its literary precursors.

Beyond illuminating that particular heritage, queer transmission brings out a potentiality conveyed by the literary tradition. "As realism proposes to give us fictions about how things really were," Andrew Miller writes of the nineteenth-century novel, "a space naturally opens up within that mode to tell us how things might have been but were not" (Miller, *The Burdens of Perfection,* 196). As Miller writes of Henry James, "James makes us appreciate what we do receive from him by inviting us to think that everything might have been otherwise" (210).[77] This "optative," "lateral prodigality" (30), which constitutes, for Miller, one of the most important ethical dimensions of the novel, is also one of the strongest claims for the interest of queer imaginings of literary tradition. That is also to say that the book's readings (more or less explicitly) adumbrate a model of transmission and tradition. Entailed, therefore, is an understanding of literary tradition vastly different from our dominant models: tradition as neither the monumentalizing of artifacts to be revered nor the displacement or destruction of prior monuments in the claiming of one's own priority. It also resists the instrumentalizing of culture that makes literature "cultural capital" (in John Guillory's phrase).[78] A rewriting that is neither a willful distortion nor an ego-projective assertion of priority, it cedes a place to what comes before without making it a monument or an authority.

One of the more provocative assertions in Bloom's *Anxiety of Influence* is that the "strong" poet can make his precursor seem indebted to him; influence can appear to work in reverse. (T. S. Eliot's model of tradition suggests a similar possibility.) Abstracted from the heroics of virility—if one thought of redeeming the past instead of, say, of Zeus castrating Cronus or of Oedipus supplanting Laius—this moment points to some of the consequences of literary transmission for one's understanding of the historicity of the work of art. ("Belatedness," Bloom writes, "seems to me not a historical condition at all, but one that belongs to the literary situation as such" [*The Anxiety of Influence*, xxv].) The time of the work of art is not the time of human experience; the readings in this book pursue some of the consequences of that insight, and suggest reasons why such an assertion need not be understood as an idealization or sanctification or "de-politicization" of art. This conception of time also has effects on the method of reading, which, while trying to register diachronic movements, may privilege the synchronic, and so may tend toward extracting texts and isolated stylistic moments from historical and narrative contexts. The broad historical scope seeks to bring into view different imaginings of tradition, and different ways writers have imagined their own relation to their distant forebears. History is one of this book's central concerns, even if its methods are not historicist. Its mode of "close reading" might similarly extract moments from their narrative contexts. As I will suggest, there are specific reasons why Faulkner asks to be read this way, but I think it is arguable that the other great prose stylists—James, Pater, Wilde, and Swinburne—also demand that procedure, if perhaps less explicitly. In part, this is simply the way I read—pursuing echoes among interrelated, isolated syntactical fragments of greater or lesser length—and I do not seek to offer a normative style of reading. Beyond that, the recombinatory method serves to bring out the potentialization inherent in the act of reading. In each case, I have tried to show how the mode of reading demanded by the text in question constitutes its mode of queer transmission. The chapters attempt to follow the texts closely enough to hear their musings on tradition, leading one to a central question for a queer tradition, and for any project that attempts to come to terms with it: the extent to which it can, in its elucidation, remain queer, and the extent to which, too, literary potentiality can be redeemed, as potential, by reading.

Part I

1

Queer Transmission and the *Symposium*

Insult, Gay Suicide, and the Staggered Temporalities of Consciousness

In *Place for Us*, D. A. Miller writes of the Broadway musical:

> Along with a very few other terms . . . , "Broadway" denominates
> those early pre-sexual realities of gay experience to which, in
> numerous lives, it became forever bound: not just the solitude,
> shame, secretiveness by which the impossibility of social integra-
> tion was first internalized; or the excessive sentimentality that was
> a necessary condition of sentiments allowed no real object; but
> also the intense, senseless joy that, while not identical to those
> destitutions, is neither extricable from them. Precisely against
> such realities, however, is post-Stonewall gay identity defined:
> a declarable, dignified thing rooted in a community, and taking
> manifestly sexual pleasures on this affirmative basis. No gay man
> could possibly regret the trade, could be anything but be grateful
> for it—if, that is, it actually were a trade, and his old embarrass-
> ments (including that of whatever gratification he was able to find
> through them) had not been retained, well after the moment of
> coming out, in the complex, incorrigible, rightly called fatal form
> of character.[1]

Like Miller's book more generally, this moment movingly and lucidly
poses some of the psychological consequences, for the gay subject, of
"queer transmission." For it seems to me that at issue here are (at least)
three kinds of questions: First, whether it is possible to make experiences
of exclusion and social isolation the ground of community, whether "the
impossibility of social integration," shared, can become a principle of social communion. Can the isolation of the closet (its solitude, its shame,
but also its unspeakable joy) be assimilated (phylogenetically speaking) to

"post-Stonewall" forms of queer belonging or (ontogenetically speaking) to a form of gay life in which one is not alone? In Miller's book, this will be the question of the "piano bar," of whether what he calls a "homosexuality of one"[2] ("in the basement") can be shared by two or more—can be a mode of seduction, or beyond that, can become a "chorus."

Second is the related question of what happens, in a psyche, to ostensibly surmounted states of alienation, the question of the degree to which one can ever leave the closet behind.[3] (That people come out at younger and younger ages portends for some the end of the closet, and yet the number of years or days or minutes one spends there matters less than the transition that must, by definition, occur—the relative youth of people who have crossed a threshold does not erase the threshold; one cannot be out without having been, if only retrospectively, in the closet.) This atavistic return of one's personal prehistory is made more complicated, Miller points out, by the ambivalence of the emotions that return. On the simplest level, triumphant accounts of coming out have to suppress a fundamental ambivalence: gay incipience makes for an experience of both destitution or isolation and "senseless joy"—and hence the strange braiding of those two, forever, in one's experience of desire. Corresponding, perhaps, to the thought (familiar, I have to believe, to any gay teen, though how would I know?) that, however tortured you might be by homophobic self-hatred, you would not give up gay desire, much as you profess to yourself that you want to—because it is the only sexual desire you know, and because, however ambivalently, it is a joy; the ambivalence of sexual pleasure in a homophobic culture is compounded by the staggered, uncoordinated temporalities of sexual development and psychosocial assimilation. The ambivalence made for complications *then,* but it must also make for complications *now* (now that one is no longer thirteen) because the pleasures and joys of adult gay life became possible not only despite but also through those early experiences of destitution. One's relation to homophobia has to be ambivalent, as, more familiarly, no doubt, one's experience of gay desire (in a homophobic culture) will always be.[4] In other terms, though we tend to talk about homophobia as if it were a formative experience (which is to say, externalized and objectifiable), to the very degree that it is formative, it is not separable from the consciousness that would come to terms with it: "the rightly called fatal form of character."

Third, and perhaps most important, the first two strands—the psychic and historical atavism of one's private homophobic *Bildung* and the question of what that formation means for the possibility of making private experiences of exclusion the ground for social belonging and erotic communion—are braided together in an intense relation to an aesthetic object. One need not understand this braiding purely in terms of erotic energy finding itself misdirected or "sublimated."[5] For perhaps all early aesthetic enthusiasms risk sentimentality (the "opposite" of aesthetic and intellectual passion in their ostensibly more dignified, mature forms): in those early sentiments, aesthetic interests, while distinguishable conceptually from inadmissible desires, become inextricable from them, if only because one also lacks (one must develop) a language to express both. Further, if those desires hit a dead end, are allowed "no real object," because of the prohibition of same-sex desire, the aesthetic interests have "no real object" because they are, in the first place, *aesthetic* enthusiasms. In one reading of Miller's book, the relation of the Broadway musical to sexual identity is purely contingent: because one felt an intense love of the form at the same time as one experienced the closet, the form is forever colored, as if metonymically. (As we will see, Pater dwells on a similar contingency: what matters for the aesthetic initiation is above all that it be an initiation—whether it is the Broadway musical or Blondie's "Sunday Girl" or Bach's Mass in B Minor seems to matter less than the way a particular form appears at a moment when a particular consciousness is ready to experience its difference from the world.) At other moments, or in other readings of the same moments, the contingency is rather in the particular historical configuration, a form of life that—living in the world at a particular time, from the 1950s, to the 1980s and '90s and the devastations of HIV and AIDS, and surviving into the twenty-first century—happens to rhyme with the particular solicitations of the musical (ultimately, in Miller's account, by way of a mode of address that simultaneously expresses and excludes one's desire, that solicits one to partake of a form of exclusion). More generally, the aesthetic enthusiasm is important because its pleasure is isolating to the very extent that it is formative.

The Broadway musical is a rich form for Miller in part because the specificity of gay reference is at once explicit and occluded (for Miller, though the musical might solicit a dream of a desire made explicit, the explicitly gay musical is a disaster). This is partly a historical matter; this particular boy's journey out of the closet happens to coincide with the emergence of the particular form of post-Stonewall homosexual legibility in the world. The Broadway musical, therefore, is a "sign," but only in retrospect:

As the archives conclusively show, not a single 12-year-old boy was ever brought before a psychiatrist, or prayed to Jesus for help, on account of his collection of original cast albums, to which neither was there any need perceived to fix warning labels. The historical uniqueness of the Broadway musical among "the signs" consists in the fact that it never looked like one: though eventually proving not a whit less indicative than those that were horrifically transparent from the moment they appeared, it involved (as much as if it had been written in invisible ink) considerable delay before its first inscriptions achieved legibility—legibility that in consequence was rarely greeted by anything but, as over the sudden strange suitability of terms as incommensurable as Mame and mom, surprise. (Miller, *Place for Us,* 17)

Like the moment in Proust to which Miller probably refers, the letters, written in invisible ink, are legible only in retrospect—which is also to say, though it tends to disappear in the subsequent realization, that the invisibility is as important as the (later) legibility (in Moncrieff and Kilmartin's translation: "Upon the smooth surface of an individual indistinguishable from everyone else, there suddenly appears, traced in an ink hitherto invisible, the characters that compose the word dear to the ancient Greeks").[6] Miller's phrase "in consequence" makes a temporal unfolding into a relation of causality; I think we are supposed to wonder whether the sleight of hand is Miller's or that of the would-be critic of personal identity whom he ventriloquizes. That, typically, others want to share the lack of surprise Miller describes attests, to my mind, to a desire to assert cognitive mastery over a temporality of consciousness not limited to gay people—although the closet provides a particularly graphic instance of it. Miller's exploration of the musical is powerful, among other reasons, because of the ways the fundamental latency of consciousness is entwined with the contingencies of a particular historical era.[7]

There would be more to say about the temporal intricacies of Miller's account of homosexual *Bildung*.[8] Read diachronically, the "signs" point to the *nachträglich* structure of queer identity; it seems to me that much of queer theory's emphasis on performativity has been an effort to deal with that temporality (even more, perhaps, than with the contingency of identity, which has monopolized the attention of many). Synchronically, the "signs" are, if not antithetical ones (signifying at once the presence and the absence of homosexuality), then signs suspended in potentiality. Condensing two times, they seem, like the word *queer* itself, simultaneously to designate and to void particular gay content, and, relatedly, to gesture toward a generalization (or, in Sedgwick's terms, a "universalizing" gloss) and a particularity (or a "minoritizing" gloss).[9] A similar structure is legible in another form of queer interpellation: words designating gay people as a form of homophobic insult.

To choose one example among many possible others: in the 1995 film *Welcome to the Dollhouse,* Todd Solondz's great paean to the stigmatizing horror of junior high school, Dawn, the homely, awkward tween doomed to suffer, among other indignities, the pained disidentification of the filmic audience, even, or perhaps especially, of those able to recognize themselves in her awkwardness or in the exorbitant, tragically out-of-tune yearnings occasioned by objects at once beyond her reach and unworthy of her reverence, suffers more tangibly from the repeated epithet *lesbo.* Although it never directly addresses the question, the film makes plain the difficulty of characterizing the homophobia of such insults; for it is clear in the film that (like the "rape" promised by one of the boys, who sets a date for it that Dawn dutifully shows up for) the term at once cites and voids its meaning. Dawn is insulted, but not, it seems, accused of being a lesbian. Heard by a lesbian or protolesbian (and we have little reason to believe Dawn is either), such an insult would have to be stigmatizing, probably not least because of the differential way the term would suddenly have content, or a protocontent, and only for her.

The equivocal status of *lesbo* as a specifically homophobic insult in Solondz's film also characterizes other forms of insult or aggression.[10] Thus I thought of Dawn recently as I was reading about the trial of Dharun Ravi and the suicide of Tyler Clementi, the first-year student at Rutgers who committed suicide after his roommate (Ravi) clandestinely filmed him having sex with another man and then disseminated (or attempted to disseminate) the recording online. It seemed to me that many observers found their thinking stalled by two different kinds of obscurities (obscurities they perhaps mistakenly thought were particularities of this case). On the one hand, it was difficult to gauge Ravi's culpability because it was difficult to know the degree to which he was animated by homophobia, or by a rationalized or conscious homophobia. On the other hand, that obscurity was paired with (and conflated with) another one: for many, the difficulty of tracing any direct path from Ravi's harassment to Clementi's death meant that to call it a crime of homophobic bias risked (for some) trivializing hate crimes and (for others) falsely accusing Ravi of such a crime. It seems to me, however, that it was precisely the ambiguity that made the story resonate so powerfully with many gay people, and with their experience of homophobia. One certainly does not lack for concrete, unambiguous, examples of explicit homophobic violence, but for most of us, most experiences of homophobic bias in fact take place along a continuum of more or less attenuated, or at least more or less legible, intentions. (Even the most graphic examples are subject to such attenuation: one recalls the rumors, some of them cultivated by his killers, that followed Matthew Shepard's murder—rumors that it was not, in fact, a bias crime.) And it is often the absence of any conscious homophobic intention in one's victimizer that makes the homophobia more excruciating, in part because it is always open to others to see in one's designation of a homophobic effect an assertion of legible, conscious homophobic motives or intentions, and to have to bear the brunt of a perceived social aggression, and a confusion that is not one's own.

The perhaps most extended journalistic account of Ravi's actions and Clementi's suicide—an essay by Ian Parker in the *New Yorker*—highlights, also without explicitly commenting on it, the continuities and the discontinuities between consciously homophobic attitudes and a homophobic teen patois that, taking homophobia as its basic syntax, trades on the voiding of sexual content (so that ultimate Frisbee, for instance, was deemed—by a wit targeting Ravi this time—"gayer than having sex with a dude").[11] Apparently homophobic language, while it might express homophobia, can also coexist more or less comfortably with pious espousals of tolerance. More than that, the insult depends on the voiding of gay content even as the association with homosexuality is what makes for the insult. That the derogatory uses of *gay* or *homo*—or even *faggot*—which one hears nearly every day on a university campus (or my university campus, anyway), often leave one feeling caught in cross fire one cannot be sure is entirely unfriendly, that as terms of derogation they probably do not for most speakers designate homosexuality, is, in one sense, the least of it. Overheard, such uses stigmatize, but the circuitous, indirect form of nonaddress may be more important than any homophobic attitude deliberately expressed. That nonaddress, moreover, would seem to be internal to the insult, which relies on the theatrical voiding of homosexuality as an imagined or imaginable referent (which is also to say, a refusal to acknowledge that the remark could be heard by a gay person) even as that reference secures the insult's perlocutionary force.

This is also a question of development and of the transmission of violence. The difficulty of tracing any direct causality between the accretive effect of particular homophobic insults and the threshold at which a particular gay boy no longer finds life livable also raises the question of how to gauge the damage of institutional and societal forms of homophobia. People can produce—and of course have produced—lucid analyses of the social operations of homophobia; at least for me, Clementi's death and Ravi's trial made tangible the blind spot that, marking the articulation of social structures as individual experience, corresponds with my own consciousness, which was where the various obscurities seemed finally to be lodged. If, therefore, it is hard to collocate the way one has to talk about the mangling effects of homophobic discourse with a sense of what homophobia has and has not done to me, that is not least because, myself a product of a homophobic world, I have no consciousness other than the one formed by my particular history with which to imagine the thought that would have transcended that formation. Even if, from one side, it is hard to determine whether homophobia describes Ravi's motivations, it is also hard to come to a satisfying account of how such equivocally homophobic insults and actions wound.

In arguing that both obscurities that seem most striking in this case— the (possibly homophobic) boy's motivations and the vulnerability of a particular gay boy to a perceived homophobic assault—come down to questions of development, I do not mean simply to say that immaturity makes culpability as difficult to gauge as reactions to others' behavior are to predict. Secured by a horizon of maturity—where motivation, culpability, and reaction would suddenly become transparent in the finished adult— the fact of development would be merely exculpatory. Thus, the conscious or rationalized homophobia that may or may not have led Ravi to behave as he did was implicitly opposed to a casual, unthought or unthinking, and (to some, anyway) thereby ineffectual homophobia that "everyone" not unusually thoughtful (or not unusually gay) allegedly shares at his age. A generalizable difficulty of gauging human motivations became the "proof" of the absence of homophobia, at a tendentiously posited "beyond" ostensibly also occupied by those considering the story; the presumption that homophobia is unambiguous may have been at stake as much as any particular exculpation. From the other side, that (asserted) clarity, in turn, anchors another one: to be or not to be out is treated as a simple binary traversed at a discrete moment of decision—as if coming out were a constative utterance, impeded, moreover, only by the limitations of one's own personal heroism. That equivocally homophobic actions could intersect a homosexuality not "fully" rationalized or articulated is a possibility not limited to gay people at an "earlier" stage of coming out. It seems to me that a persistent asynchronicity of consciousness—which makes it difficult to gauge motivations and conclusions, causes and effects—perhaps also leaves one vulnerable psychically to such equivocal affronts. The story, to my mind, is *there*. Parker, for his part, focuses almost entirely on Ravi. The complicated psychology of gay bashing exerts a fascination that is for me finally finite, and Ravi's confused intentions cannot sustain the exhaustive attention Parker gives them. Parker and others may have had laudable reasons for their relative neglect of Clementi's motives; we do not know them, and some perhaps felt that to suggest he was open to homophobic intimidation would be to deny that he was out, or might impugn the courage of that disclosure. And yet why he committed suicide is what one wants to know—and cannot. He was out to his parents and friends and was setting up dates online to have sex with men, and yet after finding out about the clandestine taping, he checked Ravi's Twitter feed thirty-eight times the day before he died (even as he also wrote messages that professed more equanimity).[12] I do not think one needs to conclude that Clementi was ambivalent about his sexuality (though who is not?) to think one might understand, viscerally, the power of homophobic insult to wound, to make thought return obsessively to verify an affront it cannot process. Though one will never know what happened, one can trace in Clementi's reaction something of the staggered temporality of consciousness—a structure that, paradoxically, invocations of "immaturity" served, above all, to obscure.

In "Reality and Realization," Eve Kosofsky Sedgwick describes the gap between "knowledge," with its propositional content, and the realization that brings it home to us; her example is mortality, and she contrasts Buddhist practice with Western epistemology.[13] The distinction is powerful for sexuality, too, as Sedgwick was certainly aware; coming out is a practice in which one repeatedly works to align one's life with a proposition whose content (perhaps even unobjectionable in the abstract) one has known for a very long time. That is why—contra received wisdom—coming out is not simply a matter of content, is not a matter of knowing, or even of announcing, that one is gay. The citing and voiding of gay content in homophobic insult must no doubt resonate in part because it corresponds to a fundamental structure of coming out. At issue, again, is both an equivocal content—gay, but not (consciously?) gay; homophobic, but not (consciously?) homophobic—and the staggered temporality of realization. This is no doubt part of what is painful for older people about contemplating gay youth; for Clementi, the knowledge of how to disclose to others his desire to have sex with men and of how to go online to find men to have sex with seems to have preceded a sense of how to integrate such desires in a livable form of life.[14] To teach is to know, if not always fully to grasp, that our knowledge comes to us staggered, out of sync with our experience and with itself, in uneven, uncoordinated zones of illumination.[15] It is not a sign of weakness or lack of courage or immaturity or internalized homophobia to experience ambivalence that leaves one especially open to forms of homophobic attack, whose wounds are thereby also difficult to gauge concretely; it is merely to say that human knowledge is fundamentally structured by forms of asynchronicity to the very extent that cognition takes place in time.

Some of the questions raised by that asynchronicity for an understanding of "queer transmission" might be illuminated by Plato's *Symposium,* which is about (among many other things) the relation between knowledge and the particular desires—indicatively men's, for boys—that lead one to discover knowledge in the world. An account of the dialogue's understanding of that question needs to address not only the various arguments—for example, the desire and pursuit of the whole in the myth of desire's origin presented by Aristophanes's unsettlingly buffoonish speech (the myth of the "rotary octopods" whose precisely detailed anatomies make clear that installed at the heart of desire is the impossibility of the reunification to which desire ostensibly aspires)[16]—but also the dialogue's framing, most notably, how to understand why Alcibiades brings the banquet to an end by drunkenly telling of his failed efforts to seduce his teacher. His remarks prevent us from reading as sublimation the pedagogical journey Socrates outlines: from a desire for a particular beautiful boy through stages of increasing generalization culminating in the apprehension of beauty itself, the apprehension for which all learning strives.[17]

In the midst of the dialogue's philosophical arguments, in other words, there is (meanwhile) a narrative—an erotic one centered on Socrates. And just after Socrates finishes his great speech in which, at least at first glance, the desire for specific male bodies disappears in the apprehension of an ideal beauty that, without particular qualities, is nothing but beauty itself, Alcibiades arrives to tell a riveting, highly distracting story about a very particular desire: his increasingly desperate and degrading efforts, as, one might note, one of Athens's most famously beautiful citizens, to seduce Socrates, its wisest, but also (physically speaking) perhaps its ugliest.[18] Alcibiades, Ellis Hanson writes, "reveals a pathos of embodiment that Socrates' admirable abstractions disavow" (Hanson, "Teaching Shame," 149). There are ways to recuperate the narrative action, if one wants the text to be unified and the "story" to support Diotima's theory of desire. But, as Leo Bersani writes, there are two forms of love in the *Phaedrus* and in the *Symposium*:

> The first, which is Platonic in inspiration, is a love consisting of the contemplation of pure Forms, a vision that, in its fullness, is reserved for the gods and in which we, as souls not yet weighted down by bodies, imperfectly participated. But once a soul is in a body, and depends on other bodies for images of those pure Forms, its relation to the remembered Forms themselves significantly changes. . . . [Even philosophers] depend on likenesses for their access to the original. . . . Even Socrates—especially Socrates, according to the jealous Alcibiades of *The Symposium*—needs to be in the company of beautiful boys; the city's meeting places are the sites of a metaphysical sociability sympathetic to the beneficent madness of love. The Platonic contemplation of ideal Forms is transformed by that sociability. (Bersani and Phillips, *Intimacies*, 80–81).

Bersani's point can perhaps be generalized; the ideas are inaccessible to experience. For Plato, Leo Strauss writes, "the true dog does not run around. The true dog is dogness, that which is common to all dogs, in which all dogs participate" (*On Plato's Symposium*, 199). Hence, Strauss's seminar on the *Symposium* emphasizes that in this dialogue—and in the dialogues more generally—one needs to pay particular attention to who is speaking. Truth is not relative, but, by writing dialogues, Plato shows that our access to it is. "The true dog does not run around": the idea would seem to make for pedagogical complications. What Bersani calls the *Symposium*'s "metaphysical sociability" one might also call the "mess" of its narrative, and it is where teaching happens: not Gods, we come to ideas with narratives around them—and with particular, desiring bodies.[19] But how does one understand the consequences of that? In the midst of the boys' wrangling for Socrates's attention, a wrangling that, Alcibiades almost implies, may be the goal of his storied pedagogical method, Socrates refuses Agathon's request to sit next to him: "How splendid it would be, Agathon, if wisdom was the sort of thing that could flow from the fuller to the emptier of us when we touch each other, like water, which flows through a piece of wool from a fuller cup to an emptier one."[20] The fantasy that knowledge could be passed by a touch is troubled not by the teacher's culpable desire to touch a beautiful pupil but by the compromising assumption that knowledge is a thing that could be contained, conveyed, or, in the jargon of twenty-first-century pedagogues, "assessed." But that debased picture of knowledge is incompatible not only with the idealization that the general tenor of the argument might lead one to expect but also with the mediation that is linked to the imperfections of our embodiment—even the teacher's body, perhaps the most conspicuous, because the most extraneous (if not inevitably the most ungainly) body in any scene of pedagogy.[21]

This paradoxically fallen form of idealization is linked, for the *Symposium,* to forgetting, which registers the role of human finitude and particularity even within the theory of abstraction presented by Socrates and Diotima. Thus, at one moment, Diotima ties the transmission of knowledge to reproduction by underlining the role of forgetting in human knowledge. If each person strives for immortality through reproduction, that striving extends far beyond the mere making of babies: because we are constantly changing, even a person whose identity appears constant must constantly reproduce him or herself. "Still more remarkable," she continues,

> is the fact that our knowledge changes too, some items emerging, while others are lost, so we are never the same person as regards our knowledge; indeed, each individual item of knowledge goes through the same process. What is called studying exists because knowledge goes from us. Forgetting is the departure of knowledge, while study puts back new information in our memory to replace what is lost, and so maintains knowledge so that it seems to be the same. (Plato, *The Symposium,* 45)

We are never the same person as regards our knowledge; if knowledge, too, is not unified or constant, its transmission is, to say the least, complicated, because it involves a series of shifting terms. If, therefore, the transmission of knowledge involves forgetting, it is partly because, for the *Symposium,* knowledge is not objectifiable (cannot flow from the emptier to the fuller cup), is not a thing. And the *Symposium* presents two different modes of its refusal of objectification, as, perhaps, of this central forgetting: however knowledge itself might (for Socrates, at least as he presents himself) withdraw into the realm of pure forms, it is (for us) indistinguishable from the medium that conveys it. That ties it to love, which, Diotima eventually has us see, is "betweenness"—between beauty and ugliness, love is an intermediary, and in a sense perhaps uncomfortable for modern eyes (or for my particular modern eyes, at any rate) insofar as betweenness also marks a rhyme between a conceptual role and the more literal role of Love himself—as an embodied presence in the world, mediating between the gods and men.[22] (As I discussed in the introduction, in Anne Carson's rendering of this dynamic in *Eros the Bittersweet,* one often has the sense that what constitutes love by getting in the way—the thwarting of consummation that keeps the current of desire flowing—is nothing other than one's own cognition, which links love and reading. If eros, for Carson, is lack, it is also reading. Reading and thought are embodied, desiring experiences to the very degree that they cannot objectify themselves.)

It is therefore all the more striking that the dialogue is framed by questions of transmission. It is possible to forget that when Socrates finally speaks, what we hear is Apollodorus's report to Glaucon of what he had previously told a stranger relating what he had heard from Aristodemus, who had learned from Socrates what he (Socrates), in turn, had previously told the gathered guests of a speech he had long ago heard from Diotima. Such effects recur throughout the dialogue (even the proposal for the tributes to love comes as a quotation—a mediation hardly necessary, as Phaedrus is there to hear Eryximachus quote his suggestion), as do markers of the human fallibility that makes uncertain each layer of transmission.[23] One cannot but suspect that this structure of transmission is related to the dialogue's claims about knowledge. If the unsublimated sexual desire of Alcibiades, the to-some-degree-unmetabolized presence of his undisciplined body in the dialogue, throws a wrench into the workings of knowledge, the failure of knowledge's transmission may be the form its creation takes. This is a striking insight for any teacher. To confront the possibility of failing to convey what one knows, and thus the possibility that knowledge—precious to the very degree that one is a teacher in the first place—might be lost, is also potentially to ask what it would mean to lose what could never be possessed, to confront the paradoxical form taken by the transmission of literary knowledge: a making of knowledge in the thwarting of its transmission.

For Martha Nussbaum, the *Symposium* presents two irreconcilable visions; the dialogue shows us the necessity of a choice it deprives us of the grounds for making: between the redoubtable, inhuman abstraction of the universal in the speech of Socrates and the all-too-human particularity of desire and narrative embodied by the intrusion of Alcibiades. Through Alcibiades, "we realize . . . the deep importance unique passion has for ordinary human beings; we see its irreplaceable contribution to understanding. But the story brings a further problem: it shows us clearly that we cannot simply add the love of Alcibiades to the ascent of Diotima; indeed, that we cannot have this love and the kind of stable rationality that she revealed to us. Socrates was serious when he spoke of two mutually exclusive varieties of vision." She continues:

> We see two kinds of value, two kinds of knowledge; and we see that
> we must choose. One sort of understanding blocks out the other.
> The pure light of the eternal form eclipses, or is eclipsed by, the
> flickering lightning of the opened and unstably moving body. . . .
> The *Symposium* now seems to us a harsh and alarming book. . . .
> It starkly confronts us with a choice, and at the same time it makes
> us see so clearly that we cannot choose anything. We see now that
> philosophy is not fully human; but we are terrified of humanity
> and what it leads to. It is *our* tragedy: it floods us with light and
> takes away action. (*The Fragility of Goodness*, 197–98)

The queerness of teaching and learning, I would suggest, lies quite beyond the desires of particular teachers or students and beyond the subject matter of any text; it might be found in the "tragedy" of this impossible choice, in the irreconcilability of universal ideas with the partial, human, desiring bodies through which we come to know them. Queer pedagogy, with all its compromising partiality, has the potential to make manifest an interference already there, already structural to knowledge itself. Against the bureaucrats who would measure and assess it, against the pedagogues who would formalize it in a method, and against, perhaps, positions (which I have myself sometimes taken) that knowledge is purely intangible, purely untransmissible—all, I have come to think, forms, though only apparently complementary ones, of voiding the content of knowledge—the *Symposium* poses a form of transmission that could be read to entail a paradoxical content for knowledge: a content that, like the role of our embodiment in learning, is constituted through its suspension. The queer tradition I examine here explores the consequences of what for Diotima in the *Symposium* is the centrality of forgetting to knowledge, and what that constructive forgetting suggests about the content of knowledge and its relation to the bodies and persons who know. I am calling that structure queer, and that it rhymes with the semisuspended content of forms of homophobic insult that have, one need hardly add, very real effects, troubles but does not perhaps completely vitiate the illuminating potential of the pedagogical interference it charts. For the question of the relation of the Platonic text to the contemporary situations with which I began restates the quandaries of both. The question of the suspension of the particular in the apprehension of the idea is the question of transmission, of its possibility; the susceptibility of the developing mind (any mind, that is, insofar as it is alive) to its material conditions—to penal institutions seeking to rid the body politic of "gross indecency"; to the nearest unthinking thug who, knowingly or not, can marshal primordial feelings of exposed loneliness and social isolation to make it believe that it is expendable; or simply, to the staggered temporalities of realization and the limited perspectives of the finite and the embodied—is at once a historical condition (poignant for those of us who yet remember a world before our ostensibly postgay present, but not necessarily more poignant than what it will be for those who follow) and the visceral posing of our own possibly unknowable historicity.

2

Forgetting *The Tempest*

A curious scene in *The Tempest* has Prospero repeatedly, even obsessively, interrupting his narration to Miranda of the circumstances of their exile from Milan with injunctions to pay attention: "dost thou attend me? . . . thou attend'st not . . . dost thou hear?"[1] Reading Prospero's weird, almost paranoiac, fear that Miranda's attention will lapse just as he is telling her (as he would have it) who she is—a tale, she notes, that he has several times begun only to break off, midstory, himself—we should, perhaps, before "explaining" it psychologically, attend to its strangeness, which links it to the play's recurrent concern with forgetfulness.[2] His narrative leads Miranda to confess both amnesia and absorption: "I not remembering how I cried out then / Will cry it o'er again" (1.2.133–34). A strange "I" that, "not remembering," can, nevertheless, cry "it o'er *again*," its gesture of encompassing its own oblivion throws into question its coherence while also asserting a kind of mastery.[3] One is led to suspect that in this transmission of the histories of a daughter and a state it is as important for Prospero to establish Miranda's forgetfulness as it is for the play to establish her capacity for sympathy.[4] To the extent that his obsessive reminders demand the forgetfulness they seem to worry about, he might be said to get what he wants; it is curious to me that, later in the play, Miranda seems to have forgotten Prospero's reassurances about the shipwreck. She allows Ferdinand to continue believing that his father perished even though she ought to know both who was on the ship (1.2.177–85) and that everyone on the vessel is safe (1.2.25–32)—"The direful spectacle of the wreck . . . I have with such provision in mine art, / So safely ordered that there is no soul— / No, not so much perdition as an hair / Betid to any creature in the vessel / Which thou heard'st cry, which thou saw'st sink" (1.2.26, 28–33).

If Miranda can be said to forget what she ought to know, such forgetting, in this earlier scene, comes to seem all but originary. Memory is less an object to be recalled than the marker of an oblivion that forms her. Small "wonder" that it is difficult to tell whether Miranda is to remember or to forget the origins she learns about. Prospero's ostensible desire to inform Miranda of her origins stalls on the seemingly more interesting question of locating one's birth, on the untraceable threshold that separates one from oblivion by constituting a beginning to memory. Dictated, for any subject, not only by the prematurity of human birth—insofar, that is, as one's existence predates one's consciousness—but also by the fact of having a beginning at all, not to know one's origins, in *The Tempest,* seems less a consequence of one's origin than foundational, as if to forget one's origins were what brought one into being in the first place. It is not simply a matter of temporal sequence; while Prospero's fascination, insofar as he thinks Miranda "is" his history, might invoke an equivocal (or equivocated) sense of separation (garden-variety parental narcissism), it also registers his fascinated inability (at least partially acknowledged) to compass her memory: "how is it / That this lives in thy mind? What sees thou else / In the dark backward and abyss of time?" (1.2.48–50). The interest of that general question overwhelms the more particular question of what Miranda remembers of their exile, and at issue is less exposition—for us, for her—than a fathomless forgetting.[5] Prospero's asserted amnesia-by-fiat seems an effort to fashion a plummet to sound a memory—it, the abyss as much as "time" is—suspected, likewise, to be fathomless, to render it a knowable oblivion: "Canst thou remember / A time before we came unto the cell? / I do not think thou canst" (1.2.38–40). That formulation—"canst thou remember / A *time*"—recalls "the dark backward and abyss of time" and also evokes what Stephen Orgel reminds us about the word *Tempest*: its root is *time*.[6] According to the pun, to forget a *time* is to forget nothing short of the play itself. Indeed, act 1, scene 2 frames the play with a series of narratives—to Miranda, to Ariel, and to Caliban—in which Prospero insists that each has forgotten origins that he can then, vicariously, recall: "Dost thou forget," he asks Ariel, "From what a torment I did free thee? . . . Thou dost" (1.2.250–53). "I must / Once a month recount what thou hast been, / Which thou forget'st," he adds (2.2.262–63). An assertion of Prospero's priority, what might have been an argument for his power (he is powerful because he, unlike the others, can remember) becomes confused with an imperative demanding amnesia, with a power that grounds itself by compelling others (and itself) to forget. These narratives rehearse, among other things, the play's larger political narrative, which, curiously, reminds the shipwrecked usurpers of their misdeeds so that they can, by Prospero's decree, be forgotten: "There, sir, stop," he says to Alonso, who is mid-apology, "Let us not burden our remembrances with / A heaviness that's gone" (5.1.198–200).

The amnesty underlying the political reconciliation Prospero crafts may itself be founded on amnesia;[7] that amnesia is, in the context of the play, bound up with the enchantment that Prospero calls his "art." As in the scene with Miranda, Prospero's "art" is at cross-purposes with the goals to which it is also necessary, and forgetfulness seems to threaten the reconciliation it achieves. At another famously weird moment, Prospero interrupts the wedding masque he stages for Miranda and Ferdinand to profess that he has, dangerously it seems, forgotten the mutiny he has baited as a restaging of the plot that left him exiled: "I had forgot that foul conspiracy / Of the beast Caliban and his confederates / Against my life" (4.1.139–41). Awakening to leave his goddesses floating, midmasque, somewhat awkwardly in the rafters, Prospero in his forgetfulness also re-plays what originally marooned him on the island: his absorption in the "volumes / I prize above my dukedom" (1.2.167–68).[8] In his rendering, moreover, his brother's usurpation is something that Prospero did to him-self: "I pray thee mark me: / I thus neglecting worldly ends . . . in my false brother / Awaked an evil nature, and my trust, / Like a good parent, did beget of him / A falsehood in its contrary as great / As my trust was, which had, indeed, no limit, / A confidence sans bound" (1.2.88–97).

There would, of course, be any number of ways to read what is, after all, a strange assertion of mastery, where neglect seems less an abdication of control than another form of it. (One also hesitates over "like a good parent": is parenting a principle of replication, or is it, instead, a principle of symmetrical inversion, in which a "good" parent produces "evil"?) One might also note the recursivity of what Prospero's machinations achieve: deposed by his brother, who makes Milan subject to Naples, Prospero, re-gaining his dukedom, marries his daughter to Ferdinand—and thus makes Milan subject to Naples. As Orgel writes, Prospero, by "marrying his daughter to the son of his enemy," excludes "Antonio from any future claim on the ducal throne" but also "effectively disposes of the realm as a political entity: if Miranda is the heir to the dukedom, Milan through the marriage becomes part of the kingdom of Naples, not the other way around. Pros-pero recoups his throne from his brother only to deliver it over, upon his death, to the King of Naples once again." Prospero, he concludes, "has not regained his lost dukedom, he has usurped his brother's" (Orgel, "Pros-pero's Wife," 12). If he usurps Antonio, he also in a sense proleptically usurps himself, replaying the initial self-usurpation, his absorption in the "volumes / I prize above my dukedom." Prospero thus also enacts what he demands of Miranda; he does not, at least in this sense, stand above her. For him, too, to lose track of himself is originary (originates the play's plot, and makes Prospero a magician), a self-loss that restitution and revenge seem only to repeat. Orgel stresses Prospero's triumph over his brother and the way his ostensible renunciation cements his authority: "If we look at the marriage in this way," he writes, "giving away Miranda is a means of preserving his authority, not of relinquishing it" ("Prospero's Wife," 12). Preserving and relinquishing his authority are difficult to tell apart on Prospero's island, and I would stress the incoherence this moment introduces into the notion of control: mastery is indistinguishable from abdication. Indeed, Antonio's usurpation of Prospero is likewise presented as a usurpation of himself. Antonio, believing his own lie, also falls into the role he has been asked to play (by Prospero, whose absorption leaves Antonio, as it were, acting duke): "He being thus lorded, . . . like one / Who, having into truth by telling of it, / Made such a sinner of his memory / To credit his own lie, he did believe / He was indeed the duke; . . . To have no screen between this part he played / And him he played it for, he needs will be / Absolute Milan" (1.2.97, 99–103,107–9). Usurping Prospero, he perhaps also enacts his brother's own mode of power. For Prospero's power over others is, above all, a power to make them lose track of themselves; his is an art of forgetfulness. Striking, then, is the contrast between his anxious demands that Miranda mark his words and the magisterial tone with which he dispenses with her curiosity: "Here cease more questions: / Thou art inclined to sleep. 'Tis a good dulness, / And give it way—I know thou canst not choose" (1.2.185–86). Whatever his power over the natural world—to conjure up storms and shipwrecks, to bedim the noontide sun—his power to compel others' attention seems less secure than his power to compel sleep.

It may be, however, that absorption is a form of forgetfulness, or even a self-forgetfulness that looks a lot like slumber. "I forget," says Ferdinand, as he performs Caliban's labor in hopes of winning Miranda's hand; "i.e., to work at my task," Orgel, in his edition, glosses it, but the simple statement of forgetfulness floats there, ungrounded, as if forgetting were, simply, what one does here. ("Ferdinand," says Gonzalo, "found a wife / Where he himself was lost" [5.1.210–1].) Ferdinand's confession is echoed by Miranda a few lines later: "But I prattle / Something too wildly, and my father's precepts / I do forget" (3.1.57–59). True love is cast as complementary forgetting. Forgetfulness does not simply structure the plot of the play, which could be rendered as the stage management of various modes of losing track of oneself and others. Repeatedly invoked in a variety of different contexts of greater and lesser importance, it forms a leitmotif in the play's language. "The latter end of his commonwealth," remarks Antonio of Gonzalo's paraphrase of Montaigne, "forgets the beginning" (2.1.155), which leads to Gonzalo's being dubbed a "lord of weak remembrance" (2.1.230). Prospero's imperatives often command Ariel, for instance, to restate what has, on- or off-stage, already been said: "Say again, where didst thou leave these varlets? / [ARIEL:] I told you, sir, they were . . ." (4.1.170–71). Prospero's repeated assertions of others' forgetting, this makes clear, in a sense commands them to forget: "Hast thou forgot / The foul witch Sycorax . . . ? Hast thou forgot her? . . . Where was she born? Speak; tell me" (1.2.256–60). That everything in the play, it sometimes seems, must, by the displaced duke's command, be retold or reenacted seems to compel the forgetfulness it also aims to forestall. In Prospero's restaging of the initial conspiracy, the would-be usurpers are done in by their forgetfulness—not only their susceptibility to Prospero's charms, and his power to make them forget themselves in sleep, but also their tendency to forget their plot, to be distracted by tangential opportunities for thievery. And the relation of the original usurpers to their later incarnations or parodists is likewise one of forgetting: "There are few yet missing of your company / Some few odd lads that you remember not" (5.1.254–55). Prospero's interruption of the wedding masque thus literally makes manifest his getting caught up in his own plot: "I had forgot" marks the moment where control and its relinquishment become indistinct.

This is one reason why the imperative in the play's famous epilogue—which could be paraphrased (almost indifferently) as "don't forget me" or "forget me"—seems less to renounce the claims made for art and its powers of absorption than to repeat them. Indeed, the play's gestures of renunciation are striking not only for the beauty of the poetry they inspire but also for the frequency with which they are repeated. The epilogue; Prospero's promise to break his staff and bury his book; the valedictory close to the masque: Prospero's renunciation of his art is troubled less because he fails to renounce convincingly than because he convincingly renounces so often. Renunciation has constituted his art from the very beginning. "Lie there, my art," he says, after the pyrotechnics of storm and shipwreck

(1.2.24); the gesture with which he puts aside his robe anticipates the "final" renunciation and links it to the forgetfulness he demands from his listeners. "I have done nothing but in care of thee," he tells Miranda just before these lines, "Of thee, my dear one, thee, my daughter, who / Art ignorant of what thou art" (1.2.15–19). The tortured syntax ("Of thee, my dear one, thee, my daughter, who") seems performatively to put in question the identity of the daughter whose attributed distraction just after this, therefore, seems the less surprising (and whose identity, seen from his perspective, might thus be paired with his, from hers: "Sir, are you not my father?" [1.2.54]). That syntax, and the paired self-loss, seem linked, further, to the pun on art. "Lie there, my art"; "who / art ignorant of what thou art."[9] The circularity of the latter formulation—to cease to be ignorant of what one is is to learn that one is ignorant of what one is, and to fill in the ignorance could only be to repeat the conditions it diagnoses, to constitute an ignorance therefore at once dispelled and perpetuated—means that it, like Prospero's renunciation, can only be repeated.

Repeated, the gesture of renunciation is nevertheless unlocatable in the play:

> Our revels now are ended. These our actors,
> As I foretold you, were all spirits, and
> Are melted into air, into thin air,
> And, like the baseless fabric of this vision,
> The cloud-capped towers, the gorgeous palaces,
> The solemn temples, the great globe itself,
> Yea, all which it inherit, shall dissolve,
> And, like this insubstantial pageant faded,
> Leave not a rack behind. We are such stuff
> As dreams are made on, and our little life
> Is rounded with a sleep.
> (4.1.148–58)

One in a series of dry runs for the relinquishment that constitutes his power, Prospero's speech replays or anticipates the play's many gestures whereby he lays down his art; that gesture, and its repetition, comes to stand in for a broader, metaphysical renunciation, figuring the dissolution of life itself. According to a well-established topos linking the ephemeral masque to life's ephemerality, the vanishing of the theatrical spectacle, which this moment rehearses, is itself a dry run for the more encompassing vanishing to come. The terving outward of the gesture perhaps accounts for the temporal strangeness; the actors, as "foretold," *were* spirits, and Prospero and Ferdinand hover somewhere between the revels announced as "ended" and the world catastrophe, the dissolution, that "shall" occur.[10] By making the vanishing of the masque stand in for the ephemerality of human existence, Prospero merges the metaphysical with the metatheatrical; unsettling the (among other things, figural) distinctions whereby one would distinguish among these various levels, he also undermines the possibility of containing the theatrical spectacle—the one that has just dissolved, or the one that now speaks to us about that dissolution. In this turn toward the metaphysical and the metatheatrical, it thus becomes difficult to tell "where" one is, not just in space but in time. (One notes a similar wavering in the redoubled simile: "like the baseless fabric of this vision . . . like this insubstantial pageant faded." *Faded* opens the possibility—however momentarily—that the pageant was not insubstantial before it faded and thus opens a gap—temporal, among other things—between "baseless fabric" and "insubstantial pageant," a gap also enacted by the tension between adjectival (function) and verbal (form) in the repeated past participles: ended, foretold, melted, faded, rounded. The disconcerting number of *and*s further locates the repetition of relinquishment within this gesture of renunciation. Likewise, his later renunciation, "this rough magic / I here abjure" (5.1.50–51), is equivocated by the verb tenses that follow it: "when I have required / Some heavenly music—which even now I do— / To work mine end upon their senses that / This airy charm is for, I'll break my staff, / Bury it certain fathoms in the earth, / And deeper than did ever plummet sound / I'll drown my book" (5.1.51–57). By the epilogue, the renunciation is presented as having already occurred: "*Now* my charms are all o'erthrown" (5.1.319; emphasis added). The renunciation is suspended in a *now* that, never present, can only be posited between a future to come and a past accomplished; as in the speech after the masque, the epilogue's repeated gestures of deixis at once bring the play into the temporal and spatial presence of its performance and make that presence curiously unlocatable, pointing to a specific place and time even as they dissolve that specificity. The final laying bare of the stage at the play's close at once dissolves theater and enfolds the entire world within its proscenium.

The long history of the play's reception as Shakespeare's own renunciation is not to be resolved—or corrected—by any more accurate account of the historical circumstances of its initial performance or chronological place in Shakespeare's oeuvre because it responds to a renunciation that is unlocatable even within the play. Even the question of the play's setting points at once inside and outside the text: diegetically, Prospero's island is in the Mediterranean, somewhere between Italy and Tunisia; figurally, it is an island much like Bermuda. The play's "real-world" referent is as much the Caribbean as the Mediterranean, a historical connection established by a text: William Strachey's "True Reportory."[11] The debate about such ostensibly dry subjects as textual sources has become heated at times because the chronology of the transmission of Strachey's letter—published in 1625, it circulated in manuscript starting (probably) in 1609—comes into contact with questions of the play's authorship.[12] The question of how and when this letter went from Virginia to England, and of how and in what form Shakespeare might have seen it, becomes crucial not just for the play's meaning but for the question of who wrote it. The anti-Stratfordians who hold that Edward de Vere, seventeenth Earl of Oxford, wrote the play have to insist that the letter is not a source because the earl died in 1604, and so could not have read it. The exasperated tone of Alden Vaughan (who counters the claims of the Oxfordians and other anti-Stratfordians) is perhaps more interesting than the (to my eyes, slightly loony) theory about the Earl of Oxford that he rebuts.[13] Shakespeare, it seems, needs to have read this letter in order to be himself, to have written the play.[14]

The abyssal question of the play's authorship is anticipated, of course, by the text; once again, its "outside" turns out to be "inside," a structure likewise figured by the play's setting, the "bare island" of the epilogue. As Mary Crane notes, the island, both in the Mediterranean and in the Caribbean, varies, as a described place, so much according to who describes it that it seems metatheatrical to the very extent to that it is an indeterminate space (or a space determinable [only] as a stage).[15] (The pairing of the masque's dissolution with that of the play itself in the epilogue puts this effect *en abîme*.) For Henry James, the abyssal question of authorship in the play presents a "torment scarcely to be borne"[16]—the torment of how the "supreme master of expression" (1216), the one human being for whom there was no interference between world and mind, no inhibition in his capacity for articulate speech, could *stop* writing: "*How* did the faculty so radiant there contrive, in such perfection, the arrest of its divine flight?" (1219); "the fathomless strangeness of his story, the abrupt stoppage of his pulse after *The Tempest* is not, in charity, lighted for us by a glimmer of explanation" (1207). The question is—from one point of view—how infinite capacity can comprise its own negation—the question, of course, of Prospero's own renunciation. For Stanley Cavell, reading James's Shakespeare by way of Ralph Waldo Emerson and Ludwig Wittgenstein, this capacity makes visible "the continuous threat of chaos clinging to his creation," an anxiety occasioned by the intuition that it is "miraculous that words can mean at all." The unsettling implication is that the rest of us are "unable to say what we will, chronically inexpressive."[17] The anti-Stratfordians perhaps recognize that, speaking all, Shakespeare cannot be himself, an intuition that emerges, symptomatically (if incoherently), in the claim that he must therefore be someone else. For James, on the contrary, the torturous fact is that Shakespeare's lapse into silence does not coincide with his death. The problem posed by Shakespeare's silence is less that of a contingent historical question of a particular writer's career, less that, even, of an unaccountable decision willingly to renounce a superhuman gift, than that the lapse into silence appears not as a boundary to human life but as internal to it, internal, indeed, to the greatest capacity for linguistic expression the world has ever seen.[18]

Strikingly, for James, this problem emerges from a question of cultural transmission. His essay collocates the torment of our inability to compass Shakespeare's silence with the torment of the failure of historical inquiry to shed any but the most meager of lights on the circumstances of his life. Intimated is a forgetting central to literary transmission, one that brings together the passage of time with the silence at the heart of an infinite potential for expression. A particular overdetermined moment in *The Tempest* comes to mind, the citation of Virgil's *Aeneid* when Ferdinand first sees Miranda: "Most sure, the goddess / On whom these airs attend," he says (1.2.421), recalling Virgil's "O, dea certe" (*Aeneid*, bk. 1, line 328). The cited moment—to modern eyes at least—is one of the stranger ones in the *Aeneid*. A shipwrecked Aeneas encounters a woman he is sure is a goddess, but his cited certainty does not extend to the more crucial fact that she is the particular goddess who happens to be his mother.[19] Aeneas recognizes his mother only after the fact, only as she walks away from him and shrouds herself in mist: "Knowing her for his mother, he called out / To the figure fleeing away."[20] The play's citation of this moment of (maternal) nonrecognition might be read as a figure for its relation to tradition: to the *Aeneid* or the *Metamorphoses*, for example, which can be recognized, perhaps, as they recede and shroud themselves in mist.[21] And the moment renders, too, with particular economy, the dynamic of forgetfulness in the play—the nonrecognition might thus stand in for the forgetfulness that Prospero extorts from his listeners that they might be absorbed. Prospero's obsessive concern with his daughter's distractedness—like the repeated scenes of self-forgetting that at once repeat the play's political plot and point "outward" to the author's renunciation, to the author (in Giorgio Agamben's terms) as a "gesture" of self-subtraction, as the originating absence at the threshold of the work that, put into play, makes reading possible and marks where it must come to an end[22]—collocates the play's psychological and political plots with a particular model of literary transmission.

The play's equivocal forgetting of its sources, in other terms, is also the question of its depiction of absorption. To spell out the connection, I might dwell further on some of the play's famous citational moments. In context, Ferdinand's citation of the *Aeneid* attempts to explain his absorption, the beautiful music that (in lines later quoted, of course, by T. S. Eliot's "The Waste Land") made him forget his grief: "Sitting on a bank, / Weeping again the King my father's wreck, / This music crept by me upon the waters, / Allaying both their fury and my passion / With its sweet air. / Thence I have followed it, / Or it hath drawn me rather; but 'tis gone. / No, it begins again" (1.2.389–95). "Most sure the goddess / On whom these airs attend" (1.2.422–23): Aeneas's certainty, on hearing Venus's voice, that she must be a goddess has become Ferdinand's, that the airs that distracted him from his grief must attend Miranda, who must be a goddess. The beauty of the airs, it seems, is associated with Miranda's apparently goddess-like beauty only superveniently; the goddess's voice, which makes Aeneas most sure, is, in the later text, Ariel's, and perhaps even in Ferdinand's mind, the deification is merely figural. In a further inversion, Aeneas, certain that he hears a goddess, fails to recognize his mother; Ferdinand, as if mistaking a girl for a goddess, recognizes his future wife (listening to music whose coming and going he cannot trace with any certainty). *Attend*—a word that, most immediately, has the connotations of a servant or retinue (and through that, perhaps, also "to wait")—also evokes Prospero's commands to Miranda: "Dost thou attend me? . . . thou attend'st not . . . dost thou hear?" (1.2.76, 87, 106).[23] ("Your tale, Sir," responds Miranda, "would cure deafness" [1.2.106].) Furthermore, to forget grief in the experience of rapture is not just the effect of the "airs"; it is their subject: Ariel's song, seemingly about Alonso's death ("Full fathom five thy father lies"), is metatheatrical to the extent that the turning of bones to coral figures the transformation of the travails of human existence to the spectacle of art, figures the seductions of the play itself. (Miranda, seeing Ferdinand, thinks he is a "spirit" [1.2.409–11], like Ariel, or like the actors in Prospero's masque. In one sense, he is exactly that: a character in the play. Likewise, Ferdinand's "O you wonder" misrecognizes Miranda as a goddess but, nodding over the character's head to the audience by way of the onomastic pun, recognizes her as "Miranda." Ferdinand's recognition of Miranda gestures at the same time toward the theatrical illusion, and toward us.)

Ferdinand, in his turn toward absorption, is pulled away from his grief by a spectacle that sings of it, leaving one to wonder whether Miranda redeems that (after all, groundless) sense of grief or reenacts it. Ferdinand's falling in love is not simply dictated by Prospero; it also echoes a similar aspect of his renunciation. His lines—"I'll break my staff, / Bury it certain fathoms in the earth, / And deeper than did ever plummet sound / I'll drown my book"—also cite Alonso's grief, earlier in the play: "my son i' the ooze is bedded, and / I'll seek him deeper than e'er plummet sounded / And there with him lie bedded" (3.3.100–102). The product of his illusion (the shipwreck), the grief is at once groundless and inconsolable, and the echo would seem to link Prospero's renunciation of his art with the grieving father's longing to join his son in death, an absorption (in an illusory spectacle) that, in this play, inevitably evokes the audience's own. Retrospectively, then, that wish for self-annihilation comes to seem continuous with Prospero's incantatory art, as if Prospero, too, longed to disappear into a grief that is not specified ("Now I want / Spirits to enforce, art to enchant" [Epilogue, 14]). In Ovid's *Metamorphoses,* I am struck by forms of inconsolable loss that come to seem indistinguishable from their claims for beauty: loss is not so much transmuted as made permanent, as the grieving are made into everlasting emblems of their loss. Cyparissus becomes a cypress to mourn forever his beloved stag; the god who changes him can but mourn him, mourning another. Niobe's tears flow ceaselessly from a heart turned to stone. And in the midst of the tale of Ceres and Proserpine, Cyan, the goddess of the waters who witnessed the young girl's rape, becomes, in her grief, a fountain: "The selfe same waters of the which she was by late ago / The mighty Goddess now she pines and wastes hirselfe into."[24] In this context, Prospero's wedding masque seems something of such an emblem, a spectacle into which the artist wastes himself. The story of Ceres and Proserpine is interrupted just before winter arrives, leaving open to question whether their appearance in the play transmutes the loss that Proserpine's yearly descent into the underworld represents, redeeming it with the marriage of Miranda and Ferdinand, or whether Ceres's loss—echoing Alonso's, of Ferdinand; Miranda's, of her mother; and even Prospero's ("I / Have lost my daughter," he says, referring to her marriage [5.1.147–48])—becomes, in the masque itself, such an Ovidian emblem of permanent commemoration.[25]

In another of the play's recursive structures, Ferdinand's first sighting of Miranda anticipates the wedding masque. The Venus whom Aeneas recognizes only belatedly is also (seemingly by way of Ovid, on whose retelling of the myth of Ceres and Proserpine the play relies)[26] excluded from the wedding masque, where, we might further note, Aeneas's belated recognition is echoed by the appearance of Juno ("High'st queen of state, / Great Juno, comes; I know her by her gait" [4.1.101–2], lines that echo Aeneas's gaze at the retreating Venus: "And by her stride she showed herself a goddess" [*Aeneid*, bk. 1, line 555]).[27] The structure of allusion moves across (at least) two planes: the movement from (mis-)recognition to belated recognition (from "Most sure, the goddess" to "Knowing her for his mother, he called out / To the figure fleeing away") would seem to imply that Ferdinand's initial (mis-)recognition is corrected (perhaps belatedly) by the masque. At the same time, the belated recognition has moved, as it were, inside the spectacle: Venus walking away becomes Juno striding toward us, and Ferdinand's gaze at Miranda has become that of Ceres, at Juno. As these contortions no doubt also suggest, the point may also be the way that citations float free of their original context. A movement away from the *Aeneid*, it is also a movement "inward"—inside the masque—and the moment might thus be said to offer an allegory of the text's understanding of absorption. If Miranda later in the play seems to have forgotten what her father told her about the shipwreck, she is also forgetting the *Aeneid*, for Prospero's reassurances that the shipwrecked mariners are safe replay the scene in the first book of the *Aeneid* where Venus is reassured by her father about the shipwreck they witness ("No need to be afraid, Cytherëa" [*Aeneid*, bk. 1, line 347]). Yet again linking Miranda to Venus, the moment suggests that when Prospero says, "Lie there, my art," he also lays aside Virgil—just as when he interrupts his masque, he turns away from Ovid (and from the conventions of the wedding masque).[28] True to the logic of the text, though, in each case, a turning away from these sources is curiously hard to distinguish from a turning toward them.

Forgetting, in other terms, describes absorption and the text's relation to precursor texts. Fittingly, one of the text's most famous citations thematizes Prospero's powerful arts of self-loss: his speech in act 5, scene 1 ("Ye elves of hills, brooks, standing lakes and groves, . . ." [5.1.33–50]) closely follows the words of Medea in Arthur Golding's translation of the *Metamorphoses*. Prospero announces his power in order to renounce it ("this rough magic / I here abjure"); Medea's incantation asserts her power. The opposition, in fact, is not one: as Orgel notes, Prospero's renunciation in this scene "is the most powerful assertion of his magic the play gives us" ("Prospero's Wife, 10). The allusion involves more than the notable verbal echoes in the speech; in context, Medea's incantation comes in a plot that uncannily echoes *The Tempest*. Medea kills Pelias, the half-brother of Aeson (Jason's father) who had usurped Aeson's throne. Prospero's renunciation in effect combines two phases of Medea's plot: she restores the youth of Aeson by slitting his throat and transfusing his veins with the potion created through the incantation Prospero quotes, but she then repeats the spectacle in order to make Pelias's daughters stab him to death by holding out the delusory promise of rejuvenating him. Her plot turns on magic's failure—or on a power that is both a powerful magic (restoring youth to the aged) and a powerful illusion of magic. (Her "magic" in the second instance is the magical counterfeiting of magic; the maddened daughters of Pelias are in thrall to a spectacle no less than are the storm-tossed mariners of the first act of *The Tempest,* and no less, one might further add, than is the play's audience, duped precisely through its awareness that it is watching a play, caught up to the extent that it cannot yet know how far "inside" the play that knowledge extends.) Prospero's invoking of Medea combines both phases, and, once again, makes his art and his renunciation of it curiously indistinct—an indistinction, moreover, that invokes self-loss or absorption.

Prospero's citation of Ovid (of Golding's translation of Ovid), like any citation perhaps, at once invokes and voids the context of the original; Medea's magic, as well as the story of Aeson and Pelias, to say nothing of Medea's later infanticidal revenge on Jason (elided at this moment in Ovid, too—it is mentioned a few lines later, but in passing), is both there and not there in the play. In other terms, the earlier text is present in *The Tempest* as forgotten. It is perhaps worth dwelling further on the question of gender in the play's forgetting: Ferdinand's "most sure, the goddess," for instance, evokes a specifically maternal nonrecognition in the *Aeneid,* and a more immediately obvious context for the play would be the various mothers conspicuously not in it: Sycorax, Miranda's mother, and the grandmother whose virtue Miranda wryly refuses to impugn. "This thing of darkness I / acknowledge mine" (5.1, 275–76): acknowledging Caliban, Prospero takes the place of Sycorax, an exchange that, as Orgel notes, is already there in Prospero's renunciation at the beginning of act 5: "In giving up his magic, Prospero speaks as Medea. He has incorporated Ovid's witch, prototype of the wicked mother Sycorax, in the most literal way— verbatim, so to speak—and his 'most potent art' is now revealed as translation and impersonation" ("Prospero's Wife," 11). I am struck by the last move in Orgel's statement, on which he does not immediately elaborate. In my understanding, Prospero's renunciation-cum-assertion of his most potent art takes the form of an impersonation (of Medea); the play's words here cite another's (Ovid's) in the form of a translation (Golding's). Uncertain transmission, ostensibly outside the text, would seem, uncannily, to be the subject "inside" it.

Orgel's essay does in a sense develop this point about translation and impersonation and links it to questions of gender, in a coda about a textual crux in the play (a coda that I think is brilliant partly because it does not explicitly develop the earlier point): a printing mishap erases Miranda from Ferdinand's imagining of his future. "Let me live here, ever. / So rare a wondered father and a wife / Makes this place Paradise" (4.1.22–24) becomes "So rare a wondered father and a wise." As Orgel explains, "The crossbar of the f broke early in the print run, turning it to a long s and thereby eliminating Miranda from Ferdinand's thoughts of wonder" ("Prospero's Wife," 13).[29] Purely fortuitously, a textual accident enacts the gendered dynamics of power that Orgel traces in the text, and the persistence of the mistake points to how much is determined by the presuppositions of readers: "We find only what we are looking for or are willing to see" (13). There is something vertiginous in the *nachträglich* structure of transmission—as if there were no text there to be seen until after it was read. That vertigo cannot but inflect our sense of the power relations in the play. That Prospero claims power by renouncing it could be read—as Orgel seems to do—to show how Prospero always wins. Yet his power is indistinguishable from his powerlessness; the epilogue, for instance, makes this explicit. And the consequences for gender are equivocal. If, in speaking as Medea, Prospero—in a move that he often repeats—appropriates maternity in the name of paternal power, that very appropriation could equally be said to subvert paternity and to outline a maternal model of transmission, just as, as Orgel notes, Prospero grounds the legitimacy of his dynasty on the word of his late wife: "The legitimacy of Prospero's heir, that is, derives from her mother's word" (1).[30] He at once claims maternity as his own (subsumes it under paternity) and explicitly undermines patrilineal inheritance.[31] Nor are such moments only about gender: the repeated severing of parenting from any visible heterosexuality is an eclipse as much of normative sexuality as of maternity. (Prospero's fantasies of giving birth to himself—and to nearly everyone else—are, in this register, queer, in addition to being megalomaniacal.) In this sense, one of the most explicitly homoerotic moments in the text—Trinculo's crawling under Caliban's cloak and the play on anal parturition it enables[32]—also parodies Prospero's claims to power.

As with that power, queer transmission is perhaps even more elusive and is linked to the text's understanding of absorption. "Wise" or "wife": part of the question, of course, is whether Ferdinand dreams of a future with Miranda or with her father. It is also worth registering that Ferdinand's typographically corrupted speech comes in the middle of the wedding masque, and, expressing his admiration for this "most majestic vision" (4.1.118), he perhaps makes it unclear where to locate the "here" where he would "live forever": is it the island or the masque, the haven far from Milan or Naples or the world within Prospero's illusion? That they double one another, and that both come within a few lines to stand in for the "insubstantial pageant" of life itself, only makes the moment more abyssal. "Here" is everywhere and nowhere, and that it has perhaps already vanished at the moment Ferdinand utters it might account for the very desire to stay there. There is a similar effect in the epilogue, if (as it were) in reverse: "this bare island" (line 8) is at once (metaphorically) the stage Prospero stands on after the play's illusion has dissipated and the island after the characters have departed. The setting of the play persists in its very vanishing, and what one "sees" at such a moment is perhaps nothing other than one's own attention. Yet again, the play's metaphysical gestures are at the same time curiously reifying. Ferdinand's expression of rapture also anticipates Prospero's own interruption; Prospero chides him ("hush, and be mute, / Or else our spell is marred" [4.1.126–27]), but the true marring of the spell takes place as Prospero comes to (*Prospero starts suddenly, and speaks; after which, to a strange, hollow, and confused noise, they heavily vanish* [4.1]) and remembers that he had forgot. The marring of the spell is inseparable from the rapture that fuels it; Prospero is never more powerful than at the moment when he says he needs us to set him free.

The question of Prospero's power, I have tried to suggest, is also the question of the play's relation to literary tradition. Prospero's power need not be understood as purely invidious, just as it need not be understood as purely redemptive.[33] More relevant might be Sean Keilen's elegant characterization of voice in his discussion of why Ovid's *Metamorphoses* has proven so productive for later writers. The recursive turn whereby each instance of "shapes transformed to bodies strange" might be said to figure writing[34]—just as Prospero's every renunciation comes to stand in for the play itself—is, he suggests, internal to the dynamics of voice in many episodes. As he writes of Diana and Actaeon,

> In a poem where the experience of objectification is always tantamount to dying, it would appear that Actaeon's survival as a subject (someone who sees) is inseparable from his status as an object (something that is seen). Or to put it another way, Ovid would have us understand that without Actaeon to see her, Diana would be invisible; and without Diana to silence him, Actaeon would have no voice.[35]

To read Prospero's equivocal forms of renunciation as a reflection on the play's own status as a work of art is not to evade the questions of gendered power and of colonialism raised by the play; rather, it has the potential to show how abyssal those questions might be. Keilen continues his discussion of Ovid in language that could also characterize the power of *The Tempest,* suggesting that Ovid's text invites us

> to ask what it means to be a work of art, as it were, from the inside of objectivity, and from this different perspective—the perspective of Narcissus's reflection in the pool or of Ovid's representation of himself at the end of the poem ("*vivam*")—to look back on the artist or beholder whose attention is limited and limiting but finally transformative. The paradoxical suggestion that lies behind these questions is that *Metamorphoses* may have taught generations of artists how to perform their craft by showing them not only what it is like to be a subject / artist but also what it is like to be an object

/ work of art: by showing them how to be open to being changed, sometimes violently, by the very things that are constituted by our own imaginations and desires. (224)

Prospero's art of forgetting links the abyssal quality of attention or absorption in the play's unsettlingly self-grounding spectacle to an analogous structure in its relation to literary tradition—enacting thereby a form of queer literary transmission. Later writers—especially Swinburne and Wilde—will dwell on the exchange Keilen notes between subject/artist and object/work of art, will dwell on the equivocal preservation of a living body and voice within the work of art, and will dwell explicitly on the erotics of that exchange. For *The Tempest,* gazing at the work of art "from the inside of objectivity," the abyssally recursive moments that imagine the play's vanishing anticipate a self-loss in the reader that may be its most redoubtable form of forgetting.

Part II

3

Tradition in Fragments

Swinburne's "Anactoria"

Algernon Charles Swinburne's "Anactoria" (in *Poems and Ballads,* published in 1865) is explicitly about the relation between erotic desire and literary transmission. Sappho's fragmented corpus—only one poem comes to us complete; the rest we have only in fragments—becomes, in the heroic couplets of Swinburne's dramatic monologue, the desired body of Anactoria, rent and reassembled by a voice riven against itself, in turn, by the extremity of desire. The poem's imperious voice—in its expression of desire, but also, I will suggest, in its appropriation of Sappho—embodies the two sides of "queer transmission"; the fragmented body of Anactoria and the voice split apart by its address to an absent, desired body make the poem's atomizing of desire one with its understanding of transmission (an extreme but signal instance insofar as the Sapphic corpus is transmitted to us by being fragmented). The questions raised by Swinburne's appropriation of Sappho—his speaking "in" the Lesbian's voice, citing her, but never attempting actually to sound like her—are not separable from the questions of voice, desire, and transmission *in* the poem. For an inevitable question for a reader of this poem is how to formulate the relation between its two most evident strands: on the one hand, its extravagant lament at a lover's desertion, which imagines her torn apart, abolished, and consumed (literally eaten up, even) by the speaker, and, on the other, its equally extravagant claims of poetic immortality, often in contrast to the beloved's merely mortal body. And in fact the transitions are notably bumpy—at one level, the poem's remarkable creation of an unforgettable voice represents a mind distracted by grief and thwarted desire. Beside itself, riveted to itself and rent apart by its furious yearning, that distracted voice unifies the poem in speaking of the experience of desire. Yet the two strands are conceptually entwined; the poem's understandings of desire and immortality are inseparable. More than that: the two preoccupations of the poem, which, disrupting each other and thereby seeming to rupture the voice that speaks them, are, in another sense, one—are one, paradoxically, in the various ruptures that cleave the voice.

For a preliminary view, the connections are clearer if one is more specific about the lament. Addressed to Anactoria, the poem is a demand, but Sappho, notably, never asks her erstwhile lover to return; her only direct request is that she not kiss anyone else: "I charge thee keep thy lips from or hers or his / Sweetest, til theirs be sweeter than my kiss."[1] Swinburne's Sappho does not so much demand anything as express a fantasy of erotic dissolution, a wish that, in its disintegration, Anactoria's body might register the power of her poetic voice. That wish appears at the beginning of the poem in a past perfect subjunctive—"I would the sea had hidden us, the fire / . . . Severed the bones that bleach, the flesh that cleaves, / And let our sifted ashes drop like leaves" (7–10)—and it becomes the explicitly violent desire that is in many ways the poem's subject: "I would my love could kill thee" (23). With that desire, then, is paired the desire implicit in the structure of address—the desire that Anactoria might be present to hear these violent words of love. The question of the poem is thus the relation between poetic utterance and the beloved's body—tortured, killed, reduced to ash—between the survival of a poetic voice and the experience of embodied desire, between an immortal voice and a mortal body.

"I would the sea had hidden us": Swinburne's Sappho wishes for a retrospective dissolution, and as the arena of this suspended happening, the poem becomes an instrument of torture:

> I would find grievous ways to have thee slain,
> Intensive device, and superflux of pain;
> Vex thee with amorous agonies, and shake
> Life at thy lips, and leave it there to ache;
> Strain out by soul with pangs too soft to kill,
> Intolerable interludes, and infinite ill;
> Relapse and relucation of the breath,
> Dumb tunes and shuttering semitones of death. (27–34)

"Device" brings together various kinds of instruments—instruments of torture such as the rack, most immediately, but also a scheme or stratagem, a figure of speech or other conventional form (as we would say a "device" to mark something motivated not by verisimilitude but by convention or the needs of a plot), even an emblematic design in heraldry (linking it to allegory). In one set of figures, Anactoria becomes a part of the poem, just as, in its central conceit, she is absent that she might be addressed. Swinburne draws out the process, and the poem becomes a device of torture. (In Shakespeare's "Nor shall death brag thou wander'st in his shade / When in eternal lines to time thou grow'st,"[2] the pun on time transforms the temporality of mortal, embodied existence into poetic meter, in which one can grow, eternally. Imagining that transformation's taking place "in time," Swinburne imagines a painful, gradual sublimation much like dismemberment or torture.) Anactoria's body thereby becomes a lyre for Sappho to play on, and her tortured screams, music:

> O that I
> Durst crush thee out of life with love, and die,
> Die of thy pain and my delight, and be
> Mixed with thy blood and molted into thee!
> Would I not plague thee dying overmuch?
> Would I not hurt thee perfectly? not touch
> Thy pores of sense with torture, and make bright
> Thine eyes with bloodlike tears and grievous light?
> Strike pang from pang as note is struck from note,
> Catch the sob's middle music in thy throat,
> Take thy limbs living, and new-mould with these
> A lyre of many faultless agonies? (129–40)

Torture makes the body expressive—albeit of a song not its own.[3] More than that, Sappho's figure for erotic torture turns Anactoria into the material of a poem, or into a figure for poetic voice; "to wring thy very spirit through the flesh" (144) might equally describe killing her and immortalizing her in poetry.

It also describes, as the poem's opening makes clear, the experience of overmastering desire: "My life is bitter with by love; thine eyes / Blind me, thy tresses burn me, thy sharp sighs / Divide my flesh and spirit with soft sound, / And my blood strengthens, and my veins abound" (1–4).[4] To divide flesh from spirit describes both the sublimation of the body "into" poetry—where a mortal body must give way to its spiritual emblem—and the experience of overwhelming desire, where the body escapes the executive control of the spirit or mind. ("My veins abound" offers a visceral image for such an experience of desire, where one's body becomes "more.") Poetry and erotic desire both separate the body from the spirit and, either by aligning the refashioning of experience into poetry with the depredations of time or by intensifying bodily experience itself, leave the body in fragments. As Anne Carson points out, in Greek poetry the experience of desire is rendered by "metaphors of war, disease, and bodily dissolution" and of "melting . . . piercing, crushing, bridling, roasting, stinging, biting, grating, cropping, poisoning, singeing and grinding to a powder."[5] Swinburne's poem thus invokes a vocabulary of violence common in Greek poetry about desire. Hence, the poem's violent desire—"I would my love could kill thee"—brings Sappho's immortalizing of Anactoria and its attendant aggressivity (the beloved must die before she can accede to this honor) together with the desire that Anactoria, hearing the poem, will herself be led to experience the limb-loosening frenzy of desire. The poem seems to hope that one will entail the other: in its wishful logic linking desire and immortalization, Anactoria's continual "life" in the poem can bear witness to her having succumbed to the dissolution asserted by Sappho's declaration of vicarious desire.

For Swinburne, however, dissolution is only half the story. The poem attempts to resolve two apparently contradictory movements: a division or fragmentation ("divide my flesh and spirit," or the "pain like mine" of the earth in "her divided breath" [236], or even the etymological echo of division in "device") and a unification or insuperable integrity ("a lyre of many faultless agonies," "thy cruel faultless feet" [18]). That resolution is crucial for the poem's linking of its erotics to literary immortality (God is a sadist because sadism becomes a principle of poetic creation). A series of words establishes circuits alternating between fragmentation and unification, preservation and loss. Imagining the dissolution of her beloved's body and of her own, Swinburne's Sappho asserts a poetic immortality indistinguishable from fragmentation, which also means that the erotic address to Anactoria (as beloved, as object of torture, as subsumed by the poet's voice, as turned into a lyre of many faultless agonies) is inseparable from this mode of poetic survival.[6] Hence the poem exploits the antithetical meanings of "to cleave": "to part or divide by a cutting blow," "to penetrate or sever," "to fall asunder," but also "to stick fast or adhere" or "to adhere or cling to" something (*Oxford English Dictionary*, 3rd ed.).[7] Used, especially, to describe a splitting that occurs, according to the *Oxford English Dictionary*, "along the grain, between fibers, at the joint, or between planes—that is, along or at internal divisions," it marks the division inherent in unification. While "the flesh that cleaves" (8) is, most immediately, the flesh that adheres (to the bone), it is also potentially the flesh that "splits"—by extension, the mortal body itself insofar as it is susceptible to alteration. (I take that to mean the "flesh" cloven not just insofar as it is subjected to violence but also insofar as it is mortal—riven, therefore, from itself and doomed by its very nature to disintegration.) Later in the poem, we read of love "colored like night at heart, but cloven through / Like night with flame" (53–54), where the verb seems to mean "split asunder" or divided, and where the parallel phrasing likewise divides "like night" from itself. Later still, this word for desire's power to divide has become a word for Sappho's immortality: "I Sappho shall be one with all these things, / With all high things for ever; and my face / Seen once, my songs heard once in a strange place, / Cleave to men's lives, and waste the days thereof / With gladness and much sadness and long love" (276–80). As the division evident in the syntactical distance separating *cleave* (like *waste*) from its auxiliary *shall,* as well as in the redoubled naming—"I Sappho"—makes clear, the immortality-ensuring unification is also a form of division.

The unification—with Anactoria and, in her claims for poetic survival, with the world—is a "mixing," which, Cecil Lang suggests, should be understood in "its obsolete (and Latin) sexual sense" (seemingly, to "join in sexual intercourse").[8] "Mix" thus links the desire to become one with Anactoria through the violent rupture of their bodies ("O that I / Durst crush thee out of life with love, and die, / Die of thy pain and my delight, and be / Mixed with thy blood and molten into thee!" [129–32]) to the mixing of bodily desire with immortality in poetry (she says of God, "Him would I reach, him smite, him desecrate, / Pierce the cold lips of God with human breath, / And mix his immortality with death" [182–84]), and with the particular mode through which she claims poetic survival:

> Yea, thou shalt be forgotten like spilt wine,
> Except these kisses of my lips on thine
> Brand them with immortality; but me—
> Men shall not see bright fire nor hear the sea,
> Nor mix their hearts with music, nor behold
> Cast forth of heaven, with feet of awful gold
> And plumeless wings that make the bright air blind,
> Lighting, with thunder for a hound behind

Hunting through fields unfurrowed and unsown,
But in the light and laughter, in the moan
And music, and in the grasp of lip and hand
And shudder of water that makes felt on land
The immeasurable tremor of all the sea,
Memories shall mix and metaphors of me. (201–14)

"These kisses": addressed to the absent Anactoria, the deictic reference is, it seems, to the poem, to its words or lines or images or music, and the spoken words that are also a kiss are imagined to have the power to "brand" Anactoria with immortality, as if immortality could be seared into the flesh. (Of seeing Venus, she writes earlier that she "heard the kiss / Of body and soul that mix with eager tears / And laughter stinging through the eyes and ears" [64–66].)

If mixing, then, names "sexual intercourse," it also names an absorbed relation to poetry (as men "mix their hearts with music"), as well as Sappho's paradoxical form of immortality, where complete dispersal becomes indistinguishable from omnipresence. The self-contradiction that characterizes the manic voice of Swinburne's poem does not simply represent the psychological state of a speaker driven to distraction by thwarted yearning; the contradictions give voice to a logic, both of desire and of poetic immortality. Alternating between an assimilation of the world ("like me shall be the shuddering calm of night" [215]) and a dispersal of the self ("I am sick with time as these with ebb and flow, / And by the yearning in my veins I know / The yearning sound of waters" [225–27]), the poem culminates in a claim of unity ("I Sappho shall be one with all these things") that leads to its closing images of dispersal:

Alas, that neither moon nor snow nor dew
Nor all cold things can purge me wholly through,
Assuage me nor allay me nor appease,
Till supreme sleep shall bring me bloodless ease;
Till time wax faint in all his periods;
Till fate undo the bondage of the gods,
And lay, to slake and satiate me all through,
Lotus and Lethe on my lips like dew,
And shed around and over and under me
Thick darkness and the insuperable sea. (295–304)

The paradoxical topography of this preservation-through-dispersal is condensed by the strange formulation "to slake and satiate me all through," where the figurative container would seem to be ruptured by that which it contains. Echoing the (also idiosyncratic) phrase "I am satiated / with seeing thee live" (23–24) (in contrast to the "eyes insatiable of amorous hours" [51], which then becomes an image of cleaving), the assertion initially seems to contradict the defiant claim that "having made me, me he shall not slay / Nor slay nor satiate" (252–53). The claim seems to be for an unslakable desire—an exorbitant lack indistinguishable from an unfathomable power to absorb the world. What then looks like a concession—"albeit he slay me," she says a few lines later (259)—is a step in the logic whereby Sappho's total fragmentation and dispersal become indistinguishable from the survival of an "I" to be satiated "all through."

This logic is enacted in various ways. The repeated image of "lips," for example, links a physical act—cunnilingus, seemingly the repeated referent for many of the poem's images—to voice: to the kisses that brand Anactoria with immortality, to the soft sighs that divide Sappho's spirit from her flesh. Repeatedly, Swinburne's images localize a sex act but also figure, by synecdoche, the poem itself (which is another way of saying why poetics is erotic for Swinburne). Labia or mouth, the image of lips is also, of course, an image of cleaving, of a division that is also a unification. One of the poem's most often repeated nouns, *lips* marks, in addition to its sexual acceptations, by synecdoche, the division between the poetic voice and various other figures: Anactoria, of course ("sweeter thy lips than mine for all their song" [122]; "Yea, thou shalt be forgotten like spilt wine, / Except these kisses of my lips on thine / Brand them with immortality" [201–3]), and God (who "filled with thirst / Their lips who cried unto him" [176–77] and whom Sappho would desecrate: "Pierce the cold lips of God with human breath" [183]). But lips also mark the boundary between the mortal body and the state it reaches through torture—as Sappho says, "[I would] Vex thee with amorous agonies, and shake / Life at thy lips, and leave it there to ache" (29–30), and asserting world-absorbing power, "Like me shall be the shuddering calm of night, / When all the winds of the world for pure delight / Close lips that quiver and fold up wings that ache" (215–17). And they mark the division between the mouth that devours and the mouth that sings: "Ah that my lips were tuneless lips, but pressed / To the bruised blossom of thy scourged white breast! / Ah that thy mouth for Muses' milk were fed / On the sweet blood thy sweet small wounds had bled!" (105–8). The falling-silent imagined at the poem's end, as her body, fragmented, is dissolved in the sea, and as "fate" can be said to "lay . . . Lotus and Lethe on my lips like dew," marks the paradoxical preservation of the voice in its falling-silent, in a unification that is also a dissolution.

More than a thematic concern for the poem, this cleaving is visible in the poem's own structure. The quasi refrains (such as the repeated images of lilies in Anactoria's hair) that gesture toward a parallelism that is then violated is one instance. It might also describe the poem's syntax, at once fragmented and accretive. The sentences are often difficult to parse, both because so many elements are sustained in parallel and because the parallelism tends to break down. The initial formulation of a fantasized dissolution is itself interrupted: "I would the sea had hidden us, the fire / (Wilt thou fear that, and fear not my desire?) / Severed the bones that bleach, the flesh that cleaves, / And let our sifted ashes drop like leaves" (7–10). More striking, perhaps, are the assertions of poetic power, which often offer long series of images to unify them by fiat:

> Blossom of branches, and on each high hill
> Clean air and wind, and under in clamorous vales
> Fierce noises of the fiery nightingales,
> Buds burning in the sudden spring like fire,
> The wan washed sand and the waves' vain desire,
> Sails seen like blown white flowers at sea, and words
> That bring tears swiftest, and long notes of birds
> Violently singing till the whole world sings—
> I Sappho shall be one with all these things,
> With all high things forever; and my face
> Seen once, my songs heard once in a strange place,
> Cleave to men's lives, and waste the days thereof
> With gladness and much sadness and long love. (268–80)

At other times, the syntax moves in the opposite direction, from a clear outline to fragmentation or a dispersal of images. What initially looks like distraction comes from this constant waxing and waning of consolidation and dispersal.

To describe the sustained and fragmented syntax is thus also to confront the poem's understanding of poetic tradition and of the erotics of poetry. The mixing and cleaving that characterizes the poem's erotics is internal to its voice. Yopie Prins draws a similar conclusion from the curious line I quoted earlier: "Memories shall mix and metaphors of me." This line, Prins writes,

> opens up multiple readings. If we take "memories . . . and meta-phors" as the double subject of "shall mix"—a zeugma—then are metaphors turning into memories, or memories into metaphors? Where do these memories originate, in Sappho or in those who remember her? Are "metaphors of me" to be read as Sappho's metaphors or the metaphors made of Sappho? Whose memories and metaphors are they, anyway? The conflation of subjective and objective genitive in "of me" makes Sappho both cause and effect of a metaphorical logic that makes it difficult if not impossible to read her as the "speaker" of this dramatic monologue. She is less a persona than a catachresis that generates a seemingly endless series of similes. (*Victorian Sappho,* 132)

The dispersal of Sappho "all over the world," Prins points out, flows from this poetic fecundity. The self-division of the poem's voice—at the limit, as Prins suggests, making it "difficult if not impossible" to read Sappho as "the poem's 'speaker'"—also constitutes that voice's power (132–33). Hence, for instance, the importance of rhetorical questions for constituting its style of imperiousness: "Ah, wilt thou slay me lest I kiss thee dead?" (79); "Ah, sweet to me as life seems sweet to death, / Why should her wrath fill thee with fearful breath?" (87–88); "Would I not plague thee dying overmuch? / Would I not hurt thee perfectly?" (133–34); "Who shall change with prayers or thanksgivings / The mystery of the cruelty of things?" (153–54); and so on. Each major section of the poem culminates in some form of unanswerable question. (The imagining of Anactoria's body as a "lyre of many faultless agonies" is also couched as a question: would I not "Take thy limbs living, and new-mould with these / A lyre of many faultless agonies?") These repeated questions in a sense restage, over and over, Aphrodite's question: "Who doth thee wrong, / Sappho?" (73–74). They also extend the self-division of the poetic voice to the (thereby equivocated) presence of their ostensible object of address. Such questions are forms of recrimination insofar as they demand an answer that they nonetheless refuse to hear. A classic rhetorical device, perhaps, in the lover's plaint, it is so not merely because the beloved is given no space to respond. In that closing off of the possibility of response, the questions also make manifest that the lover is absent—has left behind, in Anactoria's case, only a girdle to be addressed—and, beyond any particular question asked, they implicitly indict the beloved for not being present to hear read against her the charges of desertion. An appealing gesture for one deserted by her lover, it turns the beloved's absence into a testament to the speaker's power.

The claim of power, however, is not simple, and that the voice is in a sense divided against itself is also apparent in the particular mode of its imperiousness. Its commands usually take the form of jussive subjunctives: "I pray thee sigh not, speak not, draw not breath. / Let life burn down and dream it is not death" (5–6); "let our sifted ashes drop like leaves" (10); "Let fruit be crushed on fruit, let flower on flower" (13). As in the rhetorical questions that implicitly claim credit for the absence they would also transcend, it is often difficult to distinguish an assertion of power from an admission of powerlessness: "I would my love could kill thee"; "I would find grievous ways to have thee slain"; "Ah that my lips were tuneless lips"; "That I could drink thy veins as wine, and eat / Thy breasts like honey! that from face to feet / Thy body were abolished and consumed, / And in my flesh thy very flesh entombed!" (111–14); "O that I / Durst crush thee out of life with love, and die, / Die of thy pain and my delight, and be / Mixed with thy blood and molten into thee!" (129–32); "Him would I reach" (182); and so on. Each claim of power—both of poetic transcendence and erotic mastery—could equally be read as confession of thwarted yearning, even of impotence.

In the last third of the poem, these forms turn into a more definite future tense: "Memories shall mix and metaphors of me"; "I Sappho shall be one with all these things." Even here, though, it is apparent that the certainty is on the level of speech: "Yea, though thou diest, I say I shall not die" (290). The poem can render indistinct dissolution and consolidation, preservation and loss, in part because all remain suspended as purely poetic events. As verbal happening, any event in a poem is virtual happening;[9] making this explicit in the form of a wish—"I would find grievous ways to have thee slain"—the formulations of Swinburne's Sappho locate the poem's violence at the level of its utterances: this is another sense in which the poem becomes a device of torture. "I say I shall not die" is a performative assertion of power to the degree that it brackets that power within the limits of the poem—where Sappho both does and does not speak. The poem's characteristic temporality—subjunctive, past subjunc-

tive, past perfect subjunctive, and the "third conditional"—is thus inseparable from its meditations on time—on the time that, dissolving Anactoria
and Sappho both, will consign them both to the time of the poem. In this
time, omnipotence and impotence become indistinct.

At the end of the poem, the temporal suspension is even more pronounced. Its images of dissolution take the form of conditionals—
conditions that, until they are fulfilled, negate the sentence: "Alas, that neither moon nor snow nor dew / Nor all cold things can purge me wholly
through, / Assuage me nor allay me nor appease, / Till supreme sleep shall
bring me bloodless ease"—whose long series of following clauses (again,
in quasi parallel until the parallel form fragments in the elaboration of the
final clause) further multiplies the conditions. Having just declared her
immortality, Sappho then closes the poem with the seemingly negated
possibility—regretted as impossible—of her disappearance, which is nevertheless powerfully evoked in its potentiality: "Till fate undo the bondage of
the gods, / And lay, to slake and satiate me all through, / Lotus and Lethe
on my lips like dew, / And shed around and over and under me / Thick
darkness and the insuperable sea." The redoubled, intercalated parentheses
("Till fate undo . . . And lay . . . And shed"; "And lay . . . Lotus and Lethe")
syntactically mime the topography of dispersal ("around and over and
under me"), and the dissolution, suspended in negated conditions, enacts
the poetic immortality imagined as a paradoxically voice-consolidating
dispersal. The declaration of poetic power in Swinburne's poem is, repeatedly, a power that it *would* arrogate to itself. A voice divided from itself, it
is as if suspended in that yearning, and its power is, paradoxically, located
there—which makes its power indistinguishable from its impotent desire
for power, and Sappho's immortality inseparable from the purely mortal
longings of a deserted lover.

The voice of the poem is "cloven" in another sense, too. The poem represents, of course, a kind of appropriation: Swinburne speaks in Sappho's
name. That fact is foregrounded by the poem. Speaking in the voice of the
poet who was, for him, "beyond all question and comparison the greatest
poet that ever lived" (in Lang, *The Pre-Raphaelites and Their Circle*, 322),
he makes her sound—to my ears anyway—unmistakably like Swinburne.
Among other things, the sustained, long periods of Swinburne's poem are
in marked contrast to Sapphic syntax, and the impressive cohesiveness of
the poem gives voice to a poet whose work comes to us almost entirely
in fragments. The fragmented body imagined to be the result of Sappho's

desire makes that fractured literary corpus likewise a consequence of the poet's own desire. Swinburne's "appropriation" of Sappho is therefore also internal to this logic of desire—and to this poetic body that, as Yopie Prins writes of Anactoria, is "held together only by falling apart" (*Victorian Sappho,* 117).

Certain moments in the poem explicitly state the curiously inside-out relation of Sappho's voice to that of her latter-day ventriloquist. Swinburne insists that he did not translate lines from Sappho,[10] though he also admits, "Here and there, I need not say, I have rendered into English the very words of Sappho" (in Lang, *The Pre-Raphaelites and Their Circle,* 407). Sappho's lines do appear in the poem—perhaps most notably in the rendering of the "Ode to Aphrodite" at lines 73–74 ("Who doth thee wrong, / Sappho?") and lines 80–85:

> Yet the queen laughed from her sweet heart and said:
> "Even she that flies shall follow for thy sake,
> And she shall give thee gifts that would not take,
> Shall kiss that would not kiss thee" (yea, kiss me)
> "When thou wouldst not"—when I would not kiss thee!
> Ah, more to me than all men as thou art,
> Shall my songs not assuage her at the heart?[11]

At the end of this passage, it is very difficult to determine who is speaking, and to whom. The curious indeterminacy of voice is especially apparent if one reads these lines out loud—if one lends one's voice to the poem, and discovers how appropriation and the ceding of one's place to an earlier voice can become indistinct. The voice is suspended between appropriation and its source: the parentheticals foreground the quotation, and the rapid alternation of voices (and echoes among them) make explicit the merging evidenced when, quoted, Sappho's lines become the voice of Aphrodite, speaking *to* Sappho. Swinburne, quoting Sappho, seems to quote himself; he creates a Sappho who does much the same thing. And Swinburne notwithstanding, this question of voice is already there in Sappho, as Anne Carson points out about this ode: "Sappho's reverie goes transparent at the center when she shifts mid-verse to direct speech of Aphrodite. There is an eerie casualness to the immortal voice simply present in Sappho's own" (in Sappho, *If Not, Winter,* 358).[12] Sappho, Prins suggests in *Victorian Sappho,* founds the lyric tradition and the lyric voice by being transmitted to us in fragments.[13] For Swinburne's poem, the constitution of the poetic voice—cleaving to Sappho, but cloven through by her—brings together its erotics and its meditations on poetic transmission and literary tradition. Who doth thee wrong, Sappho? This great love poem, in conveying an overmastering experience of queer desire—lesbian, sadistic, masochistic, or perhaps the layered vicarious imagining or appropriation of each of them—also thereby explores the queerness of literary transmission, the suspended, here literally fragmented, content of literary knowledge and poetic power.

4

Queer Atavism and Pater's Aesthetic Sensibility

"Hippolytus Veiled" and "The Child in the House"

In Giorgio Agamben's reading of Herman Melville's "Bartleby," I noted earlier, the scrivener who would prefer not to contests "the retroactive unrealizability of potentiality,"[1] the inevitability, as one might also phrase it, of history; in the terms Agamben takes from Walter Benjamin, Bartleby brings out the capacity of "remembrance" to "redeem" the past: "remembrance is neither what happened nor what did not happen but, rather, their potentialization, their becoming possible once again" (267). Such a redemption—what Daniel Heller-Roazen calls "to read what was never written"[2]—offers an apt description of the paradoxical form of revival that characterizes both Walter Pater's historiography and his model of aesthetic sensibility. *Queer* is the term, to my mind, for both, less because they are attended by an explicit same-sex eroticism (to perceive that eroticism, it suffices to attend to the explicit statements of the texts, and this chapter, therefore, will largely take it for granted) than because historical transmission and aesthetic perception are, in Pater's account, out of phase with themselves.[3] The past for Pater, writes Carolyn Williams, "is dead and buried" and "can only be revived after a period of loss and forgetting"; likewise, "the governing fiction of development must be interrupted for knowledge to be formed."[4] In Pater, as in the other writers discussed in this study, literary history is embodied by a series of objects that—over and over again—fail to be transmitted, and aesthetic consciousness often seems to consist in the increasingly refined (and pleasurable) ways that consciousness can be experienced in its failure to coincide with itself. Read together for the exploration of queer transmission, Pater's short texts "Hippolytus Veiled: A Study from Euripides" and "The Child in the House" point to a potentiality that structures both historical recovery and aesthetic *Bildung* in Pater.

"Centuries of zealous archaeology notwithstanding," begins "Hippolytus Veiled," "many phases of the so varied Greek genius are recorded for the modern student in a kind of shorthand only, or not at all."[5] One of Pater's "imaginary portraits," and named after a lost play by Euripides— who himself revised that version in his surviving Hippolytus play—Pater's text retells the story of Hippolytus, Theseus, and Phaedra told by Euripides, Ovid, Seneca, and Racine. Continually foregrounded in Pater's text is the "imaginary" quality of this portrait, the historical reconstruction, and frank conjecture involved in the recovery the text presents, and the narrative is preceded by a kind of historiographical essay in which the transition between pre-Attic deme life and the ascendancy of Athens provides an occasion for reflection on historical transmission. "Must have been," "we can hardly doubt," "as we may fancy": such terms and their cognates recur throughout the text ("Hippolytus Veiled," 322).[6] "This is what irresistible fancy," Pater writes, "superinduces on historical developments, themselves meager enough" (325–26). What initially seems a problem specific to the attempted recovery of "Greek culture"—Pausanias's ten-volume account of his travels in Greece leaves the "minutely systematic" (323) modern student with a regretful sense of the wasted opportunities for observation that he or she would have seized—starts to seem instead a more generalized predicament. It is hard to imagine what past culture would not be transmitted by "shorthand" if only for the simple reason that no culture, however mindful of its chroniclers to come, can transmit a code sufficiently exhaustive to make legible what it has left behind, can ever write in anything but a shorthand. Time, by erasing contexts, reveals as the shorthand they always were what texts it does not obliterate entirely. Pater's retelling of the story of Hippolytus is a meditation on historical transmission and all that escapes it, on the inevitable vanishing not just of times and peoples and the gods they worshipped but of the knowledges and texts that might have supplied the context for gauging, or even registering, such a loss.

Thus, Pater writes, "The sentiment of antiquity is indeed a characteristic of all cultivated people, even in what may seem the freshest ages, and not exclusively a humour of our later world" (326). Every culture arrives belatedly; even those that seem to spring, unplanted and spontaneously, from the earth are, in this sense, "cultivated," and the moment of "freshness" where a culture could be present to itself continually recedes from view. Originary "freshness" is an illusion born of belatedness, of a temporal horizon hiding what was, in a now vanished world, the vanishing traces of what had gone before. ("In those crumbling towns," we later read, "as heroic life had lingered on into the actual, so, at an earlier date, the supernatural into the heroic. Like mist at dawn, the last traces of its divine visitors had then vanished from the land" [326–27]; Pater intimates that this structure repeats itself endlessly.)[7] The specific scene of "Hippolytus Veiled" is the "early Attic deme-life" absorbed by the ascendancy of Athens:

> One of the most curious phases of Greek civilization which has
> thus perished for us, and regarding which, as we may fancy, we
> should have made better use of that old traveller's facilities, is the
> early Attic deme-life—its picturesque, intensely localized variety,
> in the hollow or on the spur of mountain or sea-shore; and with
> it many a relic of primitive religion, many an early growth of art.
> (322)

Globalization *avant la lettre,* this amalgamation obliterates the smaller forms of life that are nevertheless preserved as absorbed traces within the ascendant culture: "Lingering on while Athens, the great deme, gradually absorbed into itself more and more of their achievements, and passing away almost completely as political factors in the Peloponnesian war, they were still felt, we can hardly doubt, in the actual physiognomy of Greece" (323). Still felt—or so "we can hardly doubt"—they thus linger on in their very obliteration.

The united preservation and loss is structural in yet another sense; Pater outlines a model of art history that calls to mind Agamben's potentiality. "Given any development at all in this manner," Pater writes,

> there must have been phases of art, which, if immature, were also
> veritable expressions of power to come, intermediate discoveries of
> beauty, such as are by no means a mere anticipation, and of service
> only as explaining historically larger subsequent achievements, but
> of a permanent attractiveness in themselves, being often, indeed,
> the true maturity of certain amiable artistic qualities. (325)

Intimated is a curiously (and appealingly) reticulated model of art history; history conceals an interconnected network of nonetheless unrelated, plural developments. Phylogeny may, in Pater's rendering of history as individual development, recapitulate ontogeny, but only insofar as ontogeny, too, shelters within it multiple uncoordinated and not necessarily hierarchically organized developments. (To be out of sync with oneself is to be alive.) "Development" (of a history, as of an artist) is thus an illusion of limited perspective; lost to view are the innumerable forms of development—startings out, and comings to "amiable" maturity—that merely intersect (or indeed are entirely skew to) the line of history. The past is in this sense "irrecoverable" because of all the innumerable unrealized worlds that, at any given moment, were possible but did not come to be.

Pater signals the reconstruction necessary to bring such unrealized worlds into view: "there must have been." Moreover, the model of reticulated developments emerges, as if in retrospect, from a sentence that initially subordinates it to a "larger" developmental scheme. "Veritable expressions of power to come" and "intermediate discoveries of beauty" initially seem to describe moments on the way toward "historically larger subsequent achievements"; only with "such as are by no means a mere anticipation" are those "intermediate discoveries" as it were desubordinated, fracturing perspective by multiplying the end points relative to which they might be said to be intermediate. The "power to come" then is likewise removed from a teleology, naming not a power that will be constituted once a specific line of development has come to fruition but a power that is itself an anticipation abstracted from any particular outcome, indeed from any outcome at all—a power, we might therefore say, of potentiality.

Such is the model of history that frames "Hippolytus Veiled"; as we will see in "The Child in the House," it is also Pater's model of aesthetic initiation and development. Before coming to the latter text, however, the narrative presented by "Hippolytus Veiled" further complicates things, and "frame" does not do justice to the relation of this historical model to the story of Hippolytus it prefaces. The narrative is easily recapitulated. Briefly, Antiope, queen of the Amazons, betrays her people through her love for Theseus—who, having vanquished the Amazons, also deserts the tergiversating queen and their son, Hippolytus, a devotee of Artemis, whose temples are coming to be neglected in favor of Aphrodite. Hippolytus later visits Athens, where his chaste beauty seduces Phaedra, his stepmother and the new queen. Her advances repulsed, she denounces the hapless youth; responding to a curse uttered by the enraged Theseus, Poseidon spooks Hippolytus's horses as he rides by the sea, causing the boy to be dragged to his death behind his chariot. Pater, in contrast to his sources, emphasizes the story of Antiope and puts the rivalry of the goddesses Artemis and Aphrodite in the context of the particular historical situation described at the beginning of his text. Thus, Hippolytus becomes an allegory for the historical situation in which he finds himself: the absorption by an ascendant Athens and its gods of local forms of worship and their autochthonous deities (figured, for Hippolytus, by Artemis) determines the story that also allegorizes it (the rivalry between Artemis and Aphrodite both determines the boy's fate—as it does in Euripides—and allegorizes a historical situation). As a son of the Amazons and a worshipper of vanishing gods, "this creature of an already vanished world" (337) himself represents the lovely creatures, "innocent things" destined, as Pater wryly puts it, to be improved "off the face of the earth," and evokes, with them, the regret we might feel for "something that could never be brought to life again" (327).[8]

Seen from the perspective of Athens's ascendency, this moment is an ending; seen from a later perspective (for instance, that of Hegel's *Aesthetics*), it is the beginning (of art). Thus, the chastity and youthful restraint emphasized by Euripides make Hippolytus, for Pater, a figure for the dawn of art history. "Fired by certain fragments of its earlier days, of the beauty, in truth, absolute, and vainly longing for more," Pater writes,

> the student of Greek sculpture indulges the thought of an ideal of
> the youthful energy therein, yet withal of youthful self-restraint;
> and again, as with survivals of old religion, the privileged home, he
> fancies, of that ideal must have been those venerable Attic town-
> ships, as to a large extent it passed away with them. (325)

In the model of art history Pater takes from Hegel, this freshness marks the perfect accord of form and content before the fall into the perplexities of self-consciousness.[9] True to that model, where such an accord can be posited only from the belated perspective of Romantic inwardness, the freshness Hippolytus embodies in his chaste body is, self-consciously, a reconstruction: those vanished Attic townships, "he fancies, . . . must have been" the "privileged home" of that ideal—a conclusion drawn, moreover, solely on the evidence of a passing away.

Hippolytus, moreover, is not only the vanished past; he is also the historicizing reader. The hero is devoted to Artemis in an age of Aphrodite; what in Pater's sources is a narrative of superhuman rivalry, of a spurned goddess and her revenge, becomes in Pater's version a boy's antiquarianism: his devotion, a figure for the passing away of graceful, superannuated

forms; and his religious observation, the historical research of the biblio-
phile. "Through much labor," we read, "at length he comes to the veritable
story of her birth" (332); "at home, . . . he is still the student, still ponders
the old writings which tell of his divine patroness" (336). The worship of
this goddess—and her survival—is figured, from the outset, by a book:

> But safely roofed beneath the sturdy tiles of gray Hymettus marble,
> upon the walls of the little square recess enclosing the deserted
> pedestal, the series of crowded imageries, in the devout spirit of
> earlier days, were eloquent concerning her. Here from scene to
> scene, touched with silver among the wild and human creatures
> in dun bronze, with the moon's disk around her head, shrouded
> closely, the goddess of the chase still glided mystically through all
> the varied incidents of her story, in all the detail of a written book.
> A book for the delighted reading of a scholar, willing to ponder
> at leisure, to make his way surely, and understand. (331)

The passage enacts the equivocal preservation-in-loss that, throughout
Pater's writings, marks his sense of historical continuity. To become a
book is to be legible, and therefore immediately alive to the inquisitive
reader, even as it is also to fade into writing, to recede from life to text,
from immediacy to history; the passage renders this double movement in
its hesitation between figural and literal registers. One hesitates, in other
words, over the figural status of this "book," which seems, as the scholar
begins to read and ponder it at his leisure, to be more than a figure, just as
the rendering of the goddess's continued life seems to equivocate on how
literally to take it: is she as if alive in the art that depicts her, or is she in
fact still alive there (perhaps insofar as her life has ever been in her artistic
rendition, and in the worship it marks)? That "still glided," moreover, is
in the past tense further leaves one to wonder about the perspective from
which it is past; in the narrative we read, she perseveres as past, survives
as vanished. A space inside the text—the "chapel of the goddess" (331)—is
figured as a book: a figural rendering of absorption "inside" the text offers a curiously "literal" rendering of one's absorption "outside" it. The figural transformations—from eloquent imageries to a "book" for delighted
reading—link the equivocal form of historical persistence embodied by
the goddess to the inside-out topography of the text and to the (I would
say, erotic) experience of reading it.

The uncertain figural status of this book presents in miniature a whole series of similar hesitations, hesitations that might be ranged under the heterogeneous "genre" of the imaginary portrait. As Hippolytus himself becomes a reader of an uncertain text, troubled, not least, is the effort of a reader of "Hippolytus Veiled" to assert a stable distance between himself and a literary "object," rendering the text both irrecoverable and uncannily insinuating—the structure, in brief, that makes aesthetic experience erotic for Pater. Similar such waverings are explicit in the text. Embedded in a text that is part essay, part myth, and part story, Hippolytus, for instance, is not just an allegory for his place in various histories and for his rendering by a text; he is also a character, and Pater's version of the story expands on his sources both in its psychological elaboration and in the historical transformation his tale is made to represent. Pater's text also refuses to subordinate one project to the other: to make character allegory, for instance, or to understand historical transformation in narrative terms driven by character. One is therefore struck by the interlocking series of repetitions that structure the text as a whole. The vanishing of Attic deme life repeats earlier vanishings and anticipates amalgamations to come; Pater's use of his sources—Euripides and Ovid, perhaps above all—and his renaming of his story after a lost play enact the reconstruction that his tale highlights as his historical method. Framed by the question of historical transmission, the story of Hippolytus—itself a narrative of transmission (of curses, paternal and maternal; of an Amazon past; and so on)—presents a series of narratives that curiously repeat one another, and the "lingerings-on" of various figures into times not their own appear, in relation to the pasts they commemorate and in relation to one another, as vestiges or lingering atavisms or the products of parthenogenesis. (*Vestige* or *atavism* might name the goddess who "still glides" but in her image in her temple.) In this story of irrecoverable pasts, everything nevertheless reappears, as if by an atavistic fatality.

Thus the tale's maternal rivalries are also repetitions. Antiope–Phaedra, Antiope–Artemis, Artemis–Aphrodite: these rivalries for the love of Hippolytus repeat each other, but they also intersect and, articulated on their own terms, resist any precise superimposition.[10] Similarly, Hippolytus's own story is also that of the Amazons, as, for that matter, is the story of Artemis—she likewise, a savage virgin to be "improved" away by the imperial ambitions of Theseus. To Artemis, we read, the beautiful chaste boy devotes himself: ". . . her maternity, her solitude, to this virgin mother, who, with no husband, no lover, no fruit of her own, is so tender to the children of others, in full heart he dedicates himself—his immaculate body and soul. Dedicating himself thus, he has the sense also that he becomes more entirely than ever the chevalier of his mortal mother, of her sad cause" (332). That he can become (or have the sense that he becomes) "more *entirely* than ever" Antiope's chevalier through his service to another enacts the intertwined rivalry and repetition in the tale, literalizing the equation of the maternal figures in their relation to him, and spelling out one of its consequences, that a relation can be more entirely exclusive by being transected by another. Antiope, too, seems almost a virgin mother, and the resurgence of her maternal instinct is itself a kind of vestige: "the heart-strings would ache still where the breast had been cut away" (328). Maternal love—and Antiope's becomes the primary topic of this imaginary portrait—thus renders the various historical lingerings-on in the text, and the meanings and desires that unfold from one's readings of shorthand. Pater's version of Artemis's birth—for him, she is the daughter of Demeter rather than of Leto—likewise hesitates between a personal predicament and an allegorical rendering of belatedness: "The late birth into the world of this so shadowy daughter was somehow identified with the sudden passing into Hades of her first-born, Persephone" (332–33). A belatedness in which birth and a "passing into Hades" are "somehow identified": this is the birth, too, of Hippolytus out of the vanishing of the Amazons and of Athens's greatness in its absorption of early Attic deme life (as it is, perhaps, the "Renaissance" that Pater repeatedly finds in a present that arrives in time to recover not the past but the still-vital traces of a disappearance: Pico della Mirandola's beautiful corpse still red with life in the grave as the embodiment of humanism's perpetual vitality, or Johann Joachim Winckelmann's discovery of the pulse of life, still "fervent" in the "relics" of ancient culture).[11]

The proliferating repetitions in the text—as Pater transforms Euripides's tale of Aphrodite's wrath to a receding series of Pietà after Pietà—point less to the consolidation of history under a single model (as anticipations or recollections of the death and resurrection of Jesus, for example) than to a series of cells, like rooms in Leibniz's Palace of Destinies. If Hippolytus is a queer figure—it is not impossible to think that Pater was drawn, in part, to a beautiful boy who, in his fierce loyalty to his virgin mother, "never noticed women" (as Edith Hamilton dryly puts it),[12] and his chastity, whatever else it does, also allows one to dwell at ravished length on his physical beauty—it is perhaps less for the easily adducible thematic reasons than for the structure of nonlinear, nonteleological transmission he embodies (atavism or parthenogenesis, but not inheritance). His virgin birth seems important less for its anticipation of Christ than for the ways it liberates transmission from procreation, recovery from presence, development from teleology. And just as, in Pater's account, the story of Theseus—and his curse—recedes from view, deemphasizing the paternal inheritance so important to earlier versions of the myth, the proliferation of maternal relations links maternal grief less to individual development (to any one person's development or to " the mother") than to a more generalized structure of atavistic fatality and recovery-through-loss. Hippolytus's very beauty—"Healthily white and red, he had a marvelous air of discretion about him . . . , as if he never could be anything but like water from the rock, or the wildflowers of the morning, or the beams of the morning star turned to human flesh" (339)—in its embodiment of the freshness of classical art, links Moses (Exod. 17; Ps. 78 and 105),[13] who will not be suffered to enter the promised land, to Artemis, born ("in sorrow") from Demeter in the "rock-hewn cubicle of the inner chamber" (332).

That relation travels laterally; maternal inheritance is emphasized because it encodes a sororal relation, linking Artemis ("somehow") to Persephone. And it is not just the two figures thus linked—Moses excluded from the promised land and a daughter consigned perpetually to return to the underworld—but the way that they are linked by the echo in Pater's language: the "water from the rock" of Hippolytus's beauty evokes the "rock-hewn cubicle of the inner chamber" of Demeter's birth without subordinating Demeter and Artemis to Moses; Pater's language produces an echo that intimates a coexistence or imprecise superimposition. Moreover, the syntax of the sentence in which the reference appears ("never could be anything but") renders, with particular economy, the setting aside of potentiality in the actualization that thereby sustains it, and the series that follows (or . . . or . . . or . . .) presents putatively interchangeable alternatives that are nevertheless not parallel in form or content and that, moreover, themselves embody different modalities of transformation. Hippolytus is thus a palimpsest, a Palace of Destinies sheltering a series of nonhierarchized realized and unrealized worlds. Such a model of historical transmission—the reticulated structure of historical development and the transmission through loss that I have called "queer atavism," the effects, more generally, of a historical model of potentiality—also extends to personal or psychological development (this another sense in which Hippolytus as *character* resists full assimilation to allegory or to a meditation on history) and to the development, in particular, of a sensibility—which, from "Diaphaneitè" to *Gaston de Latour,* might have been Pater's *only* narrative. To think of a character or sensibility as likewise structured by queer atavism—by unrealized worlds, reticulated and nonsubordinated developments, and noncommunicating cells—suggests that the recovery of one's personal history is no less vexed than the recovery of pre-Attic deme life: how much might the "minutely systematic" later observer have to regret at the opportunities for observation wasted, even as that minutely systematic observer might find that there is no identity to recover, nothing there to have been observed. It also suggests that Pater's model of historical transmission is inseparable from the queer erotics of his aesthetics.

In *Innocence and Rapture,* I discussed Pater's model of aesthetic apprehension in detail and suggested why it is also an experience of eroticism. "The Child in the House," I also argued there, narrates the coming-into-being of an aesthetic sensibility ready for rapture, attuned to the refinements of self-loss that make aesthetic perception—even mere sense perception—the domain of queer eroticism for Pater. That the narration in "The Child in the House" is fundamentally incompatible with the development it ostensibly narrates and that this interference, and temporal scrambling, paradoxically constitutes the very sensibility it cannot account for, linked, in my earlier argument, Pater's model of aesthetic apprehension to a troubling of *Bildung* in Pater, James, Wilde, and Vladimir Nabokov. I propose now to return to "The Child in the House" in the context of the queer atavism and potentiality in "Hippolytus Veiled," to read Pater's understanding of aesthetic sensibility as an instance of queer transmission.[14]

Among other things, one notices immediately the recurrent emphasis on contingency in Pater's (ostensibly) autobiographical text of aesthetic *Bildung.* "As Florian Deleal walked, one hot afternoon, he overtook by the wayside a poor aged man," Pater's text begins; "as the man told his story, it chanced that he named the place, a little place in the neighborhood of a great city, where Florian had passed his earliest years."[15] That night, Florian dreams of the place; "and it happened that this accident of his dream was just the thing needed for the beginning of a certain design he then had in view, the noting, namely, of some things in the story of his spirit—in that process of brain-building by which we are, each one of us, what we are" (223). The story likewise concludes on a note of caprice; when the family moves to a new house in a journey the child Florian had "eagerly anticipated," he discovers he has left behind a pet bird, and, on returning to rescue it, he is overcome by the sight of the empty house: "And so, with the bird found, but himself in an agony of home-sickness, thus capriciously sprung up within him, he was driven quickly away, far into the rural distance, so fondly speculated on, of that favourite country-road" (237). *Capriciously* evokes the accident of the encounter (and of the dream) that opens the story, and caprice joins the occasion for the memory with the content thereby remembered: an accidental mention of a lost home happens to occur at just the moment when Florian seeks to trace the emergence of his sensibility, and the accident uncovers the memory of a feeling "capriciously" sprung up in him as the effect of yet another accident.[16]

The story repeatedly links the emerging sensibility to a rooted sense of home—to his particular childhood home, and, by extension, to embodiment and sense perception as the material "home" of consciousness; the way that this instinct for home is made synonymous with homesickness is linked in various ways to the story's understanding of contingency. In the first place, the text repeatedly collocates two senses of *accident,* using the term to signify both a contingent event (a bird left behind or a word dropped by an old man) and a sensible quality (the material form taken by an idea or, for example, by a sensibility). "In the process of our brain-building, as the house of thought in which we live gets itself together, like some airy bird's-nest of floating thistle-down and chance straws, compact at last, little accidents have their consequence" (230). This *accident* refers both to the contingent events that shape a world of thought and to the environment in which the "brain-building" takes place: the brain's embeddedness in a material context. Indeed, Pater's very simile for consciousness—"like some airy bird's-nest"—seems to derive from the incident just narrated: Florian's removal from its nest of a starling, and the remorse he feels at hearing the plaints of its temporarily orphaned hatchlings. Pater's simile of the nest thus redoubles the effect: the trope for brain development (and its informing by a material context) is itself informed by the accident of the narrative: the material form taken by the occasion for insight, but also the accident of its being mentioned, of its coming to memory at this particular time and place. The accidents of our birth and environment (that is, our contingent worldly place, and the sensible qualities of the world in which we have a place) inform, in overdetermined ways, the people we become.

The sensibility described here, moreover, is one particularly attuned to the influences of the material world:

> How insignificant, at the moment, seem the influences of the sensible things which are tossed and fall and lie about us, so, or so, in the environment of early childhood. How indelibly, as we afterwards discover, they affect us; with what capricious attractions and associations they figure themselves on the white paper, the smooth wax, of our ingenuous souls, as "with lead in the rock forever," giving form and feature, and as it were assigned house-room in our memory, to early experiences of feeling and thought, which abide with us ever afterwards, thus, and not otherwise. The realities and passions, the rumors of the greater world without, steal in upon us, each by its own special little passage-way, through the wall of custom about us; and never afterwards quite detach themselves from this or that accident, or trick, in the mode of their first entrance to us. (226)

The "agony of home-sickness," at the end of the text, "thus capriciously sprung up within him," (237) echoes the "capricious attractions and associations" here. Further, caprice also evokes the *nachträglich* structure of causality throughout the tale. "How insignificant at the moment . . . How indelibly, as we afterwards discover": the parallelism emphasizes the temporal lag of significance, and no "minutely systematic" observer can be sufficiently observant without the benefit of hindsight. Consciousness is out of sync with itself because its development can never dispense with that "afterwards." Moreover, the rest of the text makes clear that it is not simply that the indelible impression is not apparent until later. The impression seems in fact to come back from the future, to call the sensibility into being that will then have accounted for the very urge to decipher its retrospective traces.

That paradoxical temporality informs the tale's mode of narration, and its making the narration of development inextricable from the development it ostensibly narrates. But—before turning to that structure—Pater's text renders that paradoxical temporality as a topography. The child is *in* the house but is also rendered, metaphorically, by the house; the house is an (outer) material context that comes to shape the child's (inner) sensibility but also figures both an inner world to be invaded by exterior impressions and a "material habitation" for a sensibility. In a narrative that depicts the formation of an interiority by the external world of "accidents," insides and outsides perpetually change places, and to attempt to track the relation for the text of the terms *child* and *house* is to begin to trace the inside-out topography of a sensibility. "With the image of the place so clear and favorable upon him," we read,

> he fell to thinking of himself therein, and how his thoughts had grown up to him. In that half-spiritualised house he could watch the better, over again, the gradual expansion of the soul which had come to be there—of which indeed, through the law which makes the material objects about them so large an element in children's lives, it had actually become a part; inward and outward being woven through and through each other into one inextricable texture—half, tint and trace and accident of homely colour and form, from the wood and the bricks; half, mere soul-stuff, floated thither from who knows how far. In the house and garden of his dream he saw a child moving, and could divide the main streams at least of the winds that had played on him, and study so the first stage in that mental journey. (223–24)

"Upon him . . . therein . . . to him"; the various (contradictory) spatial relations, the "gradual expansion" of a soul within a material space that it is also said to have "become a part" of (the difficulty, in fact, in that latter phrase, of determining what has "become a part" of what)—all point to the explicit difficulty of tracing a process of development. If "inward" and "outward" are "woven through and through each other into one inextricable texture," then the "tint and trace and accident of homely colour and form" will be impossible to distinguish from the "mere soul-stuff," and the formation of a sensibility will be literally impossible to trace. Hence, then, too, the temporal difficulties—the indeterminate time of "had come to be there" and the hesitation, in "actually," between an assertion of material impingement and a (more Gallic) sense of "now" or "by now" (itself at an indeterminate time, wavering, for instance, between the narrated moment of formation and the later moment of the narration).[17] The inside cannot be isolated—temporally or topographically—from the outside that informs it, making it impossible, in turn, to distinguish the formation—indeterminately acting from within and from without—that forms a sensibility.

The aesthetic sensibility narrated in the text is thus curiously groundless—without logical, spatial, or temporal origin—and contentless. The sensibility comes into being by registering a pure difference, which is why its origination can be traced to a rapture that divides it from itself, why it comes into being through the division that makes it cease to be one—ruptured by its narration and by the impossibility of that narration. "It is false," Pater writes,

> to suppose that a child's sense of beauty is dependent on any choiceness or special fineness, in the objects which present them-selves to it, though this indeed comes to be the rule with most of us in later life; earlier, in some degree, we see inwardly; and the child finds for itself, and with unstinted delight, a difference for the sense, in those whites and reds through the smoke on very homely buildings, and in the gold of the dandelions at the road-side, just beyond the houses, where not a handful of earth is virgin and un-touched, in a lack of better ministries to its desire of beauty. (225)

A comforting theory for those of us who grew up in—for example— suburban Denver instead of Paris or Venice, it suggests that aesthetic ini-tiation occurs not by way of a particular content perceived but through a purely differential relation between a sensibility and its surroundings.[18] What is internalized is not a content but a difference, "a difference for the sense": in the registration of contrasts (like the "delicious recoil" in the "Conclusion" to *The Renaissance*),[19] to "see inwardly" is both to find that such minimal differences suffice for the young mind's aesthetic delight and to perceive the intervention of difference that is itself the formation of aesthetic sensibility.[20] To see inwardly is thus both to see what one needs, aesthetically, to see and to see the inward process that is creating the aesthetically sensitive creature who will come to delight in such per-ceptions. (This is partly why, for Pater, to perceive aesthetically is ever to become a child, and why each aesthetic perception presides in this sense over the creation of a sensibility adequate to it.)[21]

Aesthetic initiation is groundless in that what it allows one to perceive is nothing other than the initiation itself. And the initiation turns out to entail a sensibility's self-division. "This house then stood not far be-yond the gloom and rumors of town, among high garden-wall, bright all summer-time with Golden-rod, and brown-and-golden Wall-flower—*Flos*

Parietis, as the children's Latin-reading father taught them to call it, while he was with them" (225). Pater's prose transcribes a perception of difference in its transmutation of terms—"garden-wall . . . Golden-rod . . . brown-and-golden Wall-flower"—and (beyond the effect of paronomasia) in a wily parallelism where morphological semblance unites diverging terms: garden-wall, summer-time, Wall-flower, even Latin-reading father. The sentence, moreover, seems to enfold two contradictory structures: is the house "among high garden-wall . . . and brown-and-golden Wall-flower," or is the wall "bright . . . with Golden-Rod and . . . Wall-flower"? At the origin of aesthetic sensibility, this description of the house refuses to decide between two contradictory, forking paths. It is therefore "fitting" that, while the house represents the unity of a sensibility with its material habitation—an aesthetic unity of body and soul, form and content, expressed as a perfect adequation of the child's sensibility and its environment—the initiation that forms a sensibility adequate to perceive it occurs through the rupture of that very unity. The "general human instinct" for home, we read, was reinforced by the

> special home-likeness in the place his wandering soul had happened to light on, as in the second degree, its body and earthly tabernacle; the sense of harmony between his soul and its physical environment became, for a time at least, like perfectly played music, and the life led there singularly tranquil and filled with a curious sense of self-possession. (227–28)

The transition between "home" and "home-like" ruptures the identity it asserts (and the child's relation to the particular place his soul "happened to light on" is also asserted to be a matter of contingency).[22]

The unity of body and soul, sensibility and environment, is posited, and rendered as "self-possession" and as Florian's tranquility and security. The sensibility, however, comes into being as those relations fall away from the unity of "perfectly played music." The aesthetic sensibility narrated here comes into being not as the embodiment of Pater's often-asserted ideal of aesthetic unity but as its rupture, and the equivocation—"for a time at least"—soon seems warranted:

> And the sense of security could hardly have been deeper, the quiet of the child's soul being one with the quiet of its home, a place "in-

closed" and "sealed." But upon this assured place, upon the child's assured soul which resembled it, there came floating in from the larger world without, as at windows left ajar unknowingly, or over the high garden walls, two streams of impressions, the sentiments of beauty and pain—recognitions of the visible, tangible, audible loveliness of things, as a very real and somewhat tyrannous element in them—and of the sorrow of the world, of grown people and children and animals, as a thing not to be put by in them. From this point he could trace two predominant processes of mental change in him—the growth of an almost diseased sensibility to the spectacle of suffering, and, parallel with this, the rapid growth of a certain capacity of fascination by bright color and choice form—the sweet curvings, for instance, of the lips of those who seemed to him comely persons, modulated in such delicate unison to the things they said or sang. (228)

A series of unities—the quiet of the child's soul and the quiet of its home, the "assured" place and the "assured" soul—prepares the way for the perception of other forms of unity: the "sweet curvings . . . of the lips of . . . comely persons, modulated in such delicate unison to the things they said or sang." The aesthetic ideal of this "unison" (a Romantic ideal of the symbol or, above, of "perfectly played music") might be rendered as a perfect unity of body and soul, form and content, inner and outer, and yet it is perceived by—or gives rise to—a sensibility that registers (as "the lust of the eye," perhaps [228]) a difference, the division between "his soul and its physical environment," a fall from identity to resemblance (from being "one with the quiet of its home" to being an "assured soul which resembled" an "assured place"—or from inclosed and sealed to "inclosed" and "sealed"), which in turn is figured as a "self-possession" ruptured, a secure house whose windows are found to have been "left ajar unknowingly."

It is for this reason that the narration of aesthetic development is both incompatible with and curiously indistinguishable from that very development. The older Florian, I argued in *Innocence and Rapture,* is a "*revenant,*" one of the querulous "home-returning ghosts" who creep in through windows left ajar (53). If, as I suggested there, it becomes difficult to tell whether the story narrates an initiation or whether (true to the *nachträglich* structure of causality in the text) the narration in fact constitutes the initiation it describes, if, that is, Florian's later return to the scene of his childhood seems uncannily to produce the aesthetically sensitive creature he will have become, this is partly because the narration of the text introduces a difference—between Florian and himself (between the reminiscing Florian and the child he was, but also between the child and itself) and between the past and itself—that can be said to constitute that very sensibility. Hence the peculiar groundlessness, again, of the aesthetic sensibility formed, and its curiously circular relation to the initiation that forms it: the material world intervenes to create a sensibility that can be described as one particularly attuned to the interventions of the material world. ("He came more and more to be unable to care for, or think of soul but as in an actual body, or of any world but that wherein are water and trees, and where men and women look, so or so, and press actual hands" [Pater, "The Child in the House," 232]. The text seeks to recover the particular world that created such a sensibility.) The text's recurrent mode of designating the remembered child—"the child of whom I am writing" (226)—links the narration of the text to the intervention of difference that traverses the child's "self-possession" in his coming to aesthetic awareness. "The child of whom I am writing" marks an interruption that paradoxically constitutes the identity it narrates: the gap in the narrative, its failure to comprise its subject, constitutes that subject.

The catalyzing perception of the text is in fact a difference. What Florian remembers is not the house as it was, nor even himself as he was when he lived there, but rather the house as different from what it was:

And that night, like a reward for his pity, a dream of that place came to Florian, a dream which did for him the office of the finer sort of memory, bringing its object to mind with a great clearness, yet, as sometimes happens in dreams raised a little above itself, and above ordinary retrospect. The true aspect of the place, especially the house there in which he had lived as a child, the fashion of its doors, its hearths, its windows, the very scent upon the air of it, was with him in sleep for a season; only, with tints more musically blent on wall and floor, and some finer light and shadow running in and out along its curves and angles, and with all its little carvings daintier. He woke with a sigh at the thought of almost 30 years which lay between him and that place, yet with a flutter of pleasure still within him at the fair light, as it were a smile, upon it. (223)

When, then, we read, immediately after this sentence, that "this accident of his dream was just the thing needed for the beginning of a certain design," we might wonder whether "this accident" refers to the accident of the dream's taking place or the particular quality—the difference between the house and itself—that characterizes the dream.

The difference is, among other things, anthropomorphizing. Implicit in *aspect*—etymologically, "looking toward or to," which comes to take on the contours of a recognizable face, as in the French *aspect,* meaning both "face" and "look"—the giving of a face becomes explicit when the "fair light" of the dream's difference is called a "smile." The anthropomorphizing of the house returns at the very end of the text in the child's "agony of home-sickness . . . capriciously sprung up within him": "But as he passed in search of [the bird] from room to room, lying so pale, with a look of meekness in their denudation, and at last to that little, stripped white room, the aspect of the place touched him like a face of one dead" (237). The older Florian's anthropomorphizing of the house is, as it were, anticipated by the child he was, just as the autobiographer turns back to consider a childish gesture of turning back and can but replay that originary return to the now empty house (itself therefore retrospectively a figure for the sensibility that is constituted almost purely as a susceptibility to being constituted). It is as if that later anthropomorphic recovery were visible in the past itself, as if Florian's capricious homesickness were a perception of the later remembrance that will have brought it into being. That it is a *dead* face suggests a redoublement of the structure of retrospection: either that the earlier moment can anticipate the later look back because, even then, the child encounters a house that is becoming a part of the past, or, more radically, that the initiatory effect proleptically visible in the child's anthropomorphizing gaze comes back to initiate precisely as a *retrospective* look at a present therefore already past, already dead. Likewise, the subject or the sensibility seemingly brought into being, groundlessly, through the very return to the grounds that will have constituted it, thus also discovers (as initiatory, through a return to the origins it also brings into being) an *empty* house.

Melancholia might offer one way to conceptualize such a structure, emblematized as it is by a dead face and an empty house, but it is very far, I think, from sadness; Pater's melancholic sensibility would seem to entail what is more strictly at stake in melancholia, a refusal of loss that here takes the form of potentiality.[23] In this sense, then, the narration of aesthetic initiation is a perception of a sort of Palace of Destinies, a potentialization or a "redemption" of the past. And that is one way, therefore, to read what is "capricious" in the springing up of homesickness in the child Florian who returns—for the first time, that is—to an empty house. Such might be a way, too, to read the text's recurrent linking of the development of aesthetic perception to death, not only in its explicit references to others' deaths as formative of his sensibility, but in its figuring of impressionability. We might hear, in other words, in the "waxen, resistless faces" of the dead he gazes upon in his visits to the Paris morgue (233), an echo of the "influences of sensible things . . . in . . . early childhood" that figure themselves ("with what capricious attractions and associations") on "the white paper, the smooth wax of our ingenuous souls" (226). Likewise, the return of the dead to "their old homes" both makes Florian such a ghost and links their rupture of the home's security to the formation of aesthetic sensibility through difference. Impressionable mind or waxen face, the boy's openness to his material surroundings—his becoming the house he is "in"—is, at the end, an openness to death.

That is the trajectory of Pater's "Conclusion" to *The Renaissance*. It also suggests another reading of the death of Hippolytus and of Pater's refusal of resurrection for him. The "queer atavism" intimated by that story is thus also a sort of aesthetic rapture: aesthetic and historical "development" join each other in the capricious perception of a dead face. For the end of that text refuses resurrection, leaving Hippolytus, like the Amazons, to exert the "prerogative of poetic protest," and to survive thereby ("Hippolytus Veiled," 327). That paradoxical survival is enacted, at the end, by Antiope, as well as by a curious narrative hiatus. Tangled in the reins of his chariot, Hippolytus is dragged home—and, as Ovid has the dead boy say, "no part of my body / was recognizable: I was just one great wound"[24]—"till he lay at length, grey and haggard, at the rest he had longed for dimly amid the buffeting of those murderous stones, his mother watching impassibly, sunk at once into the condition she had so long anticipated" (Pater, "Hippolytus Veiled," 342). Then, after a break in the text, Pater adds this epilogue:

> Later legends breaks [*sic*] a supernatural light over that great desolation, and would fain relieve the reader by introducing the kindly Asclepius, who presently restores the youth to life, not, however, in the old form or under familiar conditions. To her, surely, counting the wounds, the disfigurements, telling over the pains which had shot through that dear head now insensible to her touch among

the pillows under the harsh broad daylight, that would have been no more of the solace than if, according to the fancy of Ovid, he flourished still, a little deity, but under a new name and veiled now in old age, in the haunted Grove of Aricia, far from his old Attic home, in a land which had never seen him as he was. (342)

Pater's elastic syntax leaves unclear, perhaps, who has "sunk": to resolve it might depend on one's sense of whose death—her own, or her son's—Antiope has long anticipated. Grammatically and thematically, it is probably "he" who has "sunk," which might resolve, too, any threat of incoherence in the mother's coming back to life to count over her son's wounds. And yet the wavering, however brief, is there. The entire imaginary portrait might be said to take shape in the hiatus between a narrative (if only waveringly present) for which the mother "sunk at once into the condition she had so long anticipated" and the evocation of what "would have been" to "her, surely, counting the wounds." The text's series of self-conscious reconstructions—the lost histories that "must have been"—are here rendered as a dead mother's grief for her dead son, a family tree that, by leading nowhere, leads to everything that could have been. Lost, and thereby brought into view, is the body of a beautiful boy: the chaste beauty of Hippolytus (chastity, Antiope remarks twice, being a sort of death) stands in for the queer mode of transmission of this text, for the way that Hippolytus, like Bartleby, and like Pater's aesthetic subject, comes to redeem not what was but what was not. The closing sentence is extraordinarily moving, but it is also filled with a curiously thrilling sense of possibility, because it presents its own Palace of Destinies, describing a mother who, if she were alive, would find no more solace in one revival than in another, leaving us to wonder whether our exile in a land—ours, among many others—that has never seen him as he was is not, finally, where his beauty can most shine for us, "like water from the rock, or the wildflowers of the morning, or the beams of the morning star turned to human flesh."

Part III

5

"That Strange Mimicry of Life by the Living"

Queer Reading in Oscar Wilde's "The Portrait of Mr. W.H."

The charting of what Leo Bersani calls the "metaphysical sociability" that traverses the contemplation of ideal forms in Plato's *Symposium* led us to perceive ways in which the curiously messy narrative of that dialogue makes the vagaries of transmission central to a theory in which desire for a particular boy would seem to vanish into the contemplation of beauty as idea—beauty purified of any accidental qualities, beauty that is nothing other than beauty itself.[1] Foregrounding that process of transmission, the staging of the dialogue acts out some of the consequences of its understanding of love as a form of mediation. Transmission becomes queer not only because Socrates favors the cultivation of ideas over the creation of actual babies and links that cultivation to male intergenerational eros, but also because the text makes clear that, for us, knowledge is indistinguishable from the medium that conveys it. That makes for a paradoxically queer form of transmission, and the fact that knowledge, at one point in Diotima's speech, takes the form of a creative forgetting is perhaps not unrelated to the persistence of the boy's beauty—the beauty of Agathon or Alcibiades, Charmides or Phaedrus—within the ostensibly transcendent form of contemplation that would negate his particularity in the perception of beauty "as such." Not coincidentally (articulating as it does one strand of eroticized aesthetics that finds its source in Plato's dialogue), Oscar Wilde's remarkable story "The Portrait of Mr. W.H." spells out the paradoxical erotics of the disappearance of particular beautiful bodies and explores what it means to say that their beauty "lives on" in art. In so doing, it meditates on "queer reading"—on what it means to "recognize" desires in art, or even to be called to a particular desire by a passionate experience of aesthetic apprehension—and links queer reading to literary history. The boy disappears in the passage from embodied perception to ideal forms; he disappears, too, through the passage of time. Vanished as a particular bodily presence and as a discoverable historical referent, the boy is yet preserved, Wilde suggests, in the act of reading. Its exploration of these two forms of vanishing means that Wilde's story is at once a theory of the erotics of reading and a meditation on literary transmission and literary history.

"The Portrait of Mr. W.H." presents a reading of Shakespeare's sonnets, claiming, more specifically, to have discovered the identity of the "Mr. W.H." to whom the sonnets were dedicated (seemingly by their publisher—speaking to an uncertain degree for Shakespeare himself). It identifies "Mr. W.H." as an actor in Shakespeare's troupe named Willie Hughes—a person who, it turns out, cannot be proven to have ever even existed. It makes another argument, too, which sneaks up on one in the course of reading the story: it argues that male homoeroticism is central not just to the life but to the work of the most celebrated writer in the English literary tradition, that Shakespeare's passion for Willie Hughes transforms not only his personal existence but the plays themselves. Like Plato's *Symposium,* Wilde's text is not just a "theory"; it is also a narrative, and one of considerable complexity. In the simplest possible terms, the narrator tells us the theory of the sonnets that he heard from his friend Erskine, who heard it from Cyril Graham, a one-time boy actor and the most exquisite creature Erskine ever saw. The theory is passed from one man to another, and we are presented with a series of homoerotic relations extending "outward" from the theory: Shakespeare and Willie Hughes; Erskine and Cyril; the narrator and Erskine; and, implicitly, the narrator and his reader. And as one moves through these layers, a beautiful boy disappears with every remove: Cyril falls in love with Willie Hughes, whom he has never seen but whose existence he deduces from a text; Cyril kills himself long before the narrator discusses him with Erskine; Erskine dies before the narrator presents the story to us; and we, of course, never literally see any of them. A reading of the sonnets and the evocation of the beauty of vanishing boys each is made more passionate by its proximity to the other, and the text sets up a relation of mutual figuration between, on the one hand, a reader's absorption in a literary work and, on the other, the fascination exerted by a beautiful or beloved body.

"The Portrait of Mr. W.H." is, in many important respects, about literary transmission, and on several different levels: as a reading of Shakespeare's sonnets, it meditates on historical transmission and the knowledge that escapes it, figured as the beautiful boy who vanishes into the sonnets.

The equivocal afterlife of a beautiful body in poetry is, after all, a recurrent concern of the sonnets themselves, where repeatedly we find that, for the boy to live forever in art, he must submit himself to his vanishing as a human presence, must submit himself to the inhuman form of art. For Wilde's text, the wavering presence of that immortalized boy seems to body forth both a loss—of his embodied presence and any definitive knowledge of the historical conditions in which the sonnets themselves came to birth—and the possibility of a recovery, a presence discerned in the very yearning occasioned by the glimpsing of this loss. Narratively, too, Wilde's story is about transmission—specifically, the communication of literary enthusiasm. Presenting an interlocking series of narratives—a series of readers of the sonnets who pass their feverish discovery on to their interlocutors—the text offers a curiously economic account of literary absorption: to tell (and, especially, to write) of one's passionate relation to the theory of the sonnets is, it seems, to lose that passion, or, more ominously, one's life. On another level, the subject of Wilde's text is transmission in the sense that it is about reading and about what it means to be absorbed—about what it is that can be said to pass between exquisite text and ravished reader. On still another level, it is about recognition, about, in particular, the recognition of one's desires "in" literature. What does it mean to recognize one's own gay male desires by reading the sonnets or the writing of Oscar Wilde? These different senses of transmission, I will argue, are all linked. To consider historical transmission in the text is to consider both absorption and the story's narrative structure. Wilde's text over and over again intertwines the theory it presents with the narrative in which that theory, its Shakespearean reading, is embedded.

In one sense, the story avoids the question of historical fact. For, if the theory of the sonnets is that the "Mr. W.H." of the dedication refers to an actual boy, a boy actor who formed the cornerstone of Shakespeare's art as he did the center of his amorous passion, it is a theory that is curiously unprovable. The problem for the theory, in short, is that it relies entirely on "internal evidence";[2] there is no grounding in external "fact" to anchor the linguistic speculations. The theory proposes to find "proof" of a historical fact using as its sole evidence the language of the poems. The story thus poses, with particular economy, the problem of discerning the relations between the "insides" and "outsides" of literary texts, of linking what goes on inside them to the historical conditions outside them. This is, of course, also the question posed by the frequent deictic play of the sonnets themselves: "So long lives this," we read in Sonnet 18, "and this gives life to thee."[3] Equivocal reference is shown to be the condition of historical transmission: this is what Derrida calls "iterability."[4] Survival—here, the portability of that deictic reference to a potentially infinite series of contexts—is guaranteed precisely by the vanishing of a specific context; that is why the condition of the boy's immortality in the sonnets is his vanishing as a beautiful boy. He becomes immortal on the conditions of becoming a poem and of submitting himself to the logic of erasure that constitutes the possibility of meaning's transmission.

At one moment in the story, Wilde's narrator (at first glance, rather strangely) uses the self-referentiality of the sonnets to argue for their link to the plays. The moment marks one place where the text more or less explicitly seeks to connect the desires of the sonnets to Shakespeare's larger poetic corpus; no mere personal expression of desire that can be bracketed in the contemplation of Shakespeare's plays, the importance of the sonnets is magnified as they become forms of metacommentary, and the particular desire there expressed likewise expands to shape the plays and, implicitly, the English literary tradition in which they loom as monuments.[5] Wilde gets there, however, by exploiting effects related to iterability: of the lines (in Sonnet 18), "Nor shall death brag thou wander'st in his shade, / When in eternal lines to time thou grow'st," Wilde's narrator asserts that *eternal lines* here "clearly alludes to one of his plays that he was sending him at the time, just as the concluding couplet points to his confidence in the probability of his plays being always acted" (1168). By imagining a particular context of transmission and exploiting the oblivion of any particular context implicit in the structure of deictic reference, the narrator turns *this* in the sonnet's couplet ("so long lives this and this gives life to thee") from self-reference to a form of external referentiality and thus allegorizes the entire method of the reading—where historical reference somehow emerges from the text's self-reflexivity. (Likewise, when Sonnet 40 speaks of "this powerful rhyme," he suggests that the reference is not to the sonnet but to *Romeo and Juliet.*) The conspicuous strain in both readings—where the narrator is forced to imagine the sonnet all but physically attached to a particular play and is forced to read against the obvious meaning of the lines—brings to the fore the story's contemplation of questions of historical reference in works of art.

The self-grounding quality of the literary work is thus rendered by the story as a logical flaw: "You start by assuming the existence of the very

person whose existence is the thing to be proven" (1161). The difficulty—
dictated by historical remove, but perhaps also by the nature of the literary
artifact—of giving language a referential anchor, of moving from inside to
outside (from *hews*, say, to *Hughes*) becomes a different kind of movement
inside out: absorption. In the simplest terms, the most immediate effect of
the unprovable theory is to excite fascination.[6] ("It seemed to me that I was
always on the brink of absolute verification, but that I could never really
attain to it" [1178].) Frustrating certainty, the text brings readers inside the
text, exciting more and more language about the sonnets. ("There is really
a great deal to be said for the Willie Hughes theory of Shakespeare's Sonnets" [1201] is the final line of Wilde's story: the ultimate point is to have
a great deal to say.) And it excites eroticism. The upshot, in short, is that
men stay up all night together feverishly reading and talking about the
sonnets—a result unlikely, to say the least, if empirical verification of the
theory were achieved.

Yet however true it might be that empirical uncertainty excites an interest far greater than anything mere certainty might begin to muster, the
relation, for "Mr. W.H.," between a vanishing historical grounding and effects of fascination goes beyond this perverse fact of human psychology
and becomes clearer with a detailed consideration of absorption in the
text. The fascination excited by a literary text is rendered, first, as a blending of voices. The text enacts a reader's absorption by merging its language
with that of the sonnets—or, from another angle, by appropriating it. The
blending of voices becomes increasingly apparent in the second section of
the story. Initially, the words of the sonnets appear as evidence or as matter
to be discussed and are set off semantically and typographically; more and
more, the quotations are syntactically woven into Wilde's sentences, which
themselves begin to narrate the perceived story of the sonnets. What is
perhaps most striking to a modern reader is that Wilde does not analyze
the poems; he retells them, rendering them as a narrative. Finally, the quotations are at last unmarked, the voice of Wilde's text merging with that of
the sonnets:

> I could almost fancy that I saw him standing in the shadow of my
> room, so well had Shakespeare drawn him, with his golden hair, his
> tender flower-like grace, his dreamy deep-sunken eyes, his delicate
> mobile limbs, and his white lily hands. His very name fascinated
> me. Willie Hughes! Willie Hughes! How musically it sounded! Yes;

who else but he could have been the master-mistress of Shakespeare's passion, the lord of his love to whom he was bound in vas-
salage, the delicate minion of pleasure, the rose of the whole world,
the herald of the spring decked in the proud livery of youth, the
lovely boy of whom it was sweet music to hear, and whose beauty
was a very raiment of Shakespeare's heart, as it was the keystone of
his dramatic power? (1169)[7]

Willie Hughes becomes, almost, a perceptual human presence at the moment when the reader's voice appropriates as its own—or is absorbed
by—the words of the sonnets. It is not insignificant therefore that the first
presentation of the theory occurs in quotation and at several removes: the
narrator's rendering of Erskine's account of Cyril Graham's theory of the
sonnets. The narrative structure of the text repeats the absorption it enacts,
and the theory is made an object of literary fascination no less than the
sonnets themselves. Not only is the initial presentation of the theory in
(redoubled) quotation; the narrator, in his own quest, seems to seek to render himself, as it were, in quotation, which might be why the culmination
of his search is a letter, or, beyond the frame, another literary text. (Telling
us the theory, he attempts to reconstruct a letter he wrote that was subsequently lost, and the letter therefore joins Willie Hughes in the historical
oblivion to which fascinating objects are consigned.)

Moreover, the postulated theory shares this structure; once again, the
relation to the sonnets doubles the story discerned in them. Absorption
might describe what happens to Shakespeare in his feigned love for the
dark lady:

It is never with impunity that one's lips say Love's Litany. Words
have their mystical power over the soul, and form can create the
feeling from which it should have sprung. Sincerity itself, the
ardent, momentary sincerity of the artist, is often the unconscious
result of style, and in the case of those rare temperaments that are
exquisitely susceptible to the influences of language, the use of
certain phrases and modes of expression can stir the very pulse
of passion, can set the red blood coursing through the veins, and
can transform into a strange sensuous energy what in its origin
had been mere aesthetic impulse, and desire of art. So, at least, it
seems to have been with Shakespeare. He begins by pretending to

love, wears a lover's apparel and has a lover's words upon his lips. What does it matter? It is only acting, only a comedy in real life. Suddenly he finds that what his tongue had spoken his soul had listened to, and that the raiment that he had put on for disguise is a plague-stricken and poisonous thing that eats into his flesh, and that he cannot throw away. (1186)

At issue here—among other things—is a transition between a literary pleasure ("Love's Litany," "phrases and modes of expression," "style") and a bodily one ("the red blood coursing through the veins"), between bodies and texts. That is, of course, partly what is at stake in pursuing the traces of queer desire in literature: the question of how one moves from words and phrases and aesthetic pleasures to an embodied experience of desire. The passage explores this transition by moving in two seemingly opposed directions. The first is a distancing effect: it is one's "lips" (and not oneself) that say love's litany, and the bodily descriptions as the passage continues are similarly distanced and, as it were, aestheticized. The second, though, makes distancing a form of melding: that very aestheticization describes an experience of a body's seduction, of blood made to flow by words.

Wilde's image of the "plague-stricken and poisonous" raiment describes a form of distancing of an appearance from the essence it masks—"disguise"—where the instrument of control turns out to breach the body's boundaries. Notably, then, Wilde's trope—which invokes a traditional topos of clothes whose opposition to the body doubles the body's to the soul—implicitly links the effect of a text on a desiring body to an aesthetic ideal: one in which form and content merge, like a body and a soul, or like clothes with a body. Experienced as transport, this might be the infinite expansion that links sense perception to the infinity of the soul in Charles Baudelaire's "Correspondences," for example. Wilde's plague-stricken raiment renders that correspondence in, as it were, the opposite direction (and makes it a compulsory, involuntary condition: a garment he "cannot throw away"). The unification that Wilde's image casts as a disease is a Paterian (and Romantic) aesthetic ideal. As it is articulated in Pater's "School of Giorgione," the ideal condition of art is one in which form cannot be distinguished from content, where meaning would therefore be immediately available to sense perception: "Art," Pater writes, "is thus always striving to be independent of the mere intelligence, to become a matter of pure perception, to get rid of its responsibilities to its subject or material;

the ideal examples of poetry and painting being those in which the constituent elements of the composition are so welded together, that the material or subject no longer strikes the intellect only; nor the form, the eye or the ear only; but form and matter, in their union or identity, present one single effect to the 'imaginative reason,' that complex faculty for which every thought and feeling is twin-born with its sensible analogue or symbol."[8] As with the plague-stricken garment that "eats into [the] flesh," form and content cannot be separated; nor is the form, therefore, merely a vehicle for a content that could be expressed apart from it. Each art, Pater's essay begins by asserting, has its own essential "sensuous element" that "brings with it a special phase or quality of beauty, untranslatable into the forms of any other" (102); it would be a "mistake" to think of the different arts as each attempting to translate, in their own forms, a preexisting idea. Having defined the arts by their material embodiment, he then argues that they attempt to "alienate" themselves from their own conditions and to pass into other forms of art. That self-alienation, that striving beyond itself to the untransmissible,[9] thus leads Pater to his particular phrasing of that Romantic ideal where form and content could merge so completely that the idea could be made immediately available to sense.

This Paterian ideal is explicitly invoked, and explicitly eroticized, elsewhere in Wilde's story:

> Yes: the "rose-cheeked Adonis" of the Venus poem, the false Shepherd of the "Lover's Complaint," the "tender churl," the "beauteous niggard" of the Sonnets, was none other but a young actor; and as I read through the various descriptions given of him, I saw that the love that Shakespeare bore him was as the love of a musician for some delicate instrument on which he delights to play, as a sculptor's love for some rare and exquisite material that suggests a new form of plastic beauty, a new mode of plastic expression. For all Art has its medium, its material, be it that of rhythmical words, or of pleasurable colour, or of sweet and subtly-divided sound; and, as one of the most fascinating critics of our day has pointed out, it is to the qualities inherent in each material, and special to it, that we owe the sensuous element in Art, and with it all that in the Art is essentially artistic. (Wilde, "The Portrait of Mr. W.H.," 1173)

To the erotics of the merging of Wilde's voice with Shakespeare's, one would have to add that of his repeated appropriations of Pater, both in the tale's aesthetic theory and in its virtuoso renderings of homoerotic literary history. Wilde makes explicit the eroticism implicit in Pater—that most fascinating of critics, whose "School of Giorgione" Wilde here paraphrases. For Pater, the perception of beauty is often cast as an interaction between material bodies, and he repeatedly links the sensuous grounding of aesthetic effects to human (particularly male) bodies that both feel and are seen.[10] (The homoeroticism of aesthetic perception is explicit in Pater's essay on Winckelmann, but it is implicit throughout *The Renaissance*.) What potentially looks like an alibi—implicitly recasting love poems to a boy as an aesthetic treatise on beauty, which is to say following the ladder of sublimation in Plato's *Symposium* from Willie Hughes to beauty in general—also works in the opposite direction, eroticizing the claims of beauty and linking the ravished perception of the beautiful ideal to an encounter with a particular male body. The same could be said for Wilde's rendition of neo-Platonic aesthetics:

> It is only when we realise the influence of neo-Platonism on the Renaissance that we can understand the true meaning of the amatory phrases and words with which friends were wont, at this time, to address each other. There was a kind of mystic transference of the expressions of the physical world to a sphere that was spiritual, that was removed from gross bodily appetite, and in which the soul was Lord. Love had, indeed, entered the olive garden of the new Academe, but he wore the same flame-coloured raiment, and had the same words of passion on his lips. (1175)

However he might demur from "gross bodily appetite," it is unclear whether Love's entry into the "olive garden" sublimates desire or, on the contrary, makes the spiritual world erotic—as, indeed, for a reader, the experience of that "flame-coloured raiment" makes an allegorical figure indelibly sensual, and as, likewise, the words of passion said to be "on" Love's lips make us loath to forget that surface, and the words, and lips, we might thus almost seem to touch.

Wilde extends the Paterian argument by applying its aesthetic principles to acting—and to the love that Shakespeare bore the beautiful boy who "realised" his art.[11] That aesthetic relation is also a form of erotic commerce, and, rendered as an embodiment of art that is simultaneously a blending of voices, it extends to the text's own use of Shakespeare and, implicitly, to the reader's reading of "The Portrait of Mr. W.H." To speak Love's Litany describes what Willie Hughes does for Shakespeare, what Cyril, Erskine, and the narrator do for Shakespeare, and what a reader, more generally, does for any text: Wilde's description of ensnarement by the work of art also describes vivifying a text, or, in other terms, reading and (more literally) *acting*.[12]

It is worth dwelling, then, on the strangeness of Wilde's description of acting—among other reasons, because it leads to the paradoxical "recognitions" that this text charts as a kind of queer reading. Describing the conditions of theatrical art—which, more embodied than any other art, therefore contains possibilities (and must also address constraints) that the other arts do not—Wilde calls it "that strange mimicry of life by the living" (1173). Wilde's formulation implies, of course, an at least minimal distinction between "life" and "the living" (both words being noun forms that could be derived from the verb *to live*), so that one could be said to "mimic" the other. The living, it seems, mimic life, which suggests that their condition is something other than being alive. (Wilde's formulation would also, of course, trouble any hierarchical ordering of "life" over "mere" art insofar as "living" is not something one can presume to do outside the mimicry that constitutes art.) This also means that the material of art has in a sense entered the object of representation. Where one might expect an account of theater to emphasize the proximity of theatrical representation to what it purports to represent and to see in the identity of a material and what it renders a personification of aesthetic form—the "people" in the play are represented by people on stage, and not, for example by stone or paint—Wilde instead suggests the uncanny entry of the material into what it represents. Theatrical representation intervenes between the human and itself, a crossing of the human with the materiality of art.

That crossing then alters one's sense of what is at stake when, at the end of the text, Wilde describes absorption as a kind of recognition:

> There are few of us have not felt something akin to this. We become lovers when we see Romeo and Juliet, and Hamlet makes us students. The blood of Duncan is upon our hands, and with Timon we rage against the world, and when Lear wanders out upon the

heath the terror of madness touches us. Ours is the white sinless-
ness of Desdemona, and ours, also, the sin of Iago. Art, even the
art of fullest scope and widest vision, can never really show us the
external world. All that it shows us is our own soul, the one world
of which we have any real cognizance. And the soul itself, the soul
of each one of us, is to each one of us a mystery. It hides in the
dark and broods, and consciousness cannot tell us of its workings.
Consciousness, indeed, is quite inadequate to explain the contents
of personality. It is Art, and Art only, that reveals us to ourselves.
(1194)

One's merger with a text is described as a form of self-recognition. The
nachträglich structure of that recognition evokes *The Picture of Dorian
Gray* and the paradoxically vicarious confession that commences the various identificatory exchanges in that text; it is worth noticing the curious
facts here that, as in the longer text, the secret seems to come into being
after its revelation, that what is constituted, first, is a purely contentless
locus of secrecy, which, in *Dorian Gray,* then writes itself on a body (stains
a famous, exquisite young cheek with shame). More or less clandestinely
at stake, which is also to say more or less explicitly so, is a specifically gay
self-recognition: the recognition of one's desires, for example (to evoke
the story's own gay literary histories), in *The Symposium* or neo-Platonic
aesthetic writing or Renaissance sonnets (Shakespeare's or Michelangelo's)
or the long homoerotic tradition that, in Wilde's rendition, constitutes
the Western canon. That kind of recognition works in two directions in
Wilde's text, which powerfully evokes both kinds of experience: on the one
hand, a coming to a recognition of one's own desire "through" literature,
finding desires revealed there that one then senses, after the fact, had been
there all along, and, on the other, a recognition of gay desire "in" literature,
which Wilde renders (possibly allegorically, possibly in more literal terms)
as the centrality of homoerotic desire (for boy actors especially) not only
to aesthetics derived from *The Symposium* but to Romanticism and to the
Enlightenment. These recognitions make the text resonate powerfully, it
seems to me, for a gay reader and suggest why this text is about gay reading
and gay readers. The characters' recognition of Willie Hughes, and Shakespeare's desire for him, catalyzes these various, and variously equivocal,
recognitions.

Yet it is a very strange sort of recognition, and one that is grounded in the particular relation of idea to embodiment in acting, "that strange mimicry of life by the living." What can it mean, after all, to see oneself in a text?[13] The final pages of Wilde's story recur to the experience of absorption or fascination—in reading or in watching a play. And two different kinds of experience come together. On the one hand, we are presented with—for lack of a better term—a psychological recognition or identification. This strand is exemplified in assertions such as "There are few of us who have not felt something akin to this," for example, or the repeated substitution of pronouns that identify the speaker with the narratives of the plays and sonnets:

> Yes: I lived at all. I had stood in the round theater with its open
> roof and fluttering banners, had seen the stage draped with black
> for a tragedy, or set with gay garlands for some brighter show. . . .
> In the side boxes some masked women were sitting. One of them
> was waiting with hungry eyes and bitten lips for the drawing back
> of the curtain. As the trumpets sounded for the third time she went
> forward, and I saw her olive skin and raven's-wing hair. I knew her.
> She had marred for a season the great friendship of my life. Yet
> there was something about her that fascinated me. (1194–95)

A further blending of voices in ventriloquism, these moments seem to invite us to understand absorption as a form of identification, and identification as a mirroring, across history, of shared desires.

On the other hand, however, Wilde also renders the recognition of oneself in art in more unsettling terms:

> We sit at the play with the woman we love, or listen to the music in
> some Oxford garden, or stroll with our friend through the cool gal-
> leries of the Pope's house at Rome, and suddenly we become aware
> that we have passions of which we have never dreamed, thoughts
> that make us afraid, pleasures whose secret has been denied to us,
> sorrows that have been hidden from our tears. The actor is uncon-
> scious of our presence: the musician is thinking of the subtlety of
> the fugue, or the tone of his instrument; the marble gods that smile
> so curiously at us are made of insensate stone. But they have given
> form and substance to what was within us; they have enabled us to
> realise our personality; and a sense of perilous joy, or some touch

or thrill of pain, or that strange self-pity that man so often feels for himself, comes over us and leaves us different. (1194)[14]

One reading of this moment would emphasize a psychological conversion: the turning of art to recognizable, or at least recognized, passions within us. Yet the implication is also that these recognitions can occur only after the fact because what occasions them is fundamentally different from the passions recognized. "The actor is unconscious of our presence: the musician is thinking of the subtlety of the fugue, or the tone of his instrument; the marble gods that smile so curiously at us are made of insensate stone." In music and theater (in this reading) two disjunctive forms of rapture confront one another and thereby produce a paradoxical recognition: if one recognizes a personal passion in the work of art, there may be a mirroring of artist and spectator, but its basis is not resemblance (just as its result is not to consolidate our identity but rather to leave us, in some unspecified way, "different").[15] The communion imagined in the experience of aesthetic absorption is not psychological and is not mimetic. Whatever emotional reaction one might have to exquisitely played music, that emotion does not mirror anything felt by the performer, whose relation to the music is purely formal. (Method acting, at least in the way it is popularly rendered, looks like a vulgarism. And indeed Wilde celebrates boy actors in part because their gender—by virtue of our tendency to essentialize gender and to see it as a condition of personhood—separates actor from role and makes acting artistic to the extent that it prevents any understanding of that relation as immediate.) At the limit, then, the gods, who may smile at us, and, occasioning pleasure or rapture, may seem to mirror back to us our humanity, are "made of insensate stone."[16]

Hence, the recognition of one's desire "in" literature has the potential to identify the "soul" with something inhuman, with, even, insensate stone. The "self-pity" man feels for himself seems an effect of alienation; to give "form and substance to what was within us . . . to realise our personality" is thus not to express a psychology but to become something other, to become a form: "As from opal dawns to sunsets of withered rose I read and re-read them in garden or chamber, it seemed to me that I was deciphering the story of a life that had once been mine, unrolling the record of a romance that, without my knowing it, had colored the very texture of my nature, had dyed it with strange and subtle dyes. Art, as so often happens, had taken the place of personal experience" (1194).

To decipher "a life that had once been mine," to assert a continuity across history of shared passions, is to displace "personal experience." And art's taking the place of "personal experience" is rendered as a becoming-material of the human—a nature made into a "texture," and, like the dyer's hand, "dyed . . . with strange and subtle dyes." Hence, art may reveal us to ourselves, but "the soul of each one of us, is to each one of us a mystery. It hides in the dark and broods, and consciousness cannot tell us of its workings." Therefore, if, on the one hand, Wilde's text renders an aesthetic ideal of form merging with content in terms that implicitly eroticize it, bringing "flame-coloured raiments" and lips of flesh and blood to beauty's garden, the gay self-recognition that this aesthetic judgment makes possible is curiously—exhilaratingly—alienating.

That paradoxical recognition might also go some way toward explaining the strange economy of fascination in Wilde's text, why the theory's hold over one seems incompatible with its expression: "No sooner, in fact, had I sent it [a letter, later lost, containing his "strong appeal to Erskine to do justice to the memory of Cyril Graham"] off than a curious reaction came over me. It seemed to me that I had given away my capacity for belief in the Willie Hughes theory of the Sonnets, that something had gone out of me, as it were, and that I was perfectly indifferent to the whole subject" (1196). The narrator wavers among a series of accounts of why he lost his faith, but the common thread among all of them is a loss structural to transmission—a loss entailed by the alienating terms through which the fascination itself is described. At this moment, in other words, the narrator seems to become an artist: to identify with an inhuman, formal fascination is to cross over to a realm of indifference (indifference, at least, to the emotional terms with which the fascination has been framed). His indifference thus forms an alternative, more benign, mode of entry "into" the theory. (For Cyril and Erskine that merger entailed death.) The exteriorization of the "soul" in the recognition charted by the text might lead one to separate oneself from, as much as to identify oneself with, the soul thus constituted. The gods that smile at us are made of insensate stone. A sense of perilous joy comes over us, and leaves us different. Hence, in one reading, the recurrent series of exchanges between texts and hands:

Those stained and yellow pages had once been touched by his white hands. (1192)

A book of Sonnets published nearly three hundred years ago, written by a dead hand and in honour of a dead youth, had suddenly explained to me the whole story of my soul's romance. (1195)

This living hand: the decaying paper and the white hand, the dead hand and the living verse, seem to change places, the life of one coming at the expense of the other's death and decay. In the first instance, we get both sides of this exchange by dint of the decay of the *hand* intimated by the "stained and yellow pages" (and their foregrounded materiality), their visible decay embodying, as it were, the disappearance of that white hand, even as the explicit contrast of yellow paper to white hand moves in the opposite direction. In the second instance, the exchange is an effect of the conflation of two times: the hand was not dead when it wrote the sonnets to a boy who had not yet vanished. Read *now,* the way that death invaded the living hand at the moment of writing becomes explicit; this temporal crossing, insofar as it also describes an identificatory one, charts a perilous passage for the reader as well, whose present is likewise fused with the past tense of writing. The rhythm of fascination and indifference in the narrative progress of the story is thus a rendering of the identification or recognition described there, the curiously expropriating experience of finding one's desires written in art. In that exchange between art and life, human life encounters the unassimilably foreign temporality of the work of art: "To the present day I cannot understand the beginning or the end of this strange passage in my life" (1197).

The question of gay reading—of the relation of an embodied experience of desire to the rapture attending the reading of a literary text—is also the question of survival raised by the sonnets themselves. To be immortalized in art is an equivocal proposition, if only because one must be dead to have access to that immortality. The two blank lines that end Sonnet 126—the last sonnet to the boy, a sonnet whose pun on *render* is given flesh, as it were, by a lapsing into silence that is also a comprising of silence by a line and by a voice, as if a blank line could be *read*—make almost unbearably tangible what it might mean to live forever in art. That sonnet, not coincidentally, embodies the crisis that Agamben calls "the end of the poem."[17] Noting that the possibility of enjambment—"the opposition of a metrical limit to a syntactical limit, of a prosodic pause to a semantic pause" (109)—is the only possible way to distinguish poetry from prose and that the poem becomes formally coherent only at the end (or, in other words, in the one line of a poem where enjambment is not possible), Agamben notes that the poem is therefore defined by an element that is not poetry. "Poetry," he writes, "lives only in the tension and difference (and hence also in the virtual interference) between sound and sense, between the semiotic sphere and the semantic sphere" (109). The end of the poem thus causes a crisis: "As if the poem as a formal structure would not and could not end, as if the possibility of the end were radically withdrawn from it, since the end would imply a poetic impossibility: the exact coincidence of sound and sense" (113). Thinking in these terms about the final sonnet to the boy, it is not just the final two lines that body forth the impossibility of ending, leaving us to "read" silence. The end of the poem has invaded the poem itself. For Sonnet 126 departs from the formal structure of the other sonnets in another way: the rhyming couplet that announces the end of the poem in the other sonnets has moved "inside" the poem. The other sonnets' final couplet has become the rhyme scheme of the poem, so that one has, in a sense, nothing but endings. In this envoi that ends and coincides with the sonnet, the boy disappears into the end of the poem—vanishing and sheltered there in perpetuity.

Hence Willie Hughes cannot be found in the sonnets. The rapture of the sonnets' language both makes him viscerally present to absorbed readers and entails his disappearance:

> His true tomb, as Shakespeare saw, was the poet's verse, his true monument the permanence of the drama. So had it been with others whose beauty had given a new creative impulse to their age. The ivory body of the Bithynian slave rots in the green ooze of the Nile, and on the yellow hills of the Cerameicus is strewn the dust of the young Athenian; but Antinous lives in sculpture, and Charmides in philosophy (Wilde, "The Portrait of Mr. W.H.," 1193).

Repeatedly at issue for the sonnets is the equivocal nature of living "in" art—"in sculpture," "in philosophy," or "in" a noble line. The verse in which the boy lives forever is also a tomb; suspended in potentiality, the boy lives where preservation and oblivion become indistinct. Wilde's text makes clear that this is also the question for the reader of the literary work. To recognize oneself in art is, in this sense, to "live" there—to answer the injunction, for example, of Pater's "Conclusion" to *The Renaissance*. But to burn always with a hard gemlike flame is to confront, over and over again, life's brevity; art does not so much preserve the moment as make visible its vanishing.[18] That is another reason, then, why the recognition detailed by "Mr. W.H." seems, in certain of its formulations, so uncompromisingly austere in its refusal of psychological mirroring.

This is why the unprovability of the theory of the sonnets and the thwarting of definitive historical reference is the principle of literary transmission in this text: the disappearance of Willie Hughes into the text links his disappearance as historical fact (or historically embodied presence) to his becoming-text, his appearance as text. In that sense, therefore, the unprovability of the theory becomes the principle of transmission in the text: Mr. W.H. is "transmitted" to future readers precisely through his disappearance as a verifiable person, as a referential "fact." Absorption is incompatible with a definite historical "proof" of the existence of Willie Hughes precisely because of the text's antimimetic, antipsychological rendering of absorption. That absorption can countenance neither the discovery of definitive historical reference nor the ceding of the desire to find it; reaching out to an outside it must never grasp, its condition is the curiously suspended reference of the literary work. And what initially seems a contingent effect—of historical loss, of this particular literary mystery—turns out to be structural to literary transmission. The text's narrative of literary absorption is thus also its theory of literary history. Irrecoverable historical proof fuels eroticized fascination; the boy's living on, his perpetual preservation in the sonnets, is guaranteed by his disappearance. What is transmitted by literature, what conveys its perpetual fascination, is nothing other than a loss. Wilde's understanding of queer reading thus moves between a reification and an erasure; exciting forms of recognition—of oneself, or of one's desires, in Shakespeare's text, or in Oscar Wilde's—such reading catalyzes a form of identification where it is difficult to distinguish the postulated queer reader from his vanishing into fascination and into the inhuman temporality of art.

6

Erotic Bafflement and the Lesson of Oscar Wilde

De Profundis

> *Do you really think that at any period in our friendship you were worthy*
> *of the love I showed you, or that for a single moment I thought you were?*
> *I knew you were not. But Love does not traffic in a marketplace, nor use*
> *a huckster's scales. Its joy, like the joy of the intellect, is to feel itself alive.*
> *The aim of Love is to love: no more, and no less.*
>
> —Oscar Wilde, *De Profundis*

How splendid it would be if it were true, if shame felt this exquisite, if one's own abjection could be the occasion for a song like Wilde's. Some personal destitutions remain stubbornly unremediable, and yet Wilde's text makes me dream that to formulate my inadequacy to his upbraiding address might begin to describe the erotic appeal of "art for art's sake." How splendid that would be. Chapter 5 suggested that Wilde's "Portrait of Mr. W.H." offers a complex meditation on absorption—as a cipher of the paradoxical afterlife lived "in" the work of art, of the strange identifications excited by the vanishing of human presence in the austere form of art. In contemporary readers—often, though not exclusively, queer ones—Wilde himself, of course, inspires an investment not entirely dissimilar to Erskine's and Cyril's investment in Shakespeare and his beloved boy, and it is difficult not to view the fate of those passionate readers (as, perhaps, the fate of Dorian Gray himself), as uncanny presentiments of Wilde's own martyrdom. The complex ramifications of the way his sordid tragedy helped codify twentieth-century homosexual identity (so that his name could enable generations of gay readers to discover a name for their own desires) have been explored by astute readers such as Ed Cohen, Linda Dowling, Lee Edelman, Neil Bartlett, Ellis Hanson, Wayne Koestenbaum, and Eve Kosofsky Sedgwick. The appalling spectacle of Wilde's imprisonment, even from a century's historical remove, perhaps also appalls us because, like the return of Alcibiades in the *Symposium,* it reminds us that ideas cannot fully escape the bodies that give them birth, that ideas are housed in persons who can be subject to the intervention of a homophobic society, can be imprisoned, tortured, or killed. The recognition of a gay Wilde—or the recognition of homosexuality through Wilde—therefore occurs, at least to some extent, through the negation of his art (in part because one perhaps recognizes in the silencing of Wilde's art by a punitive social apparatus the thwarting of one's own, less lavish, gifts).

Wilde's post-trial writing is aware of that potential legacy, and it artfully recasts his martyrdom to the homophobic mores of his age as a self-willed martyrdom to art—a disappearance into the work of art like those of Mr. W.H., Cyril Graham, or Dorian Gray. Chief among his post-trial writing is *De Profundis,* Wilde's 1897 prison letter to Lord Alfred Douglas (or "Bosie"). (Wilde titled his letter as a parodic papal bull: *Epistola: In Carcere et Vinculis. De Profundus* is the name given by Robert Ross to the letter's expurgated form first published in 1905 and, conventionally, the name given to the unexpurgated version that finally appeared in 1962.)[1] This unclassifiable text has shown itself to be curiously elusive. When the letter is not simply culled for biographical data (a suspect operation in relation to this evasive, cagey, guarded, and extravagant text), it is often treated by queer critics, and even by those for whom it movingly documents (sometimes, implicitly, nothing but) the fact of oppression, as something of an embarrassment, its sentimental, vindictive, resentful, and even catty tones shaming the urbane linguistic play of the queer 1890s sophisticate. It is, unmistakably, a pained letter, and it is often a painful one to read— dramatizing a great mind distracted, baffled by impossible and demeaning circumstances, and yet still desperately in love. It also offers one of Wilde's most complex meditations on aestheticism: on the relation between art and "life," on the eroticism of aesthetic experience, and on beauty and the transmission of ideas. *De Profundis* is, ultimately, a pedagogical text, and to consider the consequences of Wilde's life and works for the question of queer reading, one must brave, perhaps, the difficulties of that imagined teaching, particularly as it is enacted by the text's exacting mode of address. The letter leads me to ask what its erotic bafflement might mean for queer literary criticism, to ask what that criticism might have to gain from a teacher who betrays it and who offers not so much liberation as the opportunity to partake in his abjection.

Wilde's trials and imprisonment offer the allure, for queer criticism, of reifying a sometimes intangible experience of oppression: look, it can say, my suffering felt like *that,* and *De Profundis* might be read—indeed, has been read—as documenting oppression in a straightforward testimonial to homophobia's cruel tariffs. Yet to discover one's own testimonial in *De Profundis* is a peculiar gesture: it is rivetingly personal and confessional, but in its most daringly shameless moments, it is unclear what has been revealed, and in its most intimately confessional moments, the confessions are made on another's behalf. It is intimately confessional and excites a kind of identification, in other words, in spite—or, rather, because—of its tendency to produce its most powerful effects of identification slantwise, or vicariously, which indirection extends beyond the fact that, as Richard Ellmann notes, "more than half" of this "dramatic monologue" is "taken up by his confession, not of his own sins, but of Bosie's."[2] Arguing against Jonathan Dollimore's contention that in *De Profundis* Wilde unequivocally reinstalls the "authentic, sincere subject" he had previously subverted, thus exemplifying, even embodying "the defeat of the marginal and the oppositional" through "ideological domination," Ellis Hanson points to, among other things, the pleasures and elusiveness of confession itself.[3] "Confession," he writes, "is a mode of pleasure for Wilde, and not just an allusion to pleasure. . . . His confessions are a splendid artifice. Every time he opens his closet, something new and strange pops out—usually another closet. . . . [In Wilde's confessions,] there is always something of the beautiful lie" (Hanson, *Decadence and Catholicism,* 290, 293).

We might consider the paradoxical pleasures of confession in *De Profundis*—and sharpen our sense of its power to thwart and enable various critical recognitions—by dwelling on its pedagogical method. "The most important thing about *De Profundis*," writes Ellmann, "is that it is a love letter," and I think that it is a love letter precisely to the extent that its goals are pedagogical (Ellmann, *Oscar Wilde,* 515). "You came to me," Wilde writes to close his letter to Douglas, "to learn the Pleasure of Life and the Pleasure of Art. Perhaps I am chosen to teach you something much more wonderful, the meaning of Sorrow, and its beauty" (*De Profundis,* 658). Sorrow, I will suggest, allows Wilde to resolve (and not to resolve) the letter's pedagogical aims ("Sorrow, . . . and all that it teaches one, is my new world" [517]), but for now, I would note how often Wilde characterizes the letter as a lesson, particularly in self-knowledge: "I could have held up a mirror to you, and shown you such an image of yourself that you would not have recognised it as your own till you found it mimicking back your gestures of horror, and then you would have known whose shape it was, and hated it and yourself for ever" (555). That the language here reminds one of Dorian Gray's equivocal commerce with his portrait suggests that Wilde's casting of the letter as a mirror—"If you have read this letter as carefully as you should have done you have met yourself face to face" (641–42)—entails not simply an excoriation of Douglas for his moral shortcomings but a complex erotics of address. Douglas is to speak the letter in Wilde's voice, to see himself less as Wilde sees him (for Wilde is still in love) than as an incarnation of self-loathing, an experience of chastisement meant to move one outside the self. The image is one's own when it mimics back one's gestures of horror, when it repudiates one as one has tried to repudiate it, when one uncannily sees one's own gesture of horror directed at oneself. It is striking that Wilde refers to what his previous letters "could have" done—"I could have held up a mirror to you"—and imagines a scene where the self-recognition is purely potential: "then you would have known." And these unwritten letters of potential excoriation are paired with the self-vindicating betrayal Wilde could have used in the trial: he could have told the court that the offenses he was accused of were Douglas's, that they had been credited, as it were, to Wilde's account. Invoking a violence it refrains from committing—"I could if I had chosen have torn you to pieces with bitter reproaches. I could have rent you with maledictions"(554–55)—it seeks to form a mirror at least ostensibly distinguishable from what he did not do, to effect the self-recognition by referring to his past restraint, to what he *could have* done.

Bosie's encounter with himself and the complex vicissitudes of identification it condenses are to induce humility and, most importantly, *shame*—one name for the alienation produced by becoming the occasion of one's own startled horror—which is inspired perhaps less by remembered behavior than by this detour through a past text and through a suspended capacity. *Shame* is one of Wilde's most mobile, multivalent, and erotic terms in *De Profundis* and *The Ballad of Reading Gaol,* as it is in *Dorian Gray*: as Lord Henry Wotton famously says in his confession on Dorian's behalf, where chiasmus marks in its very rhetoric the traces of the confession's vicariousness and power of alienation (and anticipates, and as if diagnoses, Dorian's later identificatory commerce with his portrait), "You, Mr. Gray, you yourself, with your rose-red youth and your rose-white boyhood, you have had passions that have made you afraid, thoughts that have filled you with terror, day-dreams and sleeping dreams whose mere memory might stain your cheek with shame—."[4] For Dorian, shame is inseparable from being named—he is named or addressed in variations of the second-person eight times before any content is given to his confession—which makes the shaming inseparable from the lover's address (Dear Bosie: you, you, you, you . . .). The effort to shame Bosie is also a calling out of his name by the despairing voice of love. And shame is inseparable from the peculiarly *nachträglich* constitution of Dorian's character: he is to discover, in retrospect, by being told by another, the shaming desires that will have determined his character, and it is unclear from the outset whether the shame is generated by the content of those waking dreams or by the fact that he does not know he has had them until he hears about them later from another. (That temporal structure and the vicarious illumination, even more than the sexual connotations of words like *passion, terror,* and *shame*—and perhaps more, even, than the explicitly homoerotic context—make Dorian's "confession" here resonate with the experience of coming out.) Shame marks a character's or a personality's permeability; in *Dorian Gray* and *De Profundis* one is not so much ashamed of anything in particular as one *is* insofar as one is ashamed, even as shame marks the realization of one's excess or deficiency in relation to oneself, and thus shame, for both texts, is also an erotic affect.[5] The letter's eroticism often appears in images of humiliation that echo Lord Henry's assertion of shame's power to mark the flesh: "Read the letter over and over again till it kills your vanity," Wilde writes. "You must read this letter right through, though each word may become to you as the fire or the knife of the surgeon that makes the delicate flesh burn or bleed"; "Your pale face used to flush easily with wine or pleasure. If, as you read what is here written, it from time to time becomes scorched, as though by a furnace-blast, with shame, it will be all the better for you" (*De Profundis,* 510, 511, 551).

The lesson's eroticism, however, is not simply in its imagining of the scourging of Bosie's body and soul, the scarring and scorching of his pale face and delicate flesh. The permeability that makes it an erotic affect links shame to complex forms of address and vicarious confession visible from the text's very opening: "Dear Bosie, After long and fruitless waiting I have determined to write to you myself, as much for your sake as for mine, as I would not like to think that I had passed through two long years of imprisonment without ever having received a single line from you, or any news or message even, except such as gave me pain" (509). The bumpy logic—he seems perversely to level the distinction between writing to Bosie and receiving a letter from him, asserting that, to ensure that he would not go two years without a letter, he has resolved to write one himself—makes the letter itself, in its mode of address, a mirror holding an image that Bosie will not recognize as his own until he sees it mimic back his gestures of horror. "As I would not like to think that . . .": Wilde's formulation seems at once rhetorical (he knows he has received no word)[6] and not (perhaps he really would not like to think it). The rhetorical form asserts that writing to Bosie can take the place of writing from him, even as the ostensibly literal statement makes explicit that Wilde's thought is what truly matters; it levels the distinction not just between thought and action but between Wilde's thought and Douglas's action.

The lover knows the misery of never being loved enough, of never being loved at all, since the beloved's desire cannot coincide with his own. The beloved knows, however, the imposition and presumption of desire, the lover's imperious need to which the beloved is, paradoxically, superfluous. And to receive such a letter would be to experience an unsettling form of erasure; as Douglas is preempted by Wilde, there is, in more than one sense, no room for Douglas, and the shame the letter hopes to produce is a function of that address. The address replays the structural impossibility of learning the lessons it offers: over and over, it constructs lessons that cannot be learned, offers insights that cannot be used. Shame and erotics emerge when the student is confronted by this impossibility. The address to an absent lover that becomes the occasion to preempt the lover's voice is, perhaps, a common trope in love poetry. (To go no farther than the texts I discuss here, one thinks of Swinburne's "Anactoria." Generically, love poetry overlaps with elegy because of this structural absence.) Wilde's letter, that is to say, is a love poem, and its mode of erotic address is pedagogical. Thus, the text's lessons often culminate in unanswerable questions:

> "Are you beginning now to understand a little? Is your imagination wakening from the long lethargy in which it has lain?" (556)

> "Does it ever occur to you what an awful position I would have been in if for the last two years, during my appalling sentence,

I had been dependent on you as a friend? Do you ever think of that?" (630)

"Have you imagination enough to see what a fearful tragedy it was for me to have come across your family? What a tragedy it would have been for anyone at all, who had a great position, a great name, anything of importance to lose?" (631)

How would one answer such questions? Yes? No, I don't have the imagination to see how awful I was? Wilde refashions the lover's plaint into an exam a student could never pass, a lesson that, even if it could be learned, could never be proven to have been learned.

The structure of pedagogy in *De Profundis* is not simply to be read as Wilde's rendering of what I can only imagine to be the paralyzing physical and mental constraints of prison life. No doubt part of the letter's emotional power comes from the crossing of the love affair with Wilde's subjection to prison—and from the (often self-consciously) tendentious assertions of thought's power over both. Yet the equivocal assertions of authority and the particular form of erotic pedagogy in the text are not fully determined by circumstance. Thus, there are important aesthetic continuities linking Wilde's understanding of pedagogy in his prison writing to his formulation of it in his earlier writing. Lord Henry Wotton's (for Dorian, highly influential) denunciation of influence comes to mind. The particular pedagogical demands of *De Profundis* also remind me of Wilde's fairy tales, which often begin as if preparing to give Victorian lessons in morality, only to render these lessons curiously unreadable, offering instead mini-manifestos of decadent aesthetics. The tales return again and again to beautiful but useless gestures of self-sacrifice for illusory causes or for the oblivious or unworthy, and the sacrifice's beauty often depends upon the delusion of the one who sacrifices him- or herself. Self-consciously inhabiting a didactic genre, these tales repeatedly offer paradoxical forms of pedagogy. The lovely and useless self-sacrifice of the artists in Wilde's fairy tales is, among other things, a trope for "art-for-art's sake," and the lesson in the fairy tales and in *De Profundis* is in many ways in the rigors of aestheticism. That the eponymous character in "The Remarkable Rocket" is self-important and delusional ensures that the consummation of his life remains pure—his blaze of glory serves no purpose, is not even coherently intended, and is witnessed by no one. Self-sacrifice is also at the center of

"The Nightingale and the Rose," in which the nightingale thinks that she has finally found in a smitten student a lover whose passion is adequate to the songs she sings.[7] This lover needs a red rose—his beloved will not dance with him otherwise—and there is an elaborately explained shortage of red roses. The tree who can give the nightingale this rose tells her that making it will entail her death: "If you want a red rose, . . . you must build it out of music by moonlight, and stain it with your own heart's-blood. You must sing to me with your breast against a thorn. All night long you must sing to me, and the thorn must pierce your heart, and your life-blood must flow into my veins, and become mine" (293). In lovely passages that, dominated by similes and repetition, evoke the exquisitely mannered still-nesses of *Salomé,* the story describes the bird's sacrifice to love, her song so beautiful that "the white moon heard it, and she forgot the dawn, and lingered on in the sky" (295).

The student, meanwhile, is unworthy of the nightingale, and his love, unworthy of her sacrifice. The passionate bird speaks of what she will do for love: "All that I ask of you in return is that you will be a true lover, for Love is wiser than Philosophy, though he is wise, and mightier than Power, though he is mighty. Flame-coloured are his wings, and coloured like flame is his body. His lips are sweet as honey, and his breath is like frankincense." But the uncomprehending ostensible lover merely seizes the opportunity to pontificate: "She has form . . . that cannot be denied her; but has she got feeling? I am afraid not. In fact, she is like most artists; all style without any sincerity. She would not sacrifice herself for others. She thinks merely of music, and everybody knows that the arts are selfish. Still, it must be admitted that she has some beautiful notes in her voice. What a pity it is that they do not mean anything, or do any practical good!" (294). Just as the bird in "The Happy Prince" hallucinates meaning where it is not, find-ing unmistakable signs of love in the movements of a windblown reed, the student dismisses meaningful sounds as mere "style." These inverse mistakes of interpretation ground the moral meanings of the tales. The nightingale dies, the student finds the red rose ("It is so beautiful that I am sure it has a long Latin name" [295]), but the beloved woman flings it away because it does not match her dress, leaving the student, who decides love is impractical, to return to his room to read alone. The story's pastiche of the student's superficiality and sophomoric aesthetics, however, pales next to the useless beauty of the nightingale's sacrifice and the prose it calls into being. The student's dismissal of the bird's style without substance seems a wry send-up of critiques of decadence, but the loveliness of the bird's paean to love may depend on its not being understood. The story severs an ethos of self-sacrifice from its moorings in utilitarian or moralizing ideologies, renders it a lovely, useless, aestheticist gesture. The rose dyed red with the nightingale's blood is all the more exquisite for having been discarded: the nightingale might be said to sacrifice herself not for the sake of the student's love but for the sake of the sacrifice itself. A story about misplaced identification and deluded reading offers no real lessons about either; the delusion seems to have been necessary for—but irrelevant to—the beauty of the sacrifice it inspired, made possible by the nightingale's misreading and the student's failure to learn his lesson.

If Wilde is to play the nightingale, he might need the oblivious student as the occasion for his song. And in fact I would suggest that we read the lesson of *De Profundis* as analogous to those of the fairy tales, that we think of Wilde's self-sacrifice, his casting of himself as, like Christ, a "Man of Sorrows," in terms of the nightingale's lovely, useless self-sacrifice.[8] In *De Profundis*, Wilde thus does not leave behind "art-for-art's sake" so much as sacrifice himself to it. Wilde's martyrdom to art is of a piece with the letter's treacherous mode of address: just as the letter rules out the response it would seem to crave, it spells out an aestheticist ideal to which Douglas must remain inadequate. In Wilde's prison letter, the structural impossibility of learning the offered lesson appears, among other places, in the irreconcilable semantic alternation in the often-repeated word *realize*. Bosie is asked both to "realise" what he has done—to *know* it—and to "realise" it as Wilde uses that word in *Dorian Gray* and elsewhere: to make it "real" or visible, as Dorian makes tangible ideals of beauty, gives them perceptible form. "Realise your youth while you have it," Lord Henry tells Dorian Gray (*Dorian Gray*, 22). Dorian's proleptic loss—that is, his anticipatory realization of what will have been his loss, which makes him, for the course of the novel, "forever young"—achieves the impossible task of reconciling realization as knowledge with realization as embodiment. *De Profundis* is in many ways about the incompatibility of these two imperatives and the potential eroticism of that incompatibility. On the one hand, *realize* is a term for the knowledge of his sins and himself that will bring Bosie salvation: "I saw that you realised nothing of what you had done," accuses Wilde; "I saw . . . that nothing that had happened had made you realise a single thing" (*De Profundis*, 551, 559). In this sense, he phrases the lesson as a cognitive one, a coming to knowledge of responsibility and guilt, and

this lesson is often put in terms of a forcible teaching of empathy or identification: "I have told you this account of the mode of my being conveyed
here simply that you should realise how hard it has been for me to get
anything out of my punishment but bitterness and despair" (623). Such
empathy ought, finally, to lead Douglas to realize that he is responsible,
ought to make him feel guilty:

> You can't wash your hands of all responsibility, and propose with
> a shrug or a smile to pass on to a new friend and a freshly spread
> feast. . . . It may for the moment have the charm of a new sauce or a
> fresh vintage, but the scraps of a banquet grow stale, and the dregs
> of a bottle are bitter. Either today, or tomorrow, or some day you
> have got to realise it. Otherwise you may die without having done
> so, and then what a mean, starved, unimaginative life you would
> have had. (651)

Bosie must know his responsibility and guilt and thus learn humility
and love; he must become imaginative, must learn what Wilde has been
through.

As the addressee of this letter might be made to realize, it is of course
one thing to feel guilty and quite another to make that feeling manifest
with a sufficient virulence of contrition. Wilde makes this difficulty an
aesthetic one, and *De Profundis* often speaks of "realisation" in aesthetic
terms, as the making visible or giving of material form to an ideal. Hence
in the "Preface" to *The Renaissance*, Pater's famous turning of Matthew
Arnold into an aesthete makes this giving of aesthetic form a mode of
cognition—for which aestheticist criticism aims: " 'To see the object as in
itself it really is,' has been justly said to be the aim of all true criticism whatever; and in aesthetic criticism the first step towards seeing one's object as
it really is, is to know one's own impression as it really is, to discriminate
it, to realise it distinctly."[9] And Pater repeatedly uses the word *realize* to
mean a giving of form that makes aesthetic apprehension possible. Thus
the reiterated refrain of *De Profundis* opposes *realization* to *shallowness*
(implicitly depending, perhaps, on a figure of legibility, a distinct depth of
inscription): "The supreme vice is shallowness," Wilde writes at least four
times; "everything that is realised is right" (511, 551, 585, 652).[10] Transforming, in exemplary aestheticist fashion, "whatever is, is right" to "everything
that is realised is right," the letter often speaks of "self-realisation" and

of "realis[ing] one's soul," and its aesthete Christ is praised for just such a power of *realization* (582, 602).[11] The basis of his nature "is the same as that of the nature of the artist, an intense and flamelike imagination"; Christ "realised in the entire sphere of human relations that imaginative sympathy which in the sphere of Art is the sole secret of creation" (598). His place is with the poets because "his whole conception of Humanity sprang right out of the imagination and can only be realised by it" (599). And, a little later, Wilde writes, "Feeling, with the artistic nature of one to whom Sorrow and Suffering were modes through which he could realise his conception of the Beautiful, that an idea is of no value till it becomes incarnate and is made an image, he makes of himself the image of the Man of Sorrows, and as such has fascinated and dominated Art as no Greek god ever succeeded in doing" (605–6). Achieving a Hellenism that surpasses that of the Greeks, Wilde's decadent (and Grecophone) Christ is the supreme artist of sorrow.

Thus, the imperative to Bosie is partly that he make his life into an aesthetic form, that he *realize* guilt as Christ realized his conception of the beautiful, and Wilde's appropriative address is explicitly part of the lesson: "You see that I have to write your life to you, and you have to realise it" (550). The project of the letter is thus autobiographical, but it is Bosie's autobiography, urging him to realize the life it writes. Douglas must accede to his being spoken by his lover's voice; his own voice, demanded and excluded, disappears into Wilde's unanswered and unanswerable letter. Such realization is the purpose of repentance: "Of course the sinner must repent. But why? Simply because otherwise he would be unable to realise what he had done." The sinner must not only know his sin; he must also make it real. The impossible lesson forecloses response but also makes room for that repentance. Not simply a cognitive mastery of the past, repentance's realization is a transcending, an imaginative reworking of it that evokes Dorian Gray's discovery, in the words of another, of what will have been his past: "The moment of repentance is the moment of initiation. More than that. It is the means by which one alters one's past" (*De Profundis*, 616). It is perhaps not merely willful to hear in such terms an echo of the potentiality I have linked to queer transmission. Wilde's impossible lesson in realization is a redeeming of the past that seeks to restore to it its potentiality.

Yet again, the paradoxical realization of aesthetic form—a form that embodies this redeemed potential—cannot be known: "People whose desire is solely for self-realisation never know where they are going. They can't know. In one sense of the word it is, of course, necessary, as the Greek oracle said, to know oneself. That is the first achievement of knowledge. But to recognize that the soul of man is unknowable is the ultimate achievement of Wisdom. The final mystery is oneself" (617). A past that remains to be written cannot determine a self that is knowable; paradoxically, self-realization and self-knowledge prove incompatible. For Bosie to embody Wilde's sorrow, he cannot know what he has done; he can answer the letter only by not answering it. Self-realization involves making real the self's unknowability, its opacity to itself. By structuring his autobiographical prison letter as his lover's autobiography, by formalizing the confusion of identities that allows him to forestall Bosie's two-year silence by writing his *Epistola*, Wilde makes the impossibility of the letter's autobiographical project stand in for a paradoxical realization of this opacity, enacted through the impossibility of its injunction to *realize* guilt, the impossibility, in other words, of its lesson. Thwarted pedagogy is thus the principle of its transmission, its plaint, and its erotics.

When, at the end of the letter, Wilde remarks, "I have now written, and at great length, to you in order that you should realise what you were to me before my imprisonment, during those three years' fatal friendship: what you have been to me during my imprisonment . . . : and what I hope to be to myself and to others when my imprisonment is over," the stress is partly on the impossible injunction that Douglas become what he was; or, better, what he never was (642). The impossibility of this demand stands in for the gap between *realization* as knowledge and *realization* as formal embodiment.

The pedagogy of *De Profundis* also evokes queer transmission because it turns on questions of time—inside and outside prison—that ultimately lead one to question the compatibility of the time of experience and the time of art. If Wilde repeatedly recurs to sorrow as the source of knowledge, realization, and redemption, for some readers that term anchors the text in reality, establishing the letter's historical facticity by testifying to an unmediated encounter with oppression. Sorrow, however, is not just an affective category for Wilde; it is an aesthetic and erotic one that allows him to work through the paradoxes of the letter's lessons. And the boundary between Wilde and Douglas—as between Douglas and realization—is time.

"One can realise a thing in a single moment," Wilde writes, "but one loses it in the long hours that follow with leaden feet. . . . We think in Eternity, but we move slowly through Time." Wilde formulates a mismatch between realization and temporal existence that makes Bosie's thwarted lesson the result of incarnation: of the mismatch between ideas and the (finite, temporal) bodies and minds that have them. Prison's sorrow allows insight because suffering annihilates time:

> A great river of life flows between you and a date so distant. Hardly, if at all, can you see across so wide a waste. But to me it seems to have occurred, I will not say yesterday, but today. Suffering is one long moment. We cannot divide it by seasons. We can only record its moods, and chronicle their return. With us time itself does not progress. It revolves. . . . Of seed-time or harvest, of the reapers bending over the corn, or the grape-gatherers threading through the vines, of the grass in the orchard made white with broken blossoms, or strewn with fallen fruit, we know nothing, and can know nothing. For us there is only one season, the season of Sorrow. (565)

Wilde's powerful evocation of what he subsequently claims not to know exploits the doubled signification in the trope of *occultatio* or *paralepsis* for its power to enact sorrow's paradoxical mode of knowledge.[12] Evoking the riveted stasis of pain, Wilde also enacts, rhetorically, a simultaneous knowledge and nonknowledge. From the nontime of prison, Wilde gazes back at temporal existence. Even if he evokes the repetitive regimentation of prison life, he also makes one think of the temporality of the work of art, oblivious as it is to progress or to the time of human life; the self-consciously literary topoi through which Wilde renders time's passage perhaps mark this fading of life into art. Hence he powerfully evokes an experience he cannot, perforce, know. Sorrow marks the culminating aesthetic achievement of realization and (therefore) places Wilde beyond the compass of the lesson he would offer.

Thus, on the one hand, Wilde speaks of sorrow—just as later he will speak of Christ—as an aestheticist ideal of the symbol, transforming the boredom and pain of prison into an aestheticist ideal: "I now see that sorrow . . . is at once the type and test of all great Art. What the artist is always looking for is that mode of existence in which soul and body are one and indivisible: in which the outward is expressive of the inward: in which Form reveals" (592).[13] There are many such modes of existence, he suggests, drawing heavily on Pater—Greek sculpture, for instance, or music:

But Sorrow is the ultimate type both in life and Art. Behind Joy
and Laughter there may be a temperament, coarse, hard and
callous. But behind Sorrow there is always Sorrow. Pain, unlike
Pleasure, wears no mask. Truth in Art is not any correspondence
between the essential idea and the accidental existence; it is not the
resemblance of shape to shadow, or of the form mirrored in the
crystal to the form itself: it is no Echo coming from a hollow hill,
any more than it is the well of silver water in the valley that shows
the Moon to the Moon and Narcissus to Narcissus. Truth in art is
the unity of a thing with itself: the outward rendered expressive of
the inward: the soul made incarnate: the body instinct with spirit.
For this reason there is no truth comparable to Sorrow. (592–93)

To read this moment purely as a palinode—"Man is least himself when he
talks in his own person. Give him a mask, and he will tell you the truth,"
he says in "The Critic as Artist"[14]—would be to suppress the difficulty of
(among other things) claiming that Wilde here speaks in his own voice.
His words specify how "realisation" forms an aesthetic ideal. Sorrow's
power of realization is a power of incarnation, a truth in art where form
becomes identical to meaning. There is no reflection, resemblance, comparison, or echo because there is no gap between the idea and its incarnation or embodiment, no gap between inside and outside, between body
and soul. It is not a meeting of two terms because there are not two terms.
Imagined, too, is a lesson whose sorrow will teach Bosie this unity and will
thereby unite, at last, Wilde and his lover and will allow Wilde's own letter
to Douglas to become the response he yearns for.

On the other hand, however, the annihilation of time also makes sorrow's insight inaccessible, makes impossible the unity it demands of Bosie.
Sorrow marks the impossibility of incarnation's perfection—of the perfect
adequation of meaning and form, body and soul, Wilde and Bosie—that
sorrow announces as its truth. As Wilde writes earlier in the letter, "And
in the sphere of thought, no less than in the sphere of time, motion is no
more. The thing that you personally have long ago forgotten, or can easily
forget, is happening to me now, and will happen to me again to-morrow.
Remember this, and you will be able to understand a little of why I am
writing to you, and in this manner writing" (566). "Remember this," he
writes to Bosie, and the uncertain reference of the demonstrative pronoun
this condenses the paradoxical lesson. It is not simply that Douglas must

remember what he has forgotten; he must remember what he never knew, what he could never have known. (For he is asked to realize that he is inadequate to Wilde's lesson, to realize the defects that make him unable to learn it.) He is urged to remember—and thus to realize—the very difference that makes Wilde's experience in prison inaccessible to him. In prison, there is no forgetting because there is no time; because there is no time, there is also no memory. But Douglas is asked to remember this nonforgetting.[15] Evoking the shame of Dorian Gray's metaleptic realization of his beauty, Douglas is asked to become himself by objectifying himself, to realize his sins by seeing them as another's. The pedagogy of *De Profundis* makes impossible demands, offers unlearnable lessons, pleads for a response whose possibility it simultaneously forecloses. "The secret of life is suffering" (593), Wilde writes, perhaps leaving unclear whether suffering is what life ultimately reveals or what makes life possible. The truth of the letter, it is its truth less because Wilde's indubitable suffering forms the kernel of the experience underlying the text than because the secret might be said to name the structure of knowledge and eroticism in the poem's didactic address.

Notably, the letter both does and does not avow gay desire, which might be called a secret (or an open secret) in the text.[16] At one point, Wilde writes of a "friend of ten years' standing" who told him that "he considered me quite innocent" of the charges brought in the trials.[17] Wilde's response—that though the specific charges brought against him by Douglas's father, the Marquess of Queensberry, were often untrue, still "my life had been full of perverse pleasures and strange passions, and . . . unless he accepted that as a fact about me and realised it to the full, I could not possibly be friends with him any longer" (641)—seems to affirm a kind of gay pride, to affirm the sometimes painful psychic necessity of speaking what he calls "the truth." Resisting the pressure to lie about his desire, he then makes one of his most celebrated affirmations of that desire:

> I remember as I was sitting in the dock on the occasion of my last trial listening to [Frank] Lockwood's appalling denunciation of me—like a thing out of Tacitus, like a passage in Dante, like one of Savonarola's indictments of the Popes at Rome—and being sickened with horror at what I heard. Suddenly it occurred to me, *"How splendid it would be, if I was saying all this about myself!"* I

saw then at once that what is said of a man is nothing. The point is, who says it. (641)

The shame, he seems to suggest, is not in the desire but in one's inability to affirm it, the predicament of watching as others claim the right to speak, with contempt, disdain, and knowingness, about one's desire. Reclaiming the right to speak, Wilde can be said to clear the way for the avowal of homosexual desire. While I would agree, to a certain extent, with Wayne Koestenbaum's assertion that *De Profundis* is "uncloseted" (Koestenbaum, "Wilde's Hard Labor and the Birth of Gay Reading," 181)—Wilde certainly does not deny his desire—it seems to me that Wilde's emphasis is rather on making sorrow *speak.* As Ellis Hanson writes, Wilde imaginatively transforms dumb suffering into "exquisite pain, the brilliant tragedy of his soul to which only an artist, preferably himself, can sign his name."[18] Notably, Wilde imagines not the transformation of denunciation into avowal but the transformation of denunciation into self-denunciation; the possibility of escaping the shame of being unable to affirm one's desire is never, affirmatively, averred.

Wilde's sentence here thus evokes the curious mode of address at the beginning: not liking to think that you haven't written to me, I will write to you myself. Not liking to hear myself denounced, I will denounce myself. Avowal or disavowal, the claiming of desire is at once suspended and realized—in the writing of it. The celebrated avowal, we note, is in the apodosis of a conditional: "How splendid it would be if . . ." That the protasis (the subordinate clause)—"if I was saying all this about myself"—appears in the indicative instead of in the subjunctive suggests that this imagined avowal is located not in a hypothetical (or utopian) time that could, if the conditions were right, take place, but in a past where it never took place, and that, sealed off from the possibility of ever taking place, it is also preserved in the mode of potentiality.[19] "What lies before me," he later writes, "is my past" (657). Wilde's avowal takes place as the staging of the lost possibility, the discovered impossibility, of that avowal. Just after the moment about Lockwood's denunciation, the great love letter asserts the moral value of confession: "A man's very highest moment is, I have no doubt at all, when he kneels in the dust, and beats his breast, and tells all the sins of his life" (641). Yet Wilde's sins are not his own. The lies he protests against being forced to tell are not about his desires, but about Bosie's, and the confession he arrives at by imagining the extravagant possibility of self-naming is not his own, but his lover's: "If you have read this letter as carefully as you should have done you have met yourself face to face."

In the *Symposium*, Socrates, we recall, refuses Agathon's invitation to lie down next to him and in so doing corrects the implicit understanding of knowledge as objectifiable and as if physically transferrable:

> Socrates sat down and said, "How splendid it would be, Agathon,
> if wisdom was the sort of thing that could flow from the fuller
> to the emptier of us when we touch each other, like water, which
> flows through a piece of wool from a fuller cup to an emptier one.
> If wisdom is really like that, I regard it as a great privilege to share
> your couch. I expect to be filled up from your rich supply of fine
> wisdom . . ."[20]

It may be that, as Leo Strauss writes, "this is very nasty."[21] If so, it perhaps partakes of the shame central to many forms of pedagogy—pedagogy that trades on the desire (for knowledge, approval, connection) that it elicits and (at such moments) refuses.[22] Without the solicitation, there can be no refusal, and the teacher can therefore not stand aloof from the shame. Alcibiades's return to the *Symposium* is thus both sanctifying and a little embarrassing—because compromising (not just for Alcibiades; also for Socrates). *De Profundis,* too, can sometimes be embarrassing, primarily because the need behind it is so unrepentantly overweening, so lonely, and so unassuaged. "As regards your letter to me in answer to this, it may be as long or as short as you choose" (656). Repeatedly, Wilde seems to say, *please* write. That importuning address, I have tried to show, embodies a paradoxical lesson of bafflement. And the lesson is not just Bosie's.

As readers of *De Profundis,* we are the chastened lovers of Oscar Wilde, who have failed to realize our unworthiness, who have tried to make his love traffic in a marketplace and use a huckster's scales. If our queerness derives from our thwarted yearning to recognize ourselves in Wilde's letter, to make it represent us, what lesson does *De Profundis* offer in lieu of the comforts of such recognitions? It seems clear, at the very least, that to read Wilde's love letter simply as a sincere confession is drastically to simplify its complexity. As in the fairy tales, its lessons are those of aestheticism. "The aim of Love is to love: no more, and no less" (556). As in the fairy tales, the lessons are treacherous and lead to an unconsoled martyrdom of the self in the inhuman time of the work of art. The life expressed there is suspended—annulled but also preserved—in potentiality. Our final test, perhaps, is the challenge of proving ourselves adequate to that suspension. The paradoxical pedagogy of *De Profundis* suggests that a queer literary criticism might have most to gain from Wilde's refusal to teach the right lessons, his refusal to be the exemplary gay writer we want him to be, his refusal to recognize us and to let us recognize in him the provenance of our yearnings, from his thwarting and baffling of our critical desires. Yet even to phrase it thus seems to strike a false note; it assimilates to a critical lesson Wilde's playful refusal to teach a lesson. Perhaps one way to phrase Oscar Wilde's critical legacy is thus both to underline his thwarting of our desire for him to teach the lessons we want to learn—that is, to try to grasp what is most seductive, alluring, risky, and troubling about his *queerness* and ours—and to consider our perpetual failure to remain baffled, our perhaps inevitable move to recuperate as tendentious insights the exquisite seductions of our bafflement.

Part IV

7

Lessons of the Master

Henry James's Queer Pedagogy

> *Even the disciple has his uses. He stands behind one's throne, and at the moment of one's triumph whispers in one's ear that, after all, one is immortal.*
>
> —Oscar Wilde, "A Few Maxims for the Instruction of the Over-Educated"

> *"You make me very miserable," Paul ecstatically breathed.*
>
> —Henry James, "The Lesson of the Master"

It is a striking aspect of Henry James's fiction that no one ever learns anything—or, more precisely, no one is represented learning. Initiation is often a central concern, but its centrality in any given text seems in direct relation to the tendency of the initiation itself to fade from view. Repeatedly, development—of consciousness, of knowledge—is shown to be incompatible with the narrative of development. *What Maisie Knew* is perhaps the text that gives this structure its fullest expression, but it is also there, for instance, in the logic of childhood innocence in *The Turn of the Screw*: the children are angels or they are demons. The middle reaches between those extremes are foreclosed not just by the governess's prurient delusions but by the structure of knowledge itself. In the famous moments of realization—one thinks of Maggie Verver, Isabel Archer, Lambert Strether, or, in a potentially delusional mode, even Miles and Flora's governess—what comes to be known is that one already knew, where *what* one already knew pales in importance next to the recognition of delayed recognition. Consciousness is ever belated in relation to itself; this is perhaps the shared theme of James's late fiction. As a recurrent concern, the unfathomability of realization, and consequently of consciousness, is there even in the earlier texts: to my mind, more compelling than the "international theme" is the confrontation of differentials of knowledge, which allows James to formulate, in various ways, some of the paradoxes of representing understanding in time—of representing shifting consciousness. The fact that people learn means that consciousness is not itself—is not, perhaps, representable; this is perhaps the primary reason that James is so interested in children.

Legible as a "theme" in the earlier texts—one thinks of the predicaments of Isabel Archer, Hyacinth Robinson, or even Daisy Miller, or of the pedagogical triangles of *The Bostonians* or *Roderick Hudson*—the perplexities of initiation become even more complex with the so-called major phase, as the effects of knowledge in the texts are also worked out as dynamics of reading. It is no coincidence in this regard that the series of stories about literary discipleship written in the late 1880s through the mid-1890s both represent baffled disciples and are often read as metareflections on fiction or reading. *What Maisie Knew* and *The Spoils of Poynton* might be read in these terms: both focus on aesthetic initiation, and both put the reader in a predicament not unlike that of the baffled disciples of James's tales. Thus, an experiment in point of view, *What Maisie Knew* famously limits its depictions to what Maisie perceives without limiting them to what she can understand. That difference—between perceptions and conceptions or terms—allows the novel, in the progressive shifts in that ratio, to be one of the great representations of mental development, precisely because it does not represent such development directly. (One perhaps feels as if Maisie's consciousness were represented; what is represented, however, is a series of differentials, from which we are left to deduce the consciousness and the shifts that, retrospectively, make visible its development.) At the same time, the novel is governed by an entirely different logic: what develops is not a consciousness but a system of exchange, one that is at once, on the one hand, the result of the contentious divorce proceedings that open the novel and give birth to the sordid arrangements that shift Maisie among a series of more or less culpable adults in more or less recondite relations, and, on the other, the linguistic system that is the novel itself.[1] That the novel cannot stand aloof from the parents' treatment of Maisie is one effect; the incompatibility of the narrative of development with the development it depicts is another. This great novel of the development of consciousness finally shows that development is incompatible with its depiction. Likewise, *The Spoils of Poynton* is governed by two competing systems that are both fully articulated without being hierarchically ordered or mutually governed by any other unifying principle: a perfectly compelling account of psychological motivations of desire, and a fully developed, though largely unrelated, aesthetic logic of the novel's eponymous "spoils"—one that looks, as it were, parapsychological to the extent that one takes at face value James's claim that the furniture is the main character and is what is most accorded consciousness and volition. It seems to me that there is a realization in the text, but that realization belongs to the furniture, which, quite sensibly, sets itself ablaze.

The narrator of the "The Figure in the Carpet" never gets it, never learns the secret; the narrator of "The Aspern Papers" never gets his hands on the papers and seems none the wiser for his failure. James's enthralled disciples never learn; if what is to be learned by a reader is understood to be isomorphic with what these narrators seek to learn, then the reader is never let in on the secret, either. One way to think about "The Aspern Papers" would be (as in *Spoils* and *Maisie*) to try to keep in view several narratives at the same time: on the one hand, it is a story, like *Maisie,* about a limited point of view and about the convergence of incompatible perspectives, allowing one to glimpse perspectives and motives (Juliana's desires, her machinations on behalf of Tina, and of course Tina's desires for the hapless narrator) that the story does not represent; on the other, it is also about the exorbitant yearning excited by the literary work, that its capacity to touch one might be literalized. (Part of the pain in the text comes from the thwarted effort to superimpose these two narratives, the effort to make the position of the work of art into one perspective among others, or, in other terms, to occupy it, as if one's relation to a work of art were a human or interpersonal one.) The lurid perversity of the narrator's sexual excitement—he seems to be sexually fascinated by Juliana because she had sex with Jeffrey Aspern, an "indirect" frisson of contact that, however perverse, is but a literalization of what he might experience if he succeeded in interposing himself between the letters' author and their addressee—and the narrator's increasingly delusional search render, albeit luridly, what I have to imagine is a common enough readerly fantasy: that the unfathomable commerce between text and mind that produces ideas could be represented, could be seen, and could be located in a particular body. Yet wanting to meet the author is a little like wanting to see one's own internal organs. The vision achieved, one mostly finds that that was not, after all, what one wanted: they—authors and organs—keep what they conceal. Reading is indubitably sexy; the question is whether that sexiness can be represented. Questions of perspective in the text likewise return one to scenarios of reading. Experiments with point of view in late James often raise the question of whether perspective belongs to a person; "The Aspern Papers" forces one to ask whether the reader can unify the disparate points of view it adumbrates. Reading these two strands together—its multiple perspectives and its thematization of a reader's desire for literal contact, both in some sense raising the question of whether reading is representable—suggests that perspective and point of view are, to the extent that they return us to the question of the possibility of representing consciousness, also tied to the story's exploration of literary transmission.

It is all the more striking, then, that pedagogical relations are among the most erotically invested in James's texts and are also some of the most elusive; to examine eroticism in James is inevitably to confront questions of initiation and of literary transmission. James's tales of literary discipleship are perhaps where he spells out most explicitly the eroticism of some of these larger questions; in them, scenes of pedagogy and relations of tutelage almost always carry an erotic charge, even as they tend to dissolve any firm sense of what, pedagogically, has been achieved. The intimate claustrations of master and disciple, the elaborately choreographed intensities of famished examination and reluctant exhibition that inflame the fascinations of those claustrations, the panting, breathing, groaning, caressing, throbbing, and pressing, the passionate beatings of hearts and flutterings of attention, all seem to issue in an unverifiable sense that the student has been betrayed.

The phrases above all echo verbs and phrases in "The Lesson of the Master," whose equivocal lesson turns on just such a hint of pedagogical betrayal.[2] Paul Overt has been convinced by his mentor, Henry St. George, to renounce women—and one, Marian Fancourt, in particular—for the sake of his writing. Learning that (while Paul was in self-imposed exile in Switzerland) St. George has become engaged to Marian, Paul returns home to wonder whether St. George's advice to give up "life" and Marian may not have been a self-interested ruse:

> His face was red and he had the sense of its growing more and
> more crimson. All the evening at home—he went straight to
> his rooms and remained there dinnerless—his cheek burned at

intervals as if it had been smitten. He didn't understand what had happened to him, what trick had been played him, what treachery practiced. "None, none," he said to himself. "I've nothing to do with it. I'm out of it—it's none of my business." But that bewildered murmur was followed again and again by the incongruous ejaculation: "Was it a plan—was it a plan?" Sometimes he cried to himself, breathless, "Have I been duped, sold, swindled?" If at all, he was an absurd, an abject victim. . . . Mystification bitterness and wrath rose and boiled in him when he thought of the deference, the devotion, the credulity with which he had listened to St. George. . . . He had flung himself on the sofa, where he lay through the hours with his eyes either closed or gazing at the gloom, in the attitude of a man teaching himself to bear something, to bear having been made a fool of. (181–82)

Part of what is so powerful here is the rendering of erotic betrayal: to feel betrayed carries with it the mortifying realization that one is not even the main character in the drama. That this shame calls out for further mortification in an attempt to ameliorate a little at least the latter affront—calls out for some acknowledgment of the spectacle of one's abjection—is evident in Paul's self-dramatizing gesture ("he went straight to his room and remained there dinnerless") that redoubles the shame by attempting to stage the exclusion. And the text links a bodily shock to baffled interpretation. The sense of betrayed credulity takes the form of a physical shock that, leaving Paul "breathless," writes itself on his cheek; more important perhaps than the shock of betrayal is the excruciating sense that he cannot know whether or not it was a betrayal, whether or not there was a "plan" against him. The mystification, betrayal, and bafflement are figured by corporeal violence, or rather, a corporeal violence of an uncertain figural status. As important, perhaps, as the violent figures is the foregrounded equivocation: his cheek burns "*as if* it had been smitten," and he sits "*in the attitude* of a man teaching himself to bear . . . having been made a fool of," leading one to wonder whether he is teaching himself to bear it, or merely taking the posture of one undergoing such a lesson. Paul has "the sense" of his face growing ever more crimson—no mirror appears to confirm this sense—and his gaze at the end of the passage indifferently confronts two obscurities: his eyes are either "closed or gazing at the gloom." Paul has been taught a lesson, but it is hard to formulate what that might be. And, for him, the uncertainty about the betrayal redoubles the wound, as if his own sense of betrayal were itself somehow culpable: "It was necessary to his soreness to believe for the hour and the intensity of his grievance—all the more cruel for its not being a legal one" (187). Standard-issue envy (it is difficult to profess resentment about the happiness of one's friends) is compounded by a sense of exclusion, the painful sense that he has been made the butt of a joke. Or, perhaps worse, that there was no joke, that he did not exist for the lovers at all.

If the closing moments of the story mark a pupil's disillusionment with a teacher, then such disillusionment may have been structural to the lesson. For Paul Overt, to whom St. George has said, "Look at me well, take my lesson to heart—for it *is* a lesson" (141), the lesson has been, more or less: "Do not be like me." The difficulty of placing his sense of betrayal then seems built into the very lesson: the teacher who gives the advice, if he is right to give it, cannot help proving himself inadequate to give advice, unqualified to judge what the pupil should or should not be. (At moments, one suspects that this is the only lesson one ever succeeds in conveying to one's students: don't be like me.) In one sense, such contradictions befit the other "lesson" of the story, which can be read as presenting Paul with a lesson in the duplicity of signs. Thus, Paul often seems the object of authorial satire: "Our friend was slightly nervous; that went with his character as a student of fine prose, went with the artist's general disposition to vibrate" (116). Beyond the sense that the terms of praise render Paul's own view of himself, the writerly parts that all go together indicate a potentially risible naïveté, and it might be necessary for Paul to learn betrayal and deceit because, at the beginning of the story, he is a markedly naïve reader. He often seems too bafflingly dense to warrant the interest that the older writer takes in him, perhaps most notably in his difficulties with the basic linguistic competence of understanding pronoun reference and figures of speech.[3] Paul's literary training is then partly in the obliquities of reference and in the potential of language to deceive. And St. George is described, from the outset, in terms of mismatched parts and deceiving appearances. His wife (whose "strength was not equal to her aspirations" [137]) does not look like the wife of a great writer, and that afternoon, "she looked as if she had put on her best clothes to go to church and then had decided they were too good for that and had stayed home" (120). We are told of the "ill-matched parts of [St. George's] genius," of a writer who, some say, has sacrificed "too much to manner" (118). When Overt finally sees St.

George, the writer's appearance confounds the devoted disciple's expectations; he could "have passed for a lucky stockbroker" (125). St. George's manner often jars with what he is saying, and his pronouncements do not "harmonize" with his behavior. In contrast, Overt, as his name suggests, is a good pupil because he takes everything the master says earnestly and literally. In one reading of the story's lesson, therefore, Paul must learn that literary language can deceive; he must be deceived. To learn his lesson, then, is to be duped or, rather, to be left unsure whether he has been or not. If St. George has betrayed him at the end of the text, then he has made the lesson complete: words do not mean what they seem to mean, and you cannot take my lesson literally.

Certainly such a lesson poses complications for what is called "the practice of pedagogy." The complexity of "The Lesson of the Master" also derives from the way Paul's lesson intersects questions of voice. "She looked as if she had put on her best clothes to go to church and then had decided they were too good for that and had stayed home": we come to doubt that such lines can be attributed to Paul. A perhaps recognizably "Jamesian" narrative voice, the mobility of perspective and the crossing of an imponderably knowing voice with a finely calibrated (but often unverifiable) free-indirect inhabiting of characters' views and vocabularies, subjects everything in the story to the deflation of its irony. Thus, for instance, the seemingly parodic descriptions of Summersoft, the country house where Paul first encounters Marian and St. George: the house is characterized, above all, by the unity of its signifying elements; when we are told that "the nearness counted so as distance," the reference is, as Gert Buelens writes, to "the ideal proportions and balance of the classical style in architecture and landscape design; the trick whereby the parts of a house as well as the latter's relation to the garden manage to result in a sense of distance and nearness combined."[4] One's sense that this aesthetic ideal is the object of parody in the story, which comically multiplies its aesthetic unities, floats free of any particular character's judgment or taste. The footman "appeared to wish to intimate that a person staying at Summersoft would naturally be, if only by alliance, distinguished" (115); the house's "balustrade of fine old ironwork . . . like all the other details, was of the same period as the house. . . . It all went together and spoke in one voice" (116); and the smoking room, we scarcely need to be told, "was on the scale of the rest of the place" (137). All this unity produces ludicrous effects, as when the house's beautiful pink brickwork—compared to a beautiful woman's complexion—seems to demand that even the houseguests present a unified spectacle: General Fancourt was "tall, straight and elderly and had, like the great house itself, a pink smiling face, and into the bargain a white moustache" (116, 117). Near and far, person and house, inside and out: it all goes together and speaks in one voice.

So St. George's lesson—to the very degree that it is ambiguous—relieves us from a homogenizing unity that makes a man's pink smiling face just like the house he is standing near. The explicit content of the "lesson" is that a writer must protect the sanctity of art by refusing to sell out to commercial or mercenary interests. St. George, the disqualified role model, has capitulated. Taking "the mercenary muse . . . to the altar of literature," he leads, in his own words, "the clumsy conventional expensive materialised vulgarised brutalised life of London"; even his writing desk is such that "the person using it could write only in the erect posture of a clerk in a counting house" (124, 141, 169, 161). The difficulty for Paul at the end is in knowing whether the master's capitulation is synonymous with his having married. Inverting the wisdom that marriage will bring to frivolous boys the (apparently desirable) chastisement of adult responsibility, St. George's lesson casts marriage as the gravest irresponsibility, the desertion of art for the claims of materialism and prosperity.

Yet St. George formulates the lesson in strikingly self-negating terms: asked by Paul, "You think the artist shouldn't marry?" he responds, "He does so at his peril—he does so at his cost" (168). *Cost* collates the terms of sacrifice and imperiled spiritual quest (*cost* as a synonym for *peril*) with the pecuniary considerations of the merely mercenary (*cost* as a synonym for *expense*): artistic rigor can be measured only in the very terms it is supposed to transcend. "If your idea's to do nothing better there's no reason you shouldn't have as many good things as I—as many human and material appendages, as many sons or daughters, a wife with as many gowns, a house with as many servants, a stable with as many horses, a heart with as many aches" (170). The work of art, St. George suggests, is not susceptible to quantitative measurement, but the vocabulary produced for discussing art consists precisely of terms of measurement and cost, just as a heart may be said to have as "many" aches as a stable has horses. It is thus one level of the story's irony persistently to describe writing as a commercial enterprise. Even beyond the fact that it is often difficult to believe that Paul is the great writer St. George may or may not think he is, the story makes it hard to view with any reverence the art that would be protected from pecuniary contamination.

Nor does the story make it easy to regret the lost possibilities for love with Marian Fancourt. "She's an angel from heaven," Paul exclaims, and neither he nor St. George can come up with compliments more stirring than praise for her "naturalness" (144).[5] A girl "more candid than her costume" (120), her beautiful face gives a sense "of an enthusiasm which, unlike many enthusiasms, was not all manner" (126). "You ought always to believe such a girl as that," says St. George to Paul in a lesson strikingly opposed to his later dissertations, "—always, always. Some women are meant to be taken with allowances and reserves; but you must take *her* just as she is" (139). Notably, too, in context, he asks Paul to believe a statement (that he had read Paul's book) he has just admitted was false. To accept that Marian is "more candid than her costume," one has to ignore the fact that she is wearing it; the phrase self-consciously delivers the candor to the appraising men while ostensibly assigning it to her, even as the expression itself is, of course, knowingly very far from candid. Ultimately, the naïveté of this girl "more candid than her costume" is compelling because it sets off the opposite quality "between men"; as Paul remarks of her watercolors, "naïveté in art is like zero in a number: its importance depends on the figure it is united with." The pun on *figure* links the mathematical accumulation that the text opposes to art with the calculated cynicism of weighing a girl's naïveté according to the claims of her figure's beauty. For the story, surely the point of the putatively clever pun is its betrayal of the speaker's limitations—and not merely the limits of the passion it unconvincingly mimes.

When St. George says to Paul, "If your idea's to do nothing better there's no reason you shouldn't have as many good things as I—as many human and material appendages, as many sons or daughters, a wife with as many gowns, a house with as many servants, a stable with as many horses, a heart with as many aches," the master's lesson is about the unlawful yoking of dissonant registers, on two levels. The content of the lesson decries the contamination of art by commercial interests. As a figure of syllepsis, the yoking of registers models an anarchic linguistic practice. The figure makes manifest that unity (of, for example, Summersoft) can be a linguistic illusion, like homophony—a result of language's power to link, formally, elements that have no substantive relation—and thus also makes manifest that disunity is potentially sheltered within a unified aesthetic form. It cannot escape one's attention, then, that St. George celebrates art for a unity that evokes that of Summersoft. An artist cannot marry because women, instead of having "one standard," have "about fifty." The artist, however, can consider only the claims of perfection: "He has nothing to do with the relative—he has only to do with the absolute; and a dear little family may represent a dozen relatives" (173). Yet again, St. George undermines his own lesson; his pun on *relative*—the relativized standards of an art determined by pecuniary and familial considerations and the "relatives" that may be "represented" by a family—like Overt's pun on *figure,* though more clever, as puns go, enacts the fracturing of the "absolute" he warns Overt about (and thus, by enacting its warning, makes his statement paradoxically in unity with itself). The contamination of art by the principles adduced as opposed to it end up securing what their exclusion seeks to maintain. As St. George, in their late-night colloquy, explains to Overt the different registers of life and art and suggests that the true artist pursues perfection by excluding the claims of life (167–68), we are reminded that Mrs. St. George's arrangement of his study achieves just such a purification: "The outer world, the world of accident and ugliness, was so successfully excluded, and within the rich protecting square, beneath the patronizing sky, the dream-figures, the summoned company, could hold their particular revel" (163). The selling out of art to commercialism and heterosexual entanglement seems to achieve something that looks a lot like the purified realm of art that St. George's warnings against selling out purport to protect. Yet again, one is confronted with an abyssal question of voice: is the integration of disparate registers enacted (for instance) by the self-conscious aestheticization of "rich protecting square"—"the patronizing sky" with "the dream-figures, the summoned company" whose "particular revel" evokes *The Tempest*—parodic or not, and, if so, of whom or of what?

"You can't do it without sacrifices—don't believe that for a moment," says the master, "I've made none. I've had everything. In other words I've missed everything" (169). Paul's question ends up being whether that is in fact true, whether his dinnerless smarting (his lightless smarts) are truly superior to, or even distinguishable from, a life without sacrifice. (This is a minor version of Lambert Strether's predicament in *The Ambassadors.*) Just as St. George might look unartistic because he is not an artist, because a true artist looks, paradoxically, like someone who does not look like an artist, or because there is no fundamental relation between looks and artistry, his lesson may be a just one that teaches what it proclaims, may be a deliberate attempt to dupe his pupil, may teach because it does dupe his pupil, or may produce enlightenment in spite of the master's compromised but therefore irrelevant motives. The story's narrative voice seems to comprise these options—and to keep its own counsel. The story is as deceptive as St. George himself; or rather, each may or may not be deceptive, and the predicament for both pupil and reader is perhaps in never knowing, in having but being unable to decide, whether or not they have been betrayed. The long tradition of reading these texts of literary discipleship as statements of James's aesthetic principles stumbles up against a baffling pedagogy (that is, the tales') that refuses to disclose those principles. Surely, these texts are metareflections on James's art, but it is curiously difficult to formulate how without thereby failing to read them in any detail.

Recurrently, James's stories of masters and disciples pose the question of the relation between "life" and "art." Often, too, there is a suspiciously economic understanding of that relation: questioning whether he has been duped, Paul Overt is surely right to wonder whether art obeys such economies, whether "more" attention to art entails "less" attention to life, however much one might be inclined to endorse the opposition between aesthetic and mercantile interests as a general principle. To serve the mercenary muse is no doubt to betray art; it perhaps less clear how to put such an intuition into practice. "The Aspern Papers" seems to suggest that the fascination with the author's life betrays his art. In "The Death of the Lion," the narrator explicitly says that this is the case. In that story, likewise, popularity and fame are at odds with literature, and it presents an inverse image of the "The Lesson of the Master": the disciple asks Fanny Hurter to renounce any desire to meet the great writer, who is nevertheless sacrificed, as if literally, to popular hunger (his book unwritten and its outline lost, he himself dies to make, through his death, a society lady's home more eminent). In the end, the disciple marries Fanny himself. Fanny's renunciation in that text is almost comical: she sits facing a wall for the length of an opera in order to avoid laying eyes on the great man, even at a distance, and the strain of the effort brings tears to her eyes. Fanny Hurter makes the Jamesian doctrine of the supremacy of art into a form of personal renunciation—makes it, in a sense, representable, and perhaps thereby betrays it no less than does the society lady who babbles to death a great writer. Renunciation comes to seem a structural requirement in these stories—not, I think, because James himself had any psychological interest in sexual renunciation (though for all I know he did). Rather, these texts seem interested in the difficulty of representing the commerce between authorial life and authorial creation, the difficulty of understanding life's relation to art. To my mind, to ask about the eroticism of these stories is to bring this question into view, and here one might be led to say that homosexual desire is privileged in (for example) "The Lesson of the Master" insofar as it is not represented there. To my mind, however, more important than the specific desires represented (or not represented) for the articulation of queerness in the story is the way that its paradoxical pedagogy interrupts the possibility of representing its lesson. Escaping the story's terms of economic exchange and cliché, queerness might emerge as the unspoken—but articulate—ground of pedagogical bafflement and hence of reading itself. The stories' lessons are less the dicta one might abstract than the experience of betrayal they represent—hence, it seems to me, the interest of betrayal in these pedagogical stories, as in *The Wings of the Dove, The Golden Bowl,* and *The Ambassadors,* among others.

James's corpus might be understood in terms of its (paradoxically) increasing lucidity about pedagogical bafflement and betrayal—about, in some ways, the obscurity of insight, realization, and learning. Isabel Archer's scandalous decision at the end of *The Portrait of a Lady* might be read to intimate that she has finally learned the necessity of committing, even performatively, to the consequences of one's thoughts; it might also mark the making-permanent of a failure to learn anything. What has been learned, and by whom, is an open question at the end of *The Wings of the Dove,* as unfathomable a question as what was written in the letter that is never read. Merton Densher wandering around Venice or Maggie Verver wandering around her strange garden pagoda both represent—in registers however different—something unrepresentable at the heart of realization, a bafflement that is carried to the end of both texts. But the novelistic culmination of this exploration of unrepresentable initiation and unfathomable betrayal is perhaps *The Ambassadors.* The multiplication of pedagogical relations—Chad Newsome and Mme. Marie de Vionnet, Lambert Strether and Chad, Strether and Mme. de Vionnet, Strether and Maria Gostrey, Strether and Little Bilham, even Strether and Waymarsh—and the multilateral "directions" pedagogy takes in each makes that novel more complicated than the stories, which seem, in retrospect, to isolate different modalities that the novel will run simultaneously. If there is a central "lesson," though, it is in betrayal; Strether has an infinitely finer capacity for registering betrayal than does Paul Overt. Fleda Vetch does not get Owen Gareth, does not receive even a tiny token of the beautiful things. The narrator in "The Aspern Papers," denied the papers, makes do with a portrait. Strether does not get Chad, does not get out of the whole affair, as he says, anything for himself. But, though I have to think that his pain is deeper than Overt's to the very extent that his sensibility is perfectly calibrated to register the refinements of its predicament, he does in some sense discover the pleasures of baffled enthrallment, as most of the disciples in the earlier stories do not, however much, seemingly unknowingly, they may participate in it. This is one reason, as I have elsewhere discussed, why I resist understanding Strether's predicament as a sad one.[6] James's reflections in the autobiography—where the aesthetic initiations are remarkable for being both groundless and unlocatable—suggest, in any event, how profitable a structure (the temptations of biographical criticism notwithstanding) this was for James himself. Baffled realization may be the most important content of James's representation of consciousness, just as baffled pedagogy may represent the recurrent structure of its eroticism.

In chapter 8 I will pursue some of the consequences of Jamesian pedagogy in *The Beast in the Jungle*—where the unremitting depiction of a baffled quest for realization occurs in an explicitly pedagogical relation purged (also explicitly) of any consciousness of eroticism. That tale provides the occasion, too, to consider another form of queer transmission: James's afterlife in queer theory.

8

The Beast's Storied End

It is striking that the two best readings of Henry James's *The Beast in the Jungle*—by Eve Kosofsky Sedgwick and Leo Bersani—find reason to regret its ending, viewing it as a failure of lucidity or nerve on the part of its author.[1] For both, too, what is regrettable about the end is the sudden convergence of author and character, which invests John Marcher with narrative authority or consigns the previously distanced narrator to the particular perplexities of that most perplexed of characters. "James's bravura in manipulating point of view," Sedgwick writes, "lets him dissociate himself critically from John Marcher's selfishness—from the sense that there is no *possibility* of subjectivity other than Marcher's own—but lets him leave in place of that selfishness finally an askesis, a particular humility of point of view as being *limited* to Marcher's" (Sedgwick, "The Beast in the Closet," 199). At the end, however, Marcher and James, in Sedgwick's view, unite in giving voice to May Bartram's unexpressed desires: "For this single, this conclusive, this formally privileged moment in the story—this resolution over the dead body of May Bartram—James and Marcher are presented as coming together, Marcher's revelation underwritten by James's rhetorical authority, and James's epistemological askesis gorged, for once, beyond recognition, by Marcher's compulsive, ego-projective certainties" (200). The underwriting of Marcher's "realization" with "narrative/authorial prescription" (199) means that the story does not merely depict the ravages of homosexual panic on a thereby representative character; it enacts the knowingness—the enforced and enforcing self-ignorance—that Sedgwick diagnoses as the mechanism of male homophobia. If, in the last scene, Marcher becomes "the irredeemably self-ignorant man who embodies and enforces heterosexual compulsion" (210), then the "rhetorical clinch" (199) Sedgwick also finds there has dire consequences for the story, for the genitive in her subtitle—"James and the Writing of Homosexual Panic"—might be read to diagnose a writing that does not so much depict panic as enact it. Presuming to give voice to another's desire—Marcher and James "reunited at last" in their "confident, shared, masculine knowledge," presuming to say "what [May] Really Wanted and what she Really Needed" (168)—Marcher's treatment of May, in Sedgwick's account, therefore raises the question of whether James's voicing of homosexual panic can stand aloof from that panic, and, more generally, of the extent to which one can ventriloquize another without running the risk of the voice "given" becoming one's own. At stake is not just James's distance from Marcher but the distance of his writing from homophobia.

For Bersani, at the end, the story sinks into banality. In Bersani's reading, Marcher is—to this point—a cipher of potentiality, of the suspended being that forms the impersonal ontology of Jamesian fiction. His fate, Bersani asserts, in a decisive account not just of the story but of James's late writing more generally, "is temporalized as both prior to and subsequent to its own happening, as if it were a kind of being, or a formal law, inherently incompatible with the very category of happening" (Bersani, "The It in the I," 20). *The Beast in the Jungle,* he continues a few pages later,

> thematizes the Jamesian tendency to extract all events, as well as all perspectives on them, from any specified time, and to transfer them to a before or after in which they are de-realized in the form of anticipations or retrospections. The designation of Marcher as a colorless figure aptly describes what is most original about him: he is the embodiment of the refusal of all embodiment. . . . He is a life lived as pure virtuality—at least until the moment when he loses this rare dignity by speaking of it as if it were an affective and moral failure. (23–24)

For *The Beast in the Jungle,* he concludes, finally "retreats from its images of indefinitely suspended being—refuses, that is, to allow its protagonists to maintain or to profit from their impersonal intimacy" (29).

That Marcher fails to sustain this virtuality and comes to psychologize his predicament (as a failure) need not, perhaps, mean that James himself endorses Marcher's assessment. It is at least arguable that—read in Bersani's terms—Marcher's banalizing understanding of his life depicts the difficulty of sustaining such impersonal intimacy, of remaining a "colorless figure," of not falling back into psychology. (It is open to question, too, whether depicting that sustaining as possible would be the same thing as sustaining it.) Curiously, again, something about the story makes it difficult to maintain the distance separating author, narrator, and character; "voice," spoken for another or simulating another's speech, risks becoming one's own. Bersani is more equivocal—he notes the "peculiar rhetorical inflation of Marcher's self-discovery on the final page of the story" (19)—but whatever the implicit critique of Sedgwick's privileging of May's view (which, it might be worth registering, is not necessarily merely psychologizing insofar as Sedgwick reifies a point of view that, she reminds us, the story does not give us), his reading shares with hers a suspicion of the story's end, and the convergence they find there of the author's perspective and voice with his character's.

Sedgwick and Bersani have very good reasons (reasons both dictated by their theoretical arguments and justified by the text's language) for their view of its end, but I nevertheless think that the story invites us to distinguish its view of the spring of the beast from Marcher's. The curious "rhetorical inflation" Bersani notes in the final pages comes with signs of simulated voice, signs that at least open the possibility of free-indirect discourse. The interpolated repetitions ("the escape would have been to love her; then, *then* he would have lived"),[2] the use of italics to indicate emphasis ("he had been the man of his time, *the* man, to whom nothing on earth was to have happened" [70]; "*she* was what he had missed" [70]; "this horror of waking—*this* was knowledge, knowledge under the breath of which the very tears in his eyes seemed to freeze" [71]), even the invocation of Marcher's name ("what had the man had, to make him by the loss of it so bleed and yet live? Something—and this reached him with a pang—that he, John Marcher, hadn't; the proof of which was precisely John Marcher's arid end" [69]), and, potentially, the coordination of tenses ("it had sprung as he didn't guess" [71]) all suggest represented thought or ventriloquism. The "climactic, authoritative (even authoritarian) rhythm" (Sedgwick, "The Beast in the Closet," 200) and the "peculiar rhetorical inflation" may be Marcher's (or the narrative's rendering of Marcher's view). Earlier in the story, in any event, such markers do seem to indicate represented thought—linked to the limitation (almost entirely sustained) of point of view in the story to Marcher's perspective. It is not obvious that that limitation ends as the story comes to a close. And projected voice is at issue throughout. One notes, for example, that one of the moments Bersani reads so brilliantly—"she had been living to see what would *be* to be seen, and it would quite lacerate her to have to give up before the accomplishment of the vision" (Bersani, "The It in the I," 52)—is both the statement of virtual or potential being that Bersani reads in the formulation and an instance of redoubled ventriloquism: the narrator's rendering of Marcher's rendering of May's (potentially to be baffled) wish.

At the story's end, even if some of the formal markers of free-indirect style are difficult to pinpoint,[3] we do find—as both trope and, I will suggest, theme—what might be called prosopopoeia, a trope perhaps not unrelated to free-indirect style. Gavin Alexander, who calls it "the speaking figure," examines the links between *prosopōn* (which denotes "mask," then comes to mean "face," and eventually an entire person) and *ethōs* (which means "character," especially moral character) and suggests that the speaking figure, as it becomes intertwined with *ethōs,* describes a chain linking outer appearance to inner character.[4] Emphasizing the rhetorical roots of what becomes a modern notion of character, Alexander shows how different accounts of the trope in classical rhetoric suggest (with greater and lesser degrees of anxiety) the power of words to personify (where, these writers realize, that personifying power creates a character to vouch for the reliability of the words that produced it; where persuasion, in other terms, is grounded not in moral character but in the abyssal self-grounding power of rhetoric). Emphasizing that "selfhood is always a mask" (Alexander, "Prosopopoeia," 101), Alexander suggests ways that this originally dramatic figure comes to structure narrative relations. In his terms, it allows texts to encode a range of different "rhetorical agendas" simultaneously—which is also to say that it suggests that narrative voice is perhaps never univocal. Thus, for instance, he notes that Eve's use of "subtlest" in *Paradise Lost*—"Thee, serpent, subtlest beast of all the field / I knew"[5]—has different connotations for Milton ("treacherously or wickedly cunning") and for Eve ("skillful, clever, slender, fine"). Dramatizing that language was corrupted by the fall, Milton also, in Alexander's account, says something about character and voice:

> Satan is pretending to be a speaking snake, giving us one kind of prosopopoeia. Eve is speaking words not her own—any reader would have spotted the scriptural quotation—and so we are more likely to remember that she is another prosopopoeia, simulated by an author with a theological agenda. . . . If we hear Eve's speech as a product of two different rhetorical agendas, Milton's and her own, her character will look at that moment somewhat fragile—constructed on multiple layers, and the product of competing

rhetorical motives. Prosopopoeia allows its users to adopt the voices of others; but it also has the potential to show them that when they think they are speaking in their own person, they are prosopopoeias themselves. (Alexander, "Prosopopoeia," 107)

"To adopt the voices of others" is one rudimentary way to describe free-indirect discourse; as in prosopopoeia, however, such effects of thrown voice tend to undermine rather than confirm the positing of unified "voices" that could be attributed to independent sources (author, narrator, or character). "To adopt the voices of others" is to come face to face with how little one's own voice was ever truly one's own. The blurring of author, narrator, and character at the end of *The Beast in the Jungle* might therefore reinforce the impersonal ontology of Marcher's suspended being. For prosopopoeia might be said to be linked to free-indirect style because of the effects of such ventriloquism on person or voice. In Ann Banfield's terms, free-indirect discourse (what she calls "represented thought") does not present the coalescence of two voices because sentences of represented thought have to be conceived—for various grammatical reasons—as sentences spoken by no one.[6] As she elsewhere suggests, if the narration produces language that is not, that cannot be, spoken by anyone, the corrosive effect on persons also potentially extends to characters ostensibly represented; what she calls "non-reflective consciousness" points to the possibility of representing perceptions one did not know one had (and that were never voiced or linguistic at all).[7]

Prosopopoeia and free-indirect style are thus not unrelated to the question of where one locates "homosexual panic" in *The Beast in the Jungle,* or James in relation to Marcher. To insist that the end of James's tale at least raises the possibility of free-indirect discourse is to register how "voice" there likewise encodes different "rhetorical agendas," and the effect is similarly corrosive to univocal voice and consequently to the integrity of character and author alike. To read Marcher's conclusions about the beast as giving voice to James's view of Marcher's predicament—or to read the story as expressing James's own—is to respond to the text's thematization of voice (if not, perhaps, to register it). Autobiography, writes Barbara Johnson, leads Paul de Man "toward the paradox that the asymptotic relation between a story and a proper name makes the text continue to speak well after the death of the author. The text therefore functions like a prosopopoeia, a speaking thing, and the thing that ensures this illusion of speech is the very thing that deals a fatal blow to the author's biological life."[8] The deconstructive account of prosopopoeia—as in, prominently, Cynthia Chase's discussion of the trope[9]—leads both toward the disfiguring, depersonifying potential of the figure of voice and toward its corrosive effect on the possibility of meaning what one says. Prosopopoeia as a figure of face makes manifest a constitutive (and unavoidable) forgetting—of the fact that language cannot ground itself, that its "starting, catachrestic decree" (Chase, "Giving a Face to a Name," 84)[10] cannot be isolated (cannot be made an object of knowledge or experience) and cannot be assimilated to meaning; that forgetting is constitutive to the extent that it makes meaning possible. By making explicit that "face is not the natural given of the human person" but is rather "given by an act of language," or that, in other words, "figure is no less than our very face" (Chase, "Giving a Face to a Name," 85), de Man's account of prosopopoeia, Chase suggests, brings to the fore a series of incompatibilities: between language's capacity to posit (positing, positioning, performance, act) and its capacity to mean (knowledge, representation, constatation, figure); between the materiality of inscription and the phenomenality of perception; between the gesture of grounding (definitionally outside of sequence) and the narrative or allegory that "follows" from it; between language as meaningful pattern and the unmeaning, mechanical repetition upon which it is ostensibly "built." Such incompatibilities, moreover, also cannot be known insofar as to know them forcibly resolves the incompatibilities they would presume to know. Prosopopoeia figures that ungrounded, unassimilable "decree" and the forgetting that assimilates it to experience; giving a face, it is also "defacing": humanity, personhood, and meaning are paradoxically conferred by something inhuman, impersonal, and unmeaning, and the perception of pattern (face, meaning) itself comes to seem an automatic, mechanical, and, to that extent, depersonifying, disfiguring gesture. This is one way to understand why such questions would come to the fore in autobiography, where the confrontation between writing and life is perhaps unavoidable. In slightly different terms, therefore, the trope also points us toward the disjunctive temporalities of art and life, toward what Bersani examines as the virtuality, the suspended happening, of late Jamesian fiction.[11] *The Beast in the Jungle* is surely about (among other things) the incompatibility of figural systems and "life"—an incompatibility that, I have elsewhere suggested of *The Ambassadors,* need not be read in terms of pathos.[12]

De Man's translation of prosopopoeia as the conferring of face is, Chase reminds us, idiosyncratic; what is unusual, though it has perhaps been routinized in the years since by explorations of performativity and identity, is the interchangeability, implied by his translation, of mask and face. (Chase notes that de Man separates prosopopoeia from personification: "translating *prosopōn* as 'face' or 'mask', and not as 'person', is to imply that face is the condition—not the equivalent—of the existence of the person" [Chase, "Giving a Face to a Name," 83].) The end of *The Beast in the Jungle*, of course, has John Marcher turn from his hallucination of the leaping beast to fling himself, "face down, on the tomb" of May Bartram (James, *The Beast in the Jungle*, 71). Whether we are led to dwell on the covered eyes or the presented ass may depend on how completely we think the narrative perspective can be assimilated to Marcher's own. In any event, this is only the last of many faces in the text. "The shock of the face" (of the other man at the cemetery) catalyzes the crisis at the end of the story (69), and in the scene Marcher is then led to remember, May stands up before him, "and something to his purpose came prodigiously out of her very face" (58). "It had become . . . beautiful and vivid to him," we are told a page or so later, "that she had something more to give him; her wasted face delicately shone with it. . . . They continued for some minutes silent, her face shining at him" (59). The "shock of the face" at the end also replays their initial encounter: "It led, briefly, in the course of the October afternoon, to his closer meeting with May Bartram, whose face, a reminder yet not quite a remembrance, had begun merely by troubling him rather pleasantly" (34); when remembrance does arrive—though of course Marcher gets it all wrong—it is "her face and her voice" that "worked the miracle" (35).

One way to phrase the difficulty of the story's end would be to link its problem of voice—who "speaks" here?—to the difficulty of coordinating two parallel series of faces in the tale. In the first series, *face* repeatedly appears as a way of figuring knowledge that one has or does not have, is able or not able to accept. "I thought it the point you were just making," says Marcher, "that we *had* looked most things in the face"; the worst, he then says, is that "we haven't faced that. I *could* face it, I believe, if I knew what you think it" (56). Facts to face are figured by the face of the beast: "Marcher softly groaned as with a gasp, half-spent, at the face, more uncovered just then that it had been for a long while, of the imagination always with them. It had always had its incalculable moments of glaring out, quite as with the very eyes of the very Beast, and, used as he was to them, they could still draw from him the tribute of a sigh that rose from the very depths of his being" (48). As May sinks into her obscure illness, Marcher, made to feel, "in the face of doctors, nurses," and relatives, how small a claim their shared history gives him, is brought "face to face with the fact that he was to profit extraordinarily little by the interest May Bartram had taken in him" (64). The second series involves scenarios of address. (In this, the story seems to enact the close proximity of prosopopoeia and apostrophe.[13] Prosopopoeia "gives" a face; apostrophe, by addressing an absent, dead, or abstract entity, in a sense confers one.)[14] To face is both to confront or countenance a fact and to solicit a response—possibly in vain (as when Marcher wonders whether he had not waited "but to see the door shut in my face" [58]). As he does here, Marcher repeatedly conflates the solicitation of address with the solicitation of knowledge, an elision about which May is more equivocal; when he asserts that they have looked most things in the face, for example, she asks, "including each other?" (56).

A curious moment seems almost to figure a transition between these two senses of *face* in the tale. Contemplating the surprising fact that he has misplaced his memory of having told May his secret, Marcher thinks of the time he spent imagining he was alone with his imagined beast—and "lo, he wasn't alone a bit" (38). The echoing phoneme, by drawing attention to a repetition of sound below or beyond meaning, makes graphically visible the repetition of identical letters that then seem to draw a confrontation between paired faces (*lo—alone*), and a calling out to an imagined interlocutor (*lo* as a marker of apostrophe) calls into being a world in which one is not "alone a bit." A call of despair—alone!—becomes a call *to* someone—lo!—that is also a pointing at something (implicitly to be seen and thereby to be known), and the paronomasia brings into being a loneliness-negating sociability linking Marcher, May (as knowing), and the reader (as addressed). Such is, in fact, the "community" of *The Beast in the Jungle*. Whatever the story tells us of his pacing back and forth, of her sitting, or of their excursions to the opera, one could be forgiven for imagining their intimacy as the gazing claustrations of two opposed, almost disembodied, faces—from the very beginning, when some "accident of grouping brought them face to face" (34). As Marcher then tries unsuccessfully to recover the relation he feels their past ought to have constituted for them, James writes—in one of those sentences in which the text limits itself to Marcher's point of view while leaving open possible intimations of others—"they looked at each other as with the feeling of an occasion missed" (36). The story repeatedly reminds us of their paired faces looking at each other, a single act that comprises a huge range of cognitive and affective modalities: faces seen and offered to be seen, knowing, known, addressed, believed, and above all, constituting Marcher and Bartram's particular version of enclosed sociability; just before May's death, "face to face with her once more he believed her" (61).

Prosopopoeia, in de Man's etymology, makes manifest, we noted, the interchangeability of "mask" and "face." Masks also appear in the story—it would seem, initially, as distinguished from faces, as when Marcher's social behavior is called a "long act of dissimulation": "What it had come to was that he wore a mask painted with a social simper, out of the eyeholes of which there looked eyes of an expression not in the least matching the other features" (45). As this image is developed in these pages, the emphasis falls on dissimulation, on a "real truth" (or face) hidden behind an appearance. And it is therefore impossible not to see here—impossible, that is, after one has encountered Sedgwick's reading of this moment—a figure of the closet, especially since it is somehow their relation with each other that constitutes the long act of dissimulation. As the story progresses, though, this moment is echoed by others that foreground dissimulation less than recognition or address, and the wavering in all of these figures of "face"—between a looking out toward something and a surface presented to view, between opposed directions of a gaze—becomes explicit. May, notably, has a privileged relation to Marcher's secret because she can "see" his face from both sides: "It was only May Bartram who had [unlike the "stupid world," more than "half-discovered" that fact of dissimulation], and she achieved, by an art indescribable, the feat of at once—or perhaps it was only alternately—meeting the eyes from the front and mingling her own vision, as from over his shoulder, with their peep through the apertures" (45). ("Perhaps . . . only alternately" prevents this multifaceted gaze from being "merely" figural—or merely "figural.") Made a figure of voice, face's "direction" becomes indeterminate. In other terms, *mask* here takes on the valences of the two "series" of faces and thus figures their incompatibility: on the one hand, dissimulation (when *mask* is read in constative terms—a true face or false face), and, on the other, a scenario of address. One effect is that what looks like a (potentially comforting) rendering of comprehension—what earlier on the page is called her knowing simultaneously how he felt and how he looked—becomes more uncanny when it is (as it were) figured by the direction of gazes through and at a mask.

Marcher's mask evokes at least two other images later in the story. In the first, age turns May's face into a kind of mask:

Almost as white as wax, with the marks and signs in her face as numerous and as fine as if they had been etched by a needle, with soft
white draperies relieved by a faded green scarf on the delicate tone
of which the years had further refined, she was a picture of a serene
and exquisite but impenetrable sphinx, whose head, or indeed all
whose person, might have been powdered with silver. (54)

Aging in this image is at once a fading or wearing away (as the tone of the
scarf, once delicate, has been "further refined") and an aestheticization,
an etching that turns her face to an inscribable surface (like wax). That
becoming-wax also makes the face into a signifying form: etched on the
surface of her face are "marks and signs." The curious use of *relieved* wavers
between a "subjective" or personifying sense of "gives relief to" (where the
relief given moves, in an implicit personification whose logic of exchange
also turns a viewer to fabric, from the draperies to a spectator confronted
with a view of a pure, unremitting whiteness) and a potentially unidiomatic sculptural sense of "throws into relief" (as the lines etched into her
face might turn it into a bas-relief). The soft white draperies and delicate
scarf also make her face—engraved or etched, and like wax—seem hard, a
solidification tied to her becoming a picture.

A couple of pages later, that picture, evoking Marcher's social simper,
also seems masklike because her eyes do not match her face: "She looked
at him a minute, and there came to him as he met it an inconsequent
sense that her eyes, when one got their full clearness, were still as beautiful as they had been in youth, only beautiful with a strange cold light—a
light that somehow was a part of the effect, if it wasn't rather a part of the
cause, of the pale hard sweetness of the season and the hour" (56). Aging
makes one's face a mask because it exacerbates the gap between one's appearance and one's image of oneself derived from the experience of being
the locus of a gaze (the two never do coincide, but age makes that realization unavoidable). That gap is made visible "in" her face by the difficulty
of deciding whether the "strange cold light" comes from within May or
is a reflection there of the season and the hour, an indeterminate source
of illumination further emphasized by the strange suggestion that May's
changed eyes might be the source of the season and the hour's altered glow.
Marcher's sense is "inconsequent" both because it is irrelevant and because
it is illogical—and not merely because of the troubling of causality (in one
reading, cause recedes to a metatextual reference: May's aging face "causes"
the season because it is the background demanded by a text for that face

best to appear). It is also inconsequent because of shuffled temporality: May's eyes are out of temporal sequence, shine out from a different time than her etched and impenetrable face. When May is called a sphinx, we are presented with a kind of reverse-action prosopopoeia, which is also to say that the depersonifying, disfiguring potential of conferred face (as May becomes sculptural and an image) is made explicit—as face, that is, becomes "merely" a figure: "She was a sphinx, yet with her white petals and green fronds she might have been a lily too—only an artificial lily, wonderfully imitated and constantly kept, without dust or stain, though not exempt from a slight droop and a complexity of faint creases, under some clear glass bell" (54). Face recedes from us toward figures that can more and more tenuously be said to have a face and to face us.

That wavering of face returns in what is perhaps the most uncanny image in the story when Marcher, seeking through May to recover "the lost stuff of consciousness," visits her tomb:

> He stood for an hour, powerless to turn away and yet powerless to penetrate the darkness of death; fixing with his eyes her inscribed name and date, beating his forehead against the fact of the secret they kept, drawing his breath, while he waited, as if some sense would in pity of him arise from the stones. He kneeled on the stones, however, in vain; they kept what they concealed; and if the face of the tomb did become a face for him it was because her two names became a pair of eyes that didn't know him. He gave them a last long look, but no palest light broke. (66)

Prosopopoeia, de Man writes, "is the trope of autobiography, by which one's name . . . is made intelligible and made memorable as a face" (de Man, "Autobiography as De-Facement," 75–76; quoted in Johnson, "Face Value," 182); that trope spells out the consequence of, in Chase's terms, "giving a face to a name." May's name becomes a face, but only to refuse recognition. It is striking that Marcher here attempts to read—he fixes "with his eyes her inscribed name and date"—and his effort to decipher a secret ("the darkness of death," or his secret, concealed there, or both) is figured as an effort to make stones speak by conferring on them a face. The repeated word *face* makes explicit that the catachrestic "face of the tomb" is not *yet* a face. The conditional ("if the face of the tomb did become a face for him") leaves in question whether that face *does* appear, and conditionally relieving him of one indeterminacy (the face the tomb versus the face of his friend), it consigns him to others: not only whether the face does in fact appear but also, if it does, whether it a face (only) "for him." What is uncanny about the image is the potential—there in any face—to refuse recognition and thus to cease to be a face (to make explicit its "figurality" or simply to refuse the importunings of address).[15] That refused recognition leaves the face suspended "between" animation and de-animation, as the two names become "a pair of eyes" unanimated, however, by any answering expression. The effect is further emphasized by the uncertain figural status of elements in the passage: he beats his forehead against the "fact of the secret they kept," which (almost) comes to seem a stone, and if "sense" is what would arise from the stones were his gaze answered, if "kept" or "concealed" is a secret that would answer his queries, that answering "sense" would rely not on "penetrat[ing]" the stones but on failing to do so insofar as what the stones literally conceal, what he ostensibly wants them to cease to keep, is nothing other than May's corpse.

If this mask is a cipher for the earlier ones, it is notable that the blank face eventually becomes a page. For Marcher, that transformation means the tomb loses "its mere blankness of expression" (67). "The open page was the tomb of his friend, and *there* were the facts of the past, there the truth of his life, there the backward reaches in which he could lose himself" (68). By the end of the story, it is explicit that the tomb ceases to be blank insofar as it speaks: "The name on the tablet smote him as the passage of his neighbor had done, and what it said to him, full in the face, was that *she* was what he had missed" (70). Whatever their other effects—not least, their making equivocal James's relation to Marcher, and to the particular conclusion here spelled out—the effects of simulated voice with which we began perhaps also ought to be read in relation to this speaking tomb.[16]

The tomb as an open page also has eyes, which now can be said to see him: he loses himself from time to time at her tomb

with such effect that he seemed to wander through the old years with his hand in the arm of a companion who was, in the most extraordinary manner, his other, his younger self; and to wander, which was more extraordinary yet, round and round a third presence—not wandering she, but stationary, still, whose eyes, turning with his revolution, never ceased to follow him, and whose seat was his point, so to speak, of orientation (68).[17]

Among the many things to wonder about—many of which follow from the indeterminate figural status of this image—is the phrase *so to speak,* which wavers between its conventional meaning of "as it were" or "in accordance with the figure" and a more literal sense of orienting him by speaking or in order thereby to speak. That question seems, in turn, to be related to the interference between figural and literal registers when revolving eyes are said (depending on how one parses the paired uses of "whose") to become a seat of orientation. And it seems related, too, to the similar difficulty of distinguishing figural meanings of "seat"—location, position, base, or even the "abiding or resting place (of departed souls)" (*Oxford English Dictionary*)—and a literal anatomical reference or physical description of the tomb—the ass, or what it sits on.

When I remarked earlier that the final image hesitates between covered eyes and presented ass, I therefore did not speak facetiously—a word seemingly related less to faces than to pornography, though James's story seems to register the illegitimate etymology peering out from the beginning of the word.[18] For the transactions among these various faces in the story often invoke (or induce) spatial and corporeal disorientation. One might be led to wonder, for instance, how a seat, "stationary" and "still," can nevertheless have eyes that "never ceased to follow him" as he walked "round and round" it. The image is as uncanny as the tomb that does not know him, for the speaking tomb thus seems—front and back—to be nothing but face. Likewise, the encounter with his "fellow mortal" that catalyzes the story's climax is confusing not only because of the movements among person, figure, and face and the difficulty of distinguishing the faces of persons from the faces of tombs, but also because of the difficulty of determining which way the man is facing. The face of a fellow mortal, "one grey afternoon . . . looked into Marcher's own, at the cemetery, with an expression like the cut of a blade." This face "alone forbade further attention, though during the time he stayed he remained vaguely conscious of his neighbor, a middle aged man apparently, in mourning whose bowed back, among the clustered monuments and mortuary yews, was constantly presented" (68–69). Where it perhaps initially seems possible that there are two other men, it is made explicit that there is but one "neighbor," whose face forbids further attention, whose back is "constantly presented," and who later delivers the "shock of the face." There are ways to resolve the question of how a figure whose back is constantly presented nevertheless has a face that forbids further attention (most easily, perhaps, by articulating them as moments in a sequence—a face forbids attention and then turns away so the back is thereafter constantly presented). The back with a face, however, is not unprecedented in the story.

Of Marcher's secret and its power to remain constantly a presence even in the absence of any reference to it, we read, "Such a feature in one's outlook was really like a hump on one's back. The difference it made every minute of the day existed quite independently of discussion. One discussed of course *like* a hunchback, for there was always, if nothing else, the hunchback face" (44). The literal referent here is, I think, obscure—what *is* the hunchback face?—but the possibility of a face becoming a back (or vice versa) is matched by the strangeness of a "feature" in one's "outlook" being like "a hump on one's back." "A feature in one's outlook" itself suggests a reversal, in which a way of looking becomes a thing seen and, figurally anyway, part of a face, a face that, moreover, figures the recognizability of a particular face looking at this feature (as May is said to be a "feature of features" in Marcher's existence, and her condition, a disfigurement of his outer person [53]). That latter reversal appears in several other moments, such as, for example, when Marcher bemoans his loss of distinction after May's death: "The terrible truth was that he had lost—with everything else—a distinction as well; the things he saw couldn't help being common when he had become common to look at them. He was simply now one of them himself" (66–67). However one resolves the meaning of the assertion, the literal implication is that Marcher was now one of the things he saw.

When at the end, then, "the two men were for a minute directly confronted" (69), it is perhaps not unwarranted to render *confronted* as "sharing a face": the two share a face insofar as they face each other. This complicated (even impossible) anatomy, where faces opposite merge and thus, like the back with a face, face away from themselves, echoes earlier moments with Marcher and May. When it dawns on him that she knows his secret, he blushes: "Then it was that while he continued to stare, a light broke for him and the blood slowly came to his face, which began to burn with recognition" (38). When a face "burn[s] with recognition," where *is* the recognition? Is it "in" the face, or in the gaze at it? The shock of the face and what is said to him full in the face: the face is literally both what is seen and what receives the impression. This effect is compounded by the fact that Marcher is (seemingly, literally) lit by a figural burning: he blushes in response to May's question ("has it ever happened?") through which, the story tells us, "she burnt her ships" (38)—which might also lead one to wonder where "a light broke for him."[19] That her face is repeatedly said later to "shine" at him evokes this earlier moment (59), when her (ostensibly figural) action seems (literally) to illuminate his face. It is as if what is to happen to Marcher will happen (only) to his face, leaving him unable to perceive it; it is clear from the very beginning that whatever is to happen to him will appear other than "natural," will appear "strange," or in other words, will be perceptible, only to May—or, as Marcher puts it, "Well . . . say to you" (40).

The closing revelations—if they are revelations—strike me as instances of free-indirect style not only because they seem to be Marcher's more than the narrative's alone but also because Marcher's secret is vicarious from the beginning. The shared face and the back-as-face provide visual analogues for the uncertain locus of perception and voice when a face becomes a locus (or object) of address. To be unsure of where James is in relation to Marcher is to repeat an uncertainty structural to Marcher's secret. Hence these disorientations are entirely consonant with the initial rendering of that secret, which (like Dorian Gray's) appears in a second-person address from another (with the added mediation that the second-person report informs him of what he himself once said): "You said you had had from your earliest time, as the deepest thing within you, the sense of being kept for something rare and strange, possibly prodigious and ter-rible, that was sooner or later to happen to you, that you had in your bones the foreboding and the conviction of, and that would perhaps overwhelm you" (39). (For a reader, this is redoubled eavesdropping—we learn of the secret by overhearing May's speech to him, which reports his own to her.) Among other things, this structure clarifies why it is that Marcher unaccountably tells May his secret and then forgets he has. Raising the possibility that their unique relation is unique only insofar as she alone responds to the solicitation of his confidence—if he forgot once, why could he not have forgotten twice or more?—it also intimates that the secret was never his to begin with. (In this regard, all those moments where May—or her mortality—is said to be a feature of *his* face are legible as something other than his selfishness and, like the moments when he perceives [or fails to perceive] his secret "in" her face, intimate less narcissism than this curi-ously expropriated version of consciousness.)

The Beast in the Jungle repeatedly offers puns on the word *expression*: when we are told that Marcher's situation turned almost fresh, "usually under the effect of some expression drawn from herself"—and "her expressions doubtless repeated themselves" (46)—we inevitably hear "expression" to mean both a phrase and a "signifying" face, and in the latter case, therefore, it is difficult to tell whether the expression drawn from her appears on his face or hers. At the beginning, the passage I quoted earlier—"It led, briefly, in the course of the October afternoon, to his closer meeting with May Bartram, whose face, a reminder yet not quite a remembrance, had begun merely by troubling him rather pleasantly"—continues: "It affected him as the sequel of something of which he had lost the beginning. He knew it, and for the time quite welcomed it, as a continuation, but didn't know what it continued, which was an interest or an amusement the greater as he was also somehow aware—yet without a direct sign from her—that the young woman herself hadn't lost the thread" (34). *It* seems to refer to May's face, which suggests that her face affects Marcher as a "sequel," and the possibility at least emerges of reading every instance of that proliferating pronoun as likewise referring to his interlocutor's face. The turning of a blank face to an open page no doubt belongs to this movement, and to a more literal choreography of "turning" in the story.[20] At the end, of course, Marcher, "instinctively turning . . . flung himself, face down, on the tomb" (71); read in terms of knowledge, the moment initially seems to mark a refusal—a turning away from what he might countenance or face. For a reader, however, it is striking that Marcher's gesture repeats May's earlier one when, "her face shining at him," he only expectantly gapes: "She gave way at the same instant to a slow fine shudder, and though he remained staring—though he stared in fact the harder—turned off and regained her chair" (59). (She repeats this gesture in their final interview: "She turned her eyes away" [62].) Confronting the tomb that refuses to speak, Marcher is "powerless to turn away" (66); once the tomb becomes "an open page," May's eyes seem to distill that gesture—to become a pure turning (or a turning that is—from every point—a turning away, and thus a turning that *never* turns away).

This choreography complicates one's reading of the story's end because it can no longer be read purely as an evasion of insight: if Marcher repeats May's gesture of turning away, he turns from us as she turned from him to the extent that his face has become a page for us to read. It is curious that turning away in *The Beast in the Jungle*—as May turns from Marcher, and Marcher, from us—does not seem to mark (as it often does in other James texts) a turning away from knowledge. It is not a refusal to "face" something because, more often than not, it is a turn *toward* a face. It seems rather to be a withdrawal—one that both refuses another's address and constitutes (in turn) a form of knowledge. A refusal and a solicitation: it is a back constantly presented that presents the shock of the face. Read in terms of knowledge, the final turn might suggest an evasion. Read in terms of address, however, it dramatizes the trope of apostrophe: "The lyric poet normally pretends to be talking to himself or to someone else: the spirit of nature, a Muse, a personal friend, a lover, a God, personified extraction, or a natural object. . . . The poet, so to speak, turns his back on his listeners."[21] That means that the lyric is an utterance "overheard," which is evocative (as it were) of the mediations of voice in *The Beast in the Jungle.* One might also emphasize that apostrophe—or "aversion"—consists in this gesture of turning.[22] Apostrophe, Jonathan Culler writes, is "the turning away from actual listeners to address absent or imagined interlocutors";[23] apostrophe's invocations "turn away from empirical listeners by addressing natural objects, artifacts, or abstractions" (Culler, "Apostrophe," 60). Marcher's turn at the end of the story might thus be read as a *figure* of address. As such, it embodies the reversals inherent in structures of address: the absent entity addressed in the lyric so that it might, in turn, address (and animate) the speaker; the de-animation and disfigurement implicit in that claimed power of animation and ventriloquism; the difficulty of distinguishing face from voice, which is also to say, of deciding the "direction" of one's view at or through a mask. The closing gesture of the story—to compound the difficulties it raises—both presents a *figure* (asks to be read in a constative register) and *addresses* us (performs or enacts the structure of address). Marcher, we noted, repeatedly conflates the solicitations of address with those of knowledge and therefore reads the dilemmas of the story entirely in terms of a hidden secret. Not to perceive the multivalent registers of voice of the story's close is in a sense to read as Marcher does. The multiple "rhetorical agendas" that can be registered in free-indirect discourse force one to confront the multifaceted, equivocal reversals of address and personification that the story depicts and enacts.

Part of the difficulty of the story's end is also the indeterminate figural status of that "figure" of address. Faces and address in *The Beast in the Jungle,* therefore, ought perhaps to be read in relation to the figural indeterminacy of late James. Marcher, Ruth Bernard Yeazell notes, seems motivated by metaphor, and in fact the story's plot repeatedly treats figures as if they were literal.[24] What prevents Marcher and May from marrying is just such a literalization:

Something or other lay in wait for him, amid the twists and turns
of the months and the years, like a crouching beast in the jungle.
It signified little whether the crouching beast were destined to slay
him or be slain. The definite point was the inevitable spring of the
creature; and the definite lesson from that was that a man of feeling
didn't cause himself to be accompanied by a lady on a tiger-hunt.
Such was the image under which he had ended by figuring his life.
(James, *The Beast in the Jungle*, 43–44)

The odd causality (perhaps not unlike a season determined by the sorrows
of May's changing face) suggests that Marcher's closet contains James's late
style. The odd anatomy of faces that seems to spell out the crossing of epistemological and vocative senses of *face* can also be understood in terms
of the difficulties that emerge when a trope of address (prosopopoeia or,
perhaps, free-indirect style) becomes a thematic element in the text—to
be seen there, addressing, and, seen, addressed. The proliferation of faces
curiously literalizes the text's own mode of address. Marcher's turn at the
end, as he throws himself face down on a tomb that is a name that has
become a pair of eyes that has become an open page, makes him, I noted,
May Bartram to our John Marcher and presents us a back with a face. With
Marcher face down on the tomb, his face and the face of the tomb at last
meet. It may be that the text thereby becomes a voice by giving us a face—
thereby turning us to the things that are, Barbara Johnson suggests, the
human ideal of the person.

Not the least striking aspect of Sedgwick's reading of the tale in this
context is its own status as a form of prosopopoeia. I do not mean simply
the essay's own voicing, and the pause certain phrases in the first person
must necessarily give one now—"I am convinced, however . . ."; "I hypoth-
esize that what May Bartram would have liked for Marcher, the narrative
she wished to nurture for him" (Sedgwick, "The Beast in the Closet," 203,
207)—but also, as that last instance suggests, its highly identificatory ventriloquizing of May's desires. And that ventriloquism comes with its own
versions of apostrophe:

She seems the woman (don't we all know them?) who has not
only the most delicate nose for but the most potent attraction
toward men who are at crises of homosexual panic. . . . Though,
for that matter, won't most women admit that an arousing nimbus,

an excessively refluent and dangerous maelstrom of eroticism, somehow attends men in general at such moments, even otherwise boring men? . . . To speak less equivocally from my own eros and experience, there is a particular relation to truth and authority that a mapping of male homosexual panic offers to a woman in the emotional vicinity. (209)

It is difficult to separate the theory from its vicarious relation to male desire—to say nothing of its production, often by proxy, of effects felt vicariously in turn. (Do we *all* know them? And surely it is no accident that what "most women" would admit is phrased, unmistakably, as only one woman in the world would have phrased it.)[25] To judge from others' responses to this essay, it was not merely the perfect fit of "my own eros and experience" at the moment I first read it that led me to respond as I did—a response solicited, strangely, by an essay addressed not to me but to others, about me. "Lo, *he* wasn't alone a bit"; "speak ye unto the rock before their eyes" (Num. 20:8): for me, it was an essay less heard than overheard and soliciting to the very extent that it excluded me, an essay that constituted a community I felt less enabled to join than authorized to imagine for others. "It wasn't till after he had spoken that he became aware of how much there had been in him of response."[26] One might also wonder why it was in a reading of James that Sedgwick produced her theory of homosexual panic (which is to say, of male heterosexuality)—a theory still powerful, still incontrovertible, even today when the reigning dispositif of tolerance and marriage-for-all will not let anyone stop proclaiming how virtuously free of panic the world at last is. Surely, neither the theory nor the reading would live for us if the story were merely the (albeit perfect) example. "Imagine a possible alterity" (Sedgwick, "The Beast in the Closet," 200): what seems exorbitant—by which I mean powerful and, even now, unexpected—in Sedgwick's epochal, field-founding reading of James's tale responds to the multiple ways this story is about the unanswered, unanswerable yearnings of imagined address.

Part V

9

"My Spirit's Posthumeity" and the Sleeper's Outflung Hand

Queer Transmission in *Absalom, Absalom!*

> . . . *I said to the mountain,*
> *what becomes of things:*
> *well, the mountain said, one*
> *mourns the dead but who*
> *can mourn those the dead mourned;*

—A. R. Ammons, "Continuing"

> *The ivory body of the Bithynian slave rots in the green ooze of the Nile,*
> *and on the yellow hills of the Cerameicus is strewn the dust of the young*
> *Athenian; but Antinous lives in sculpture, and Charmides in philosophy.*

—Oscar Wilde, "The Portrait of Mr. W.H."

Literary tradition raises the question of survival and of the artifacts whose possible preservation means that they belong to a time beyond that of any human being. To live "in sculpture" or "in philosophy" is therefore an equivocal proposition; such a sublimation cannot leave one as one "is," and, for Wilde, immortality (in the paradox Dorian Gray embodies) is achieved through one's vanishing, just as the continuity of culture is secured, in Pater's renaissance, through a series of discontinuities. Art makes present not the moment but its vanishing; "humanism" gives us to see the perpetual fading away of the human.[1] I propose to read William Faulkner's *Absalom, Absalom!* in this perhaps unlikely context; its link to Pater and Wilde—and, beyond that, to a long tradition of queer aesthetics—goes far beyond the tableau of Charles Bon's mistress visiting his grave: "It must have resembled a garden scene by the Irish poet, Wilde," the "magnolia-faced woman" with her "thin delicate child with a smooth ivory sexless face" whom "Beardsley might not only have dressed but drawn."[2] Largely removed (except in this scene) from explicit decadent tonalities, the novel—in its models of transmission and history and, more broadly, the understanding of time that animates it—shares with aestheticism what, to my mind, is a large part of its queer allure.[3]

For anyone seeking to unveil the homoerotic subtext of *Absalom, Absalom!*, the first challenge would be to make that unveiling seem as startling as its almost total neglect by the novel's critics suggests it ought to be.[4] Such thematics are hardly a subtext; to notice them it suffices to attend to the letter of the text. Among many other such moments:

> Because Henry loved Bon. He repudiated blood birthright and material security for his sake. . . . Because he loved Bon . . . he (Henry) who could not say to his friend, *I did that for love of you; do this for love of me.* (71, 72)

> Yes, he loved Bon, who seduced him as surely as he seduced Judith. (76)

> It was because Bon not only loved Judith after his fashion but he loved Henry too in a deeper sense than merely after his fashion. Perhaps in his fatalism he loved Henry the better of the two, seeing perhaps in the sister merely the shadow, the woman vessel with which to consummate the love whose actual object was the youth. (86)

> It was not Judith who was the object of Bon's love or of Henry's solicitude. She was just a blank shape, the empty vessel in which each of them strove to preserve, not the illusion of himself nor the illusion of the other but what each conceived the other to believe him to be—the man and the youth, seducer and seduced, who had known one another, seduced and been seduced, victimized in turn each by the other, conquerer vanquished by his own strength, vanquished conquering by his own weakness, before Judith came into their joint lives even by so much as girlname. (95)

It is open to a reader to understand such lines in a context so thoroughly marked by homophobic presumption that the love that dare not speak its name is free volubly to speak its name because that name can safely be assumed to name something else. Yet the forthrightness makes one suspect that one is not in such a context at all, just as one almost dares ask oneself, as Shreve feels Quentin shaking in bed, how many beds they have (or use) in their Harvard dorm room (288). (The other boys in *The Sound and the Fury* call Shreve Quentin's "husband"; that the earlier novel seems to cast that as a comment on Quentin's conflicted relation to female sexuality and on the consequent disruption, for him, of homosocial relations, does not make the knowingness there any simpler to understand.)[5] Whereas heterosexuality in *Absalom, Absalom!* is nearly always thwarted—one thinks of Ellen's wedding or Judith's trousseau or Rosa's lovelorn poetry, her "barren" youth, or her engagement—male same-sex love affairs are remarkable for not seeming particularly unrequited: Henry and Bon have a good six years together, and Shreve and Quentin, somewhere between a long evening and 103 years. (By the time one traverses that affair, the question of what it means to have an object leads one to question whether Miss Rosa's desires—like, in consequence, those of Judith and Ellen—can be called unrequited, makes one speculate about the way her passion might likewise transform desire into something queer.)[6] It takes a cultivated obliviousness to fail to notice that a good dorm-room story—for Shreve anyway—is best heard (and told) naked; the novel continually reminds us of Shreve's noctilucent flesh and of the fact that, to our gaze on their conversation, he almost always looks nude. For Quentin, too, the culmination of the story involves taking off his clothes: "Then he was lying on the bed, naked, swabbing his body steadily with his discarded shirt, sweating still, panting" (298).

The markers of time—"then he was . . . sweating still"—are perhaps more central to the queer eroticism of *Absalom, Absalom!* than either Shreve's "naked torso pink-gleaming and baby-smooth, cherubic, almost hairless" (147) or Quentin's naked, sweating, panting body. *Absalom, Absalom!* is a love story—several such—between men; even if one sometimes suspects that the pyrotechnics of the novel's historical scope and its telling of the bloody history of a continent were merely the occasion for two roommates to express their love in their lamp-lit Cambridge dorm room, the love is inextricable from that bloody history, from the telling itself, and from the intertwining of the telling with the story told.

That intertwining prevents the homoeroticism from being merely thematic: a story about two boys in love (Charles Bon and Henry Sutpen) told by two boys (Quentin and Shreve) as a way of speaking their love. It *is* such a story, of course, but the movement of that love from the story to its telling makes the novel queer in a much more radical sense and suggests that the explicit thematic homoeroticism of such moments indexes (I would also say "transmits") a queer structure. A novel about telling, *Absalom, Absalom!* is structured as a series of (often redoubled) scenes of narration: Miss Rosa and Quentin, Mr. Compson and Quentin (telling of Sutpen's words to Quentin's grandfather, with the intervening conveying of the story to Mr. Compson left largely implicit), and Shreve and Quentin, with other minor repetitions of the same structure. Intercalated with each other narratively, these (re)tellings overlap but do not coincide, and each presents a complicated, layered narrative of its own. It is worth recalling, too, the obvious fact that the novel, about transmission in the sense that it is about telling, is also about transmission in the sense that it is about a failed dynasty—Thomas Sutpen's failure to transmit anything but this failure to transmit. That failure does prove transmissible: from Haiti to New Orleans, where the renounced marriage returns threatening incest and miscegenation, to Sutpen's Hundred, where fratricide (Henry's killing of Bon) ends both the threat posed to the dynasty by the possible marriage and the dynasty itself. Sutpen's Hundred goes up in flames, and Sutpen's line disappears with Jim Bond ("whereabouts unknown" [309]). The novel's allegorical dimensions—the Sutpen story, that of the Civil War, and that of an America rent from the beginning by a bloody history of "race"—raise the stakes of that failure, as does the layering of mythical retellings: of the misfortunes of the House of Atreus, for example, or the biblical narrative of Absalom, Amnon, Tamar, and David. The allegorical layers repeat—in the very fact of their layering—the characters' preoccupation with a past that never passes away.

That Sutpen transmits a failure to transmit intimates a failed transmission that is curiously indistinguishable from transmission itself. If it is often the case in this text that narratives fail to be told, and even if the past seems doomed to irrecoverable obscurity, its resurgence and atavistic recrudescence also mean that the past, if never fully told, also never fully disappears: the House of Sutpen is the house of Atreus and of David, just as Quentin and Shreve come to embody the story they tell. Time is out of joint; to phrase simply an effect far from simple, its understanding of transmission makes *Absalom, Absalom!* a novel about queer time.

Words and Flesh

These modalities of thwarted transmission are framed at the beginning by Rosa Coldfield's exorbitant desire that words might become flesh:

> And opposite Quentin, Miss Coldfield in the eternal black which she had worn for forty-three years now, whether for sister, father, or nothusband none knew, sitting so bolt upright in the straight hard chair that was so tall for her and her legs hung straight and rigid as if she had iron shinbones and ankles, clear of the floor with that air of impotent and static rage like children's feet, and talking in that grim haggard amazed voice until at last listening would re-nege and hearing-sense self-confound and the long-dead object of her impotent yet indomitable frustration would appear, as though by outraged recapitulation evoked, quiet inattentive and harmless, out of the biding and dreamy and victorious dust. (3–4)[7]

As the novel unfolds, Rosa's fantasy—or the fantasy she is made here to embody—comes to mark two seemingly opposed relations to time. In the first, her desire is shown to be a fantasy, and her wish, therefore, a mono-maniacal illusion, albeit one shared by all inhabitants of a vanquished South, or by all those whose caste and "race," or, despite these, whose in-vestment in whatever ideal that South represents, allows them to regret the passing of that vanished world: to lose the war is a hitch in time that leaves survivors to reenact defeat, pursuing the illusion that to recover the lost time would be to recover experience itself. The dust, biding, is, even in the fantasy of a recapitulation that would cease to be one, ever victorious, and Rosa is consigned to a perpetual mourning that lacks even an object to mourn—"sister, father, or nothusband none knew." From another angle, however, such recovery is what telling achieves; the past comes back in its fully embodied immediacy. On the one hand, lost or illegible texts excite the fantasy and demystify the illusion of their impossible recovery, and thwarted love dreams in vain of its revindication or redemption; on the other, telling, and particularly the telling of loss, acquires an exorbitant power to conjure from the biding dust the tangible forms of the ghosts that haunt it.

Such a hesitation is visible in the sentence's irresolute grammar: one is confronted with two divergent (quasi-)parallel structures, the first pairing "sitting" with "talking" and the second pairing "she had iron shinbones" with "at last listening would renege." The sense of the sentence, in other words, leads one to understand *would* in "would renege . . . would appear" as if it were governed by an "as if"; grammatically, though, the sentence has Miss Rosa "talking until at last listening would renege . . . and the long-dead object . . . would appear." *Would* hesitates between a conditional or hypothetical and a real past (or even a habitual past),[8] and the following "as though" then suggests either restatement or qualification, "as though by outraged recapitulation evoked" marking either a hypothetical parallel to the power of speech to conjure a long-dead object or a hypothetical statement of the particular mode of such recovery (a recovery itself not subject to doubt). What does it mean, then, for "listening" to "renege" and "hearing-sense" to "self-confound"? If listening (which becomes a noun with agency, an abstraction, as it were, given body) desires or denounces or goes back on a promise, the verb lacks an object; likewise, the self-confounding of hearing-sense (where the redundancy of the compound noun seems to strive for a similar concretization) indicates a sense turned reflexive. Hearing, turned back on itself, bodies forth a long-dead object, by defeating itself, or by throwing itself into confusion, making itself lose its presence of mind, or, in an obsolete, chiefly scriptural meaning, by abashing itself or putting itself to shame. Sense—"conquerer vanquished by his own strength, vanquished conquering by his own weakness"—grasps its object by confounding itself, and the object, long dead, is brought forth within a grammar in which a verb unidiomatically voids its object in favor of an objectless reflexivity.

Even if this moment with Miss Rosa suggests that outraged recapitulation might hope to overcome time, and that baffled sense might hope to encounter its object by confounding itself in reflexivity, for Mr. Compson, the loss of immediacy is a consequence of recapitulation. In one version of history in the novel, this is the predicament of those living in a defeated South, "the deep South dead since 1865 and peopled with garrulous outraged baffled ghosts" (4). Quentin ("still too young to deserve yet to be a ghost but nevertheless having to be one for all that, since he was born and bred in the deep South the same as she was" [4]) "had grown up with that; the mere names were interchangeable and almost myriad. His childhood was full of them; his very body was an empty hall echoing with sonorous defeated names; he was not a being, an entity, he was a commonwealth. He was a barracks filled with stubborn back-looking ghosts still recovering" (7). The echoing of names, which is repeatedly evoked (and is itself echoed in the text, as in the recurrent parenthetical glossings of pronouns with their nominal referents, of which more later), here marks a turning-hollow of the body. Outraged recapitulation travels its circuit in reverse and leaves the living disembodied. Quentin's body, made an echoing memorial, or, even less grandiosely, a barracks abandoned but for its haunting ghosts, becomes a confederation of the dead. This strand of the novel is that of unresolved mourning and ambivalence ("yes, I have been listening too long" [116]; "*I don't hate it! I don't hate it!*" [303]), and it excites a fantasy—Miss Rosa's at the beginning, for instance—of becoming, at last, oneself, as Mr. Compson imagines it was possible for people

> of a dead time; people too as we are and victims too as we are, but victims of a different circumstance, simpler and therefore, integer for integer, larger, more heroic and the figures therefore more heroic too, not dwarfed and involved but distinct, uncomplex who had the gift of a loving once and dying once instead of being diffused and scattered creatures drawn blindly limb from limb from a grab bag and assembled, author and victim too of a thousand homicides and a thousand copulations and divorcements. (71)

This, one of the many moments when the novel's prose seems out of all proportion to what occasions it (in this showing, too, "that curious lack of economy between cause and effect which is always a characteristic of fate when reduced to using human beings for tools, material" [94]; Mr. Compson wonders simply whether there is enough light on the porch to read by), offers a more visceral version of Quentin as commonwealth: a body assembled of mismatched parts amalgamated, where the violence of dismemberment is indistinguishable from the violence of assembly. "Drawn blindly limb from limb" and "drawn . . . from a grab bag and assembled": to *drawn* as "pulled apart" and as "taken from" one might add *drawn* as "depicted"—where, moreover, the merger of "author" and "victim" parallels that of homicide, copulation, and divorcement. To recover the past, one imagines, would allow one, at last, to love "once" and die "once," and to inhabit a body once again whole.

As the pun on *drawn* suggests, the falling away from bodily immediacy is—initially—framed as a move from body to text, where, moreover, the loss of immediacy is figured as an *illegible* text. And the major narrative sections—Mr. Compson's narrative to Quentin as it is interwoven with Miss Rosa's and, more markedly, Quentin and Shreve's late-night Cambridge colloquy—are framed by illegible texts: Bon's letter to Judith (given to Quentin on the porch where, Mr. Compson fears, there will not be enough light to read it) and Mr. Compson's letter to Quentin about Rosa's death, which sandwiches almost the entirety of the Harvard section and which Quentin stares at even though the semi-levitation induced by its fold makes it, we are repeatedly told, indecipherable from where he is sitting. "Maybe I can read it here all right," Quentin says of the first letter, though it will be thirty pages before he has a chance to try (71). Whatever promises of clarification attend the suspense of such letters—they do always arrive at their destination but take pages on pages of novelistic prose to do so—they are as indecipherable read as they were when unreadable, which makes these indecipherable texts stand in for an irrecoverable past and for the novel's understanding of transmission. "They," Mr. Compson says of the long-dead people whose inscrutable understandings of the world have left it as we find it,

> dont explain and we are not supposed to know. We have a few old
> mouth-to-mouth tales; we exhume from old trunks and boxes
> and drawers letters without salutation or signature, in which men
> and women who once lived and breathed are now merely initials
> or nicknames out of some now incomprehensible affection which
> sound to us like Sanskrit or Chocktaw; we see dimly people, the
> people in whose living blood and seed we ourselves lay dormant
> and waiting, in this shadowy attenuation of time possessing now
> heroic proportions, performing their acts of simple passion and
> simple violence, impervious to time and inexplicable—Yes, Judith,
> Bon, Henry, Sutpen: all of them. They are there, yet something is
> missing; they're like a chemical formula exhumed along with the
> letters from that forgotten chest, carefully, the paper old and faded
> and falling to pieces, the writing faded, almost indecipherable, yet

meaningful, familiar in shape and sense, the name and presence of volatile and sentient forces; you bring them together in the proportions called for, then nothing happens; you re-read, tedious and intent, pouring, making sure that you have forgotten nothing, and made no miscalculation; you bring them together again and again nothing happens: just the words, the symbols, the shapes themselves, shadowy inscrutable and serene, against that turgid background of a horrible and bloody mischancing of human affairs. (80)

"Letters without salutation or signature" (like Bon's shoe-polish letter: "the dead tongue speaking after the four years and then after almost fifty more . . . without date or salutation or signature" [102]) offer an image for a text that is indecipherable insofar as all texts exceed those who write them; the letter's indecipherability indexes its truncation by time, which removes writer and addressee and the contexts that gave them birth to leave a text that then makes manifest an indecipherability, and a loss, internal to writing. Writing, to the extent that it is transmissible, is in this sense always a dead tongue speaking.

Mr. Compson's two comparisons are nevertheless different in crucial respects. Both offer images for historical distance and alienation, but in the first (presuming, as he seems to do, that one knows neither Sanskrit nor Choctaw), one is able to perceive the difference. In the second, the script is "*almost* indecipherable, yet meaningful, familiar in shape and sense" (emphasis added); one can decipher the formula, but "nothing happens." This formula becomes "inscrutable" in its very decipherment. The transition suggests a parallel between "we see dimly people . . . impervious to time and inexplicable" and "the words, the symbols, the shapes themselves, shadowy inscrutable and serene." The passage moves from "inexplicable" people and a vanished past to a loss more difficult to locate. Persons become symbols or shapes—decipherable but inert—who, in their transition to texts, take on legibility at the same time that they become inscrutable. Historical transmission is thus explicitly tied to a fading-away of human life into textual forms, leading us to question, for example, whether "the shapes themselves" are persons or letters. That shift, in turn, is implicitly tied to the Civil War: the texts are the same, those figures seen against "that turgid background" seeming to speak and write, or to be written, in a familiar tongue, but the world is so changed that they no longer retain their meaning. That is perhaps the sense in which *inscrutable* is synonymous with *serene*; the texts are legible but—precisely insofar as human beings have become legible texts—they are without salutation or signature, do not address us, stare placidly beyond us to a time after our disappearance.

Missed Experience, Belatedness, and Telling

For Mr. Compson and for Miss Rosa, it initially seems that their predicament is a function of belatedness—a predicament to which, Mr. Compson imagines, an antebellum South was not subject. In this text, however, to arrive too late in history—and thus to be a grab bag or commonwealth— might be to recover most authentically the experience of the lived past. Everyone—not just Quentin, Shreve, Rosa, and Mr. Compson but also Henry, Bon, Judith, Ellen, and Sutpen—is out of sync with his or her own life, shaped by a past never experienced or experienced only secondhand as narrative. To be "a widow without ever having been a bride" (10) is less a peculiarity of Judith's fate (or even of her generation's youth lost to war) than an emblem of experience *tout court* in the novel. Thus, that "bowed and unwived widow" (110), like everyone else, misses even the start of the war. It is not just Quentin and Shreve who miss "what is probably the most moving mass-sight of all human and mass-experience, . . . the sight of young men, the light quick bones, the bright gallant deluded blood and flesh dressed in a martial glitter of brass and plumes, marching away to a battle" (97) because they were born too late, or just Rosa, who does because she was too young and her father too opposed to secession, but also Henry, Bon, and Judith, who, although the right age and ostensibly there, miss it, too (as we are told in a passage whose evocative power seems in inverse proportion to the immediacy with which anyone in the novel can be said to have seen the spectacle described):

> . . . and Judith not there and Henry the romantic not there and Bon the fatalist, hidden somewhere, the watcher in the watched: and their current flower-laden dawns of that April and May and June filled with bugles, entering a hundred windows where a hundred still unbrided widows dreamed virgin unmeditant upon the locks of black or brown or yellow hair and Judith not one of these: and five of the company, mounted with grooms and body servants in a forage wagon, in their new and unstained gray made a tour of the State with the flag, the company's colors, the segments of silk cut

and fitted but not sewn, from house to house until the sweetheart of each man in the company had taken a few stitches in it, and Henry and Bon not of these either. (97–98)

Likewise, Bon goes to university too late (if in fact he ever was the "right" age for the experience [98]), and the generations in the Sutpen–Coldfield clan are almost comically scrambled:

Miss Rosa who in actual fact was the girl's aunt and who by actual years should have been her sister and who in actual experience and hope and opportunity should have been the niece, ignoring the mother to follow the departing and inaccessible daughter. (55)

Rosa, telling of "*the miscast summer of my barren youth,*" who "*had been born too late,*" who had been taught "*to listen before I could comprehend and to understand before I even heard*" (117, 118, 112), initially seems to enact a psychosexual etiology of the "old maid," and her obsessional prurience ("the spinster doomed for life at sixteen" [59]), the precocious sexualization that dooms her, in the common wisdom to which that nomenclature belongs, to miss sex altogether (it hardly matters whether the missed sex dooms her to a regressively overinvested interest in it or whether the particular style of interest has as a consequence the missing of what most obsesses it). That specialty erotics, however, comes likewise to embody the experience of temporality and history in the novel—a queer one where generations come out of order and experiences refuse to coincide with themselves in time.

Thus (in another figure born of literary inbreeding), the sexually hyperaesthetic virgin, morbidly fixated on the sexual experience of others, appears here as a creature whose belatedness creates an evocative erotic sensibility:

I was not spying, who would walk those raked and sanded garden paths and think "This print was his save for this obliterating rake, that even despite the rake it is still there and hers beside it in that slow and mutual rhythm wherein the heart, the mind, does not need to watch the docile (ay, the willing) feet"; would think "What suspiration of the twinning souls have the murmurous myriad ears of the secluded vine or shrub listened to? What vow, what promise, what rapt biding fire has the lilac rain of this wistaria, this heavy rose's

dissolution, crowned?" But best of all, better far than this, the actual
living and the dreamy flesh itself. Oh no, I was not spying while I
dreamed in the lurking harborage of my own shrub or vine as I be-
lieved she dreamed upon the nooky seat which held invisible imprint
of his absent thighs just as the obliterating sand, the million finger-
nerves of frond and leaf, the very sun and moony constellations
which looked down at him, the circumambient air, held somewhere
yet his foot, his passing shape, his face, his speaking voice, his name:
Charles Bon, Charles Good, Charles Husband-soon-to-be. (119)

Rosa can say, "*I was not spying while I dreamed*" in part because her not-
spying gazes on no scene of love she might vicariously share but on an
absence—one from which is obliterated even the footprint that could attest that a presence had been there. It is hard to call this eroticism "unrequited," though, or (therefore) to oppose belatedness to self-presence.
"*Held somewhere . . . his passing shape*": the absence can be, at the same
time, a preservation because absence is here the registration of a shape.
The print, "*the invisible imprint of his absent thighs,*" "*the million finger-*
nerves of frond and leaf," even the crowning "*lilac rain of this wistaria*" as
scent or petals enfold a figure from above, are at once sensuous images
of contact between surfaces and registrations of a disappearance that extends, as obliterating sand and dissolving rose attest, even to the material
imprinted.[9] She is not spying on the lover who died before her arrival,
moreover, because "*the lurking harborage*" of "[her] *own shrub or vine*"
is another such enclosure enfolding absence—like, we might extrapolate,
the quotation marks that enclose the (self-consciously rhetorical) forms
attributed to that (also vanished) I "*who would . . . think.*" Those poetic
forms, moreover, imply a presence that they do not assert but merely question; the rhetorical questions, and their elaboration, allow us to perceive
a form that they nevertheless refrain, in the strictest sense, from positing.
Her belatedness allows her to bear witness to a vanished object, to make
present—"*held somewhere*"—a vanishing.

What initially seems the particularly ratcheted-up sensuality of a sexuality denied its meet object in fact describes the ontology of experience
(not just Rosa's, but everyone's) in the novel:

It is not the blow we suffer from but the tedious repercussive anti-
climax of it, the rubbishy aftermath to clear away from off the very

threshold of despair. You see, I never saw him. I never saw him dead.
I heard an echo, but not the shot; I saw a closed door but did not
enter it. (121)

. . . because I never saw him . . . For all I was allowed to know, we
had no corpse; we even had no murderer. (122, 123)

"*A shot heard only by its echo*" (123); "*we had buried nothing. No, there had*
been no shot" (127): belatedness puts in question not one's relation to an
event whose facticity can be assumed but the event itself.[10] "*Yes, more than*
that: he was absent, and he was; he returned, and he was not; three women
put something into the earth and covered it, and he had never been" (123).
The *and*s hesitate among a variety of different relations: logical coordination
("and therefore . . ."), simultaneity, and temporal sequence. It seems to me
that they ask to be read in all of these senses at once, which produces a series
of logical and temporal scramblings culminating in "*he had never been.*"

Among other effects, "*he had never been*" intervenes afterwards to negate
"*he was.*" The temporal reversal ("*There had been no shot. That sound was*
merely the sharp and final clap-to of a door between us and all that was, all
that might have been—a retroactive severance of the stream of event" [127])
marks the particular temporality of narrative, where the (logically) later
(ostensibly subordinate) time of telling comes to shape the time of events
told.[11] The temporality of narrative thus allows it to become Rosa's "lurking
harborage" or the impressible seat or sand or crowning lilac rain that held
somewhere yet his passing shape. Narrative thus has the power to repoten-
tialize the past, to bring out the potentiality encrypted in actualization (and
encrypted there to the very extent that it is actualized).[12] Perhaps better,
the making manifest of potentiality is brought out by the fluidity of time in
Absalom, Absalom! "A shot heard only by its echo" defines, with particular
economy, one's encounter with an event known only through narrative.

In this novel, it also defines the war, which is repeatedly called an "interval." The interval between "before" and "after," the central shaping event
of *Absalom, Absalom!*—even, in fact, its subject (as the convergence of its
various classical and biblical allusions and as the catastrophe that fuels
the narrative)—the war is less an event than a hiatus. "*That night which*
was four years long" (137), the "interval of four years" (102), is described
as a period of waiting: "It should have been all; that afternoon four years
later should have happened the next day, the four years, the interval, mere

anti-climax: an attenuation and prolongation of a conclusion already ripe to happen, by the War, by a stupid and bloody aberration in the high (and impossible) destiny of the United States. ... Henry waited four years, hold-ing the three of them in that abeyance, that durance, waiting" (94).[13] And after the waiting, the crisis, Bon's death, is not described, and comes to mark another interval: "*a shot heard, faint and far away and even direction and source indeterminate, by two women, two young women alone in a rot-ting house where no man's footstep had sounded in two years—a shot, then an interval of aghast surmise above the cloth and needles which engaged them, then feet, in the hall and then on the stairs, running, hurrying, the feet of a man*" (108). Striking in this regard is Bon's noncourtship of Judith: "There was no time, no interval, no niche in the crowded days when he could have courted Judith" (77). For Henry, on the other hand, Bon's ex-istence is nothing but an interval; suggesting that Rosa's not-spying gaze espies a series of invisible imprints truly left (only) after the fact by her speculations about their love (and that her lurking harborage is the niche love needs), it also makes Henry's and Bon's war more or less explicitly a courtship. And in this sense the narration of events introduces an interval, a hiatus separating experience from itself. Hence, if belatedness separates one, as by narrative distance, from an event one can (in this logic, there-fore) only tell but not experience, then the central "event" of the novel, the war, *is* such an interval: an experience transmitted to the extent that it is missed. Moreover, therefore, it is to the precise extent that the interval of their conversation intervenes between themselves and events that Shreve and Quentin—with their own night, 4 or 43 or 103 years long, and their own lurking harborage or niche—have their love story, too, and, in their outraged recapitulation, bring to life the past they were born too late to experience.

Distance and Absorption; Merger and Fault

But I am getting ahead of myself. Those moments that posit an alienation from experience often invoke the name: to be denied self-presence (as a mere wandering ghost in a defeated South) is to be a mere name, "an empty hall echoing with sonorous defeated names" (7); as Rosa says, "*I never saw him. I never even saw him dead. I heard a name*" (117). Or, yet again, when her not-spying on a vanished love attenuates a bodily presence in the assertion of its preservation: "*His foot, his passing shape, his face, his speaking voice, his name*" (118). This is the sense, too, in which the novel uses the word *shibboleth*: "*But let flesh touch with flesh, and watch the fall of all the eggshell shibboleth of caste and color too*" (112). In spite, and even through, this assertion of absence, however, the name takes on an incantatory or conjuring power—to become a presence (enacting, among other things, the particular atavistic durability of that "*eggshell shibboleth*"):[14] "The starved and ragged remnant of an army having retreated across Alabama and Georgia and into Carolina, swept onward not by a victorious army behind it but rather by a mounting tide of the names of lost battles from either side—Chickamauga and Franklin, Vicksburg and Corinth and Atlanta" (276). Or: "*Charles Bon, Charles Good, Charles Husband-soon-to-be.*" Thus, perhaps, the similar transition in the novel's use of David's lament (in 2 Sam. 18:33), the echoing name, mourning turned to incantation, from "O my son Absalom, my son, my son Absalom! . . . O Absalom, my son, my son!" to *Absalom, Absalom!* That is another way, it seems to me, in which to read the repeated parenthetical renamings in the Harvard section—"he (Bon)"; "he (the demon)"; "she (Judith)": as polyphony and as incantation of the name.

In question are the relations among the different registers of the novel: its palimpsest of received texts (David and Absalom; Clytemnestra, Cassandra, and Agamemnon; and so on), its narratives (Sutpen; Henry, Bon, and Judith; Rosa; Wash Jones; and so on), and its narrative whose subject is narrative, its story of absorption. That narrative is marked by a transition between different kinds of relations to the spectacle the story presents. At some moments, foregrounded is an immediacy that nevertheless exteriorizes the scene viewed as a spectacle—however viscerally it is experienced. "Quentin seemed to watch" (14); "It seemed to Quentin that he could actually see them, facing one another at the gate" (105); "It seemed to Quentin that he could actually see them: the ragged and starving troops" (154); "It seemed to him that if he stopped the buggy and listened, he might even hear the galloping horse; might even see at any moment now the black stallion and the rider rush across the road before them and gallop on" (290); "It seemed to him that he could still hear her whimpering" (292). Such formulations recur throughout the text, and although they do, paradoxically, assert an immediacy greater than that of the eyewitness ("He could see it; he might even have been there. Then he thought *No. If I had been there I could not have seen it this plain*" [155]), they are less immediate than what the storytelling will achieve later. The repeated "seemed," like the specifications of "to him" or "to Quentin," has a distancing effect, explicitly highlighting the potential illusion. (Notably, too, the same formulation is applied to Quentin's relation to a narrative he hears or imagines as to his relation to an event he actually experienced and its capacity to return in memory: "It seemed to him that he could still hear her whimpering.")

Such markers of distance disappear in the middle of the Harvard section, which reaches its climax of represented absorption with the culmination of the Henry–Bon narrative, falling off (as in the last two instances above) when the story returns to Miss Rosa:

> Shreve ceased. That is, for all the two of them, Shreve and Quentin, knew he had stopped, since for all the two of them knew he had never begun, since it did not matter (and possibly neither of them conscious of the distinction) which one of them had been doing the talking. So that now it was not two but four of them riding two horses through the dark over the frozen December ruts of that Christmas eve: four of them and then just two—Charles–Shreve and Quentin–Henry. (267)

Telling produces a rhythm of differentiation and merger, a movement in and out of absorption where presence is posited and withdrawn and where Quentin and Shreve merge with their story and with each other and then are individuated again: "First, two of them, then four; now two again" (275); "two, four, now two again, according to Quentin and Shreve, the two the four the two still talking" (276). In one reading, telling brings the figures back into presence, where, then, the scene of absorption, where the two would register their existence as four, disappears just as any differentiation between Quentin–Shreve and Bon–Henry does. One effect of this transition—"the two the four the two"—is to make explicit how "the two" differ from themselves once they are traversed by narrative. "Quentin had not even put on his overcoat, which lay on the floor where it had fallen from the arm of the chair where Shreve put it down. They did not retreat from the cold. They both bore it as though in deliberate flagellant exaltation of physical misery transmogrified into the spirits' travail of the two young men during that time fifty years ago, or forty-eight rather, then forty-seven and then forty-six, since it was '64 and then '65": the boys' increasing absorption mirrors (and, inversely, is mirrored by) the movement of Henry and Bon forward, toward them, in time (275–76). The erotic merger of Quentin and Shreve ("it did not matter . . . which one had been doing the talking") is paired with their merger with their objects of contemplation, and paired with a narrowing temporal gap where time moves forward and backward at the same time.

And, again, the narrative merger is indistinguishable from that of love:

> They stared at one another—glared rather—their quiet regular breathing vaporising faintly and steadily in the now tomblike air. There was something curious in the way they looked at one another, curious and quiet and profoundly intent, not at all as two young men might look at each other but almost as a youth and a very young girl might out of virginity itself—a sort of hushed and naked searching, each look burdened with the youth's immemorial obsession not with time's dragging weight which the old live with but with its fluidity: the bright heels of all the lost moments of fifteen and sixteen. (240)

> She must have seen him in fact with exactly the same eyes that Henry saw him with. (75)

> In fact, perhaps this is the pure and perfect incest: the brother realising that the sister's virginity must be destroyed in order to have existed at all, taking that virginity in the person of the brother-in-law, the man whom he would be if he could become, metamorphose into, the lover, the husband; by whom he would be despoiled, choose for despoiler, if he could become, metamorphose into the sister, the mistress, the bride. (77)

A courtship that is also innocence's initiation into the passage of time, a fluidity that has yet to become a weight, Quentin and Shreve's merger with each other in telling the tale is thus erotic (among many other reasons) in that it replays the "perfect incest" that characterizes the desire in the story they tell: "that single personality with two bodies both of which had been seduced almost simultaneously by a man whom at that time Judith had never even seen" (73). The structure of desire—homosocial or homoerotic or incestuous or all of these—thus is also the inverse of the split personalities in the novel: Sutpen becoming two people as he contemplates being turned away from the front door of the plantation; Quentin as "two separate Quentins" (4) or as "commonwealth."

But it is a repetition of that split, too, insofar as in these mergers (with each other and with Henry and Bon), Quentin and Shreve encounter their own thoughts and words, alienated, in another. Quentin's commonwealth-forming division from himself was attributed to a belatedness that left him to experience events only as circuited through narrative. The Harvard section (in particular) transforms that alienation to an erotic merger by narrating, and narrating just such a merger. That narrative—of a "happy marriage of speaking and hearing" where "it did not matter to either of them which one did the talking" (253)—is told, among other ways, in the novel's choreography of italics and quotation marks and parentheses. The italics, which sometimes take the place of quoted speech and sometimes mark ventriloquized thought, also seem to indicate a simultaneity of events otherwise unrepresentable in language, which has to proceed linearly (Quentin remembering Miss Rosa's or his father's words while he is also talking or listening to Shreve, for example). They also serve to make visible in the text's own typography its patchwork of overlapping voices. At moments, this palimpsest suggests mediation, as when Quentin tells to Shreve what he heard from his father, who heard it from his father, who heard it from Sutpen (who often speaks as if he heard it from himself—as, in the soliloquy where he imagines what it would be to own a fancy rifle, he did). Quentin, as speaker, is again a commonwealth. At other moments, voices seem even more literally to merge, and that kind of mediation takes place both between people, and, in localized scenes of telling, in speakers' relations to themselves. Thus, when Quentin repeatedly says "yes" in chapter 6, one is uncertain whether he is automatically responding to Shreve (while his thoughts pursue their own course) or whether the represented (italicized) language is Shreve's, giving voice to Quentin's thoughts.[15] ("Don't say it's just me," Shreve says, "that sounds like your old man" [210], responding to something that Quentin seems not to have said out loud, giving us the impression that Quentin's thoughts are transparent to his Canadian roommate. Such a blurring is a relatively simple instance of a more generalized phenomenon in the text.)

To stay with chapter 6, there is a choreography here, too, as the repeated "yes" appears in quick succession early in the chapter, returning to punctuate the dialogue in larger segments, and forming a unifying refrain in several registers: in Quentin's intervening represented thoughts (*"Yes, I have had to listen too long"* [158]; *"Yes, I have heard too much, I have been told too much; I have had to listen too much, too long,* thinking, *Yes almost exactly like father"* [168]; *"Yes* he thought *Too much, too long")* and in the narrated, ostensibly voiced telling both in Cambridge ("Yes, who to know if he said anything or nothing" [169]) and at the Sutpen graves, another remembered Mississippi conversation that Quentin narrates in Massachusetts ("Yes. They lead beautiful lives—women" [156]; "Yes, Clytie, who stood impassive beside the wagon that day" [158]). One effect of this one-word leitmotif is to make different times and places present in a single layer of the text as narrated, making it visibly a palimpsest, and compressing time so that the events of the story, Mr. Compson's conversation with Quentin, and Quentin's discussion with Shreve all seem to take place at once. Thus, when, at several moments, Quentin's thoughts intervene (*Yes, too much too long*) it is impossible to tell where they intervene from—whether his thoughts interrupt Mr. Compson or Shreve—and the location of the narrative voice thus wavers among various represented times.

Nor do the italics have an entirely homogenous function; in the course of the chapter, they largely indicate Quentin's thoughts, but they also represent quotations within quotations, as well as the narrated thoughts of figures in the tale Mr. Compson tells. Typographically, therefore, it is difficult to distinguish inside from out—"interiors" and "exteriors" of persons or of narrative "frames" alike, distinctions necessary for the coherence of transmission. By the close of the chapter, it becomes all but impossible to differentiate among the various voices:

He had to brush the clinging cedar needles from this one also to read it, watching these letters also emerge beneath his hand, wondering quietly how they could have clung there, not have been blistered to ashes at the instant of contact with a harsh and unforgiving threat: *Judith Coldfield Sutpen. Daughter of Ellen Coldfield. Born October 3, 1841. Suffered the Indignities and Travails of This World for 42 Years, 4 Months, 9 Days, and went to Rest at Last February 12, 1884. Pause, Mortal; Remember Vanity and Folly and Beware* thinking (Quentin) *Yes. I didn't need to ask who invented that, put that one up* thinking *Yes, to too much, too long. I didn't need to listen then but I had to hear it and now I am having to hear it all over again because he sounds just like father: Beautiful lives—women do.* (171)

The italics represent both a gravestone (thus adding its engraved words, and the traditional ventriloquized injunction of the epitaph, to the palimpsest of voices in the chapter, and visibly assimilating those voices to the voices of the dead) and Quentin's thoughts, which, moreover, quote his father's words (156). At some point before the middle of the next page, the italicized language becomes Shreve's—"*But you were not listening, because you knew it all already, had learned, absorbed it already without the medium of speech somehow for having been born and living beside it, with it, as children will and do: so that whatever your father was saying did not tell you anything so much as it struck, word by word, the resonant strings of remembering...*" (172)—which Quentin, in turn, answers: "'Yes,' Quentin said" (174). (That pages 143–75 seem—if I haven't missed something—to be enclosed in parentheses also suggests that most of chapter 6 is an interruption or a superimposition. Yet an interruption of what, or a superimposition of what on what, is unclear: the narrative thread interrupted by the parenthesis does not return until chapter 9. The parentheses make visible some other, unspecifiable narrative topography where no voice can be said to have an "inside" in which to "contain" another, and no narrative scene [telling or told] or temporality remains discrete, retains a unity or coherence that would allow one to conceptualize it as enfolding or enfolded by another.)[16]

The various markers of superimposed speech and thought tax one's efforts to track or describe them, however clear one might (momentarily) imagine oneself in one's own reading. But the blurring of voice also becomes an explicit topic of the novel. Thus, the repeated glossing of pronouns, which seems to be part of the call-and-response rhythm of Quentin and Shreve's midnight colloquy, gives way to explicit statements about their not being necessary:

"And now," Shreve said, "we're going to talk about love." But he didn't need to say that either, any more than he needed to specify which he he meant by he, since neither of them had been thinking about anything else; all that had gone before just so much that had to be overpassed and none else present to overpass it but them, as someone always has to rake the leaves up before you can have a bonfire. That was why it did not matter to either of them which one did the talking, since it was not the talking alone which did it, performed and accomplished the overpassing, but some happy marriage of speaking and hearing wherein each before the demand, the requirement, forgave and condoned and forgot the faulting of the other—faultings both in the creating of the shade whom they discussed (rather, existed in) and in the hearing and sifting and discarding the false and conserving what seemed true, or fit the preconceived—in order to overpass to love, where there might be paradox and inconsistency but nothing fault nor false. (253)

The marriage of speaking and hearing is perhaps the only "happy" one in this text; the only major wedding that manages to take place in a novel of unwived widows begins in an empty church and ends in tears and a hail of thrown vegetables. In this description of Quentin and Shreve's happy marriage, I would dwell on the echo of "fault": the "faulting of the other" forgiven, condoned, forgotten in the "overpassing" to love, where there "might be . . . nothing fault nor false" (where Bon, moreover, becomes "bonfire").[17] The story of the pursuit of the architect makes me read the initial "faulting" as "losing the scent," as hounds, or a storyteller, might "fault" (losing the scent is part of any story worth staying up all night to hear—in a Mississippi swamp as in a Harvard dormitory).[18] That forgiven faulting carries with it the gap or break denied by the second "fault," and the latter negated fault specifies not—as one might expect—the unity of lovers so much as the unity of a discourse about love. The merger here is thus multiple: it is a merger between lovers (at least by association or connotation if not strictly by the letter of the sentence) and between speakers and their objects ("the shade whom they discussed [rather, existed in]"); it is also a merger between a structure of identification (Shreve and Quentin with Henry and Bon) and a topic of discussion ("he didn't need to say that either, any more than he had needed to specify which he he meant by he"). One seems to be able to have an analogous relation to "he" and to "and now . . . we're going to talk about love." The movement from a *faulting* that needs to be forgiven to a *fault* that is not there thus marks a transition but also—in the term's multivalence, in the disparate ways a fault-negating merger takes place—a fault, while the fault of *fault*'s difference from itself also embodies a merger (of persons with texts) that represents the negation of the *fault,* the negation cast here as the truth of love. (To be more explicit: condensed in the pun is the text's understanding of narrative transmission, and the way its paradoxical merger-as-division and transmission-as-loss become a story of love.)

This moment occurs just after Henry's touching declaration of love to Bon: "He fumbled, groped, blurted with abrupt and complete irrelevance . . . his face scarlet but his head high and his eyes steady" (253), and the "faulting" in the discourse without "fault" reminds us that this scene is, after all, a scenario invented by the Harvard roommates—where "fault" evokes, too, Henry's "abrupt and complete irrelevance." ("'Is that so? The whiskey's your side. Drink or pass'" [253].) The echo makes Henry's love for Bon, and Shreve and Quentin's merger with the object of their story, an occasion for their faultless merger with each other. Striking, then, is the question of voice: who is speaking here? There are many such moments, particularly in this section of the novel, where a narrative voice emerges to comment, particularly on Shreve and Quentin's narrating of the story. Because the question of voice and of who is speaking is so foregrounded by the variously differentiated markers of direct and indirect speech—even when it does not matter whether it is Quentin or Shreve who speaks, we are allowed to forget neither the scene of narration, the freezing dorm room, and their vaporizing breath, nor the telling, which has to be spoken, to be "overpassed"—moments such as this one seem to imply another, unlocatable scene of narration: a couple that encompasses Quentin and Shreve as they encompass Henry and Bon. The possibility of a "psychological" explanation for the echo—*faulting*'s emergence from *fault* motivated, more or less unconsciously even, by the story told just before this about hunting the architect of Sutpen's house (a hunt in which the hounds repeatedly lose the scent)—suggests a narrative voice curiously permeable to the story it narrates. The quasi-free-indirect imitation of voice (or semantic resonance) enacts a "faultless" merger between narrator and "object" of narration. (This effect is also mimicked, in a comic mode, by Quentin and Shreve when they mime Sutpen's language—"that wife who would be adjunctive to the forwarding of that design" [203–4], for instance). Likewise, when the novel describes in shorthand Quentin and Shreve's becoming Henry and Bon—"the two of them (the four of them) held in that probation" (267)—the effect is both explicitly to identify the gesture of glossing with Quentin and Shreve's absorption into the story and, again, to expand the described process of absorption outward by positing another scene of narration (the scene of reading) and, implicitly, another erotic pair, a narrator and a reader (a reader's voice thereby made visible within the text), who eventually will not need such parenthetical glossings. This couple would thereby reenact Quentin and Shreve's reenactment of Henry and

Bon—of the story that is, for them in turn, a reenactment of (biblical, classical, historical) texts (inside-outside-inside; text-action-text: "the two the four the two").[19]

One way that the novel figures the "fault" in narrative that enables its faultless mergers is the temporizing imperative *wait,* which, in the Harvard section, is an index of absorption. It appears at crucial moments— "*wait,*" says Clytie to Rosa, "*Don't you go up there*" (111), and Quentin and Rosa, approaching Sutpen's Hundred, repeatedly tell each other to wait ("Wait," he said, "do you really want to go inside?") (292, 293, 294). And it is, of course, Quentin and Shreve's refrain. At one moment, we are told that Shreve did not say "Wait" before leaving the room to put on his bathrobe; the register of *wait,* this makes explicit, is something other than and more important than whatever purely practical exigencies a half-naked boy might face listening to a tale of the South in a frigid Harvard dorm room. Rather, often serving as a demand for recognition in a story moving too quickly for one's cognitive grasp (as when Shreve, thinking Melicent Jones had a son, cannot follow Quentin), its punctuating of the narrative establishes a relation between teller and hearer, between them both and their story, and between hearing (or telling) and cognition. An interjection of incredulity ("Wait. You mean that this old gal, this Aunt Rosa—" [243]), it often means "I don't understand." (It can thus mean something like the opposite of wait: skip ahead to what will allow me to understand—a demand that is never satisfied [you'll have to wait].) It increasingly loses that connotation to become an interjection of aroused absorption. It is therefore striking that, in the Henry–Bon narrative, it is a temporizing demand (meaning "I need more time to understand"):

> He stood looking at the innocent face of the youth almost ten years his junior, while one part of him said *My brow my skull my jaw my hands* the other said *Wait. Wait. You cant know yet. You cannot know yet whether what you see is what you are looking at or what you are believing. Wait. Wait.* (251)

> Henry said, "Wait. Wait. Let me get used to it." And maybe it was two days or three days, and Henry said, "you shall not. Shall not" and then it was Bon that said, "Wait. I am your older brother: do you say *shall not* to me?" And maybe it was a week, maybe Bon took Henry to see the octoroon and Henry looked at her and said,

"Aint that enough for you?" And Bon said, "Do you want it to be
enough?" and Henry said, "Wait. Wait. I must have time to get
used to it. You'll have to give me time." . . . "but you'll have to wait!
You'll have to give me time." (272, 273)

Cognition needs time to catch up to what it already knows—this interval
is one of the crucial ways thought is out of sync with itself in Faulkner.
(In *Light in August*: "Memory believes before knowing remembers.")[20] The
war is repeatedly called an "interval" or "durance" or "probation" because
it marks the lapse between realization and action, the period of waiting
in which Henry and Bon catch up with their realizations and the novel's
action catches up with itself. It is striking, therefore, that this cognitive
disjunction—time out of joint—produces narrative: Quentin (and therefore we and Shreve) hear Mr. Compson's tale because Quentin has to wait
for it to be late enough to pick up Miss Rosa, for example. (And, in another
register, the represented action—of Quentin or of Rosa or of Henry and
Bon—turns out to consist primarily in waiting, as for that matter, does
the activity of the novel's reader, who continually has to wait: for Bon's or
Mr. Compson's letter, for the culmination of Quentin and Rosa's drive to
Sutpen's Hundred.) This movement from cognitive exigency to the temporality of narrative (the interval that allows a story to be told), along
with the movement of *wait* from "inside" to "outside," from Henry and
Bon to Shreve and Quentin, makes the term an erotic one in *Absalom,
Absalom! Wait* becomes an index of eroticism when the suspense of telling (or hearing) merges with the story itself, when, therefore, cognition
is shown visibly to be traversed by narrative delay. When, then, the first
thing Henry says to Bon early in the morning after he has learned that Bon
is part black[21] is "Wait," the imperative that commences the final interval
in which Bon and Henry move toward the shot that will at last align their
actions with their knowledge (or, perhaps, will leave thought and action
permanently out of sync) also reads as an erotic consummation (284).

An Erotics of Telling: Self-Confounded Listening-Sense and the Suspended Presence of Words Made Flesh

At the culmination of the Harvard section, Quentin and Shreve return to
the suspension of empirical certainty that Rosa experiences as temporal
lag ("I heard an echo, but not the shot"). That suspension corresponds to

the interval required by cognition in *Absalom, Absalom!*; insofar as that interval is the space of narrative, the temporal lag in thought extends outward from within psyches to relations between people and between generations and times. The lag in cognition may extend beyond even one's lifetime; one's spirit might literally be doomed to posthumeity. The reversal in the quasi-pedagogical relation between Quentin and his father ("'Your father . . . seems to have got an awful lot of delayed information awful quick, after having waited forty-five years. If he knew all this, what was his reason for telling you that the trouble between Henry and Bon was the octoroon woman?' 'He didn't know it then. Grandfather didn't tell him all of it either, like Sutpen never told Grandfather quite all of it.' 'Then who did tell him?' 'I did.'" [214]) thus marks the way that telling begins to take priority and that time starts to run in reverse. The priority of Quentin's version over his father's derives from its further remove from the story because it does not come, the novel makes clear, from any clarified relation to "actual" events. Transmission is made possible by stories in which the tellers do not tell "quite all of it"; that gap leaves room for cognition, and for love.

Thus, for the boys at Harvard, a foregrounded uncertainty about the story's empirical grounding marks their absorption with each other and, paradoxically, with their tale. They come closest to the Sutpen story when they are least sure of what in fact happened because at this moment the story told merges most completely with its telling. The uncertainty makes visible that merger, their taking each other "up in stride without comma or colon or paragraph" (225):

> They stared—glared—at one another, their voices (it was Shreve speaking, though save for the slight difference which the intervening degrees of latitude had inculcated in them . . . it might have been either of them and was in a sense both: both thinking as one, the voice which happened to be speaking the thought only the thinking become audible, vocal; the two of them creating between them, out of the rag-tag and bob-ends of old tales and talking, people who perhaps never existed at all anywhere, who, shadows, were shadows not of flesh and blood which had lived and died but shadows in turn of what were (to one of them at least, to Shreve) shades too, quiet as the visible murmur of their vaporizing breath. (243)

The echo of the comparison a few pages earlier ("They stared at one another—glared rather— . . . not at all as two young men might look at each other but almost as a youth and a very young girl might out of virginity itself") makes explicit the link between the blending of their voices (their joint-thinking become audible) and a scene of eroticism, and between both of these and their merger with their story (taking the parts of the variously amalgamated Henry, Judith, and Bon). Here, the material grounding of the story is literally vaporized, turned to ghosts without reference but thereby given a *material* presence in the bodies of Quentin and Shreve—more precisely, not in their bodies but in the "visible murmur" of respiration, of bodies not so much present as deducible from a trace they leave (in the earlier moment, we read of their breath "vaporising faintly and steadily in the now tomblike air"). The long parenthesis introduces another form of enactment by allowing one to read, simultaneously, "their voices . . . quiet as the visible murmur" and "shades . . . quiet as the visible murmur"; their voices are thus turned to the shades whom the roommates both invent and become; they are left the tangible, "visible" traces of a vanishing. And these effects are linked to the visible intervention of an interval of text, a parenthesis that interrupts but also represents a merger or a simultaneity (a murmur that is, perhaps, visible without being audible). Thus, later, when the text foregrounds the posited nature of the story told—"so Shreve and Quentin believed . . . according to Shreve and Quentin . . . which Shreve had invented and which is probably true enough . . . whom Shreve and Quentin had likewise invented and which was likewise probably true enough. . . . And Bon may have, probably did" (268)—the vanishing of certainty corresponds to a motion closer both to each other and to Henry and Bon, in an erotic commingling that is also a turning of proximate bodies to vaporizing breath.

The interval of cognition in the novel—"Wait!"—suggests that the becoming-text that turns persons to "inscrutable and serene" shapes seen against the "horrible and bloody mischancing of human affairs" may traverse consciousness from within. The spirit's posthumeity (the consequence of narrative's power to make coalesce a merger that is also an alienation, a fading that is also a becoming-proximate), which turns Quentin, in a long-dead South, to a commonwealth, may be generalizable. It may be, simply, the condition of consciousness. The vanishing of empirical certainty in Shreve and Quentin's tale thus corresponds to the self-confounding of hearing-sense, which brings forth its long-dead object from the victorious dust. Experience and the belatedness that misses it become curiously indistinct, just as the outraged recapitulation that strives impotently to recall the object of its frustration becomes indistinguishable from the happy marriage of speaking and hearing that achieves such a recovery. This is the sense in which I read the recurrent markers of deixis in the Harvard section of the novel: "*that* dead summer twilight—the wistaria, the cigar-smell, the fireflies—attenuated up from Mississippi and into *this* strange room, across *this* strange iron New England snow" (141; emphasis added). The contrast of *that* to *this* brings into view Quentin's removal in time and space from Mississippi and his father. Yet it also brings into view another vanished locale: "this strange iron New England snow." The *this* asserts both an immediacy and a vanishing. As the novel draws to a close, *now* marks less a definitive temporal moment than a blurring between two or more times (and likewise, *here,* less a particular place than a conjoining of spaces):

He could hear her panting now. (291)

. . . telling himself that if Henry were there now, there would be no shot to be heard by anyone. (291)

He remembered it, lying here in the Massachusetts bed and breathing faster now, now that peace and quiet had fled again. (295)

"Dont you go up there, Rosie" and Miss Coldfield struck the hand away and went on toward the stairs (and now he saw that she had a flashlight; he remembered how he thought, "it must have been in the umbrella too along with the axe"). (295)

What initially seems an event's definitive locating marks a merging of narrated and narrating time (as is especially clear in the collocation of "now he saw that she had a flashlight" with "he remembered how he thought": perception travels from Mississippi to Harvard).

The implied closure, then, after we have learned it was Henry whom Rosa found at Sutpen's Hundred, serves less to cordon off the narrated time from the space of narration than to indicate their blurring: "It was quite cold in the room now; the chimes would ring for one at any time now; the chill had a compounded, a gathered quality, as though preparing for the dead moment before dawn" (298). Thematically, Quentin's thoughts dwell on the consequences of this blurring ("Nevermore of peace. Nevermore of peace. Nevermore. Nevermore. Nevermore" [298]). The collocation of *now* with a narrative past tense ("He lay still and rigid on his back with the cold New England night on his face" [298]) brings out another aspect to the deictic reference: namely, its power to concretize a vanished context, to make visible a vanishing. *Now* and *here* link that vanishing to writing, link endurance and disappearance. And preservation or transmission is linked to the fading of the event's certainty, the fading that draws Shreve and Quentin, reader and text, closer together. The erotics of *Absalom, Absalom!* is an erotics of telling—but an erotics of telling's power to make present a vanished past and to make it present, like the exquisite "interval" of Pater's "gem-like flame," precisely in its vanishing.

The belatedness that dooms Miss Rosa and Quentin—commonwealth or barracks filled with back-looking ghosts—to outraged recapitulation is tied to writing as an attenuation of presence but also (paradoxically, therefore) to an erotic communion that is a form of historical connection. A pendant to the evocation of outraged recapitulation's power to call long-dead objects back from the biding dust is, perhaps, Miss Rosa's meditation on the difference between memory and remembering. The latter term calls to mind Mr. Compson's "diffused and scattered creatures drawn blindly limb from limb from a grab bag and assembled," from a grab bag that, for Mr. Compson, characterizes what it means to live in a belated time. What initially seems to overcome that dismemberment—touch rather than text, a body, and a consciousness, unified, rather than split—seems instead to repeat it:

> *Once there was—Do you mark how the wistaria, sun-impacted on this wall here, distills and penetrates this room as though (light-unimpeded) by secret and attritive progress from mote to mote of obscurity's myriad components? That is the substance of remembering—sense, sight, smell: the muscles with which we see and hear and feel—not mind, not thought: there is no such thing as memory: the brain recalls just what the muscles grope for: no more, no less: and its resultant sum is usually incorrect and false and worthy only of the name of dream.—See how the sleeping outflung hand, touching the bedside candle, remembers pain, springs back and free while mind and brain sleep on and only make of this adjacent heat*

some trashy myth of reality's escape: or that same sleeping hand, in
sensuous marriage with some dulcet surface, is transformed by that
same sleeping brain and mind into that same figment-stuff warped
out of all experience. Ay, grief goes, fades; we know that—but ask the
tear ducts if they have forgotten how to weep.—Once there was . . . a
summer of wistaria. (115)

It may be that remembering recovers an immediacy of experience, but
Rosa's terms posit that immediacy in the same gesture that renders its
"substance" inaccessible. While Rosa seems to privilege immediacy—
the body's encounter with facticity as opposed to the "figment-stuff" the
mind makes of it—embodiment here marks something more like the
self-division occasioned by narrative insofar as there is no person, or no
person unified with his sensuous experience, but only a sense perception
that, accessible only to the part that in whatever sense can be said to feel
it, divides the sleeper from himself as surely as does the dream to which
the mind transforms the candle's heat. The very assertion of immediacy, in
other words, forbids reading that sleeping hand as synecdoche and therefore leaves dismembered what it would fain remember.

The assertion of immediacy, moreover, is framed by various gestures
of mediation: the recurrent imperatives ("see how . . ."; "ask the tear
ducts . . ."), like the interrogative ("do you mark how the wistaria . . . ?"),
repeatedly posit an intervening, and to that extent alienated, consciousness necessary to perceive (to see, ask, mark) the immediacy it therefore
also negates, a consciousness that the almost musical refrain of "once there
was" makes manifest is a function of narration. Likewise, the repeated
gestures of deixis point us not to a recovered, remembered body but to
the scene in which we are told about it. To receive the wisdom of the tear
ducts, in other terms, one needs to ask them. The novel makes this paradoxical immediacy the stuff not just of texts but of destroyed texts. At a
striking moment, Judith delivers to Quentin's grandmother the letter she
received from Bon ("We have waited long enough" [104]). She delivers it
less that it might be preserved than that it *might* be destroyed. Her ratio-
nale links its preservation to the possibility of its destruction. "Me? You
want me to keep it?" Quentin's grandmother asks.

"Yes," Judith said. "Or destroy it. As you like. Read it if you like or
dont read it if you like. Because you make so little impression, you

see. You get born and you try this and you dont know why only you keep on trying it and you are born at the same time with a lot of other people, all mixed up with them, like trying to, having to, move your arms and legs with strings only the same strings are hitched to all the other arms and legs and the others all trying and they dont know why either except that the strings are all in one another's way like five or six people all trying to make a rug on the same loom only each one wants to weave his own pattern into the rug; and it cant matter, you know that or the Ones that set up the loom would have arranged things a little better, and yet it must matter because you keep on trying or having to keep on trying and then all of a sudden it's all over and all you have left is a block of stone with scratches on it provided there was someone to remember to have the marble scratched and set up or had time to, and it rains on it and the sun shines on it and after a while they dont even remember the name and what the scratches were trying to tell, and it doesn't matter. And so maybe if you could go to someone, the stranger the better, and give them something—a scrap of paper—something, anything, it not to mean anything in itself and them not even to read it or keep it, not even to bother to throw it away or destroy it, at least it would be something just because it would have happened, be remembered even if only from passing from one hand to another, one mind to another, and it would be at least a scratch, something, something that might make a mark on something that *was* once for the reason that it can die someday, while the block of stone cant be *is* because it never can become *was* because it cant ever die or perish." (100–101)

Notably, Judith's two sets of figures both turn on overlapping terms: the "strings" shared by marionettes and looms, and the "scratches" on marble that are to be distinguished from the "scratches" made on "something" that can be "is" because it can be "was." Because, in the initial figure, the strings are attached to the arms and legs that the people try to move, the image seems to be of marionettes who do not realize who is pulling the strings, but it is also a figure for an uncontrollable embeddedness in a context, for the way that one's actions affect—and, vice versa, are affected by—everyone else's. Agency similarly disappears in the second figure, where those attached strings seem to feed (dangerously, one imagines) into a loom, and the loom of fate, by dint of being patterned by everyone, is controlled by no one. The overlap in the figures' ground becomes, in the second figure, a linguistic one—of two diverging but indistinguishable terms: the "scratch" indicating both survival and oblivion, the "scratch" made on persons as opposed to on marble.

Tellingly, it is the scratch on the more mutable surface that is the more lasting. Judith locates survival not in the assertion of her agency (as, for instance, Sutpen does, in his desire to wrest Sutpen's Hundred from the wilderness and make it endure beyond the war that will spell its permanent obsolescence), but in giving herself over to another's will. Insisting that Quentin's grandmother can read the letter or not, destroy it or preserve it, Judith gives herself over to contingency. Writing must occur on a mutable surface because transmission is secured not by permanence and immutability but by the possibility of destruction; to be "remembered," in Judith's account, is to seek preservation not in another's mind or on a marble slab, but in a mutable transmission, a passing between hands and minds. It is in this sense, it seems to me, that the illegible texts—Bon's letter, which is the one Judith discusses here, and Mr. Compson's, to Quentin, in the Harvard section—frame the erotics of transmission in *Absalom, Absalom!* Held like ice melting in our hands, writing makes for the interval that is that of erotic possibility and of our vanishing:

> Quentin hearing without having to listen as he read the faint
> spidery script not like something impressed upon the paper by a
> once-living hand but like a shadow cast upon it which had resolved
> on the paper the instant before he looked at it and which might
> fade, vanish, at any instant while he still did: the dead tongue
> speaking after the four years and then after almost fifty more,
> gentle sardonic whimsical and incurably pessimistic, without
> date or salutation or signature. (102)

As Bon's letter concludes, "*I now believe that you and I are, strangely enough, included among those who are doomed to live*" (105).

The "happy marriage of speaking and hearing," and the interval, hiatus, durance it introduces, has two sides in the novel, I have suggested: mourning or ambivalence (Quentin as commonwealth or barracks) and erotic possibility (lurking harborage or nooky seat). The novel makes these two indistinguishable, which—far beyond its explicit homoeroticism—makes it queer. That queerness, moreover, is linked—in uncontrollably ambivalent ways—to the history of racialized violence that is, simply, the history of America. For the *interval* we have addressed here has another name when it is localized as a place: the island, probably Haiti, where Sutpen went to make his fortune and that is in many ways the structural center of the novel, marking its narrative origin in the trans-Atlantic slave trade.[22]

> A little island set in a smiling and fury-lurked and incredible indigo sea, which was the halfway point between what we call the jungle and what we call civilization, halfway between the dark inscrutable continent from which the black blood, the black bones and flesh and thinking and remembering and hopes and desires, was ravished by violence, and the cold known land to which it was doomed, the civilized land and people which expelled some of its own blood and thinking and desires that had become too crass to be faced and borne longer, and set it homeless and desperate on the lonely ocean—a little lost island in a latitude which would require ten thousand years of equatorial heritage to bear its climate, a soil manured with black blood from two hundred years of oppression and exploitation until it sprang with an incredible paradox of peaceful greenery and crimson flowers and sugar cane sapling size and three times the height of a man and a little bulkier of course but valuable pound for pound almost with silver ore, as if nature held the balance and kept a book and offered a recompense for the torn limbs and outraged hearts even if man did not, the planting of nature and man too watered not only by the wasted blood but breathed over by the winds in which the doomed ships had fled in vain, out of which the last tatter of sail had sunk into the blue sea, along which the last vain despairing cry of woman or child had blown away;—the planting of men too: the yet intact bones and brains in which the old unsleeping blood that had vanished into the earth they trod still cried out for vengeance. (202)

This island—with "the same weary winds blowing back and forth across it and burdened still with the weary voices of murdered women and children homeless and graveless about the isolating and solitary sea" (204)—is an *interval,* a "halfway point" in a geographical passage and a human narrative.[23] And this recounting of the history of chattel slavery presents in visceral and viscerally desublimated form the transformation of human bodies not only into material prosperity and, literally, into objects for human use, but into beauty (a sublimation enacted, too, in the aestheticized tones of the passage—also made visible in the contrast between the writing's lovely cadence and its grotesque imagery). The monstrous "accounting"—"a soil manured with black blood," the blood turned to sugar cane—issues in a survival that is also a disappearance. The slave revolt, then, is cast as another form of agricultural sublimation and as a voice that survives the body's vanishing: "the yet intact bones and brains in which the old unsleeping blood that had vanished into the earth they trod still cried out for vengeance."

To my mind, more crucial for the novel than Quentin's final statement of ambivalence ("I don't hate it" [303]) is Shreve's remark just before it: "In a few thousand years, I who regard you will also have sprung from the loins of African kings. Now I want you to tell me just one thing more" (302–3).[24] The history of the North American continent appears here as the interval between the beginning of the slave trade and a final, total miscegenation. (In the novel's "grammar," incest and miscegenation are interchangeable; writing a new anthropology, the founding prohibition of America would be, Shreve intimates, the prohibition of miscegenation, and redemption could occur only through the overturning of that prohibition and the unraveling of the social form it founded.) That *utopia* might also describe the depiction of Haiti gives one pause in understanding Shreve's comment in unambiguously redemptive terms. (*Go Down, Moses,* I will suggest in the next chapter, attempts to leave us suspended between these two utopias: a queer, anti-Oedipal disruption of patrilinearity and its horrible literalization in the American history of "race.") Rosa's perhaps analogous comment—"let flesh touch with flesh, and watch the fall of all the eggshell shibboleth of caste and color too"—can be read to mark a similar kind of "redemption": as a mutable transmission, or passing between hands and minds, like that which Judith imagines with Quentin's grandmother, rather than any imagined genuine contact to transcend the illusory constructions of the mind. That fleeting, paradoxically intangible touch is the substance of remembering. For the time is also impossible: "I who regard you . . . will also have sprung. . . . Now I want you to tell me." Generalizing the Harvard scene to encompass the novel's reading (where "I who regard you" can become any reader of the text—or any reader as invested as Miss Rosa is in the evocative powers of recapitulation, in the hearing-sense that might at last self-confound), the gesture erases that posited reader as much as it does Shreve, who, bodying forth the *now* of narrative desire, vanishes in the interval between a present regard and a past that is yet to come.

10

"Vanished but Not Gone, Fixed and Held in the Annealing Dust"

Initiations and Endings in *Go Down, Moses*

William Faulkner has not, to my knowledge, been claimed as part of any gay or queer tradition; his name has perhaps never appeared on any list of a queer canon stretching from Socrates and Plato to Shakespeare and Christopher Marlowe to Pater and Wilde to Woolf and Stein to Proust and Jean Genet. That fact may be attributable to our anecdotal knowledge of Faulkner's life—reinforced by a lingering sense that queer texts are written by queer persons, or that literature expresses the life of the author by mirroring some putatively primary, extraliterary experience—or to a more or less sophisticated sense that Faulkner (with Joyce, against Woolf and Proust) represents butch (male) modernism. That he is not often read in relation to queerness attests more to the resilience of homophobic modes of reading than to any unresponsiveness on the part of his texts to queer reading—even when that is understood to mean merely an openness to registering homoeroticism. As with *Absalom, Absalom!, The Sound and the Fury,* and indeed almost all of Faulkner's texts, to perceive the homoerotic thematics of *Go Down, Moses,* it suffices simply to pay attention. Uncle Buck and Uncle Buddy are less glamorous than Quentin and Shreve, but their relationship is even more explicitly a same-sex marriage. Cultured gay Victorians were, it has often been remarked, confronted with the daily paradox that their society's most esteemed form of knowledge—Greek philosophy and culture—contained explicit celebrations of the homosexual desire whose very existence, if they were to accede to the highest realms of cultural privilege, they had to deny. Then, as now, to be the guardian of cultural tradition is more or less fundamentally not to read it. It would be wishful to imagine that literary or cultural knowledge had even remotely the cachet in contemporary American life that it did for the Victorians; to the extent that that culture provides a literary education, it demands a not entirely dissimilar obliviousness to the homoeroticism of Dickinson, Melville, Walt Whitman, Mark Twain, Willa Cather, and Faulkner—to name only the most obvious of American writers.

My purpose here is not to reclaim Faulkner as a queer writer—however worthwhile such a project might be—but to pursue the complications of queer transmission as a multivalent question in his work. For all that Uncle Buck and Uncle Buddy have a same-sex marriage in everything but name (while Quentin and Shreve, at least to the knowing Harvard undergraduates around them, have the name, too),[1] what seems most queer about *Go Down, Moses* is its understanding of transmission, in more and less obvious senses. Queer transmission is a central, explicit concern of Faulkner's text and is also implicitly thematized by the mode of reading it demands. Thus, on the most evident level, the text is about transmission in a specific sense—the transmission of the patronymic and of property— and about the ways both can go awry.[2] It is *queer* transmission, therefore, because it disarticulates inheritance, tradition, and pedagogy from biological reproduction and—moreover—pursues a paradoxical form of transmission as the failure of transmission. The text is more concerned with lateral relations and with men (one never knows the names of several important mothers), and names recur without thereby seeming to be passed down by fathers—Carothers McCaslin; McCaslin "Cass" Edmonds; Carothers "Roth" Edmonds. Fathers in the text are, in Hortense Spillers's phrase, "removed . . . from *mimetic* view."[3] "Was," the first section of *Go Down, Moses,* in this sense, is indicative; on one level it is the story of two sets of parents—Ike's and Lucas Beauchamp's—but the text makes those parental pairings the result (and in more than one way the relatively trivial result) of avuncular relations. Uncle Buck might be Uncle Ike's father, but that relation is never named in the course of the story, where he—with Buddy and Hubert—remains one among many uncles. In this story, and in the text as a whole, heterosexuality almost never takes center stage except as failed, grotesque, or lost; the world of *Go Down, Moses* is a world of brothers and uncles. The family tree is curiously involved and static, as if it replayed its end (for all genealogies eventually dead-end) at every stage of its putative (and highly complicated) "growth."

"By the distaff"; "chancery dying wishes mortmain possession or whatever": it would be forgivable to imagine that a reading of *Go Down, Moses* could consist, simply, in untangling the genealogy of the McCaslin–

Edmonds–Beauchamp family, in plotting the exfoliations of its family tree.[4] Indeed, the narrative of "Was" is, for the story's opening section, consigned to an initially ungrounded deictic reference: "*This* was not something participated in or even seen by himself."[5] The refractions of narrative perspective that follow—seemingly, Isaac McCaslin's sense of events he heard about from McCaslin Edmonds, who, a boy at the time, was not centrally involved in them—mirrors the genealogical indirection that, far more than the plot that follows, is the opening's central focus. Isaac, "a widower now and uncle to half a county and father to no one," hears of it from "his elder cousin, McCaslin Edmonds, grandson of Isaac's father's sister and so descended by the distaff, yet notwithstanding the inheritor, and in his time the bequestor, of that which some had thought then and some still thought should have been Isaac's, since his was the name in which the title to the land had first been granted from the Indian patent and which some of the descendents of his father's slaves still bore in the land" (3). *Go Down, Moses* gradually unravels these relations, but the confusion is very much to the point, for what one discovers is a genealogy more reticulated than linear. All genealogies, perhaps, are reticulated, if one views them from "above" and not from any governing perspective (oneself, for example); this one is more so because one's focus comes to rest on structural symmetries (folding laterally or vertically) and inversion. To follow the "story" from "Was" to "Go Down, Moses" is gradually to fill in a genealogy—one that could be called *queer* for any number of reasons.

As the opening of "Was" makes clear, genealogies also mark the paths of property transmission—with which the text is preoccupied, from Ike's renunciation in "The Bear" to Lucas's inheritance to the details of the logging leases that destroy the woods in which Ike hunts to (even) the question of who owns Rider's house in "Pantaloon in Black" ("when he put his hand on the gate it seemed to him suddenly that there was nothing beyond it. The house had never been his anyway" [135]). For any number of readings of *Go Down, Moses,* its central question is the relation between property and names—and the social order that stands behind (supports, but also is supported by) instances of this kind of transmission. Whether Ike is inside or outside the world of his (many) fathers is partly a question of whether transmission—and Oedipality—remains intact after his renunciation of property in "The Bear." (That is one part of what makes the story's genealogies "queer": it is an effect one could call, following Lee Edelman, "No Future.")

Go Down, Moses is about another sense of transmission, too: of knowledge and cultural history. One version of transmission approximates biological inheritance, and it functions as a kind of cultural atavism: the heritage of slavery and the Civil War returns, like an intergenerational phantom, to mark the lives of characters more or less cognizant of its effects. (It is said of Carothers "Roth" Edmonds in "The Fire and the Hearth" that "the old curse of his fathers, the old haughty ancestral pride based not on any value but on an accident of geography, stemmed not from courage and honor but from wrong and shame, descended to him" [107].) It would be more than possible to read the disrupted forms of paternal transmission as instances of this equivocal historico-cultural transmission: Hortense Spillers's elucidation (in "Mama's Baby, Papa's Maybe") of the effects of the patronymic's foreclosure in African American culture under slavery (which is perhaps to say, too, the foreclosure of culture *tout court*) would illuminate *Go Down, Moses,* where the "inheritance" of slavery has made all inheritance illegitimate.

Atavistic quasi transmission occurs alongside more conscious forms of initiation, such as Sam Fathers rubbing the blood of a slain deer on Ike's face or the cultural knowledge whose internalization it is meant to mark. "The Old People" and "The Bear" are stories of pedagogy: most obviously, Ike learns the ways of the woods from Sam Fathers. The canonization of "The Bear"—and at many different levels of American culture—suggests that, for some forms of reading anyway, the story is not incompatible with the perpetuation of culture. Inside the text, however, and even at a glance, it is striking how little these quasi-pedagogical forms of transmission offer Oedipal or patrilinear culture. Initiation points to another form of queer genealogy: it integrates Ike not into a community grounded in the father's name but into an avuncular world, and it leads to the repudiation of property. Born to an uncle, as he will become one, Ike is also raised by uncles: Sam Fathers primarily, but also McCaslin Edmonds, General Compson, Major de Spain, and, perhaps, Old Ben. The major pedagogical relations, moreover, never overlap with parental relations. (Originally "Had Two Fathers," Sam Fathers embodies the truth that paternity, when multiplied, ceases to be paternity, possibly because it becomes avuncular. With the possible exception of Mr. Compson's relation to Quentin, pedagogical relations in Faulkner are nearly always avuncular. In *Intruder in the Dust,* for example, Charles Mallison has a father, but the privileged relation is with his uncle, Gavin Stevens. In *The Mansion* and *The Town,* the locus is displaced even further, from Gavin to V. K. Ratliff—whose first names, we eventually and rather strangely learn, are Russian.) It would be moving too quickly, however, to presume that, whatever sort of community initiation produces or fails to produce, it nevertheless produces knowledge. Ike, we learn in "The Bear," becomes an extremely good woodsman; to that extent, he learns. But it is a striking fact that throughout *Go Down, Moses,* the transmission of knowledge fares no better than the transmission of property does.

That latter claim will need spelling out. For the moment, though, an initial, unavoidable question is how to understand thwarted transmission in *Go Down, Moses.* There are—for a preliminary formulation—two contexts, two sets of questions that frame the importance of property transmission in the text. The first is the relation between the natural world and human forms of property and meaning. Can land be owned? What effects do human systems of meaning have on natural landscapes? The second is the heritage of slavery and its effect on property relations and patronymic transmission—the peculiar institution, by treating human beings as property, made property itself illegitimate, a condition perhaps forever entailed on all America's remotest posterity.[6] Ike, we will see, wants to assimilate these two questions—in hope thereby of redeeming both through a single gesture of renunciation. The next set of questions—again, for a preliminary formulation—bear on the relation between property transmission in those two contexts and the various forms taken by the transmission of knowledge and culture in the text. The question of whether Ike's redemption "works" is, partly, a question of how one assimilates (or resists assimilating) these various kinds of transmission. Far more than the presence or absence of gay thematics, what makes the text fertile ground for queer reading is the various ways that local and global effects in Faulkner's prose continually return us to this conundrum, of whether these multiple registers can be assimilated in a unified reading of the text.

Thematically, one central question of *Go Down, Moses* is—in a variety of modalities—transmission. Formally, the question is coherence; as is well known, what sort of object the text presents is an unresolved—and far from trivial—question. Originally calling the text *Go Down, Moses and Other Stories,* Faulkner later insisted that the text was a novel. The question of formal coherence repeatedly emerges, not just in the relation of specific sections ("Pantaloon in Black" in particular) to a larger whole, but in the individual sections conceived as autonomous parts; this question of coherence is perhaps especially visible in the often perplexing endings of the different sections.

As I have phrased things so far, the formal and thematic registers are (perhaps misleadingly) assimilable. The opening of "Was," by joining the transmission of stories and the transmission of names and property, suggests that such assimilation is a crucial question for the text, and, therefore, that the text's formal coherence might bear on the relations among the various forms of transmission I have adumbrated so far: "This is not something participated in or even seen by himself, but by his elder cousin, McCaslin Edmonds, grandson of Isaac's father's sister and so descended by the distaff, yet notwithstanding the inheritor, and in his time the bequestor." Or again: "not something he had participated in or even remembered except for the hearing, listening, come to him through and from his cousin McCaslin born in 1850 and sixteen years his senior and hence, his own father being near seventy when Isaac, an only child, was born, rather his brother than cousin and rather his father than either, out of the old time, the old days" (4). If one formal question posed by "Was" is the relation between its frame narrative and the grotesque story that follows (about a poker game where the stakes are two slaves, Tomey's Turl and Tennie, and an unmarried sister, Miss Sophonsiba), given that one indirect result is Ike's birth, then one possibility would be to align the refracted genetic relations with the substitution of hearing and listening for witnessing and participation. Participation becomes vicarious, and paternity becomes avuncular. Hence the conjoining in both formulations (and in the opening as a whole) of thwarted transmission of property and skewed patrilineal relations with the turn from immediacy to mediation, presence to absence. One inevitably knows one's origins only by hearsay; it is striking here that that common human predicament explicitly unsettles paternity and inheritance. A division within Ike—visible in the alienating formulation "by himself"—unites two forms of alienation, and the sentence thus brings together his nonpresence in the story that follows and his renunciation of property. Another way to put it, which would summarize a major strand of *Go Down, Moses*: Ike substitutes telling for inheritance, or inherits a story instead of a parcel of land.

Yet the narrative that follows immediately warns us against parallels: in the child's view, "it was a good race" (5) and "it was the best race he had ever seen" (8) describe (first) the pursuit of a fox in a house (comical for everyone but the fox) and (second) the pursuit of a man. Point of view is the story here (and in more than one way), shaping the boy's pleasure in these races, for instance, and the reader's compromising sharing of it. Indeed, another description of the substitution effected by the story would emphasize what is grotesque about the narrative that follows. Property relations are less repudiated than sublimated. A poker game deciding black and female lives is rendered as a just-so story about cantankerous old men; the reader who cannot see the human lives for the poker game is not unlike the boy who fails to register the differences between the "races" he sees. The question of which story one attends to replays a larger strain in the text's depiction of failed transmission: seen from the angle of queer theory (or indeed from any perspective fatigued by Oedipal understandings of culture), failed transmission looks utopian, while to focus on race (not the contest of speed this time, but the other kind) brings into view the realization of such a world in slavery—in the latter instance, because of the invasion of familial structures by a total objectification of African American persons held as property.[7] That split is played out here as a dynamic of attention: which story or stories one attends to in "Was." This is a problem of reading, of how one produces a unified account of what one reads, which is also to say of how one decides what to ignore. What from one angle leads to telling as an avuncular utopia, eschewing property and patronymic inheritance, becomes, from another angle, a form of willful, and possibly complicit, blindness.

That is, of course, Isaac McCaslin's problem in a nutshell. But it also perhaps forces us to return to the thematic questions as I have phrased them so far, and it may be that my initial formulations were insufficiently abstract. Repeatedly, *Go Down, Moses* presents confrontations between disjunctive, incompatible systems: nature and property, for example, or (I would argue) sexuality and race. This is perhaps one reason why the debate between Ike and McCaslin at the center of "The Bear" is at times almost incomprehensible: they talk at cross-purposes, and that their terms appear to overlap only makes their respective vocabularies more unassimilable. Old Moses, we learn in "Was," is a dog; the realm of animality and the register of biblical reference are superimposed but never fully assimilated. Both lie on top of another pair of superimpositions visible in the text's title: the appropriation of the spiritual, which also possibly ironizes (and possibly does not) Ike's identification with Moses, and that song's figuring of the plight of black people held as slaves by the plight of the Jews held in Egypt. Miss Sophonsiba insists that they call Hubert's plantation Warwick after the earldom that, in her view, he ought to have inherited; "it would sound as if she and Mr. Hubert owned two separate plantations covering the same area of ground, one on top of the other" (9). This image of disrupted property relations also offers an image for the text's conflicting, superimposed systems. So, likewise, does the description of a dying Sam Fathers: "He lay there—the copper-brown, almost hairless body, the old man's body, the old man, the wild man not even one generation from the woods, childless, kinless, people-less—motionless, his eyes open but no longer looking at any of them" (236). The morphological similarity (between childless and motionless, for example) forcibly assimilates separate registers while making visible that forcible assimilation. Similar in effect are the repetitions and redoubled modifications: "The copper-brown almost hairless body" becomes "the old man's body," which in turn becomes, first, "the old man" and then "the wild man." Metonymical transitions, these movements produce an effect less of modification or grammatical subordination than of superimposition—of different bodies, different qualities, different contexts. From one angle, the text's recurrent figural alignment of animals and African Americans marks a compromised effort at redemption (as, from another angle, it might be read as a [possibly facile] way to critique an "unnatural" system of racial oppression).[8] It strikes me, however, that one confronts in such figures an imperfect superimposition of distinct systems. To that extent, the questions of whether the text is "one"—whether its stories can be assimilated—and of whether its explorations of nature, patrilinearity, and race can be articulated together are *the* questions of the text's meaning.

Furthermore, the superimposed systems are never merely binary. Thus, for instance, there is never any simple binary opposition of black to white in the text; there is always (at least) a tertiary relation among black, white, and Native American; likewise: not nature and property, merely, but nature and property, property and race, property and telling; telling as written transmission and telling as speaking; the time of narrative and the time of nature (each differently opposed to the time of patrilineal succession and each differently opposed to the time of human history); and so on. I will trace some of these strands in the pages that follow. Theoretical exposition inevitably lags behind fiction in this respect because analysis needs to separate systems that fiction can keep running simultaneously. The lack of any convincingly articulated relation between the strands focusing on—for example—animals and race is not a failure so much as a way of marking and enacting complex interrelations of systems that remain autonomous. (This may partly be why fiction and poetry offer more compelling theorizations of race and sexuality than—so far—theorists have been able to: these forms do not need to assimilate overlapping systems and hence do not necessarily reify one or the other by attempting to imagine relations "between" them.) Repeatedly, moreover, the confrontation of two or more incompatible systems is in turn superimposed on analogous confrontations—where neither the terms nor the modalities of confrontation precisely line up.

Even if I am right to suggest that Faulkner's writing makes especially evident the power of literary texts to surpass theoretical ones—exactly to the extent that they can leave suspended or unresolved relations among multiple, unhierarchized systems—it is also the case that queer theory led me to value such a potential in literary texts.[9] Implicitly, part of the stakes of the reading that follows is the question of whether queer theory can comprise its own outside, can shade into what I have been calling "close reading,"[10] and whether it can comprise its outside in another way, too, by offering a name to that which exceeds it: implicitly, the claim here is that such close reading of Faulkner's text can better register the complexity of sexuality's interactions with "race" or ecology, for instance, than can any mere adding of one or both as a factor within queer analysis (or than can imagining an "intersection" between disciplines or theoretical approaches).[11] The chapter will not seek, in other words, to include "race" (or "eco-criticism") within queer theory. If it seeks to spell out an aspect left largely undeveloped in chapter 9's reading of *Absalom, Absalom!*—namely, the relation of a queer reading to questions of "race"—it will do so somewhat obliquely, through the concept of transmission. The approach to queerness itself will likewise be oblique. My hope is that the other chapters of the book have provided a context that makes evident the relevance for queer theory of the questions I pursue in this chapter. To spell out the connection between the text's thematic preoccupation with queer transmission and these questions of reading—of the coordination (or not) of multiple systems of meaning—is, very broadly, to reflect on queer theory as a mode of literary reading.

Initiations

Abstractly, then, *Go Down, Moses* moves alternately toward and away from globalizing terms: toward assimilation and resolution of these different systems and, in turn, toward the puncturing or unsettling of such resolutions.[12] This is the more precise sense, too, in which the text is about initiation: as an effect of pedagogical transmission. Formally, initiation poses the question of the relation among the various kinds of (thwarted) transmission for *Go Down, Moses*. But the superimposition of different registers in a consciousness is also the content of initiation. In Faulkner more generally initiation is rarely about the transmission of knowledge or the joining of a community (however much sections of *Go Down, Moses* might seem to invite such a reading). More often, initiation is understood as a temporal discontinuity that arises from a sudden, forced superimposition of incompatible systems. One thinks of Thomas Sutpen lagging behind his experience at the plantation door (and behind what he then discovers he already knew) in *Absalom, Absalom*,[13] or of Charles Mallison in *Intruder in the Dust* flinging money at Lucas Beauchamp. There the emphasis is perhaps less on the particular mistake than on a cognitive asynchronicity, a mind out of sync with perception and with a body's actions: "In the same second in which he knew she would have taken them he knew that only by that one irrevocable second was he forever now too late, forever beyond recall."[14] That Charles—who, in this putative coming-of-age novel increasingly comes to be called Chick—obsessively repeats the initiation points to what is evident in the "first" one, namely, that, as an occurrence, its temporality is curiously scrambled. That "progression" is very much of a piece with the novel's repeated insistence that only a child or a woman would have believed Lucas, and would have gone out to the graveyard to dig up a body. That the adventure (and insight) is to make him a man exposes a fundamental difficulty: to be a man would prevent one from having the realization necessary for becoming one. That novel's hackneyed portrayal of clinging motherhood fits here: women and the children they want to prevent from becoming men are internal to the men produced by excluding the woman- and childlike, which might also be why Charles becomes a man by becoming (a) Chick. That is also why, again in Faulkner more generally, the narration of such scenes is never separable from the initiation. Arriving after the fact and knowing too much, the narration repeats the temporal and cognitive discontinuity that is the initiation itself.[15] For "Was," "The Fire and the Hearth," "The Old People," and "The Bear" in particular, the question is both whether initiation "works" and whether initiation is compatible with its narration. As in Pater's "Child in the House," that it is not compatible is, paradoxically, often the content of the initiation itself.

A set piece even more condensed than the description of Thomas Sutpen's visit to the plantation door in *Absalom, Absalom!* is the extraordinary opening of chapter 6 of *Light in August,* which describes the relation—central to narratives of initiation in this novel and in Faulkner more generally—between memory and knowledge:

> Memory believes before knowing remembers. Believes longer than recollects, longer than knowing even wonders. Knows remembers believes a corridor in a big long garbled cold echoing building of dark red brick sootbleakened by more chimneys than its own, set in a grassless cinderstrewnpacked compound surrounded by smoking factory purlieus and enclosed by a ten-foot steel-and-wire fence like a penitentiary or zoo, where in random and erratic surges, with sparrowlike childtrebling, orphans in identical and uniform blue denim in and out of remembering but in knowing constant as the bleak walls, the bleak windows where in rain soot from yearly adjacenting chimneys streaked like black tears.[16]

The question of whether memory "is" anywhere is marked by the uncertain level of abstraction—"memory believes," for instance, or "in knowing constant as the bleak walls"—that leaves unclear whether memory remembers a place, is a place, or is figured by a place. Memory, the figuration of memory, and a place all come together in the spatial incoherence of the description: the multiple, often incompatible modalities of interiority, the superimposition of multiple, differently scaled spatial relations (among purlieus, fence, and compound, for instance) visible in the proliferation of different, incompatible senses of "in." The spatially incoherent figures render an enclosure within the orphanage, the uncertain "location" of memory and a past "inside" a person (a past, moreover, that is the writing of an exterior world "within" a self, or in other words, formation), and the multiple, again often not hierarchized, patterns of subordination in Faulkner's prose (where what seems to be a parenthetical aside or subordinate element then shifts its logical or grammatical relation to elements that follow it in a sentence). That memory does something other than remember is a related difficulty. Similar are three other, highly Faulknerian effects: the conjoining of a series of modifications without punctuation to indicate their relation ("big long garbled cold echoing building"), the use of compound adjectives like "sootbleakened" and "cinderstrewnpacked," and the compound verbs followed by unidiomatic objective complements ("knows remembers believes a corridor"). All these are closer to syntactical superimposition than to subordination. (Paratactic superimposition, one might call it.) The orphanage is both the form and the content of Joe Christmas's memory; also implicit is the fact that Christmas's past, and his memory, are contained "in" the novel's prose. When his "insides" become the "insides" of the book, interiority as such becomes incoherent. The passage thus represents the scrambling of consciousness introduced by the paradoxical temporalities of human development. Moreover, the prose here demands from a reader a different kind of cognitive activity than that which would produce a unified narrative (of development or of subjective memory, for example): not to produce a hierarchized order of subordinated ideas for which spatial relations might offer an image but, rather, to perceive multiple, unhierarchized, often unrelated spaces and systems simultaneously. Such would be a way to phrase, very schematically, what I would call queer reading in Faulkner, and it thus enacts the perplexities of development and transmission that this passage figures as an incoherent space.

"The Bear," famously, presents two different narratives and two different initiations: Ike's initiation as a hunter and his discovery of his family's heritage of forcible interracial incest, a narrative obliquely told in the family's business ledgers.[17] A series of vignettes of initiation in *Go Down, Moses* might help frame what is at stake in those narratives in "The Bear." These vignettes strike a chord that resonates with many similar scenes in Faulkner that portray, as an initiating or transformative experience, the superimposition of three different, disparate temporalities: personal experience, history, and narrative. Thematically, the problem is that one arrives belatedly in the world and that one must therefore come to know its terms; there needs to have been a moment when one became aware of one's ideological and historical world. Learning must occur, and it must occur in time. But because history and personal experience unfold in different temporalities, their encounter occurs outside of both. Logically, the moment of initiation must exist, but the cognition that makes it initiating can, like the infant itself, only ever arrive belatedly. Thus, initiation, no matter how securely it seems tethered to a particular event, marks a transaction among different, disparate times. Not unified in the time of experience, it can never occur and can never be narrated as an event. Such, at least, is my understanding of why such moments in Faulkner are represented as parables that take on a symbolic (and therefore an extranarrative) resonance. (That Thomas Sutpen's initiation is repeatedly described as occurring out of time is perhaps representative, and his trip "down" the mountain to the world of plantations [a passage in the text, moreover, in which one's uncertainty in the face of a quasi-narrative, quasi-allegorical hybrid register is signal] permanently disorients him temporally.)

Among other effects of this structure and the archaeological simultaneity of the mind is a coexistence of contradictory registers, even perfectly conscious ones, in which thought shifts paths in one register as a result of an insight to which another register remains blithely oblivious. Hence, I think, the relevance for initiation and formation of a sociological fact that one learns reading Faulkner if one has learned it nowhere else: for many southern white people, particularly white people of a certain social class, institutional and ideological systems of racism coexisted with intensely close personal relations with African Americans—relations that, insofar as many such white children were raised by black servants as quasi siblings with their own children ("foster brothers" as Faulkner calls Roth and Henry [107]), one might simply call familial. The dedication of *Go Down, Moses*—"To Mammy / CAROLINE BARR / Mississippi / [1840–1940] / Who was born in slavery and who gave to my family a fidelity without stint or calculation of recompense and to my childhood an immeasurable devotion and love" (brackets in original)—not only looks like an epitaph engraved as if on a headstone over the entire text, but also points to the centrality of such familial relations for all the sections that follow. As Quentin Compson notes in *The Sound and the Fury,* both racism and particular beloved black people are "home" to him.[18] Such a structure leads one to question strategies of social amelioration grounded in efforts to foster personal acquaintance with oppressed minorities (strategies that create tolerance perhaps no more than zoos or pet adoptions create vegetarians): people's elastic capacity to make personal acquaintances exceptions to their treasured biases (which is less a particular pathology of racists than a consequence of finite perspective and of knowledge's embeddedness, for any human who comes to it, in time) and the fatigue one feels at having one's existence perpetually drafted into the service of continuing education for bigots are but two of the many reasons to resist such projects. But such a structure also leads one to question many (especially redemptive) representations of minority consciousness. It seems to me a nontrivial and underremarked fact of gay development in a homophobic climate, for example, that one's awareness of gay desire (as a source of anxiety, perhaps, but also as a source of joy) occurred at the same time as, but was not necessarily integrated with, a growing mastery of homophobic social codes—which meant both that the "trauma" was not the discovery of homophobia so much as the learned necessity of articulating those two systems together and that, even after the discovery of this putative necessity, one's desire and one's ideological interpellation followed parallel, and not always integrated, paths.[19] Coming out attempts to unify these through narrative and therefore must misrepresent gay development to the very extent that it attempts to represent it.

The repeated scenarios in Faulkner that present a sudden encounter with "race" point to a similar structure of consciousness. "The Fire and the Hearth" presents a pair of such scenes: the descent of "the old curse of his fathers" to Carothers Edmonds and the nearly lethal confrontation between Lucas Beauchamp and Zach Edmonds in Edmonds's bedroom. Among the more striking aspects of the latter scene is the disappearance of proper names—Zach and Lucas, raised as brothers, become "the white man" and "the negro" (and Zach's wife, who dies in childbirth, is never anything but "the white man's wife" [45]):

> Then Lucas was beside the bed. He didn't remember moving at all. He was kneeling, their hands gripped, facing across the bed and the pistol the man whom he had known from infancy, with whom he had lived until they were both grown almost as brothers lived. They had fished and hunted together, they had learned to swim in the same water, they had eaten at the same table in the white boy's kitchen and in the cabin of the neighbor's mother; they had slept under the same blanket before a fire in the woods. (54)

Strikingly, just after this, we read:

> "For the last time," Lucas said. "I tell you——" And then he cried, and not to the white man and the white man knew it; he saw the whites of the negro's eyes rush suddenly with red like the eyes of a bayed animal—a bear, a fox: "I tell you! Don't ask too much of me!"

I was wrong, the white man thought. *I have gone too far.* But it was too late. (54)

The contrast between the invoked childhood intimacy and the impersonal generic designation (repeated throughout this section) marks the inscription of a larger ideological system in the register of personal experience. These repetitions lead one to read the confrontation as an allegory of race—specifically, racial oppression as an experience of sexual dispropriation.[20] Assimilating their personal history to an impersonal allegory, where the voiding of a shared past is therefore both the initiation and its rendering (as allegory), this moment (and several subsequent moments) simultaneously crosses Lucas's and Zach's interiorities. Earlier, when the narration repeatedly refers to Zach as "the white man," the designation seems to be Lucas's: representing his perspective, the narrative shows us his awareness of race. With "*I was wrong,* the white man thought," the italicized representations of Zach's thought coexist with the depersonalizing designation, and the intimation seems (if only momentarily) unavoidable that Zach views himself as "the white man." The violence at the end of the scene is "almost like an embrace" (56); that intimacy is both erotic and impersonal, taking shape, when read in the context of the rest of the scene, through a crossing of their interiorities that also voids their history of personal intimacy.

The entire scene, I noted, feels allegorical. That effect of impersonality might derive from (or perhaps drive) the sense that it is both allegorical and *experienced* as allegorical. Just after "the incredibly loud click of the miss-fire," we read, "That had been a good year, though late in beginning after the rains and flood: the year of the long summer. He would make more this year than he had made in a long time, even though and in August some of his corn had not had its last plowing. He was doing that now, following the single mule behind the rows of strong, waist-high stalks and the rich, dark, flashing blades" (56). The transition is disconcerting because one's initial impression that the year was good *because* it was the year he tried to shoot Zach Edmonds derives from the fact that one is, narratively speaking, out of time and left disorientingly at sea for many lines about where to locate "that" and "now." For one is in neither of the two moments one might initially expect: neither just after the "embrace" in the bedroom nor at the moment where the flashback began, Lucas's conversation with Edmonds (Zach's son) about George's still—where Edmonds's age (he is forty-three) leads Lucas back to the evening of Edmonds's birth, the mother's death, and Molly's departure for Zach's house to raise Henry and Carothers. Instead, it seems that *now* is an unspecified moment after the misfire (a moment when, moreover, nothing has been resolved: "This time he spoke aloud: 'How to God,' he said, 'can a black man ask a white man to please not lay down with his black wife? And even if he can ask it, how to God can the white man promise he wont?'" [58]).

The scene figures Lucas and Zach's integrating a shared personal history with their identities as "the white man" and "the negro"; the repeated emphasis on a temporal telescoping is trivialized if one sees in it merely the traces of psychological trauma. Repeatedly, Lucas anticipates a later view: "It was as if he stood already in the bedroom itself, above the slow respirations of sleep, the undefended and oblivious throat, the naked razor already in his hand" (50), or later, he "entered the bedroom which it seemed to him he had already entered . . . facing again the act which it seemed to him he had already performed" (51). Such moments—in which the events are, as it were, contaminated by their later narration and are thus paradoxically experienced as remembered—seem markers of unassimilated temporal systems. One enters history through personal experience, but experience and history remain discontinuous. The section offers a beautiful image for such a confrontation:

> He was waiting for daylight. He could not have said why. He squatted against a tree halfway between the carriage gate and the white man's house, motionless as the windless obscurity itself while the constellations wheeled and the whippoorwills choired faster and faster and ceased and the first cocks crowed and the false dawn came and faded and the birds began and the night was over. (51)

The telescoping of time seems to represent the coexistence of multiple temporal frameworks: Lucas's life, the wheeling of the constellations, and the sun-synchronized choiring of the whippoorwills. The quasi-cinematic image and the contrast between him, "motionless as the windless obscurity itself," and the faster movements of the constellations and birds point to their disparate markings of temporal rhythm. The constellations seem to move faster because the birds are said to; if they "choir" faster as the constellations wheel faster, then the effect is a rhythmical one—more birds or sounds to a particular measure of time might make the singing sound "faster"—that in effect collates a steady movement with a mobile perspective, collates disparate temporal frames while maintaining their difference (his motionlessness creates the effect of motion). The temporal telescoping is also created by the prose, where the repeated *ands* establish a beat against which the conjoining of disparate, longer or shorter elements creates the effect of speed.

Whatever "lessons" are learned here, moreover, seem fundamentally untransmissible. Fathers and sons repeat the same experience, but the experience is neither transmitted nor discussed. Carothers Edmonds's suspicions about what occurred between Zach and Lucas are never confirmed; what he does learn from his father is his belated relation to his father's experience:

> Then the boy could read what was in his face. He had seen it before, as all children had—that moment when, enveloped and surrounded still by the warmth and confidence, he discovers that the reserve which he had thought to have passed had merely retreated and set up a new barrier, still impregnable;—that instant when the child realizes with both grief and outrage that the parent antedates it, has experienced things, shames and triumphs both, in which he can have no part. (111)

Carothers's relation to Henry explicitly parallels Zach's to Lucas (both pairs were born the same year, 1898 and 1874, respectively, and were raised as foster brothers); the two set pieces are repetitions without being fully symmetrical. Carothers's experience is repeatedly cast as an inheritance—"the old curse of his fathers" (107) or "his heritage" (110)—and the particular experience of race that descends on him is inseparable from the incomprehensible paternal experience that leads to the intuition that his father "antedates" him. "But it was too late," we read, of the moment when Carothers finds that he is to eat alone, not as a member of Molly's family but as that family's master (110), and he eats alone for the rest of the story. Likewise, earlier: "Then one day he knew it was grief and was ready to admit it was shame also, wanted to admit it only it was too late then, forever and forever too late" (109). (If he repeats his father's experience, it is less from any particular insight Zach might convey—we in fact never know what he learns or does not learn from it—than from a belatedness his son seems, retrospectively, to have inherited: "*I was wrong,* the white man thought.... But it was too late.")

Two things seem especially striking about the narrative as it is presented. The first is the absence of any specifiable or even speculated-upon reason for Carothers's behavior: nothing spurs it, and nothing leads up to it. "Then one day the old curse of his fathers . . . descended to him. He did not recognize it then" (107). Second, the scene is framed by a remarkable temporal compression. After Lucas demands his inheritance from Isaac,

> within a year he married, not a countrywoman, a farm woman, but a town woman, and McCaslin Edmonds built a house for them and allotted Lucas a specific acreage to be farmed as he saw fit as long as he lived or remained on the place. Then McCaslin Edmonds died and his son married and on that spring night of flood and isolation the boy Carothers was born. (106)

That telescoping frames the idyll that is, in turn, punctured by his father's curse, an existence untroubled by any questions about his relation to the black family he is repeatedly said to "accept":

> Still in infancy, he had already accepted the black man as an adjunct to the woman who was the only mother he would remember, as simply as he accepted his black foster-brother, as simply as he accepted his father as an adjunct to his existence. Even before he was out of infancy, the two houses had become interchangeable: himself and his foster-brother sleeping on the same pallet in the white man's house or the same bed in the negro's and eating of the same food at the same table in either, actually preferring the negro house, the hearth on which even in summer a little fire always burned, centering the life in it, to his own. It did not even need to come to him as part of his family's chronicle that his white father and his foster-brother's black one had done the same; it never even occurred to him that they in their turn and simultaneously had not had the first of remembering projected upon a single woman whose skin was likewise dark. One day he knew, without wondering or remembering when or how he learned that either, that the black woman was not his mother, and did not regret it; he knew

that his own mother was dead and did not grieve. There was still
the black woman, constant, steadfast, and the black man of whom
he saw as much and even more than of his own father. . . . And
besides, he was no longer an infant. He and his foster-brother rode
the plantation horses and mules, they had a pack of small hounds
to hunt with and promise of a gun in another year or so; they were
sufficient, complete, wanting, as all children do, not to be understood, leaping in mutual embattlement before any threat to privacy,
but only to love, to question and examine unchallenged, and to be
let alone. (106–7)

The temporal compression that moves from McCaslin to Zach to Carothers
in a single sentence continues in the narration of his prelapsarian life—
moving, without further marker, from "still in infancy" to "even before he
was out of infancy" to "besides, he was no longer an infant." That compression assimilates the narrated experience to the structure of *Bildung*
by marking as remote the temporal perspective from which it is seen. It is
therefore all the more striking that the "learning" described in a sense never
takes place: "one day he knew, without wondering or remembering when or
how he learned that either." The negations—"it did not even need to come
to him . . . it never even occurred to him that they . . . had not"—which
render an unquestioned sense of belonging, assimilating Carothers to the
black family so long as his relation to it, like the continuity of his and his
father's experience, is not questioned, constitute knowledge (and convey it
to the reader) not as something learned but as something unnecessary to
learn. "It never even occurred to him that they in their turn and simultaneously had not had the first of remembering projected upon a single woman
whose skin was likewise dark." Known without having been learned, the
knowledge can also only equivocally be said to belong to anyone; that formulation alienates the remembering from the boy, just as it leaves memory
groundless. (Where is the first of remembering projected *from*?)

But perhaps the most striking aspect of the passage is its dizzying series of different forms of parallelism. "They in their turn and simultaneously" links Lucas and Zach to each other and to Carothers and Henry, as
"likewise dark" brings together Molly and another posited mother surrogate, for example. But there are also the two interracial relations he never
thought to question, the different realizations he does not know or remember that he has had, and even, on a different level, the various syntactical

pairings: "his white father and his foster-brother's black one," "wondering or remembering," "when or how," "as much and even more," "horses and mules." Pairing or parallelism (and the pairing of disjoint forms of parallelism) starts to seem the very topic of the passage. That formal preoccupation is perhaps most striking in the lesson he does not remember learning: "one day he knew . . . that the black woman was not his mother, and did not regret it; he knew that his own mother was dead and did not grieve." The descent of the father's curse seems at once to interrupt that parallelism and to be generated by it. Among the striking effects is the pairing of two unregistered forms of loss—the death of his mother and the loss of Molly as a mother surrogate—in which, again, there is realization without its having taken place. Also striking is one's momentary sense that "the black woman" names two different people, which derives from the intercalation of two separate oppositions: the white woman and the black woman as lost in opposed ways (on the one hand) and lost mothers and present women (on the other): "He knew . . . that the black woman was not his mother. . . . There was still the black woman, constant, steadfast." The contradiction is a marker less of disavowal than of parallel, unintegrated systems: his knowledge of their (actual) familial relation and his experience of physical proximity ("the black woman was not" [his mother]; "there was still the black woman"). The physical details, paired with the insular relation with Henry, create a physical enclosure that takes the place of family. The "lesson" delivered to the seven-year-old boy is especially brutal because it makes explicit racial hierarchies by depriving him of a mother and a lover. And it does so by forcing him to bring into relation different registers, which is also to say, to understand the ways that the physical presence and bond are governed by (hierarchized) relations between families and between races. Here, the text seems to refuse to Carothers what Ike ostensibly does find: a compelling substitute for missing familial bonds. That it is the curse of his fathers that brings it on suggests that Carothers is excluded not because he lacks a family but because he does not lack one. Whereas Ike (as I will discuss) seems to imagine that this substitution could take place under the aegis of a unifying concept or name (which perhaps dooms him ever to repeat the patrilinear relations he ostensibly seeks to escape), the possibility (at least) emerges here of evading that kind of unification. It could be that to resist such unification is merely to be oblivious—the racialized hierarchy under which they live is, after all, a fact, and for Roth to continue as if Molly took care of him (merely) because she loved him would be to be oblivious indeed—and yet it might also be to maintain that evocative, perhaps, as Faulkner says, universal, childhood wish "not to be understood."

The descent from "foster-brother" to "the white man" can be read in two different registers. Most clearly, the designation marks the intervention of "race," its rewriting of personal relations according to a cruder logic formed by a larger, transpersonal history. In the context of *Go Down, Moses,* however, it also asks to be read in terms of a becoming-impersonal in the text's paradoxical forms of *Bildung.* For "The Old People" and "The Bear" need not be read as charting a progression toward a name: from "the boy" to Isaac or Ike.[21] Initiation would seem to give him a name (or rather, two), but it never takes place, and neither *Ike* nor *Isaac* in fact ever fully replaces *the boy* or *a boy.* "There was a man and a dog too this time," begins "The Bear," and as later recollected, experience moves toward the impersonal forms of the indefinite pronoun:

> He had only to look at McCaslin's eyes and it was there, that summer twilight seven years ago, almost a week after they had returned from the camp before he discovered that Sam Fathers had told McCaslin: an old bear, fierce and ruthless . . . ; an old man . . . ; a boy who wished to learn humility and pride in order to become skillful and worthy in the woods but found himself becoming so skillful so fast that he feared he would never become worthy because he had not learned humility and pride though he had tried, until one day an old man who could not have defined either led him as though by the hand to where an old bear and a little mongrel dog showed him that, by possessing one thing other, he would possess them both; and a little dog, nameless and mongrel and many-fathered. (282–83)

Such passages evoke the indefinite pronouns that Gilles Deleuze counterposes against the compulsive need displayed by psychoanalysis to transform them into possessives and into Oedipal relations: "*an* animal . . . *a* horse, *a* chicken, . . . *a* stomach, *some* eyes, . . . *a* father,"[22] and it would be more than possible to trace a relation between the becoming he links to such indefinite forms and what "The Bear" calls "the communal anonymity of brotherhood" (246).[23] "The indefinite article," writes Deleuze, "is the indetermination of the person only because it is the determination of the singular"; Deleuze gives as an example of "a life" the confrontation with death in Charles Dickens's *Our Mutual Friend*—"between his life and his death, there is a moment that is only that of *a* life playing with death. The life of the individual gives way to an impersonal and yet singular life that releases a pure event freed from the accidents of internal and external life, that is, from the subjectivity and objectivity of what happens." And yet he also says that one should not limit "*a* life" to this moment between (for "the indefinite life does not itself have moments . . . but only between-times, between-moments"): "*A* life is everywhere."[24] For Faulkner, the fact that this moment occurs here—as Ike and McCaslin argue about Ike's desire to repudiate his inheritance—suggests the possibility of reframing Isaac's repudiation as anti-*Bildung,* in which retrospection leads not to a personality or a thereby unified subject but to impersonal forms, the *tableaux vivants* of "a boy," "an old man," "an old bear," and "a little dog," where the boy, moreover, is bereft even of the modifying adjectives afforded the others. This Faulknerian *Bildung* leads to a vanishing of subjectivity, just as, in another register, patronymic inheritance leads not to the transmission of names and property but to a vision of the communal negation of property; even the dog is "nameless and mongrel and many-fathered."

That *Bildung* does not work, that it neither produces a subject who has learned from an experience nor integrates him into a larger community grounded in patronymic continuity, could nevertheless be narrated in negative form: as a "lesson" that leads to Ike's renunciation of property. Ike seems to desire such a resolution, which would also unify many different registers in the text. More than one difficulty confronts such a reading, however. Perhaps most important, this trajectory toward "a boy" uncomfortably echoes the trajectory from "foster-brother" to "the white man," where the ostensibly impersonal form points to the personal taking-on or interiorization of racial categories. The "communal anonymity of brotherhood" is in one version constituted and in another negated by the movement toward impersonal forms. The difficulty of the relation between the two major sections of "The Bear"—the hunt for the bear and the reading of family ledgers—is, in part, the difficulty of understanding the relation between these two pairings of "a boy" and "the white man." For its part, the text suspends articulating a single relation between these terms, leaving the two systems of meaning unarticulated. The challenge, perhaps, is whether such a suspension can be sustained without itself becoming a "lesson" or a principle of unification.

To spell out that suspension—and to explore some of its consequences—it is perhaps necessary to dwell further both on the thwarting of formation or *Bildung* in "The Bear" (and in *Go Down, Moses* more generally) and on the resolution Ike imagines. At a curious moment just after the killing of the bear, we read,

> [Boon] did not wait to let Sam try to walk this time. He carried him into the hut and Major de Spain got light on a paper spill from the buried embers on the hearth and lit the lamp and Boon put Sam on his bunk and drew off his boots and Major de Spain covered him and the boy was not there, he was holding the mules, the sound one which was trying again to bolt since when the wagon stopped Old Ben's scent drifted forward again along the streaming blackness of air, but Sam's eyes were probably open again on that profound look which saw further than them or the hut, further than the death of a bear and the dying of a dog. (234–35)

What is curious, it seems to me, is the text's leaving the perspective of the boy, which it also does at other important moments, most notably when Sam dies, when the narrative leaves the camp, to return to it, and the boy, only after Sam's burial. (Opening in "Was" with "not something participated in or even seen by himself," the text moves, in "The Bear" toward other versions of formation-by-hearsay.) Here, the repeated *and*s set up a series—it seems, of events that take place or actions that are taken—so that "and the boy was not there" is made analogous to "Boon put Sam on his bunk." It therefore seems possible to read "and the boy was not there" not as a comment about the boy's location but as an intimation that, at this crucial, formative moment in his own history, the boy does not exist—joining thereby "a bear" and "a dog." His physical removal from the scene crucial to his formation intimates a structure where it is as if his existence and the experience that forms him take place on separate planes.

Temporal Foldings and Unfoldings: The Disjunctive Times of the Animal, Human History, Genealogy, and Narrative

The possibile disjunction between the boy's life and the experiences that form him is intimated by other moments in "The Old People" and "The Bear." These sections outline (at least) four different temporalities: of animal existence, of human history, of genealogical transmission, and of narrative. The question of whether initiation "takes place"—and of whether

"The Bear" can be said to produce a transmissible insight—is the question of whether the first two are assimilable to the second two (just as the ecological disaster limned by the text could be read as the forced assimilation of the first and second). The question of transmission will return us to the various ways these temporalities are (and are not) coordinated by the text. Even before considering that coordination, we see that narrative time in *Go Down, Moses* is strikingly discontinuous, and not merely because of the different times during which the various sections take place or their disparate temporal pacings. One is struck, for instance, by the telescoping of lives—Isaac McCaslin's, especially, but, in effect, everyone's: between the discrete narrative sections, and sometimes even within those sections, one moves through years, or even from boyhood to old age or death with nothing in between. The text strains (which is also to say makes visible) one's attachment to characters (and to characters as developing), as almost any text does that extends its purview beyond individual lives or the span of a generation: the character whose boyhood misery one cathects is suddenly an old man or even a dead ancestor, more or less irrelevant to the dramas currently on view. (The mention of McCaslin's death in "The Fire and the Hearth" after he has been the boy observer in "Was" is one instance, though of course he returns as a young man in "The Bear.") Similar in effect are those repeated moments in "The Bear" in which the boy's growing older is condensed into single sentences in the form of a list: "Still a child, with three years then two years then one year before he too could make one of them" (186). Likewise, not insignificant for constituting the text's elegiac tone are reminders that the locus of perception is much later than the events told, comprising, in fact, Isaac's entire life: "He had his own gun now, a new breach-loader, a Christmas gift; he would own it and shoot it for almost seventy years, through two new pairs of barrels and locks and one new stock, until all that remained of the original gun was the silver-inlaid trigger-guard with his and McCaslin's engraved names and the date in 1878" (196). This *now* is explicitly a narrative past tense and intimates a perspective like this one:

> ... and Isaac McCaslin, not yet Uncle Ike, a long time yet before he would be uncle to half a county and still father to none, living in one small cramped fireless rented room ... with his kit of brand-new carpenter's tools and the shotgun that McCaslin had given him with his name engraved in silver and old General Compson's

compass (and, when the general died, his silver-mounted horn too) and the iron cot and mattress and the blankets which he would take each fall into the woods for more than sixty years and the bright tin coffee-pot. (286–87)

The near-exact repetition of the opening of "Was" ("a widower now and uncle to half a county and father to no one") leads one to wonder about *still*. Beyond the grammatically most likely (if somewhat strange) assertion that Ike becomes uncle to all without becoming a father (as if becoming an uncle somehow carried with it that risk), does the asserted continuity belong to the text (to a repeated statement that is "still" true) or to the life of one "still father to none"? Does it extend from beginning to end of the more than sixty years of Ike's hunting life, or from "Was" to "The Bear," where, notably, the progression "forward" in fact moves backward in time? Potentially stranger is the opening of section 3: "It was December. It was the coldest December he had ever remembered" (217). Idiomatically, the meaning may simply be that it was the coldest December he had experienced, but the past perfect is striking, intimating a collapsing together of narrated and narrating times (as of memory and experience), which also has the effect of dissolving a character (and specifically the character whose development is ostensibly on view).

Such narrative temporalities are not uncommon mechanisms in coming-of-age fiction; the elegiac tone of the genre may derive less from its nostalgia for lost youth than from that anticipation of retrospection, which reminds us that events are seen from the perspective of the consciousness they form, and thus of the "finished" human being the young character becomes. Such reminders establish the governing structure of *Bildung* and thereby make development representable as a teleology, but they also encrypt within it the vanishing of youth. (Coming-of-age fiction, even when it ostensibly addresses youth, is a genre for the middle-aged and elderly—even if possibly also for those among the young who are prodigies of proleptic nostalgia.) Thus:

dwarfed by that perspective into an almost ridiculous diminishment, the surrey itself seemed to have ceased to move (this too to be completed later, years later, after he had grown to a man and had seen the sea) as a solitary small boat hangs in lonely immobility, merely tossing up and down, in the infinite waste of the ocean while the water and then the apparently impenetrable land which it nears without appreciable progress, swings slowly and opens the widening inlet which is the anchorage. (187)

Like the moment when Lucas stands immobile beneath the whirling stars and choiring whippoorwills, perspective creates effects of motion and stasis, distance here figuring both the limited temporal perspective that makes a life, as it is lived, seem infinite, and a retrospective view that makes that life, once lived, seem but an instant. The pathos of coming-of-age narratives no doubt has something to do with its jamming together of those two incompatible "views." Faulkner's text, unlike lesser texts in this genre, does not force that incompatibility to remain implicit; its queerness derives in part from the way that making-explicit prevents the unification of temporal points of view through retrospection. "The Bear" can be—and no doubt has been—read to emphasize the power of the retrospective view to reify a retrospective viewer. In the context of the more specific temporal structures of the text, however, such moments register not as the assimilation of different times to the governing consciousness structured by *Bildung* but as the mutual interference of incompatible temporalities. For Ike as "the boy" and as "the old man" is one among many other pairings of disjunct times in the text. And the boy was not there.

The temporal superimpositions are even more complicated, however, and the structure of *Bildung* is just one layer. There are, as I noted, (at least) four different temporalities in this section of the text. The opening of "The Old People" establishes a temporality of animal life that will return throughout this section and "The Bear": "At first there was nothing. . . . Then the buck was there. He did not come into sight; he was just there" (157). Likewise, the tracks of the bear seem to appear to the boy as he follows them:

Even as he looked up he saw the next one, and, with it, the one beyond it; moving, not hurrying, running, but merely keeping pace with them as they appeared before him as though they were being shaped out of thin air just one constant pace short of where he would lose them forever and be lost forever himself, tireless, eager, without doubt or dread, panting a little above the strong rapid little hammer of his heart, emerging suddenly into a little glade and the wilderness coalesced. It rushed, soundless, and solidified—the tree, the bush, the compass and the watch glinting where a ray of sunlight touched them. Then he saw the bear. It did not emerge, appear: it was just there, immobile, fixed in the green and windless noon's hot dappling, not as big as he had dreamed it but as big as he had expected, bigger, dimensionless against the dappled obscurity, looking at him. (200)

The bear disappears as it appeared: "Then it was gone. It didn't walk into the woods. It faded, sank back into the wilderness without motion as he had watched a fish, a huge old bass, sink back into the dark depths of its pool and vanish without even any movement of its fins" (200–201). The times of the buck, bear, and bass seem momentarily to intersect with that of the boy; the animals' instantaneous appearances mark the unmodulated moments when the overlaps begin. One way, then, to phrase the question of whether "The Bear" presents a lesson that Isaac can learn or an insight a reader could formulate is to ask whether the encounter with animal life is assimilable to narrative time. The deer, perceived, is "already running, seen first as you always see the deer, in that split second after he has already seen you, already slanting away" (157); suggesting not only that the deer has quicker perceptions than "you" do, the moment also intimates that the deer's emergence necessarily escapes perception: the deer allows one to perceive one's own failure of perception and to perceive one's belatedness—to see not the time of the deer but one's difference from it.

"The boy," we read, "did not remember that shot at all. He would live to be eighty, as his father and his father's twin brother and their father in his turn had lived to be, but he would never hear that shot nor remember even the shock of the gun-butt. He didn't even remember what he did with the gun afterward" (158). More interesting to me that any psychological explanation for the amnesia is the intimation that the shot is unremembered because the time of the animal is not assimilable to the time of narrative exposition, which would also mean that the events of the story cannot be assimilated to a coming-of-age narrative. And those moments of temporal telescoping suggest that development, too, may follow a temporal unfolding unassimilable to its narration: "In less than a second he had ceased forever to be the child he was yesterday" (175). To read the text as a coming-of-age tale or as a narrative of development involves submitting such instantaneous moments to a narrative unfolding. (In both sections, the syncopation of the animal's instantaneous appearance against a tattoo of narrative sequence—"Then it moved. . . . Then it was gone" (200); "Then Sam Fathers touched his shoulder. . . . Then the buck was there" (157)—dramatizes a larger effort to assimilate animal life to a temporality of development.)

There are (again, at least) two ways that the text articulates animal life with such narrative unfolding: one renames the instantaneous atemporal life of the animal "anachronism," while the other renames it "eternity." The first is what allows the story to articulate its coming-of-age narrative with the wilderness's disappearance through logging and industrialization. (The rendering of that disaster is a lesson that makes the story, for some readers—as a recent top-fifty books list in *Newsweek* phrased it—"the best environmental novel ever written," which it might very well be, of course: articulated with a narrative of development, the disappearance of the woods becomes pedagogically assimilable.)[25] The discontinuous narrative moves from remembered childhood to an ecological disaster that is not so much narrated as presented as having already happened. Along with the gaps in the novel's rendering of Ike's life, its temporal ellipses foreground the rapidity of the destruction effected by logging. From the perspective of that rapid destruction, any life—bear or buck, squirrel or dog—is on borrowed time and is, in the march of human history, an anachronism.

Yet the description of the buck's and the bear's instantaneous appearance and disappearance is not exactly the same temporal structure as "anachronism."[26] The bear and the loggers inhabit different temporalities, but anachronism assimilates both to a common temporal measure, one that the text ostensibly links to a psychological logic. Compared (moreover) to a locomotive, the bear, "the shaggy tremendous shape . . . ran in his knowledge before he ever saw it. It loomed and towered in his dreams before ever he saw the unaxed woods where it left its crooked print" (185). This primordial presence is assimilated to consciousness as anachronism:

It was as if the boy had already divined what his senses and intellect had not encompassed yet: that doomed wilderness whose edges were being constantly and punily gnawed at by men with plows and axes who feared it because it was wilderness, men myriad and nameless even to one another in the land where the old bear had earned a name, and through which ran not even a mortal beast but an anachronism, indomitable and invincible out of an old dead time, a phantom, epitome and apotheosis of the old wild life which the little puny humans swarmed and hacked at in a fury of abhorrence and fear like pygmies around the ankles of a drowsing elephant;—the old bear, solitary, indomitable, and alone; widow-ered childless and absolved of mortality—old Priam reft of his old wife and outlived all his sons. (185–86)

The boy's consciousness, out of sync with itself, divines what it cannot encompass, figuring the bear's "anachronism" as a shuffling of genera-tions. That last figure coordinates an unfathomable temporality with the time of human generations (for one can be childless without outliving any sons)—and with meaning and human history, albeit in origins that vanish into mythology. (If Priam does outlive his sons, it is only by a few moments—he is killed by Pyrrhus just after Polites is. Faulkner's reference might suspend Priam in that moment. If the point is rather Priam's prolific progeniture turned to naught, then the final phrase makes an existence out of time representable by submitting it to paternity [and childlessness becomes, therefore, an outliving of one's sons]. Old Ben is made a father, if only by negation.) The rendering of a clash of disjunctive worlds as an effect of scale (pygmies hacking at an elephant) also brings to the fore the clashes of register in the passage (scale and time; logging, natural history, and Greek mythology; psychology and eschatology; "mortal beast" and "anachronism"; and so on). The striking phrase *absolved of mortality* per-haps echoes *apotheosis* (as quasi synonym for "epitome" and Assumption, and also in its strict meaning of being raised to the level of a god) by link-ing the religious echoes in *absolution* to the word's less common meanings of solution, conclusion, or completion (and to one meaning of *absolve*: "to set free"). That *absolution* also echoes *abhorrence* (literally echoes, that is, in sound) suggests—as all these elements do—that the collation of dispa-rate registers may be the point.

The last sentence of the passage embodies, even in its form, an assimi-lation of registers that is—insofar as the strain is visible—incomplete. The clash of registers appears in quasi oppositions—such as "mortal beast" to "anachronism" (or mortality to solitude), in which, again, the structure is not simply binary. On the one hand, the time of the bear is articulated against, first, the temporality of the boy's unconscious—the *nachträglich* structure as the bear looms in his dreams before he ever encounters him ("it seemed to him that at the age of ten he was witnessing his own birth" [187])—and against, second, the temporality of human history, inexorably

marching toward a world with highways, logging companies, and gas sta-
tions, but no bears. It remains a question not only whether the instantane-
ity of the bear is compatible with either of these times, but also whether
the compatibility or noncompatibility of the first pair is analogous to that
of the second. The question of whether the encounter with the bear can be
narrated—whether it can be made a lesson that can be learned—emerges
from these multilayered forms of possible coordination. All of this, in
turn, is (I would say, imperfectly) superimposed on the question of genealogy and property transmission. Presuming a more perfect translation
among these various registers, Ike, by his reasoning, can, by opting out
of property transmission, opt out of the temporality of human history in
favor of the temporality of the bear. And vice versa. The compatibility of
these various systems—the possibility of linking them through narrative
and rendering them as a transmissible "lesson"—is what is at stake (what
is asserted by) the epiphany at the end of "The Bear." And that assimilation
is largely a matter of coordinating different temporal rhythms.

Thus, in his argument with McCaslin about his repudiation of property inheritance, Ike—somewhat perplexingly, at first glance—is oddly
specific about the time of the property's illegitimacy. "I can't repudiate it,"
he argues;

> it was never mine to repudiate. It was never Father's and Uncle
> Buddy's to bequeath me to repudiate because it was never Grand-
> father's to bequeath them to bequeath me to repudiate because it
> was never old Ikkemotubbe's to sell to Grandfather for bequeath-
> ment and repudiation. Because it was never Ikkemotubbe's fathers'
> fathers' to bequeath Ikkemotubbe to sell to Grandfather or any
> man because on the instant when Ikkemotubbe discovered, real-
> ized, that he could sell it for money, on that instant it ceased ever to
> have been his forever, father to father to father, and the man who
> bought it bought nothing. (245–46)

Perplexing, it seems to me, is the repeated temporal specification—if the
property was *never* anyone's to be sold, how can it then *become* inaccessible to sale at any particular instant? Was ownership possible before one
realized land could be exchanged for money, and if so, in what sense was
it ownership? The repeated *because* makes a logical sequence of a baffling
temporality: the instant of Ikkemotubbe's realization dispossessed not only

him but also, and retroactively, his father and his father's father. Hence, what might initially appear to be a logical chain turns out, with the final *because,* to disclose entirely circular reasoning. (Causality seems to be a way of articulating an instant within a temporal progression.) Among other things at stake is the bare fact of correlation—"on that instant"—that allows realization and illegitimacy to be located in time. Correlation, however, proves to be as disruptive as it is unifying. The reflexive effects are perhaps condensed in the nonprogression signaled by paronomasia: from Ikkemotubbe to Ike, where one moves in a circle but (also) ends up at a different place from where one began.

Such recursive structures also mark Ike's descriptions of the sharecropping that displaces slavery as landowners' privileged form of exploitation—descriptions in which, against Ike's claims about property, merely to perceive the circularity has little purchase on the oppressive structure:

> The desk and the shelf above it on which rested the ledgers in which McCaslin recorded the slow outward trickle of food and supplies and equipment which returned each fall as cotton made and ginned and sold (two threads frail as truth and impalpable as equators yet cable-strong to bind for life them who made the cotton to the land their sweat fell on), and the older ledgers clumsy and archaic in size and shape, on the yellowed pages of which were recorded in the faded hand of his father Theophilus and his uncle Amodeus during the two decades before the Civil War, the manumission in title at least of Caruthers McCaslin's slaves. (245; see also 281)

The effect of the remarkable simile could be conceptualized as another instance of the collating of unrelated figural systems. On the one hand, "frail as truth and impalpable as equators" signals the abstraction of trade based on money, an abstraction that alienates labor and links the exploitation described to symbolization or (in the text's more general figuration) writing. On the other, equators (which return later in Ike's reference to God's using a "simple egg to discover to them a new world where a nation of people could be founded in humility and pity and sufferance and pride of one to another" [247]) figure a closed circuit (like the round earth—without, in human time at least, imagined corners). In that figure, the movement around the world (like the movement of slaves, materials, and goods from Africa to the New World and between the Old and the New

Worlds) stands in for the food and supplies turned to cotton, whose material characteristics no doubt also suggest frailty and impalpability. In the first system, embodiment might seem to be an antidote for abstraction; direct exchange, it is possible to imagine, could make labor cease to be alienated. The second system, however, makes clear that there is no opposition between abstraction and embodiment. The sweat that falls on the land binds the exploited laborers to it, becoming another form of impalpable but cable-strong threads.

Repudiation, Eternity, Epiphany, Redemption

Ike wants to escape this closed circuit, and he attempts to do so, as the rest of "The Bear" demonstrates, through a more authentic, unabstracted relation to the land. The sweat that falls on the ground mimics ownership, and Ike's circular reasoning (it was never mine to repudiate because it was never father's because it was never anyone's: "The man who bought it bought nothing") seems perilously close in form to the equators. The redemption that Ike attempts to effect through repudiation proceeds according to a not entirely dissimilar logic, through correlation: linking what is repeatedly called Eunice's "repudiation" (259) (her suicide) to his own (repudiation, not of life but of property), for example, or his "I'm free" with Fonsiba's (285, 268).[27] Submitting the atemporal instant of the animal to a temporal system that can call it "anachronism" or subsuming the various temporalities of "The Bear" to a unifying narrative of character development is thus not unlike the system of exploitation Ike would escape. The image later of the stereopticon could, in this sense, be read as an image for exchange as ownership, for correlation as redemption, and for the text's own mechanisms: "As the stereopticon condenses into one instantaneous field the myriad minutia of its scope, so did that slight and rapid gesture establish . . ." (284).[28] The forms of the *Bildungsroman* or coming-of-age story are thus intimately related to the redemption that Ike tries to effect, for they, too, try to superimpose two times (thereby producing "the appearance of solidity"), to make the narration and the narrated time into a single stereoscopic image.

Whereas "anachronism" attempts to link disjoint temporalities on a common scale, the redemption Ike seeks proceeds by rephrasing the ex nihilo appearance of the animal—its time unassimilable to that of narrative—as "eternity." And eternity will finally bring us to the epiphanic vision of unity that (almost) closes this section of the text. In this logic, the buck Ike shoots in "The Old People" is immortal: "The wagon wound and jolted between the slow and shifting yet constant walls from beyond and above which the wilderness watched them pass, less than inimical now and never to be inimical again since the buck still and forever leaped, the shaking gun-barrels coming constantly and forever steady at last, crashing, and still out of his instant of immortality, the buck sprang, forever immortal" (171).

Thus the end of "The Bear" rewrites *Paradise Lost* (minus Eve). Encountering a snake in a wilderness doomed to destruction leads Ike not to the Fall but to a sense of immortality and eternal continuity: Ike salutes the snake as Sam Fathers did the ghostly deer in "The Old People" (314). Ike's grandfather, and what we know of him, perhaps makes one wonder, a little, if the salute might have sardonic intent, if not on Ike's part then on the story's. In any event, one question (and a way to phrase the problem of the text's ending) is whether the salute presents a synthesis of two belief systems (where "the Fall" takes the place of Sam's ancestors) or a jarring collision of incompatible contexts. If "The Bear" is the "best environmental novel ever written," it is so, for many, because the salute marks the culminating moment of an ecological lesson, one that ostensibly redeems both the history of slavery and the ecological disaster destroying the world of Ike's childhood. (As a possibly ironic consequence, Ike, in this scene, is perfectly oriented, thanks to his training by Sam Fathers and the bear, in a world that no longer exists.) This culminating moment could thus be read as the transcendence of property relations and of human time in a vision of the eternity of nature. The markers of the logging company are "lifeless and shockingly alien in that place where dissolution itself was a seething turmoil of ejaculation tumescence conception and birth, and death did not even exist" (312). The disappearance of the woods is rewritten as the disappearance of the graves into the woods ("there was no trace of the two graves anymore at all" [312]), and if one momentarily wonders whether "death did not even exist" is the metaphysical assertion it seems to be or merely a literal assertion that the specific graves have vanished, that wavering would seem to be resolved by the epiphany that follows: the peppermint candy Ike leaves for Sam is gone, too,

> not vanished but merely translated into the myriad life which
> printed the dark mold of these secret and sunless places with

delicate fairy tracks, which, breathing and biding and immobile, watched him from beyond every twig and leaf until he
moved, moving again, walking on; he had not stopped, he had
only paused, quitting the knoll which was no abode of the dead
because there was no death, not Lion and not Sam: not held fast
in earth but free in earth and not in earth but of earth, myriad yet
undiffused of every myriad part, leaf and twig and particle, air
and sun and rain and dew and night, acorn oak and leaf and acorn
again, dark and dawn and dark and dawn again in their immu-
table progression and, being myriad, one: and Old Ben too, Old
Ben too; they would give him his paw back even, certainly they
would give him his paw back: then the long challenge and the long
chase, no heart to be driven and outraged, no flesh to be mauled
and bled. (313)

"Not in earth but of earth": to become part of the earth is to experience
a dissolution that paradoxically leaves one intact, "myriad yet undiffused
of every myriad part"; disintegration, by making one a part of the earth,
also makes one whole. The loss of flesh turns death to transcendence: a
vision of redemption, a secular Assumption. Likewise, the timelessness of
the buck has seemingly been assimilated to eternity, has been in this sense
redeemed, and Ike's biblical language in his discussion with McCaslin has
been reconciled with the lessons of Sam Fathers. The moment could be
read as unifying the disparate registers of the text in a timeless vision of
redemption. Such, one might say, is Ike's education in the wild.

"The Bear," of course, does not end here, just as *Go Down, Moses* does
not end with "The Bear"—nor even with "Delta Autumn."[29] Instead, "The
Bear" ends with a bathetic scene with Boon Hogganbeck, banging like
a madman on his dismantled gun, seated beneath a tree swarming with
trapped squirrels. The section's final line—"Get out of here! . . . They're
mine!" (315)—explicitly punctures the epiphany that precedes it, reassert-
ing the claims of property (as if, perhaps, Ike's confrontation with a potentially lethal snake has left him unable to redeem death or to view the
dissolution of the self into myriad life with the placidity he initially seems
to). It therefore also unsettles the reconciliation of the various temporal
strands in the story—most immediately, unsettled is the possibility of narrating the time of nature, and thus of redeeming, by narrating as epiphany

or lesson, both natural destruction and the historical inheritance of the treatment of human beings as property.

This is the form of redemption as it is stated in "Delta Autumn," where it begins to be troubled, if only because it marks a repetition:

> Then suddenly he knew why he had never wanted to own any of it, arrest at least that much of what people call progress, measure his longevity at least against that much of its ultimate fate. It was because there was just exactly enough of it. He seemed to see the two of them—himself and the wilderness—as coevals, his own span as a hunter, woodsman, not contemporary with his first breath but transmitted to him, assumed by him gladly, humbly, with joy and pride, from that old Major de Spain and that old Sam Fathers who taught him to hunt, the two spans running out together, not toward oblivion, nothingness, but into a dimension free of both time and space where once more the untreed land warped and wrung to mathematical squares of rank cotton for the frantic old-world people to turn into shells to shoot at one another, would find ample room for both—the names, the faces of the old men he had known and loved and for a little while outlived, moving again among the shades of the tall unaxed trees and sightless brakes where the wild strong immortal game ran forever before the tireless and belling immortal hounds, falling and rising phoenix-like to the soundless guns. (337–38)

In an effect not unlike that of the stereopticon, immortality appears through the correlation of different temporal measures: not only that of his life and those of the men he loved, but also that of human life and the time of the woods. One cannot be "coeval" with the woods, and it will do nothing to detract from the beauty of the passage to say that the resolution is unearned and registers, in "Delta Autumn," as a delusion. The problem, in brief, is that the atemporal structure of redemption is indistinguishable from an atavistic repetition. On the one hand, this moment marks the culmination of the promise of an earlier image of the Delta—an image in which driving into the Delta becomes a journey back in time, and in which the Delta's own cycles (as the river flows into the sea, and the sea, back into the river) become a hopeful figure for regeneration, as if the time that has obliterated the Mississippi forests could flow backward as the river does, and as Ike's mind does in the narration of his past:

> In caravan they ground on through the ceaselessly dissolving afternoon, with skid-chains on the wheels now, lurching and splashing and sliding among the ruts, until presently it seemed to him that the retrograde of his remembering had gained an inverse velocity from their own slow progress, that the land had retreated not in minutes from the last spread of gravel but in years, decades, back toward what it had been when he first knew it: the road they now followed once more the ancient pathway of bear and deer, the diminishing fields they now passed once more scooped punily and terrifically by axe and saw and mule-drawn plow from the wilderness' flank, out of the brooding and immemorial tangle, in place of the ruthless mile-wide parallelograms wrought by ditching and dyking machinery. (325)

On the other hand, that resolution is undermined because it intersects another form of repetition: Edmonds's incestuous interracial relation and his desertion of the mother and child repeats the act that Ike sought to redeem: Carothers Edmonds's desertion of his incestuous lover and the bequest that scandalizes Ike in "The Bear."

"Delta Autumn" seems despairing both because Ike's sense of redemption seems illusory and because, in the larger arc of the narrative of realization, he seems curiously impermeable to education: "Old man, . . . have you lived so long and forgotten so much that you don't remember anything you ever knew or felt or even heard about love?" (346). It is not just that Ike's renunciation is made to seem inhuman (leading one to reread the sections in "The Bear" about Ike's wife, for instance). His shaking as he lies in the tent in "Delta Autumn" (347) repeats that of "The Old People" and "The Bear," as if the represented education had never occurred, and therefore making the vision of "the shaking gun-barrels coming constantly and forever steady at last," and with it, the buck's immortality, seem a willful illusion. The formulation of Ike's epiphany is striking, too ("Then suddenly he knew . . ."), insofar as it suggests that Ike does not yet know what he already knew at the end of "The Bear." His intuition of the immortal hunt (achieved by the juxtaposition of "two spans") largely repeats the epiphany of "The Bear," where the different temporalities are ostensibly unified (and unified as narrative) in the natural cycles of birth, death, decay, and rebirth. A question that emerges in "Delta Autumn"—which is inevitably, too, a question of whether *Go Down, Moses* coheres as a novel or should be read as a collection of discrete stories—is whether the story's developments undermine the redemption of "The Bear" or merely make explicit the tensions within it.

Again, one can discover the seeds of the problem farther back. The reconciliation punctured by Boon's bathetic proprietary outburst is set up in stages in the story. It is striking that the elegiac descriptions of Ike's boyhood seem nostalgic less for the experience of hunting than for the talking that accompanied it, leading one to wonder what has in fact been lost with the disappearance of the older hunters and the woods if Ike can still talk (as, in "Delta Autumn," he prodigiously does). According to the text's logic, talking is like being there because, unlike writing, it is not mediated:

> He was sixteen. For six years now he had been a man's hunter. For six years now he had heard the best of all talking. It was of the wilderness, the big woods, bigger and older than any recorded document:—of white man fatuous enough to believe he had bought any fragment of it, of Indian ruthless enough to pretend that any fragment of it had been his to convey; bigger than Major de Spain and the scrap he pretended to, knowing better; older than old Thomas Sutpen of whom Major de Spain had had it and who knew better; older even than old Ikkemotubbe, the Chickasaw chief, of whom old Sutpen had had it and who knew better in his turn. (183–84)

The epiphany at the end is, arguably, framed here by the opposition between "the big woods" (with the "humility" of a true relation to them) and the presumption of owning, inheriting, or selling land—a presumption the text links to writing. The sentence structure perhaps leaves in question whether it is the woods or the talk about them that is "bigger and older than any recorded document," which thus opposes both "the best of all talking" and the woods themselves to writing—writing like the marking of property on a deed or in the family ledgers. Talking's priority over writing is linked to a physical presence—a more immediate one, and a bigger one:

the best game of all, the best of all breathing and forever the best of all listening, the voices quiet and weighty and deliberate for retrospection and recollection and exactitude among the concrete trophies—the racked guns and the heads and skins—in the libraries of town houses or the offices of plantation houses or (and best of all) in the camps themselves where the intact and still-warm meat yet hung, the men who had slain it sitting before the burning logs on hearths when there were houses and hearths or about the smoking and blazing of piled wood in front of stretched tarpaulins when there were not. (184)

When the refrain returns later in the story, it asserts the continuity of bodily experience: "He felt the old lift of the heart, as pristine as ever, as on the first day; he would never lose it, no matter how old in hunting and pursuit: the best, the best of all breathing, the humility and the pride. He must stop thinking about it" (223). The palpability of both descriptions seeks to redeem the exploitation—impalpable as equators—of property ownership. The lift of the heart links telling to the assertion of nature's eternity at the end of the text and, potentially, makes the time of the animal narratable. As before, both—and the privileging of speech and presence over writing—repeat the sweat falling on the land, which is the other thread, cable-strong, that binds the exploited, keeping them, one might say, from being "absolved." If one escapes (or thinks one escapes) the antinomy here, it is perhaps through the multiple, unhierarchized relations of subordination in the sentence. If experience seems to level the distinction between the hunt and talking about it, the long series seems to make indistinguishable libraries, offices, and the camps themselves. The protean syntax perpetually reshapes itself as one reads, so one is not sure (for instance) if it is the "voices" or the "trophies" (themselves indistinguishably guns, heads, and skins) that are "in" the libraries, offices, or camps. The long series of modifications (for . . . among . . . in . . . of . . . of . . . in . . . where . . . before . . . on . . . when, and so on) mimes the sentence's basic structure, which is to keep paired alternatives (camp or house, fire or hearth)—themselves subject to variation—in view simultaneously. A question, perhaps, is whether one registers that simultaneous perception as unification, or whether the parts remain disparate in one's stereoscopic view.

At such moments, one is led to wonder about the relation between two forms of mediation: "the best of all talking" and the forms of symbolization (represented by the ledgers) that attempt to submit land (and persons) to ownership. A similar assertion of telling's reifying power—again with speaking opposed to writing—is made early in "The Old People":[30]

> And as he talked about those old times and those dead and vanished men of another race from either that the boy knew, gradually to the boy those old times would cease to be old times and would become a part of the boy's present, not only as if they had happened yesterday but as if they were still happening, the man who walked through them actually walking in breath and air and casting an actual shadow on the earth they had not quitted. And more: as if some of them had not happened yet but would occur tomorrow, until at last it would seem to the boy that he himself had not come into existence yet, that none of his race nor the other subject race which his people had brought with them into the land had come here yet; that although it had been his grandfather's and his father's and his uncle's and was now his cousin's and someday would be his own land which he and Sam hunted over, their hold upon it was actually as trivial and without reality as the now faded and archaic script in the chancery book in Jefferson which allocated it to them and that it was he, the boy, who was a guest here and Sam Fathers' voice the mouthpiece of the host. (165)

Ike, I noted, attempts to exchange property for a story, and if—as a depiction of absorption in narrative—this moment figures the text's own power to captivate, it casts that power in redemptive terms, a power to make the vanished present, to make time go backward, to return to life the victims of history. It therefore also links narrative's temporal reversibility to the cyclical time of nature, and thus to the epiphany at the end of "The Bear" (as narrative combination and multivalent redemption). Yet again, the problem is knowing whether such transcendence can be experienced or, if experienced, can be told. One difficulty is perhaps apparent in the boy's sense that "he himself had not come into existence yet." As in the moment later in "The Bear"—"and the boy was not there"—in this assertion of telling's power to make a past present, moreover, the boy's absorption while listening to a compelling story is tied to the redemptive capacity of nature's cyclical temporality ("death did not even exist") and to a subjugated people's power to transcend the temporality of (white) history. But that multilayered redemption also erases the boy who is ostensibly the subject who learns. It is striking that the (we know, counterfactual) future posited here (Ike does not in fact inherit the land, as he does not have children, which the text speculates about at another moment) is indistinguishable from other moments of temporal telescoping; a later retrospective view and a free-indirect narration of Ike's past speculations about what his future "would" look like are made indistinct. That indeterminacy is exactly the state of absorption achieved by the stories the boy listens to—except that the vanishing "subject" is no longer the boy but the later perspective on him. It is perhaps not surprising, given all of this, that the insight baffles formulation as a lesson anyone in particular has learned, and that the epiphany achieved at the end of "The Bear" may be incompatible with its narration.

That strain is evident, too, in that the story's celebration of telling over writing and property takes a conspicuously rhetorical form: "the best of all talking . . . the best game of all, the best of all breathing, and forever the best of all listening." The parenthetical repetition of the phrase later—"in the libraries . . . or the offices . . . or (and best of all) in the camps themselves" marks a kind of transcendence (a disappearance of particularity: "best game of all . . . best of all breathing . . . best of all listening . . . best of all"). It also creates a sort of stutter—especially visible in "or (and"—while making explicit the rhetorical patterning both by violating the pattern (moving from a superlative to a comparative) and by making apparent the rhetorical inventiveness of the refrain. Listening is made analogous to breathing, which sets up the assertion of natural perseverance as bodily presence through the very rhetorical patterning that a less mediated form of speech would ostensibly circumvent. Read in this context, the epiphanic moment of "The Bear" leaves audible echoes of textuality in its phrasing of myriad life: "not vanished but merely translated into the myriad life which printed the dark mold of these secret and sunless places with delicate fairy tracks."

The hinge that allows the text—at least provisionally—to present the time of the animal as eternity and as a narratable epiphany underlying its ecological and racial redemptions is John Keats's "Ode on a Grecian Urn." That poem allows Ike to make the ex nihilo appearance of the deer and bear into images of aesthetic wholeness.[31] McCaslin reads the poem to him to explain why, when he had the chance, Ike did not shoot the bear. It is notable that the explanation is McCaslin's, not Ike's (who remains more equivocal, not to say confused, about his motives), and it is strange, too, that McCaslin focuses on the second stanza rather than the fourth, where the animal sacrifice that does not take place is perhaps closer, thematically, to "The Bear" than is unrequited love. It is also striking how lame McCaslin's gloss of the poem is—something highlighted further by his repeated, and insistently pedagogical, "Do you see now?" Two movements in Keats's poem seem especially relevant to Faulkner's text. The first is the transformation of narrative interruption in freeze-frame images into a unified image for eternity; that transition makes the aesthetic fact of the images on the urn—their status as images and their immobility—a figure for the urn's own perseverance through time (just as the instantaneous appearances of the buck and bear come to mean immortality, and just as, at the moment of the bear's death, the falling bear, with Boon and Lion, appear as "statuary").

Second, the poem's famous conclusion—often taken to be synonymous with its message, a message that is, moreover, the central lesson of the aesthetic education, and hence the lesson underlying the novel of development—is given in quotation marks. The urn figures aesthetic eternity, and gives a lesson, when it can be made to speak, and yet that proclamation is in a sense perpetually deferred—to that moment "when old age shall this generation waste," speaking its ostensibly comforting lesson "in midst of other woe / Than ours," to us insofar as we are not there.[32] Only by inhabiting a world after our disappearance does the urn cease to be a "silent form" for us. That the "silent form" speaks unites the spoken couplet with the "unheard" melodies that, in the poem's conceit, figure aesthetic apprehension (therefore, too, both the difference between an urn and a poem and the surmounting of that difference). The voice of the silent form in the midst of other woe than ours is the voice of the poem. To the very extent that the poem itself achieves immortality, the reference of "this generation" will remain a present deixis, therefore leaving its speech perpetually deferred until after a wasting that is perpetually yet-to-occur. ("that is all / Ye know on Earth, and all ye need to know" can therefore feel more than a little privative, and in more than one way.) Ike's vision of "the shades of the tall unaxed trees and sightless brakes where the wild strong immortal game ran forever before the tireless and belling immortal hounds, falling and rising phoenix-like to the soundless guns" asserts the perpetuation of the woods by aestheticizing them, by making them one of the unheard melodies of Keats's poem. (The assimilation of registers is visible in the double entendres of "shades of . . . unaxed trees" and "sightless brakes," which oscillate between physical description and ghostly [or dead] presences.)

The closing epiphany of "The Bear" seems to quote Keats, turning the unfading girl to a transcendent nature, and Keats's "happy boughs" that cannot shed their leaves to forms that defy death by shedding them: "Then he was in the woods, not alone but solitary: the solitude closed about him, green with summer. They did not change, and, timeless, would not, anymore than would the green of summer and the fire and rain of fall and the iron cold and sometimes even snow" (308). The grammatical suspension in the sentence (where summer and fall seem to be parallel to "sometimes even snow," possibly because of an omitted "of winter") is paired with another kind of suspension: a three-page memory of hunting with Ash after he killed his first deer that interrupts the epiphanic language. After that interruption, the seasons return: "—; summer, and fall, and snow, and wet and saprife spring in their ordered immortal sequence, the deathless and immemorial phases of the mother who had shaped him" (311). The assertion that "still the woods would be his mistress and his wife" points to the substitution of natural cycles for the unrequited love in Keats ("*He's talking about a girl*" [283]). Also striking is the interruption itself (like, perhaps, the beautiful substitution of "snow" as a metonymy for "winter"). Here is Ike's own rendering of why he did not shoot:

> somehow it had seemed simpler than that, simpler than somebody talking in a book about a young man and a girl he would never need to grieve over because he could never approach any nearer and would never have to get any further away. He had heard about an old bear and finally got big enough to hunt it and he hunted it four years and at last met it with a gun in his hands and he didn't shoot. Because a little dog—But he could have shot long before the fyce covered the twenty yards to where the bear waited. (284)

Hearing about an old bear is opposed to "talking in a book," but I am also struck by the suspended sentence, "Because a little dog—" (a little dog "nameless and mongrel and many-fathered"). On one level, the text mimics thought or speech, and the thought is suspended because Ike dismisses the explanation of the dog even as he raises it ("But he could have shot"). But the interruption leaves us with the mere positing of the little dog and mimics in form the interruption of the epiphany later—and likewise the tonally jarring end of "The Bear" itself.

Ruined Totalities and the Ventriloquism of Grief: The Thwarted Lessons of "Pantaloon in Black"

In one reading, then, the invocation of Keats's poem assimilates the intuition of nature's deathless renewal to a perception of aesthetic plenitude, and that perception enables the redemption of the story Ike reads in the ledgers. His renunciation is, in this reading, a positing of an aesthetic whole (or a "globalizing term," in the vocabulary I used to describe the movements of Faulkner's prose). It unifies the stories of *Go Down, Moses*— ecological destruction, "race" or the history of slavery and the genocidal conquest of native peoples, and experiences of initiation and learning— and redeems them in a narrative of *Bildung,* or developing insight. It is therefore striking that *Go Down, Moses* perpetually ruins its own aesthetic unifications. The tonally puncturing end of "The Bear" is one example; that of "Delta Autumn" is another. But the most notable ruined whole is, of course, nothing other than *Go Down, Moses* itself, which is at once a novel and a collection of loosely related stories. As John Limon points out, the problem section is "Pantaloon in Black," where the McCaslin–Edmonds– Beauchamp clan appears only as almost unnamed owners of the land on which the story of Rider—in many other ways a tonal departure from the rest of the text—takes place; whether or not *Go Down, Moses* is a novel, Limon writes, depends "on the success one has in integrating 'Pantaloon in Black' into it" ("The Integration of Faulkner's *Go Down, Moses,*" 421). The quandaries I have been describing in "The Bear" are condensed in the story, largely as effects of voice. It is all the more striking, therefore, that the formal coherence of this particular story also poses the question of the possibility of transmission—what Limon brilliantly shows is the impossibility of understanding Rider.[33] The first half of the story offers a wrenchingly beautiful evocation of grief, only then to turn, jarringly, in the second half to an oblivious sheriff's deputy who, moreover, fails to convey even his limited understanding to his hurried (and possibly even-more-awful) wife. That Rider's grief fails entirely to register for him beyond the crudest of racial stereotypes is condensed by a movement that is perhaps the inverse of the coalescences and assimilations of the rest of the text, as the deputy tells the story to his wife:

> "Ketcham went in and begun peeling away niggers until he could see him laying there under the pile of them, laughing, with tears big as glass marbles running across his face and down past his ears and making a kind of popping sound on the floor like somebody dropping bird eggs, laughing and laughing and saying, 'Hit look lack Ah just cant quit thinking. Look lack Ah just cant quit.' And what do you think of that?"
>
> "I think if you eat any supper in this house you'll do it in the next five minutes," his wife said from the dining room. "I'm going to clear this table then and I'm going to the picture show." (154)

The ostensibly redemptive aestheticization of death at the end of "The Bear" here turns tears to "glass marbles"—tears that, falling, moreover, perhaps evoke the threads, cable-strong, that bind exploited people to the earth. The repetition of *think* dramatizes a series of failed transmissions insofar as it fails to cohere in a singular register of meaning.[34] That each person seems to mean something different by the term makes manifest the untransmissibility of interior states.

That untransmissibility is also thematized by the use of dialect: the deputy's ventriloquizing of Rider's utterances discomfitingly echoes the story's own. For also notable earlier is the contrast between Rider's own words and the story's renderings of his emotions (perhaps better, of the world as it appears beside those emotions, or, as it were, startled by them into appearing). Among many other instances:

> "Hah," he said. "Dat's right. Try me. Try me, big boy. Ah gots something hyar now dat kin whup you."
>
> And, once free of the bottom's unbreathing blackness, there was the moon again, his long shadow and that of the lifted jug slanting away as he drank and then held the jug poised, gulping the silver air into his throat until he could breathe again, speaking to the jug: "Come on now. You always claimed you's a better man den me. Come on now. Prove it." He drank again, swallowing the chill liquid tamed of taste or heat either while the swallowing lasted, feel-

ing it flow solid and cold with fire, past then enveloping the strong steady panting of his lungs until they too ran suddenly free as his moving body ran in the silver solid wall of air he breasted. (143)

That the story shares with the deputy this common mode of ventriloquism is distressing, for part of what is so moving about the first section of the text is the contrast between Rider's inarticulateness and the grief that is conveyed by the evocative power of the narration, not so much to describe grief as to describe the natural world—in ways that, at least until section two, do not immediately strike one as appropriative.[35]

This is also because grief makes Rider experience his own voice as ventriloquized. To my mind, the "navel" of the story is Rider's plea to the ghost of his wife:

But this time as soon as he moved she began to fade. He stopped at once, not breathing again, motionless, willing his eyes to see that she had stopped too. But she had not stopped. She was fading, going. "Wait," he said, talking as sweet as he had ever heard his voice speak to a woman: "Den lemme go wid you, honey." But she was going. (136)

What is almost unbearably moving about this moment is not only the simplicity of the desire and not only the apostrophe (as a mode of address that makes manifest the absence it also claims to surmount) in the form of an intimate term of endearment. Nor is it simply the contrast between the gentleness of the imploring and the "blood and bones and flesh too strong" (137)—the embodiment that, even were he not so hyperbolically strong, separates him from Mannie, no matter how much he wills himself to be "motionless" and not to breathe. Perhaps most evocative is the externalization of Rider's view of himself—"talking as sweet as he had ever heard his voice speak to a woman"—where it is not just that he hears himself speak but that "his voice" takes on an agency separate from his own, as if hearing his voice were for him a different, and separable, experience from that of talking. When the story—and perhaps even the deputy—renders (with markers of dialect) his voice as others would hear him, the effect is therefore not necessarily opposed to Rider's own experience of grief.

The story's language, I noted, often counterposes Rider's inarticulate speech against a natural world seemingly startled into appearance by his grief. The ventriloquism and that contrast replay Rider's own wish: for his too-strong breathing flesh to merge with "the bottom's unbreathing blackness." The deputy's ventriloquism is diametrically opposed to this evocation of grief. The story's disruption of the unity of its point of view—its switch to the sheriff's deputy and his failed effort to interest his wife in Rider's story—dramatizes a failure of transmission, of the very grief that the story has itself just movingly conveyed. But as this moment with Mannie suggests, such a failure *is* in some sense the story's moving depiction of grief. Another astonishing moment figures this paradoxical form of transmission. Rider leaves Mannie's funeral to return to their house:

> It was middle dusk when he emerged from [the woods] and crossed the last field, stepping over that fence too in one stride, into the lane. It was empty at this hour of Sunday evening—no family in wagon, no rider, no walkers churchward to speak to him and carefully refrain from looking after him when he had passed— the pale, powder-light, powder-dry dust of August from which the long week's marks of hoof and wheel had been blotted by the strolling and unhurried Sunday shoes, with somewhere beneath them, vanished but not gone, fixed and held in the annealing dust, the narrow, splay-toed prints of his wife's bare feet where on Saturday afternoons she walked to the commissary to buy their next week's supplies while he took his bath; himself, his own prints, setting the period now as he strode on, moving almost as fast as a smaller man could have trotted, his body breasting the air her body had vacated, his eyes touching the objects—post and tree and field and house and hill—her eyes had lost. (133)

Rider's loss is conveyed by a moving series of erasures: the road is empty except for the traces of vanished traffic, which in turn take the form of layers of obliterated traces—Mannie's prints lost among the weekday marks of hoof and wheel that have themselves been "blotted" by the churchgoers. "The absence itself," Limon writes, "is absent (as Mannie is first a ghost and then an absent ghost), and all is dust" ("The Integration of Faulkner's *Go Down, Moses*," 433). The footprints extend the repeated synecdoches: marks of hoof and wheel, "the strolling and unhurried Sunday shoes." (Later, it is likewise his prints that move.) The tender evocation of "the narrow, splay-toed prints of his wife's bare feet"—where the synecdoche, again, gives way to a vanished trace—makes her present as vanished: "Somewhere beneath them, vanished but not gone, fixed and held in the annealing dust." *Annealing* leads one to imagine the print baked or fired, as in clay, yet the image seems more paradoxically to assert that the print is preserved in its very vanishing—as *blotted* could mean both "blotted out" and "set," as ink might be. (Likewise, at the beginning of the passage, those figures not on the road are made present as absences, as negations.)

The rhythmical beauty of the prose relies on a similar effect. That beauty centers on the pairing of "his body breasting the air her body had vacated" with "his eyes touching the objects . . . her eyes had lost." The various effects of the sentence—the contrast between her absence and the presence of the objects emphasized by the repeated conjunctions uniting monosyllabic nouns ("post and tree and field and house and hill"); the parallels ("his body . . . her body . . . his eyes . . . her eyes") that link his body to present progressive and hers to past perfect verb forms; the rendering of his loss of her as *her* loss of the world; the further attenuation of possible action for her in the movement from *vacated* to *lost*; even the curious formulation of "his eyes touching," which creates an immediacy of sense perception that is taken from her—are, as it were, annealed by the rhythmical pairing of "her body had vacated" and "her eyes had lost." The beauty of that last phrase depends largely, I think, on the trochee of *body* and the dactyl of *vacated,* which lead one to expect analogous forms—so that *eyes* and (especially) *lost* take on a greater emphasis because of the two- and three-syllable rhythms we hear behind them. In that rhythmical echo, the fact that we hear *lost* with the three syllables of *vacated* keeping time behind or under it, it is as if we hear the footprints "somewhere beneath them, vanished but not gone, fixed and held in the annealing dust."

Another curious detail is the appearance of *rider* as a common noun in the list of those not on the road, which echoes the perplexing moment just before Rider kills the man at the dice game: "one who was called Rider and was Rider standing above the squatting circle" (147). Limon convincingly reads this moment in terms of namelessness and failed community; it "implies that for his six months of married life, he had been called but had not been 'Rider.' All the antirites of 'Pantaloon in Black' fail to give Rider a new name for a new stage of his life, and 'Rider' brings him back to an old one" ("The Integration of Faulkner's *Go Down, Moses,*" 433). The earlier moment, where *Rider,* who has just been addressed by "his aunt's messenger" ("Wait, Rider," 133), is shadowed by a common noun that mimes his name, likewise points to a malfunctioning of naming. A Rider that becomes "no rider" (where, rather, "no rider" bodies forth the failure-to-appear of the proper name) perhaps evokes the generalizing of "Ike" to "a boy" or of "an old man" to "and the boy was not there." As with the double narrative of "Was," the stakes of that disappearance are in each case different, and the effect of the double articulation is to suggest that Ike strives to redeem a history of disenfranchisement by repeating it. (We find a particularly economical formulation of this structure in "Delta Autumn," where the woman says to Ike, "James Beauchamp—you called him Tennie's Jim though he had a name—was my grandfather. I said you were Uncle Isaac" [344]. That Ike initially misunderstands—hears what we might call "the communal anonymity of brotherhood," the anti-Oedipal avuncular world that makes him "uncle to half the county and [still] father to no one" instead of a specific familial reference—points, for her, to a different history: "you called him Tennie's Jim, though he had a name.")

Naming and the Question of Queer Reading

To focus on names and namelessness brings to the fore—even with just a few examples—its structure of noncommunicating or noncoordinated oppositions. Uncle Ike escapes the name by dint of having too many; Tennie's Jim (né James Beauchamp) is deprived of one, where that deprivation is a cipher not for communal anonymity but for a radical disenfranchisement. That Rider (aka "Spoot," aka, perhaps, a name we never learn) does not have a name (and, raised by an aunt and uncle, cannot remember his parents [132]) can be read in relation to Tennie's Jim and his namelessness or, in another way, to Ike and his renunciation, but in many ways it is not analogous to either. Old Ben—unlike the "men myriad and nameless even to one another"—has "earned" a name. And in "Delta Autumn," names are the cipher for a genocidal European expansion and for the disappearance of the land and the "old time" alike:

> the land across which there came now no scream of panther but instead the long hooting of locomotives: trains of incredible length and drawn by a single engine, since there is no gradient anywhere and no elevations save those raised by forgotten aboriginal hands as refuges from the yearly water and used by their Indian successors to sepulchre their fathers' bones, and all that remained

of that old time were the Indian names on the little towns and usually pertaining to water—Aluschaskuna, Tillatoba, Homochitto,
Yazoo. (325)[36]

In localized moments, it is possible to articulate coherent relations among
these different forms of naming and namelessness. The kinds of contradictions that appear, however, when one attempts a more globalizing coordination, or even when one traverses certain conceptual pairings, points
to a larger structure of noncommunicating systems. That structure poses
problems for any reading of the text as a novel of development, or for articulation of a synthesizing version of the text's take on race, sexuality, history, consciousness, and the natural world.

The difficulty therefore extends beyond even the contradiction between
the contexts of the avuncular anti-Oedipal world that Ike attempts to coordinate with the timeless renewal of the natural world and with the disappearance of the name that is the heritage of slavery. "Pantaloon in Black,"
Limon writes,

> is the inverse of the parable, if a parable is based on the disparity
> between a story and its significance, a disparity which dissolves at
> the precise moment the story's interpreter joins the community
> (his understanding of the significance *equals* his admission to the
> community). The meaning—or let us better say the lesson—of the
> story "Pantaloon in Black" is apparent enough, and is what I have
> been describing; but the story itself, the story of which the lesson is
> that we cannot understand such stories—is what I do not have and
> cannot have, given the failure of a community to cohere in which
> Rider—or consequently, Faulkner—can manipulate signs to make
> his grief intelligible. Of course, it is always possible simply not
> to care about what I have called "the story"; we can even call our
> inability to understand the story, "the story." ("The Integration of
> Faulkner's *Go Down, Moses*," 436–37)

It seems to me that *Go Down, Moses* is also such a parable. As such, it poses
a particular challenge to an account of queer transmission, and one that
goes beyond even the rhyme between an avuncular queer utopia and the
radical voiding of property by the dehumanizing proprieties of slavery:
the question of whether the paradoxical transmission through thwarted

transmission I have charted in this book can avoid becoming another form of synthesis. The risk is perhaps especially clear at those moments where the potentialization of narrative—the text's imagining of counter-factual futures for Ike, for instance, perhaps even its foregrounding of the incompatibility of *Bildung* and its narration, which consigns the text (as *Bildungsroman*) to a sort of potentialization in the very realization of its epiphanic "lesson"—appears itself to be offered as a redemption of the history of "race," appears to replay Ike's globalizing renunciation even as it suspends it. Another way to phrase the "parable" of *Go Down, Moses*: Can close reading remain faithful to a text? Can it resist becoming mere theory? Can queer theory allow one to think its outside? Rider's untransmissible grief—"the story" we do not get, and in a sense the grief the text conveys as inexpressible—offers an image for queer transmission and therefore leads one to wonder whether it is possible to trace the impossibility, repeatedly thematized in the text, of assimilating initiation or knowledge to their narration, without thereby turning story's failure into "the story," without thereby unifying the disjunctive registers of the text in another globalizing term and thus repeating, at another level, Isaac McCaslin's equivocal, com-promised gesture of redemption.

Acknowledgments

No book can be written without the help of many others, and to pretend to acknowledge that help carries risks beyond that of forgetting essential people: that one might expose a hidden desire to contain, within bounds, an indebtedness one also seeks thereby to have done with is perhaps less troubling than the possibility that one might, in the bombast of confessed indebtedness, reveal a worse imposition, that of seeking to make others' generosity the evidence of an achievement worthy of it. Nevertheless, I cannot pass over these debts in silence. Antonín Dvořák, learning of the death of Josefina Čermáková, revised the end of the third movement of his Cello Concerto in B Minor, adding the melody from his song "Laßt mich allein," which she had loved. According to Yo-Yo Ma (whose source seems to be the conductor David Alan Miller), Dvořák wrote of this revision that those who knew him would understand; for those who did not, he continued, it did not matter. Those who know me will understand.

This book began its life as an undergraduate seminar at Boston College; thanks to the students who made it one of the best classes I have ever taught—especially Megan Holmberg, Tyler Thompson, and Chris Kramaric. Crucial material support was provided by a Research Incentive Grant at Boston College, by the College of Arts and Sciences at Boston College, and by a fellowship from the John Simon Guggenheim Memorial Foundation. At the University of Minnesota Press, thanks once again to Richard Morrison for his lucid and tactful advice, and to Erin Warholm-Wohlenhaus. Thanks also to Nicholas de Villiers and to the other outside reader for the Press for their generous and constructive suggestions for the manuscript. I am also grateful to Kathy Delfosse for her meticulous and invariably thoughtful copyediting and to Megan Holmberg for the lucid and subtle attention she brought to the preparation of the index.

Sections of the book were presented at Cornell University, Columbia University, Indiana University, Williams College, Boston College, and Boston University and at a series of conferences, including MLA and Narrative. Thanks to my hosts, to the organizers of panels, and to the audiences who responded generously to my work. Among those hosts, and among those who read and commented on chapters, who talked to me about ideas I developed here, who asked suggestive questions, who provided research assistance, and who helped me in more indirect (but often not insubstantial) ways: David Agruss, Ash Anderson, Eva Badowska, Caetlin Benson-Allott, Ti Bodenheimer, Mary Crane, Matt DeLuca, Andy Donnelly, Mary Favret, Zach Forsberg-Lary, Katherine Franke, Jim Giguere, Hollis Griffin, Dan Humphrey, Kristin Imre, Sean Keilen, Greg Kenny, Jim Kincaid, Niko Kolodny, Andrew Kuhn, Rob Lehman, Katherine Lieber, Emma Limon, John Lurz, Ellen McCallum, Madhavi Menon, Andrew H. Miller, James Najarian, Rob Odom, Reeve Parker, Joe Rezek, Jake Russin, Eric Savoy, Karen Swann, Mikko Tuhkanen, Dagmar van Engen, Georgia Warnke, Audrey Wasser, Carolyn Williams, and Yin Yuan. Once again—and particularly because this book is so much taken up with close reading—I want to thank those who taught me to read and write, especially Cynthia Chase, Steve Fix, Ellis Hanson, and Chris Pye. If I don't do either well, it is not their fault; they could not have done more. John Limon read both chapters on Faulkner when they were at their longest and most inchoate; the sheer number of pages would be enough to warrant separate mention, even had he not also been so lucid helping me see the point of what I had written.

It scarcely seems decent to thank those friends who have made my immediate world livable, but I risk the presumption because not to thank them, once thanks were being given, would be unthinkable: Henry Russell Bergstein, Katherine Biers, Amy Foerster, David Kurnick, Joe Nugent, Kolin Ohi, Derí Ó'hUiginn, Frances Restuccia, and Oleg Tcherny. Nor does it seem decent to thank my mother, Dee Ohi, who gave me my first, and most important, training in reading and literary transmission. A few of this book's many debts to Daniel Heller-Roazen are made explicit in the text; the true extent of those debts he knows, and it is a pleasure for me to know in turn that I need not try to say how unimaginable it would be to have written this book without him. Because they are dogs, what Milly and Seymour Bergstein know of my gratitude or my love will be neither augmented nor diminished by anything I write here; I am nevertheless grateful for the solace of their company ("because a little dog—").

Finally, however strange it might seem to dedicate to my father a book that is, at least in part, about non-Oedipal forms of transmission, that may be precisely the point: for shared music, and for the many adventures of thought that his example and presence have made possible for me, this book is dedicated to Jim Ohi.

Notes

Introduction

1. Wordsworth, *The Prelude*, bk. 5, line 164 (in both 1805 and 1850 versions), in *William Wordsworth: The Prelude, 1799, 1805, 1850*, ed. Jonathan Wordsworth, M. H. Abrams, and Stephen Gill (New York: W. W. Norton, 1979), 160–61.

2. Daniel Heller-Roazen, "Tradition's Destruction: On the Library of Alexandria," *October* 100 (Spring 2002): 133–53, 133. The idea for this book began with my reading of this article; the book is also indebted to Heller-Roazen, *Echolalias: On the Forgetting of Language* (New York: Zone Books, 2005).

3. The quotation in this passage is from Walter Benjamin, *Gesammelte Schriften,* ed. Rolf Tiedemann and Schweppenhäuser, vol. 2, pt. 1 (Frankfurt am Main: Suhrkamp, 1972–89), 204; Heller-Roazen's translation.

4. Eve Kosofsky Sedgwick, *Epistemology of the Closet* (Berkeley: University of California Press, 1990).

5. Cited by Alfred Kazin, "Jews," *New Yorker,* March 7, 1994, 62–73, 68; New Yorker Digital Archive, http://www.newyorker.com/magazine/1994/03/07/jews. It is possible that Kazin's source is James Atlas, "Chicago's Grumpy Guru," *New York Times Magazine,* January 3, 1988, http://www.nytimes.com/1988/01/03/magazine/chicago-s-grumpy-guru.html.

6. See Eve Kosofsky Sedgwick, "The Beast in the Closet: James and the Writing of Homosexual Panic," in *Epistemology of the Closet,* 180–212. Scholars have pointed out that this structure is markedly different for women. See especially Sharon Marcus, *Between Women: Friendship, Desire, and Marriage in Victorian England* (Princeton: Princeton University Press, 2007).

7. See especially Eve Kosofsky Sedgwick, "Paranoid Reading/Reparative Reading," in *Touching Feeling: Affect, Pedagogy, Performativity* (Durham, N.C.: Duke University Press, 2003), and Sedgwick, *The Weather in Proust,* ed. Jonathan Goldberg (Durham, N.C.: Duke University Press, 2012).

8. See Sedgwick, *Epistemology of the Closet,* and Lee Edelman, *Homographesis: Essays in Gay Literary and Cultural Theory* (New York: Routledge, 1994).

9. This paragraph is indebted to Katherine Biers.

10. For a reading of Sedgwick's "Jane Austen and the Masturbating Girl" that emphasizes a different side to her pedagogy than the one usually celebrated (as "enabling," for instance) in accounts of her writing, see Bonnie Blackwell, " 'O,

Soften Him! Or Harden Me!': Childbirth, Torture, and Technology in Richardson's *Pamela*," *Genders* 28 (1998), http://www.genders.org/g28/g28_osoftenhim.html. "I believe that the erotic trajectory which gives shape and energy to 'Jane Austen and the Masturbating Girl,'" Blackwell writes, "is a seduction whereby readers are lured into a theater for pleasure, and then punished for seeking it there" (para. 59). See also Heather Love, "Truth and Consequences: On Paranoid Reading and Reparative Reading," *Criticism: A Quarterly for Literature and the Arts* 52, no. 2 (2010): 235–41.

11. Kevin Ohi, *Henry James and the Queerness of Style* (Minneapolis: University of Minnesota Press, 2011), 28.

12. One specific sexual and historical context that is largely absent from this book is the history of HIV/AIDS, which, Nicholas de Villiers pointed out to me, is unfortunately invoked by the term *transmission*. Certainly, there would be much to say about the forms of discontinuity the epidemic has created in modern queer culture, as well as about the kinds of affiliation and the unexpected consequent sense of continuity for (some) survivors, and about how the history of the epidemic shapes contemporary understandings of queer history and transmission. Such a discussion, however, is beyond the scope of this book, and is, frankly, something better undertaken by someone with different sensibilities (and forms of expertise) than mine. For a consideration of (among other things) *transmission* in both senses, see Leo Bersani, "Shame on You," in Bersani and Adam Phillips, *Intimacies* (Chicago: University of Chicago Press, 2008), 31–56.

13. Lee Edelman, *No Future: Queer Theory and the Death Drive* (Durham, N.C.: Duke University Press, 2004).

14. D. A. Miller, *Place for Us: Essay on the Broadway Musical* (Cambridge, Mass.: Harvard University Press, 1998).

15. On this last point, see also the beginning of Elaine Scarry's *On Beauty and Being Just* (Princeton: Princeton University Press, 1999). I discuss Miller's *Place for Us* in greater detail in chapter 1.

16. See, among other examples, Carolyn Dinshaw, *How Soon Is Now? Medieval Texts, Amateur Readers, and the Queerness of Time* (Durham, N.C.: Duke University Press, 2012); Elizabeth Freeman, *Time Binds: Queer Temporalities, Queer Histories* (Durham, N.C.: Duke University Press, 2010); Jane Gallop, *The Deaths of the Author: Reading and Writing in Time* (Durham, N.C.: Duke University Press, 2011); E. L. McCallum and Mikko Tuhkanen, eds., *Queer Times, Queer Becomings* (Buffalo: SUNY Press, 2011); and Peter Coviello, *Tomorrow's Parties: Sex and the Untimely in Nineteenth-Century America* (New York: New York University Press, 2013).

17. Lauren Berlant, *Cruel Optimism* (Durham, N.C.: Duke University Press, 2011); Judith Halberstam, *The Queer Art of Failure* (Durham, N.C.: Duke University Press, 2011). Halberstam's account of forgetting would be relevant to my argument, though her emphasis (I take it, a salutary valorizing of forgetting) differs

from mine not only because my context here is literary tradition, specifically, but also because my interest is in forgetting as a paradoxical mode of preservation. On forgetting, see Halberstam, *The Queer Art of Failure,* 69–86.

18. This may be the place to register that the queer tradition explored in this book is largely a male one, extending from Plato to Faulkner. I have resisted limiting the claims by gender (referring, for instance, to "gay male literary transmission") because I think the book's arguments—especially the general sense of the queerness of literary transmission but, to some extent, also the conveying of a specifically queer tradition—could also illuminate writing by women. The question of men's appropriation of female voices comes up explicitly in chapter 3, on Swinburne, and indeed, Sappho is a prime instance of the dynamic of queer transmission as I describe it here. Partly, the focus on a "male" tradition is an accident of my particular erotic and literary investments. Partly, it is an accident. At one time, the book was to have included chapters on John Donne's self-conscious appropriation of a female voice in "Valediction: Of the Book," on George Eliot, on Virginia Woolf, and on Anne Carson. But, partly, too, it is a consequence of the particular aesthetic tradition (again, starting with Plato) that underlies the thinking about tradition that I trace.

19. See, for example, Eve Kosofsky Sedgwick, "Queer and Now," in *Tendencies* (Durham, N.C.: Duke University Press, 1994), 1–20.

20. Sedgwick, "The Beast in the Closet," 197.

21. Samuel Johnson, "Preface," *A Dictionary of the English Language,* in *Johnson on the English Language,* ed. Gwin J. Kolb and Robert Demaria Jr., vol. 18 of *The Yale Edition of the Works of Samuel Johnson* (New Haven: Yale University Press, 2005), 73–113.

22. My reading of Johnson's preface is deeply indebted to Stephen Fix. It was he who first drew my attention to the fascinating complexity of Johnson's surprisingly intimate, personal voice in the preface.

23. This point, among many others, I owe to Stephen Fix.

24. Jesper Svenbro, *Phrasikleia: An Anthropology of Reading in Ancient Greece,* trans. Janet Lloyd (Ithaca, N.Y.: Cornell University Press, 1993).

25. See also Bernard Knox, "Silent Reading in Antiquity," *Greek, Roman, and Byzantine Studies* 9 (1968): 421–35.

26. "In the eyes of those early readers, writing did not by itself *represent* the voice that, at least sometimes, was supposed to transcribe it. Writing was not yet autonomous in relation to the voice, which it was supposed to trigger in order to become complete. Before this vocalization, writing did not represent something any more than letters typed haphazardly by a monkey do to us. But writing would *produce* a representation if it but gave birth to a sound sequence that, unlike the written word, could be considered as a representation of the writer's voice (fictitious though that voice might be). Before the invention of silent reading, writing

did not represent a voice. It was not yet the image of a voice; it only aimed to produce a voice that would 'represent the same by means of the same'" (Svenbro, *Phrasikleia*, 164–65).

27. Stephen Booth, who does not directly address the figure of breath, writes, of the first eight lines of this sonnet, that the experience of understanding them "(as opposed to what is understood from them) is one of so many simple alternations and alternatives to pairs of alternatives that the actual experience of plodding through them is like a physical experience of relationships that are literally metaphysical—an experience of perceiving stolidly physical patterns (of paired lines and pairs of paired lines) that are both reductively simplistic in their interrelation and too multifariously complex to think about." Booth, in *Shakespeare's Sonnets*, ed. with an analytic commentary by Stephen Booth (New Haven: Yale University Press, 1977), 275.

28. "*Psukhḗ*," which comes to be translated in Latin as *anima*, is etymologically "connected with *psúkhein* 'to breathe' as in 'definitely perceived as a breath' [*Iliad* 20.440]. For an entire philosophical tradition stretching from Anaximander to Diogenes of Apollonia, *psukhḗ* was composed of air and was virtually synonymous with respiration. . . . It is thus 'by the body that the spirit [*psukhḗ*] signifies what it signifies [*sēmaínei hà àn sēmaínēi*],' as Plato expresses it in the *Cratylus*. 'And for this reason it is justly called a *sêma*.' The body is not only the 'tomb' (*sêma*) of the *psukhḗ*, but also the 'sign' or 'signifier' (*sêma*) that the *psukhḗ* uses. . . . Into this framework we should set an analogy that became current in late rhetoric, namely the analogy 'body : Spirit :: sign : meaning.' The *Scholia to Hermogenes* state, 'For the Ancients, the *lógos* was called a living being [*zôion*] and, just as a living being consists of a *psukhḗ* and a body, so the *lógos* consists of a *psukhḗ*, namely meaning [*enthumḗmata*] and a body, namely the linguistic form [*phrásis*]'" (Svenbro, *Phrasikleia*, 138–40, quoting from Plato, *Cratylus* 400b–c and *Scholia to Hermogenes, Perì staséōn*, in *Rhetores Graeci* 14.204.25–205, 4 Rabe). Shakespeare's line is probably also a reference to Deuteronomy. The Lord says to Moses (in the Geneva Bible of 1587), "Now therefore write ye this song for you, and teach it the children of Israel: put it in their mouthes, that this song may be my witnesse against the children of Israel"; "And then when many aduersities and tribulations shall come vpon them, this song shall answere them to their face as a witnesse: for it shall not be forgotte out of the mouthes of their posteritie: for I knowe their imagination, which they goe about euen now, before I haue brought them into the lande which I sware" (Deut. 31:19, 21; http://collections.chadwyck.com.proxy.bc.edu/bie/). I owe this reference to Elaine Scarry, *The Body in Pain: The Making and Unmaking of the World* (Oxford: Oxford University Press, 1987), 239. Thanks to Mary Crane for advice on which translation of the Bible to consult here.

29. Anne Carson takes issue with this argument: "The remarkable humorlessness of this line of interpretation seems to belie not only the terms in which the

ancients themselves speak of written works of art (e.g., *poiema, kosmos, charis*), but also the spirit of freedom in which artists like Simonides play through the possibilities of meaning available conjointly to writer and reader within a piece of language. Perhaps exchange of power need not always mean abuse of power. Meaning, after all, exists to be exchanged." Carson, *Economy of the Unlost: (Reading Simonides of Keos with Paul Celan)* (Princeton: Princeton University Press, 1999), 84n28.

30. See Svenbro, *Phrasikleia,* 189–97.

31. *Erastḗs* is traditionally translated as "lover"; *erṓmenos,* as "beloved"—the teenaged boy who is the object of pederastic desire. *Kalós,* Svenbro notes, is the laudatory term for a beloved—"beautiful"; *katapúgōn* is a derogatory term that Svenbro renders in French as *enculé* and that his translator renders in English as "buggered" (Svenbro, *Phrasikleia,* 189; for the French edition, see Svenbro, *Phrasikleia: Anthropologie de la lecture en Grèce ancienne* [Paris: La Découverte, 1988], 210). *Kalon* (something which is *kalos*), notes Martha Nussbaum in a chapter on the *Symposium* in which she translates the term as *the beautiful,* "is here such a broad moral/aesthetic notion that it might be more accurate to render it as 'valuable' and the corresponding noun as 'value.' . . . It may, then, actually be a single unifying notion of value in terms of which we are to see the special values such as justice and wisdom. It is clear, at any rate, that the *kalon* is supposed to include everything that is relevant to the experience of passionate love, including the love of institutions and sciences—everything that is loveable in the world." Nussbaum, *The Fragility of Goodness: Luck and Ethics in Greek Tragedy and Philosophy* (Cambridge: Cambridge University Press, 1986), 178. On *erastḗs* and *erṓmenos,* and on *kalos,* which K. J. Dover says means "'beautiful,' 'handsome,' 'pretty,' 'attractive' or 'lovely' when applied to a human being, animal, object or place, and 'admirable,' 'creditable' or 'honorable' when applied to actions or institutions," see Dover, *Greek Homosexuality,* updated and with a new postscript (Cambridge, Mass.: Harvard University Press, 1989), 15–16. For Dover, "the Greeks did not call a person 'beautiful' by virtue of that person's morals, intelligence, ability or temperament, but solely by virtue of shape, colour, texture, and movement" (16).

32. See H. I. Marrou, "Pederasty in Classical Education," in *A History of Education in Antiquity,* trans. George Lamb (Madison: University of Wisconsin Press, 1956), 26–35.

33. Michel Foucault, *The History of Sexuality,* vol. 2, *The Use of Pleasure,* trans. Robert Hurley (New York: Vintage Books, 1990), 215. Jean-Claude Milner argues that Foucault's text examines antiquity through the lens of modern sexuality. Milner, "Pleasure's Treble," trans. Justin Clemens, *S: Journal of the Jan van Eyck Circle for Lacanian Ideology Critique* 3 (2010): 40–63; translation of Milner, "Le Triple du plaisir," *Constats* (Paris: Gallimard, 2002), 65–130. "There is in ancient coitus neither *philia* nor beauty" (beauty is defined as that which causes pleasure; on *philia,*

see below, and see also note 37, below) he writes, and, therefore, "the sexual act, as such, is not a pleasure. It is situated at the impossible point of pleasure. There is not, one cannot have, sexual pleasure. . . . Coitus is the experience of a radical impossibility" (Milner, "Pleasure's Treble," 48, 49). For the moderns, all pleasure is sexual; for them, "every pleasure has sexual pleasure as horizon" (56). For the ancients, on the contrary, "pleasure has as its fundamental paradigm the starving man who eats, the parched man who drinks. Against this standard, every pleasure is measured and legitimated." He continues, "The relation of the thing to the body is fundamentally thought as incorporation. Thus the causes of pleasure are governed according to the ways that permit incorporation" (42). Therefore, "sexual pleasure is the pleasure that one body can cause another body. If it exists, sexual pleasure therefore consists in this: that one body incorporates another. But this is impossible. Impossible through penetration" (47). Moreover, if the model for ancient pleasure is incorporation, one should not understand incorporation on the model of (modern) nutritional assimilation: "The physical body welcomes as one of its essential parts the thing that is not of it. . . . Drinking and eating are the horizon of ancient pleasure, but in ancient drinking and eating, the ingested substance remains essentially distinct" (44). The atom is not divisible. (On this fundamental distinction between the ancients and the moderns—between multitudes and magnitudes, between a universe in which one is indivisible and a universe in which it is divisible—and the contrasting forms of harmony [and disharmony] they entail, see Daniel Heller-Roazen, *The Fifth Hammer: Pythagorus and the Disharmony of the World* [New York: Zone Books, 2011].) Hence the importance of *philia,* which is (anemically) translated as modern "friendship"; *philia* regulates the interaction of atoms according to a model of hospitality (the metaphorical rendering of cannibalism—the point to which all pleasure-as-incorporation tends), and thus also serves to tie the regulation of the natural body to that of the social body. "Not coitus alone, but every encounter between beings endowed with a body has cannibalism for its ultimate horizon—if at least it should be organized by pleasure" (Milner, "Pleasure's Treble," 48); cannibalism, however, is "the forbidden *par excellence,*" and "there is therefore no remedy for the failure of penetration." *Philia* ruptures the "trilemma" to which every human community would in consequence of this otherwise be submitted: "Prohibit every encounter, which is the end of all community; or permit universal devoration, which the end of every body; or prohibit every pleasure." *Philia* "authorizes pleasures and even pleasant human encounters for those who must have renounced the only properly human pleasure of devouring each other" (45). If "friendship" seems an inadequate translation of *philia,* that is because in a modern regime of sexual pleasure and assimilation, *philia* is no longer necessary. For the ancients, on the contrary, "friendship is not an attenuated variant of love, but the salvation of the world—of the golden chain that holds the world by rings of *philia* and beauty" (45). For Milner, then, "the use of pleasure" is also a mistranslation; "aphrodisia" can mean pleasure only if "we exclude the sexual act as such and relate them to the laws of hospitality" (49n8). "Use," he later argues, belongs to the regime of modern sexuality (57–58): because modern pleasure is founded on use, *philia* becomes unnecessary.

34. For Foucault's reading of Plato, see *The Use of Pleasure,* 229–46. For Milner's account of how Plato's arguments respond to the relations among pleasure, coitus, and love, see Milner, "Pleasure's Treble," 52–54. Philosophy, he suggests, represents the possibility of knots among pleasure, coitus, and love; all three cannot be "knotted," and Plato and Lucretius represent the two possible paths, knotting pleasure and love by excluding coitus (Plato) or knotting pleasure and coitus by excluding love (Lucretius) (Milner, "Pleasure's Treble," 52). Plato's "stratagem," he seems to suggest, is to secure the possibility of "knotting" pleasure and love (only between men and boys) by prohibiting penetration (or "coitus," the third strand), which follows from the fact that "if penetration in itself is the very experience of the impossibility of incorporation, then it is the experience of the impossibility of pleasure" (53). For the relation to pleasure to be possible, "penetration must be forbidden, but, for it to be forbidden, it must be physically possible. There would then be sexual pleasure only where penetration is supposed physically possible and shameful in regards to custom; but it is supposed at the same time only possible and shameful among men; between women, it is supposed physically impossible; between man and woman, it is not in itself shameful. Conclusion: only men can forbid themselves the sexual act and thereby knot pleasure and love" (53). For the ancients, the central relation is pederastic; in the modern dispensation of pleasure, on the contrary, the relation between men and women becomes central, and philosophy comes to neglect the relation between men and boys. For another account of this question of reciprocity in the context of the *Symposium,* and the reversal whereby "Alcibiades begins as the beautiful *erōmenos,* but seems to end as the active *erastēs,* while Socrates, apparently the *erastēs,* becomes the *erōmenos,*" see Nussbaum, *The Fragility of Goodness,* 188.

35. Svenbro's reading of the *Phaedrus* is considerably more complicated than my account suggests. See Svenbro, *Phrasikleia,* 198–216.

36. Bersani writes, "The soul that pursues 'that which really is what it is' is, then, not pure lack, an empty desiring receptacle; it has a recognizable moral character. It is individualized not in the way that personalities are, to our modern psychological understanding, individualized. Rather, it has what might be thought of as a general, universal, individuation. The lover seeks to make the lover like himself, but this has nothing to do with the specularity of a personal narcissism" (Bersani, "The Power of Evil and the Power of Love," in Bersani and Phillips, *Intimacies,* 82).

37. See Milner, "Pleasure's Treble," for a different account: "If we agree that all figures of encounter . . . allow themselves to be summarized by the word *philein;*

if we agree that every fulfillment of an encounter lets itself be summarized by the word *kalos,* we will have illuminated the aphorism to *kalon philon esti.* . . . The beautiful is distinct from us, it is said, but we receive it as allied" (45). (*Kalon philon esti*: J. Wright translates this proverb, which is quoted by Theognis, as "the beautiful is friendly," but, notably, Milner's remarks here concern, centrally, how to translate these terms, and, especially, whether *friendly* is an adequate rendering of *philon.* Translation in Plato, *Lysis,* trans. J. Wright, in *The Collected Dialogues of Plato, Including the Letters,* ed. Edith Hamilton and Huntington Cairns [New York: Bollingen Series 71 of Pantheon Books, 1961], 160 [216c].) This, I think, is the sameness that Bersani valorizes, which takes on a different, if related, complexion, in Milner's philological account of pleasure. "*Philia* is alliance [*apparentement*] affirmed. It therefore supposes a point from which this affirmation issues. This point is named the Same. Far from being obtained from an abstraction from resemblances, its potency consists in affirming the Same beyond resemblances and dissemblances. Through it are read in synonymy the co-belonging of the *polis* and the co-naturality of *phusis.* Saying that pleasure is related to us (*philon*) is only to say that it is governed by the Same. The thing causes a pleasure of the body insofar as the relation of pleasures grasps what there is of the Same in the cause and in the effect. It is not at all that the body and the thing are indistinct or confused. . . . Pleasure qua pleasure is only the material mark of what there is of the Same between a thing and a body that are really distinct; reciprocally, the sanction of what there is of the Same between thing and body will only be a pleasure" (Milner, "Pleasure's Treble," 45).

38. Bersani, *Is the Rectum a Grave? and Other Essays* (Chicago: University of Chicago Press, 2010); Bersani and Ulysse Dutoit, *Forms of Being* (London: British Film Institute, 2004); Bersani, "Psychoanalysis and the Aesthetic Subject," *Critical Inquiry* 32, no. 2 (Winter 2006): 161–74.

39. Anne Carson, *Eros the Bittersweet* (London: Dalkey Archive Press, 1986), 115.

40. For Carson's reading of the *Phaedrus,* see 117–73. For her reading of the passage from Sophocles, see 111–16.

41. In Carson's discussion of Sappho's Fragment 105a, for example, "the reach" that embodies the erotic dilemma includes both the apple forever beyond our grasp and the poem cut off by the vagaries of historical transmission at the moment of reaching (*Eros the Bittersweet,* 26–29). In addition to *Eros the Bittersweet,* see also her translations in and her introduction to *If Not, Winter: Fragments of Sappho,* trans. Anne Carson (New York: Vintage Books, 2003). On the transmission of Sappho, see also my discussion of Swinburne in chapter 3 below.

42. *Stereoscopy* also appears as a term in Wimsatt's *The Verbal Icon*: "The verbal object will be viewed by the critic in a kind of stereoscopic perspective that makes it look somewhat like a physical object." W. K. Wimsatt, *The Verbal Icon* (Lexington: University Press of Kentucky, 1954), 263; cited in Oren Izenberg, *Being*

Numerous: Poetry and the Ground of Social Life (Princeton: Princeton University Press, 2011), 12–13; 195n40.

43. Virginia Woolf, *Moments of Being* (San Diego and New York: Harvest Books, 1985), 65. This initial description of ecstasy becomes crucial for Woolf's articulation of moments of being.

44. Elsewhere I suggest that "the desire to see the world without oneself" in it might describe the erotics of voyeurism; if that is the case, then voyeurism might offer a way to reconceive the erotics of cinema spectatorship. See Kevin Ohi, "Voyeurism and Annunciation in Almodóvar's *Talk to Her*," *Criticism: A Quarterly for Literature and the Arts* 51, no. 4 (Fall 2009): 521–57.

45. See Kevin Robb, "Poetic Sources of the Greek Alphabet: Rhythm and Abecedarium from Phoenician to Greek," in *Communication Arts in the Ancient World,* ed. E. A. Havelock and J. P. Hershell (New York: Hastings House, 1978), 23–36.

46. In *Autobiography of Red,* Carson writes, "'How does distance look?' is a simple direct question. It extends from a spaceless / within to the edge / of what can be loved." Carson, *Autobiography of Red: A Novel in Verse* (New York: Vintage Contemporaries, 1998), 43.

47. T. S. Eliot, "Tradition and the Individual Talent," in *Selected Prose of T. S. Eliot,* ed. Frank Kermode (New York: Harvest Books and Farrar, Straus and Giroux, 1975), 37–44, 40.

48. "Someone said: 'The dead writers are remote from us because we know so much more than they did'. Precisely, and they are that which we know" (Eliot, "Tradition and the Individual Talent," 40).

49. Johnson, "Preface," 113; Oscar Wilde, *The Picture of Dorian Gray,* ed. Isobel Murray (Oxford: Oxford University Press, 1981), 54.

50. Carson's reference is to the chapter on Velázquez's *Las Meninas* in Michel Foucault's *The Order of Things*: "The spectacle he is observing is thus doubly invisible: first, because it is not represented within the space of the painting, and, second, because it is situated precisely in that blind point, in that essential hiding-place into which our gaze disappears from ourselves at the moment of our actual looking." Foucault, *The Order of Things: An Archeology of the Human Sciences,* trans. Robert Sheridan (New York: Vintage Books, 1994), 4.

51. In the preface to the second edition of *The Anxiety of Influence,* Harold Bloom writes, "I never meant by 'the anxiety of influence' a Freudian Oedipal rivalry, despite a rhetorical flourish or two in the book." Bloom, *The Anxiety of Influence: A Theory of Poetry,* 2nd ed. (Oxford: Oxford University Press, 1997), xxii. Or more recently: "My ways of writing about literary influence have been widely regarded as relying on Freud's Oedipus complex. But that is just wrong, as I have explained before, to little avail." Bloom, *The Anatomy of Influence: Literature as a Way of Life* (New Haven: Yale University Press, 2011), 9.

52. Bloom's language of "virility" no doubt derives (also) from Wallace Stevens. See Stevens, "The Figure of the Youth as Virile Poet," in *Collected Poetry and Prose,* ed. Frank Kermode and Joan Richardson (New York: Library of America, 1997), 666–85.

53. Wallace Stevens, "The Creations of Sound," in *The Collected Poems* (New York: Vintage Books, 1954), 310.

54. Gilles Deleuze, "Bartleby; or, The Formula," in *Essays Critical and Clinical,* trans. Daniel W. Smith and Michael A. Greco (Minneapolis: University of Minnesota Press, 1997), 68–90, 84.

55. For a related, but more polemical, account of education, an account that addresses questions of transmission in the context of academic disciplines, see Halberstam, *The Queer Art of Failure,* 6–18. My thinking about education has been shaped by, among other texts, Bill Readings's *The University in Ruins* (Cambridge, Mass.: Harvard University Press, 1996) and Jacques Rancière's *The Ignorant Schoolmaster: Five Lessons in Intellectual Emancipation,* trans. Kristin Ross (Stanford: Stanford University Press, 1991).

56. See, for example, Adam Gopnik, "Why Teach English?," *New Yorker,* August 27, 2013, http://www.newyorker.com/online/blogs/books/2013/08/why-teach-english.html.

57. Jean-Claude Milner, *La Politique des choses* (Paris: Éditions Verdier, 2011).

58. Leo Bersani suggests that—on the contrary—teaching, like (he provocatively suggests) cruising, should be understood on the model of impersonal intimacy. See his "Sociability and Cruising," *Umbr(a): A Journal of the Unconscious,* 2002: 9–23.

59. Andrew H. Miller, *The Burdens of Perfection: On Ethics and Reading in Nineteenth-Century British Literature* (Ithaca, N.Y.: Cornell University Press, 2008).

60. The possibility of reading in Bloom's Oedipal metaphors a struggle internal to expression evoked the writing of Stanley Cavell, whose idiom is very different from Bloom's but who is important for Miller. Bloom, I noted, links a difficulty within expression to "our universal fear of domination, of our being trapped by nature in our body as a dungeon" (Bloom, *The Anxiety of Influence,* 57). (This is likewise the problem of pain in Scarry's *The Body in Pain*; in a sense, one makes a world in order to escape being trapped in one's body as a dungeon.) In *The World Viewed,* what Cavell calls the "acknowledgment of silence" seems to involve a registering of a similar difficulty internal to expression. If synchronization of sound and image in the "talkie" tends to produce an artificial illusion of the coming together of conviction and intelligibility, the acknowledgment of silence seems to involve embodiment in at least two ways: figures of corporeal existence suggest that the silence, acknowledged, would be lived or experienced, rather than simply known, even as those figures also stand in for what remains incommunicable in

the individual mind, and for what stands in the way of knowing other minds, or saying one's own. This central preoccupation of Cavell's is also, of course, a problem of transmission. Cavell writes, "But there is a further reality that film pursues, the further, continuous reality in which the words we need are *not* synchronized with the occasions of their need or in which their occasions flee them. I have in mind not the various ways dialogue can stand at an angle to the life that produces it; nor the times in which the occasion is past when you can say what you did not think to say; nor the times when the occasion for speech is blocked by inappropriateness or fear, or the vessels of speech are pitched by grief or joy. I have rather in mind the pulsing air of incommunicability which may nudge the edge of any experience and placement: the curve of fingers that day, a mouth, the sudden rise of the body's frame as it is caught by the color and scent of flowers, laughing all afternoon mostly about nothing, the friend gone but somewhere now which starts from here—spools of history that have unwound only to me now, occasions which will not reach words for me now, and if not now, never. I am not asking for more stream-of-consciousness. . . . I am asking for the ground of consciousness, upon which I cannot but move." Cavell, *The World Viewed: Reflections on the Ontology of Film,* enlarged ed. (Cambridge, Mass.: Harvard University Press, 1979), 148. That "ground of consciousness" is as if embodied in this passage by, among other things, the beauty of the writing, and perhaps less by the particular images than by the juxtaposition, in a series, of both incommensurate ideas and nonparallel syntactical forms. The experience of watching film captures this particularity, and, for Cavell, is an experience like those he describes here. It comes in contact with this zone of silence, even as watching film was one of the inexpressible seductions that made him who he is: "St. Augustine stole a pear; lots of children have. Rousseau got a spanking with his pants down; lots of little boys have. Why seems it so particular with them? Everybody has his stolen pear, and his casual, permanent seductions; if they are to know their lives, those are to be known" (154).

61. Miller's book leads me to reconsider the argument I made about Pater in *Innocence and Rapture: The Erotic Child in Pater, Wilde, James, and Nabokov* (New York: Palgrave Macmillan, 2005), where I tended to downplay questions of ethics to avoid a moralistic account of his writing (which tempts many critics, particularly when they draw a contrast between his ethics and Wilde's). Miller offers one a way to consider the ethical dimensions of Pater's eroticization of aesthetic apprehension.

62. See, for example, Miller's discussion (in *The Burdens of Perfection,* 29–31) of Harry Shaw's *Narrating Reality: Austen, Scott, Eliot* (Ithaca, N.Y.: Cornell University Press, 1999) or, later in the text, his discussions of Neil Hertz, Eve Kosofsky Sedgwick, and Christopher Herbert. Miller, that is, is as interested in their particular mode of writing (which he links to a strand of Victorian responses to skepticism; the experience of reading as an unfolding of thought has its roots, he

suggests, in a mode of casuistry through which Victorians responded to the problem of other minds).

63. Miller discusses the Victorian concern with the "weakness of will" in terms of perspective: third person and first person, initially. Third person would seem to be a privileged form for the Victorians—a "view from nowhere" (*The Burdens of Perfection,* 58; his reference is to Thomas Nagel, *The View from Nowhere* [New York: Oxford University Press, 1986]) that entails a curiously "vicarious" (Miller, *The Burdens of Perfection,* 59) relation to experience. That allows for an "objective," dispassionate view of ethical choices, but it has the effect of eviscerating the will: "Identifying with spectators looking at me, treating what I will or will not do as a matter of empirical knowledge, allows for certain kinds of description of my inner life; it allows for the testing of that life; and it allows of the making of predictions based on an assessment of my past behavior. But it also can obscure the fact that what I do is a matter of making commitments" (Miller, *The Burdens of Perfection,* 63). Whereas the "third-person" view could be a way of obscuring agency (it might be an evasion of ethical responsibility because it obscures the fact that one has agency in one's actions), the first-person view cannot know whether it is a sham, "a flattering pretense of control over one's actions." While "neither perspective . . . denies the truth of the other" (64), the difficulty of surmounting the gap between them seems to restate the problem of skepticism. He explores this dynamic via Charles Dickens's *Hard Times* and George Eliot's *Daniel Deronda.* Eliot, especially, "characteristically dramatizes the tension between a theory of morality that stresses the importance of perspective . . . and an unflagging belief in the duty of choice" (70). Perfectionism provides a "therapy" (71), he suggests, for this problem: "One way I can now characterize perfectionism is as providing, against the perspectives of the first and third person—and indeed motivated by the epistemological and ethical quandaries that the differences between those perspectives generate—a rich elaboration of second-person relations, all they can offer and all that they cannot" (72). (The second person, he notes, does not eclipse the other two perspectives so much as "coordinate" them, "and not always smoothly" [74].) Marriage in the Victorian novel, therefore, is, for Miller, not (purely) social ideology; it also functions as an allegory for the workings of the novel, where the "orchestration of readerly perspective" serves as "a therapy for the infirmities of the will" (78). (That ends up being a matter of both eliciting and frustrating a second-person relation to the text.)

64. Miller quotes Cavell's *The World Viewed,* 100.

65. Christopher Herbert, *Culture and Anomie: Ethnographic Imagination in the Nineteenth Century* (Chicago: University of Chicago Press, 1991).

66. See, for instance, John Guillory, *Cultural Capital: The Problem of Literary Canon Formation* (Chicago: University of Chicago Press, 1993), and the writings of Pierre Bourdieu.

67. See, for instance, Sean Keilen's discussion of the nightingale in relation to figures of sexual violation, figures, he persuasively suggests, through which early modern texts thought about their relation to their Latin precursors. Keilen, *Vulgar Eloquence: On the Renaissance Invention of English Literature* (New Haven: Yale University Press, 2006). (I do not mean to suggest that Keilen's book does not also offer generalized reflection—and very illuminating reflection—on literary tradition.)

68. Giorgio Agamben, "Bartleby; or, On Contingency," in *Potentialities: Collected Essays in Philosophy,* ed. and trans. Daniel Heller-Roazen (Stanford: Stanford University Press, 1999), 243–71, 265.

69. Agamben, "Bartleby," 266; Herman Melville, "Bartleby," in *Billy Budd and Other Stories* (New York: Penguin Books, 1986), 1–46.

70. Aristotle, *Metaphysics* 1047a24–26, quoted in *Potentialities,* by Agamben, 264.

71. Daniel Heller-Roazen, "Editor's Introduction: 'To Read What Was Never Written,'" in *Potentialities,* by Agamben, 1–23, 21.

72. "In natural language, at least, it is simply not possible for one linguistic term to signify another without the second as a result losing its character of being a linguistic term and appearing as a mere object" (Heller-Roazen, "Editor's Introduction," 4).

73. Heller-Roazen links the "absolute anaphora" that Agamben sees in Bartleby's formula to the Platonic "thing itself": "Agamben," he writes, "can be said to develop fully what is already implicit in the Platonic nomination of the Idea, by which the anaphora 'itself' (*auto*) is simply added to a thing's name to arrive at the Idea of the thing. . . . It suffices to add 'itself' to any thing's name, Plato seems to say, for it to step forth as an Idea. And this 'saving of phenomena' . . . is possible, Agamben leads us to think, because every utterance is in essence nothing other than the irreparable exposition of the 'thing itself,' the very taking place of language as the potentiality for expression" (Heller-Roazen, "Editor's Introduction," 21). On the "thing itself," see Heller-Roazen, "Editor's Introduction," esp. 5–9, and Agamben, "The Thing Itself," in *Potentialities,* 27–38.

74. On the "indifferent truth of the tautology," see Agamben, "Bartleby," 264.

75. On this redemption in Benjamin, see also Katherine Biers, *Virtual Modernism: Writing and Technology in the Progressive Era* (Minneapolis: University of Minnesota Press, 2013).

76. Benjamin, *Gesammelte Schriften,* ed. Tiedemann and Schweppenhäuser, vol. 1, pt. 3, p. 1238; cited (and translated) in Agamben's *Potentialities,* 1. Benjamin takes the phrase from Hugo von Hofmannsthal, *Death and the Fool* [*Der Tor und der Tod*]; see *Three Plays,* trans. Alfred Schwarz (Detroit, Mich.: Wayne State University Press, 1966), 65; cited in Werner Hamacher, "The Second of Inversion: Movements of a Figure through Celan's Poetry," in *Premises: Essays on Philosophy*

and Literature from Kant to Celan, trans. Peter Fenves (Cambridge, Mass.: Harvard University Press, 1996), 337–87, 383n41. "Agamben suggests," Heller-Roazen writes, "that 'what was never written' in the course of all communication, linguistic and historical, is the fact that there is language; and he shows that this fact is 'never written' in the precise sense that it can only enter into 'writing' and the *gramma* in the form of a presupposition. Yet this fact can, nevertheless, be 'read': exposed, it can be comprehended in its existence as potentiality. 'To read what was never written' is in this sense to bring to light, in what is said and thought, the 'thing itself' by which anything is expressible; it is to return everything that has ever been said to the event of its taking place in its pure potential to be said (or not to be said)" ("Editor's Introduction," 22). For another gloss of this phrase, see Hamacher, "The Second of Inversion," 383–87.

77. At this moment, Miller glosses a passage in Maurice Blanchot. This moment might also encapsulate an important strand of Miller's compelling reading of James, and the sense of potentiality evoked here—put in terms of lives that might have been otherwise—is the subject of Miller's beautiful, moving chapter "On Lives Unled" (in *The Burdens of Perfection,* 191–217), which offers rich readings of Charles Dickens's *Dombey and Son* and Henry James's "The Jolly Corner," "The Beast in the Jungle," and *The Ambassadors.* For another powerful account of potentiality in the (this time, American) novel, see Biers, *Virtual Modernism.*

78. Guillory, *Cultural Capital.*

1. Queer Transmission and the *Symposium*

1. Miller, *Place for Us,* 26.

2. "For I was attempting to impart to him that homosexuality of one which—even had he accepted it, or were himself to return the favor—must have restrained either of us from ever joining the other across a crowded room. The proper use of 'Some Enchanted Evening' was not, I concluded, and can never be, to court another man, who hearing it would only return to the archaic condition or one dreamed all alone—like me, as I replayed the song 'again and again' after the still wonderful guy had gone" (Miller, *Place for Us,* 22–23).

3. In an essay that—along with the writings of a few others—could be called inaugural for queer theory, Judith Butler suggested that because one can only be "out" in relation to a closet, one can in some sense never come out: the fantasy of outness repeatedly produces the very closet it would leave behind. See Butler, "Imitation and Gender Insubordination," in *The Lesbian and Gay Studies Reader,* ed. Henry Abelove, Michèle Aina Barale, and David Halperin (New York: Routledge, 1993), 307–20.

4. For a reading of Miller (and, specifically, of this particular passage) in relation to this ambivalence, see Heather Love, *Feeling Backward: Loss and the Poli-*

tics of Queer History (Cambridge, Mass.: Harvard University Press, 2009), 19–21. On Miller's book, see also David Halperin, *How to Be Gay* (Cambridge, Mass.: Belknap Press, 2012), 90–107; on this particular passage, see 93–105.

5. For the classic statement of the relation of (one form) of homosexual desire to sublimation, see Sigmund Freud, *Leonardo da Vinci and a Memory of His Childhood,* trans. Alan Tyson, ed. James Strachey (New York: W. W. Norton, 1990; repr. of *The Standard Edition,* 1953–74).

6. Marcel Proust, *In Search of Lost Time,* vol. 4, *Sodom and Gomorrah,* trans. C. K. Scott Moncrieff and Terence Kilmartin; rev. D. J. Enright (New York: Modern Library, 1993), 18.

7. In other terms, yet again, the emergence from the closet thwarts social communion more than it enables it: "So those of us in whom his experience is still being lived remain not far from where we were before: feeling if anything more forsaken now that everyone knows what it signified than we did when no one did (for we shared in the ignorance as we cannot share in the knowledge that ignores what Barthes called the 'obtuse' dimension of the signifier)" (Miller, *Place for Us,* 19).

8. See also Kathryn Bond Stockton, *The Queer Child; or, Growing Sideways in the Twentieth Century* (Durham, N.C.: Duke University Press, 2009).

9. See Sedgwick, *Epistemology of the Closet,* 1–2.

10. On the subject of insult, see also Didier Eribon, *Insult and the Making of the Gay Self,* trans. Michael Lucey (Durham, N.C.: Duke University Press, 2004).

11. Ian Parker, "The Story of a Suicide: Two College Roommates, a Webcam, and a Tragedy," *New Yorker,* February 6, 2012, http://www.newyorker.com/reporting/2012/02/06/120206fa_fact_parker#ixzz1rEVUmvBs.

12. "Technology experts noted that Mr. Clementi had checked Mr. Ravi's Twitter feed 38 times in the two days before he jumped to his death from the George Washington Bridge. The man who was with him, identified in court only as M.B. because prosecutors consider him a victim, testified that the men heard people joking outside the room and that Mr. Clementi seemed upset by it." Kate Zernike, "Defendant Won't Testify in Rutgers Case," *New York Times,* March 12, 2012, http://www.nytimes.com/2012/03/13/nyregion/defendant-dharun-ravi-wont-testify-in-rutgers-dorm-spying-trial.html; print edition, March 13, 2012.

13. Eve Kosofsky Sedgwick, "Reality and Realization," in *The Weather in Proust,* 206–15.

14. For this last point I am indebted to a conversation with David Kurnick.

15. It occurred to me recently that a strangely common epiphenomenon of the dissemination of tolerance in a sense registers this temporal structure. Repeatedly, when I teach texts or films with references to or depictions of gay sexuality, even very tame ones (a kiss is enough), a certain number of students will tell me—after elaborate avowals of tolerance and the trotting forth of exculpatory gay friends, and so on—that it would have been fine if only I had warned them first. That most "gay content"

hardly registers as "gay content" when one is gay (representing as it does, simply, what one might call one's life) makes it difficult to remember the often unexceptional moments in question; because these moments seem most often to boil down to the designating of homosexuality, one's own sexuality seems thereby to demand that one fashion a giant cowbell to warn the unwary of one's (gay) approach. Not to do so, according to the implicit logic, is unfairly to accuse these unwary but tolerant people of the homophobia to which their startled recoil attests. Beyond that, however, I am also struck by the way that representations of gay desire seem to call forth confrontations with the temporal structure of cognition and realization. For an example in France of the complaint I am describing, see Clarice Fabre, "Après la projection de 'Tomboy,' des élèves m'ont dit: 'L'homosexualité, c'est péché,'" *Le Monde,* December 24, 2013, http://www.lemonde.fr/culture/article/2013/12/24/apres-la-projection-de-tomboy-des-eleves-m-ont-dit-l-homosexualite-c-est-peche_4339340_3246.html#xtor=EPR-32280229-[NL_Titresdujour]-20131225-[titres].

16. "Rotary octopods" comes from Anita Sokolsky, "The Resistance to Sentimentality: Yeats, De Man, and the Aesthetic Education," *Yale Journal of Criticism: Interpretation in the Humanities* 1, no. 1 (1987): 67–86, 75. The anatomical transformations (the way that Aristophanes has Zeus move the genitals around on the unfortunate halved creatures) that make sex possible also make impossible the reunification of the split bodies for which sex strives. (For this latter point, I am indebted to a class with Christopher Pye.) Leo Strauss points to another curious aspect of the anatomical details: "Where did Apollo get the additional skin required so that there were even additional wrinkles that had to be smoothed out? He acts as if the skin of the whole man were now available for the half man, which of course is a mistake." (Strauss suggests that one of the half-men, skinned, might simply have been discarded.) Strauss, *On Plato's Symposium,* ed. Seth Benardete (Chicago and London: University of Chicago Press, 2001), 130. Martha Nussbaum points out that the acknowledgment of the impossibility of physical union conceals a more profound difficulty. Physical union (in the imagined welding together of the lovers by Hephaestus) "is a far simpler miracle than the one that would have to take place if they were really to become one. For these creatures have souls; and their desire for unity is a desire of the soul, a desire of desires, projects, aspirations." The fantasy of union with another raises the problem of the soul's unity with a body: "Hephaestus' tools could do nothing to satisfy their desire—unless their souls, in intercourse, had first become thoroughly fused with their own bodies." Any distance, therefore, from that merger will ruin the union, and no one could see such a fusion as something other than a loss of wholeness: "One miracle presupposes a greater miracle: to get to be the whole, you first have to be willing to be the half." She then points out a further difficulty that arises even if the first two are surmounted: "For what they thought they most wanted out of their passionate movement turns out to be a wholeness that would put an end to

all movement and all passion. A sphere would not have intercourse with anyone. It would not eat, or doubt, or drink. . . . It would be complete. . . . Erōs is the desire to be a being without any contingent concurrent desires. It is a second-order desire that all desires should be cancelled." The speech thus points to something like the paradox explored by Anne Carson's *Eros the Bittersweet*; in Nussbaum's words, "We would like to find a way to retain our identity as desiring and moving beings, and yet to make ourselves self-sufficient. It takes considerable ingenuity" (Nussbaum, *The Fragility of Goodness,* 175–76).

17. For his account of the importance of the movement away from coitus (legible in Socrates's refusal of Alcibiades, as in, more generally, the movement from sexual desires directed toward a particular boy to the apprehension of beauty "as such") and of why the "knotting" of pleasure and love has to take the form of prohibiting sex between men and boys, see Milner, "Pleasure's Treble," 40–63, esp. 51–54. I give a brief account of his argument in several notes to the introduction above. Ellis Hanson writes that Socrates is "the impossible pedagogical ideal, desire in the service of truth alone." Hanson, "Teaching Shame," in *Gay Shame,* ed. David M. Halperin and Valerie Traub (Chicago: University of Chicago Press, 2009), 132–64, 147. In *The Fragility of Goodness,* Nussbaum emphasizes the strangeness and the forbidding austerity of this ideal, as well as its formidable abstraction. She brings out, first, the strangeness of a hidden assumption underlying one of the logical steps in the exchange with Agathon that precedes the speech of Diotima, the step in which Socrates has Agathon admit that if one loves, one lacks beauty. This assumption underlies the theory of abstraction that is spelled out in Diotima's speech, and the presupposition is that all beauty is the same—the idea that the comedy of Aristophanes's speech in a sense stumbles over and that Alcibiades will refuse. Underlying Socrates's equanimity, it is, Nussbaum writes, "a startling and powerful vision": "Just try to think it seriously: this body of this wonderful beloved person is *exactly* the same in quality as that person's mind and inner life. Both, in turn, the same in quality as the value of Athenian democracy; of Pythagorean geometry; of Eudoxan astronomy. What would it be like to look at a body and to see in it exactly the same shade and tone of goodness and beauty as in a mathematical proof—exactly the same, differing only in amount and in location, so that the choice between making love with that person and contemplating that proof presented itself as a choice between having n measures of water and having $n + 100$?" (*The Fragility of Goodness,* 180). To see, moreover, the mind and soul of Socrates as interchangeable with laws, and with the administration of laws: "what would it be like, finally, to see not just each single choice, but all choices (or at least all choices involving love and deep attachment) as similarly unvariegated? These proposals are so bold as to be pretty well incomprehensible from the ordinary point of view" (181). Ultimately, the depiction of Socrates has us register, she suggests, what is sacrificed by the giving up of the particular, what we lose with

the equanimity and invulnerability that Socrates would seem to achieve, shows us "what Diotima could only abstractly tell: what a human life starts to look like as one makes the ascent. . . . Is this the life we want for ourselves? Is this the way we want, or need, to see and hear? We are not allowed to have the cozy thought that the transformed person will be just like us, only happier. Socrates is weird. He is, in fact, 'not similar to any human being.' We feel, as we look at him, both awestruck and queasy, timidly homesick for ourselves. . . . We need to see ourselves more clearly before we can say whether we would like to become this other sort of being, excellent and deaf" (184). (Nussbaum quotes from her own translation of the *Symposium*; she references 221C–D in the dialogue. For the longer passage to which she refers, see Nussbaum, *Fragility of Goodness*, 167.)

18. Nussbaum emphasizes the importance of the particularity of Alcibiades's story. Against Socrates, Alcibiades proposes, in Nussbaum's account, this: "There are some truths about love that can be learned only through the experience of a particular passion of one's own. If one is asked to teach those truths, one's only recourse is to recreate that experience of the hearer: to tell a story, to appeal to his or her imagination and feelings by the use of vivid narrative" (*The Fragility of Goodness*, 185). For Alcibiades, the "lover's understanding," she writes, "yields particular truths and particular judgments." Love "is an integrated response to the person as a unique whole" (190, 191); in Nussbaum's reading, Socrates's inhuman abstraction, and the self-sufficiency that Alcibiades loves in him, negates, or even refuses to acknowledge, this uniqueness. ("Inside the funny, fat, snub-nosed shell, the soul, self-absorbed, pursues its self-sufficient contemplation" [183].)

19. For a powerful, provocative meditation on this fact, see Hanson, "Teaching Shame"; on the *Symposium,* see especially 145–51.

20. Plato, *The Symposium*, trans. Christopher Gill (New York: Penguin Books, 1999), 7. Strauss links this moment to his discussion of Socratic irony. From Agathon's point of view, he notes, "this is very nasty" (Strauss, *On Plato's Symposium*, 33).

21. Again, from Anita Sokolsky: "For is not the teacher's body the most awkward and extraneous element in the classroom?" (Sokolsky, "The Resistance to Sentimentality," 71–72).

22. Leo Strauss draws out a fascinating implication of these "intermediary" entities: "If there are ideas in any sense, there must be something which are not ideas, and above all there is something connecting the two realms. It follows from the very distinction between ideas and nonideas, that there are no ideas of the connecting link" (Strauss, *On Plato's Symposium*, 199–200). By this logic, there can be, he notes, "no idea of love" (200).

23. Strauss suggests a historical reason for the curiously specific lapse of time in the framing of the *Symposium*: the gap in time corresponds to the absence of Alcibiades from Athens. The banquet, Strauss notes, must have taken place in 416 (the year Agathon won first prize). Alcibiades, who, called back shortly after he

left on an ill-fated expedition to Sicily, fled to Sparta and could not return to Athens (for fear of a death sentence) because he was blamed for the profanation of the Eleusinian mysteries, "the most sacred mysteries in Athens" (*On Plato's Symposium,* 14), a profanation that occurred the year before the expedition. Alcibiades, Strauss notes, returned to Athens in 407, which is why the story can now be told. He further hypothesizes: "A profanation of mystery occurs only when someone reveals it to another who is not already initiated. . . . I suggest tentatively that the dramatic play underlying the *Symposium* is that here you get the true report of what happened in 415 or 416" (14–15). As he says later: "The mysteries divulged were not those of Eleusis but mysteries told by an entirely different priestess from Mantineia[,] . . . and the man who divulged them was Socrates himself" (24). (That other priestess is, of course, Diotima.) For another account (focusing on Alcibiades) of the historical background of the dialogue, see Nussbaum, *The Fragility of Goodness,* 165–71. Noting that there is a temporal delay even in this frame narrative—"the dialogue itself takes place two days after the reported Glaucon conversation; and it takes place between Apollodoros and an anonymous 'friend' "—Nussbaum offers the intriguing "conjecture" that the murder of Alcibiades explains the sense of urgency felt by the unnamed friend (who, unlike Glaucon, knows that the banquet took place years earlier): "In any case we are surely intended to tie the dialogue very closely to the death, to think of Alcibiades as dead, or dying, even while 'he' speaks, and to see the oligarch's fear of a love that would reunite Alcibiades and Athens as one of the fears that led to the killing" (170–71).

2. Forgetting *The Tempest*

1. William Shakespeare, *The Tempest,* ed. Stephen Orgel (New York: Oxford University Press, 1987), 1.2.76, 87, 105. All citations from *The Tempest* are from this edition; references are to act, scene, and line(s). References to Orgel's criticism will indicate the essay title; otherwise, references to Orgel are to his notes and commentary on this edition of *The Tempest.*

2. Orgel, for example, writes, "Prospero's expostulations take the form of demands for attention and reassurance. Miranda makes it clear that her attention is in no danger of wandering, but her father's violence is retrospective, the playing out of an old rage, and Miranda is not really its object" (16).

3. *Attend me*: as the echo of the French *attendre* might suggest, the imperative is to pay attention but also to wait on or for him, to give oneself over to the vacant time (which Ariel might know) between commands.

4. In an essay about William Wordsworth's *The Borderers* that, among other things, suggests that "Wordsworth's fascination with the motif of forgetfulness derives . . . in large part from *The Tempest,*" Reeve Parker traces the forgetfulness

of *The Tempest* in relation to a disavowed parricidal wish—a wish to escape a bondage to memory and narrative encoded in an ostensibly protective paternal embrace—that is itself predicated, for Prospero, on forgetting his own self-usurpation. Parker, "Reading Wordsworth's Power: Narrative and Usurpation in *The Borderers*," *ELH* 54, no. 2 (Summer 1987): 299–331, 317. For Parker, the sympathy generated at this moment of *The Tempest* is not unrelated to the forgetfulness: "Pity is the fiction that displaces the truth of self-usurpation" (321).

5. For Christopher Pye, the insistence in this scene on establishing Miranda as a *tabula rasa* ("a pure, groundless ground secured in the determinate interval between matter and spirit") is linked to the play's exploration of the self-generating, autochthonous structure of the aesthetic—and to the relation of the play's understanding of the aesthetic to questions of historical and material inscription. Pye, "Storm at Sea: *The Tempest*, Cultural Materialism, and the Early Modern Political Aesthetic," *English Studies* 94, no. 3 (2013): 331–45, 337. That problem of the aesthetic is, he suggests, at once that of subjectivity as culturally inscribed and that of historical inscription. History does not intervene from the "outside" of the play; it is internal to the play's meditation on its self-constituting grounds, which is also to say that the question of the "aesthetic" in the play cannot be bracketed in favor of historical or contextual questions. (It would be a mistake to think that history intervened on the aesthetic, as something external to it; "precisely in its totalizing movement, the aesthetic solicits and provokes history as the trace of an inassimilable cause, an infraction that occurs neither exactly from within nor from without" [343].) More generally, Pye's argument thus underlines the stakes of forgetfulness in the play—in the movement between absorption and distraction.

6. "*Tempestas*, the tempest of the title, has as its root *tempus*" (Orgel, 49–50).

7. Nicole Loraux, *The Divided City: On Memory and Forgetting in Ancient Athens*, trans. Corinne Pache with Jeff Fort (New York: Zone Books, 2002).

8. Orgel also notes that magic is what caused Prospero his problems in the first place. Orgel, "Prospero's Wife," *Representations* 8 (Autumn 1984): 1–13, esp. 10.

9. This pun also appears in *Romeo and Juliet*: MERCUTIO: "Why, is not this better / now than groaning for love? / now art thou sociable, now art thou Romeo; now art / thou what thou art, by art as well as by nature: / for this drivelling love is like a great natural, / that runs lolling up and down to hide his bauble in a hole." *The Riverside Shakespeare*, ed. G. Evans and J. J. M. Tobin, 2nd ed. (London: Houghton Mifflin, 1997), 2.4.76–80.

10. *Foretold* here might also mean "as I told you before," referring to Prospero's aside to Ferdinand during the masque.

11. The other textual connection is Gonzalo's citation of Montaigne's "Of Cannibals"; see *The Complete Essays of Montaigne*, trans. Donald M. Frame (Stanford: Stanford University Press, 1958), 150–58.

12. See Alden T. Vaughan, "William Strachey's 'True Reportory' and Shake-

speare: A Close Look at the Evidence," *Shakespeare Quarterly* 59, no. 3 (2008): 245–73. Vaughan critiques (most immediately) Roger Stritmatter and Lynne Kositsky, "Shakespeare and the Voyagers Revisited," *Review of English Studies,* n.s. 58 (2007): 447–72. Both articles rehearse some of the crucial milestones in the critical history of the letter's relation to *The Tempest.*

13. Kathy Delfosse pointed out to me the pun I wish had been intentional: the originator of the Oxfordian theory of authorship was J. Thomas Looney.

14. I owe this point—and the references to Vaughan, the anti-Stratfordians he rebuts, Strachey, and Orgel's "Prospero's Wife"—to Mary Crane.

15. Mary Thomas Crane, *Shakespeare's Brain: Reading with Cognitive Theory* (Princeton: Princeton University Press, 2001), 190–200. See also Hortense Spillers, "Who Cuts the Border? Some Readings on America," in *Black, White, and in Color: Essays on American Literature and Culture* (Chicago: University of Chicago Press, 2003), 319–35; and Jonathan Goldberg, *Tempest in the Caribbean* (Minneapolis: University of Minnesota Press, 2004). That the island is in both the Mediterranean and the Caribbean is, of course, a major crux of criticism of the play—particularly with regard to considerations of the play's relation to Bermuda and Strachey's "True Reportory."

16. Henry James, "Introduction to *The Tempest,*" in *Literary Criticism,* vol. 1, *Essays, English and American Writers* (New York: Library of America, 1984; originally published in *The Complete Works of William Shakespeare,* ed. Sidney Lee, vol. 16 [New York: George D. Sproul, 1907]), 1205–20, 1215. I discuss James's essay in much greater detail in my "Hover, Torment, Waste: Late Writings and the Great War," in *Henry James and the Queerness of Style,* 109–47.

17. Stanley Cavell, "Henry James Reading Emerson Reading Shakespeare," in *Emerson's Transcendental Etudes,* ed. David Justin Hodge (Stanford: Stanford University Press, 2003), 237.

18. Versions of some of the sentences in this paragraph appeared in my *Henry James and the Queerness of Style,* 142.

19. The strangeness of this moment was pointed out by Carl Phillips during a reading at Boston College in 2004.

20. Virgil, *The Aeneid,* trans. Robert Fitzgerald (New York: Vintage, 1990), bk. 1, lines 406–7.

21. On Virgil in *The Tempest,* see (in addition to Orgel's notes to the Oxford edition), J. M. Nosworthy, "The Narrative Sources of *The Tempest,*" *Review of English Studies* 24 (1948): 281–94; John Gillies, "Shakespeare's Virginian Masque," *ELH* 53, no. 4 (Winter 1986): 673–707; Jan Kott, "*The Aeneid* and *The Tempest,*" *Arion: A Journal of Humanities and the Classics* 3 (1976): 424–51; Kott, "*The Tempest*; or, Repetition," *Mosaic* 10 (1977): 9–36; Michael Mack, "The Consolation of Art in *The Aeneid* and *The Tempest,*" in *Reading the Renaissance: Ideas and Idioms from Shakespeare to Milton,* ed. Marc Berley (Pittsburgh: Duquesne University Press),

57–77; John Pitcher, "A Theatre of the Future: *The Aeneid* and *The Tempest,*" *Essays in Criticism* 34 (1984): 193–215; David Scott Wilson-Okamura, "Virgilian Models of Colonization in Shakespeare's *Tempest,*" *ELH* 70, no. 3 (Fall 2003): 709–37; and Robert Wiltenburg, "*The Aeneid* in *The Tempest,*" in *Shakespeare Survey* 39 (1987): 159–68. See also Mary Fuller's (compellingly titled) "Forgetting *The Aeneid,*" *American Literary History* 4, no. 3 (1992): 517–38.

22. Giorgio Agamben, "The Author as Gesture," in *Profanations,* trans. Jeff Fort (New York: Zone Books, 2007), 61–72. It is perhaps because of this dynamic of a mastery that is indistinguishable from a relinquishment and self-forgetting, and because of the difficulty of distinguishing Prospero's renunciation from the absorption that has constituted his art, that Prospero provides an epigraph to Agamben's essay "Genius," in *Profanations,* 9–18. Most fascinating, that essay's final turn to a letting-go of genius itself is compared to Prospero's at last setting Ariel free.

23. Prospero says to Ferdinand in act 1: "One word more: I charge thee / That thou attend me: thou dost here usurp / The name thou owest not; and hast put thyself / Upon this island as a spy, to win it / From me, the lord on't" (1.2.452–56).

24. *Ovid's Metamorphoses: The Arthur Golding Translation of 1567,* ed. John Frederick Nims (Philadelphia: Paul Dry Books, 2000), bk. 5, lines 534–35, on page 112.

25. See Mack, "The Consolation of Art in *The Aeneid* and *The Tempest.*" Mack does find a consoling power for art in *The Tempest*; to my mind, his article is perhaps more powerful in its account of the inconsolable in the *Aeneid.*

26. John Gillies writes, "We can be quite certain that Shakespeare's Ceres is based on Ovid both because the idea that Venus and Cupid 'plot' the rape of Proserpine is uniquely Ovidian (*Metamorphoses* 5. 459–80) and because Shakespeare's use of the homely word 'stover' (4. 1. 63) can be traced to Arthur Golding's description of Ceres (5. 435)" (Gillies, "Shakespeare's Virginian Masque," 693–94). It strikes me that the lines about Venus and Cupid also cross the story of Proserpine in Ovid with that of Dido in the *Aeneid,* where, like Proserpine in Ovid, Dido is the victim of the machinations of Venus and Cupid. (Michael Mack notes that, in an Ovidian context, there is no reason for Ceres to fear that Venus will accompany Juno; in the *Aeneid,* however, "Juno does in fact ally herself with Venus to plot the marriage of Aeneas and Dido" [Mack, "The Consolation of Art in *The Aeneid* and *The Tempest,*" 68].) In *The Tempest,* Iris's reassurances on this point— "Of her society / Be not afraid" (4.1.91–92)—curiously echo Caliban's reassurances to Trinculo and Stefano: "Be not afeard: the isle is full of noises / Sounds and sweet airs, that give delight and hurt not" (3.2.144–45).

27. This echo is also noted by Nosworthy, "The Narrative Sources of *The Tempest,*" 289.

28. Jan Kott writes, "During the Vitruvian revival the mythological setting be-

came an obligatory convention in the Stuart masque. What is unexpected is a violent interruption of the Feast of Harvest in *The Tempest*; this is contrary to all the conventions of the wedding masque which invariably ended with the presentation of gifts to the young couple and a festive choral epithalamium." Kott also notes that the interruption here recalls the disruption of the hunt "preparing us for the wedding pageantry of Dido and Aeneas" in the *Aeneid*. Kott, "*The Aeneid* and *The Tempest*," 438.

29. As Orgel notes, the disappearance of the crossbar was first noticed by Jeanne Addison Roberts; see her "'Wife' or 'Wise'—*The Tempest* 1. 1786," *University of Virginia Studies in Bibliography* 31 (1978): 203–8.

30. Orgel also notes the play's complex relation to the claims to the throne of Elizabeth and James. See "Prospero's Wife," 8–9.

31. As Orgel notes, it is striking that Caliban claims the island because it was his mother's, and not (as would perhaps be the more obvious argument) because he was there first ("Prospero's Wife," 5). Prospero, declaring Caliban illegitimate, claims the island as his own; as Orgel implies, though, thus to supervene Caliban comes perilously close to identifying with him—as Prospero's later acknowledgment perhaps suggests. In a fascinating reading, David Scott Wilson-Okamura sees in Caliban traces of Virgil that Shakespeare came to by way of Marlowe: "Marlowe provided Shakespeare with something that was missing from the records of the Virginia Company and the Bermuda shipwreck. The treachery, ingratitude, and even the intransigence that Prospero and Miranda attribute to Caliban are all in Strachey's report to potential stockholders. But Caliban is more than these things: on the contrary, his is the voice that does not appear in the investor prospectus. And for that voice, Shakespeare went, not to the New World, not even to the Old World, but to Virgilian Africa: the world of Dido and Aeneas, and (let us not forget) of Iarbas. He did so, I am suggesting, by way of Marlowe because Marlowe heard a note in Virgil's mindsong that the commentators had missed: the outrage of the dispossessed, the voice of the indigene who talks back" (Wilson-Okamura, "Virgilian Models of Colonization in Shakespeare's *Tempest*," 728).

32. See Goldberg's brilliant reading of this scene, *Tempest in the Caribbean*, 54.

33. Mary Crane makes a similar point in *Shakespeare's Brain*—see 178.

34. For a beautiful reading of Ovidian metamorphosis in relation to writing, see Daniel Heller-Roazen, "The Writing Cow," in *Echolalias: On the Forgetting of Language* (New York: Zone Books, 2005): 121–28.

35. Sean Keilen, "*Metamorphoses*, Its Tradition, and the Work of Art," in *Approaches to Teaching the Works of Ovid and the Ovidian Tradition,* ed. Barbara Weiden Boyd and Cora Fox (New York: Modern Language Association, 2010), 219–224, 223. For a beautiful meditation on Diana and Acteon, see Pierre Klossowski, *Le Bain de Diane* (Paris: Gallimard, 1980).

3. Tradition in Fragments

1. Swinburne, "Anactoria," as printed in *The Pre-Raphaelites and Their Circle,* ed. Cecil Lang (Chicago: University of Chicago Press, 1975), lines 19–20. Hereafter cited in parentheses by line numbers.

2. Sonnet 18: "Shall I compare thee to a summer's day?" *Shakespeare's Sonnets,* ed. Booth, 19.

3. Yopie Prins suggests that to "catch the sob's middle music" is to make "the voice catch or stop before the words, in order to catch a melody that is beyond words and purely musical." Prins, *Victorian Sappho* (Princeton: Princeton University Press, 1999), 127.

4. Yopie Prins, who quotes the first twelve lines of the dramatic monologue, points out that it is a rewriting of Sappho's Fragment 31 (Prins, "Swinburne's Sapphic Sublime," in *Victorian Sappho,* 116). (This fragment is also crucial for Anne Carson's *Eros the Bittersweet*; see 12–17.)

5. Carson, *Eros the Bittersweet,* 39, 40–41.

6. I would therefore disagree with Jennifer Wagner-Lawlor's claim, in her illuminating and complex reading of the poem, that the claims of immortality are ironized by our knowledge of the fragmentation of the Sapphic corpus: "Sappho's claims are powerful—but Swinburne's irony provokes at another, deeper level here: her claim of transcendence highlights for the reader the fact that our knowledge of Sappho's original work is severely limited by the survival of only the smallest fragments of her corpus. 'Sappho' is the great original whose work has been almost entirely lost, recalling the textual medium's vulnerability to the possible damage, distortion, or, in this case, near erasure that can occur over time. Sappho existed to Swinburne, as still to us, primarily through translation and interpretation, through the voices of others, not her own. Obviously this is the circumstance of the poem itself, and Swinburne forces us to be fully aware of the irony of the authority of 'Sappho's' voice here, when it is clearly a textual construct of his own as a nineteenth-century poet." Wagner-Lawlor, "Metaphorical 'Indiscretion' and Literary Survival in Swinburne's 'Anactoria,'" *Studies in English Literature, 1500–1900* 36, no. 4 (Autumn 1996): 917–34. For other crucial readings of the poem, see Richard Dellamora, "Poetic Perversities of A. C. Swinburne," in *Masculine Desire: The Sexual Politics of Victorian Aestheticism* (Chapel Hill: University of North Carolina Press, 1990), 69–85; Thais Morgan, "Swinburne's Dramatic Monologues: Sex and Ideology," *Victorian Poetry* 22, no. 2 (Summer 1984): 175–95; Morgan, "Mixed Metaphor, Mixed Gender: Swinburne and the Victorian Critics," *Victorian Newsletter* 73, no. 1 (Spring 1988): 16–19; and Camille Paglia, "Romantic Shadows: Swinburne and Pater," in *Sexual Personae: Art and Decadence from Nefertiti to Emily Dickinson* (New Haven: Yale University Press, 1990), 460–88.

7. Prins also points this out: "Here, as so often in Swinburne's verse, the verb

'to cleave' is used antithetically—meaning both 'to join' and 'to separate'—in order to describe a body held together only by falling apart" (Prins, *Victorian Sappho,* 117).

8. From the *Oxford English Dictionary,* 3rd ed., http://www.oed.com.proxy. bc.edu/: "Mix: . . . 1c. *poet* To cause (eyes) to meet in an exchange of glances; (also) to join, clasp (hands). *Obs. to mix one's thigh with:* to have sexual intercourse with . . . 3a. *trans.* To unite (a person or persons) in dealings or acquaintance; to bring together; to associate; †to join in sexual intercourse (*obs.*). Freq. *refl.* Now *rare* . . . 3b. *intr.* To have sexual intercourse. Usu. with *with.* Now *rare."*

9. Leo Bersani writes, "This is the virtuality of art which, even when it designates or portrays specific human figures or particular places and acts, has already removed them from the field of designation. Represented happening in art, however meticulously detailed, is inherently unspecifiable happening" (Bersani, "The It in the I," in *Intimacies,* by Bersani and Phillips, 26).

10. "I have striven," he wrote, "to cast my spirit in the mould of hers, to express not the poem but the poet" (in Lang, *The Pre-Raphaelites and Their Circle,* 407).

11. The other important subtext for the poem, Swinburne notes (in Lang, *The Pre-Raphaelites and Their Circle,* 406), is the "Ode to Anactoria" (Fragment 31). See the translation by Anne Carson in *If Not, Winter,* 62–65, and her commentary on the poem in *Eros the Bittersweet,* 12–17.

12. For Carson's translation of the ode, see Sappho, *If Not, Winter,* 3–5.

13. That transmission, for Prins, involves a breaking apart and reassembling of the body that she links to the sublime in Longinus—and to the various ways that both Sappho's and Swinburne's poetic works have been transmitted. Prins also suggests that one understand sadomasochism in particular and passion in general as metrical in Swinburne, and she reads this meter in the context of Victorian prosody, particularly classical meter as it can be adapted by English: "What we read as passionate expression in Swinburne is the passion of meter itself: a pathos not inherent in the utterance of a lyric subject, but in subjection to a formal principle" (Prins, *Victorian Sappho,* 155). For Prins, this subjection to the formal principle of meter is therefore also a principle of self-loss rather than self-assertion. What, formally, is transmitted is another (if related) question, and one of her more fascinating suggestions is that, in Swinburne's rendering of Sapphic meter, meter, as a formal principle, is visible rather than audible. "Despite Swinburne's virtuosity . . . in creating an English analogy to long and short quantities in Greek, what we hear is their inaudibility. . . . Indeed the closer Swinburne comes to perfecting the Sapphic stanza, the less audible it becomes, for Sappho's song can only be made 'visible' by the conversion of rhythm into a metrical pattern: a visual representation of meter that seems to be 'made of perfect sound,' because it is now without sound" (145). To suggest that meter in Swinburne is sadomasochistic is therefore also to register not only an eroticization of form but a

288 · NOTES TO CHAPTER 3

submission of the body (and even psychological particularity) to a purely formal, abstract principle—that, qua formal principle, is itself without content. In Coventry Patmore's "Essay on English Metrical Law," Prins points out, "the division of time is . . . figured in spatial terms: 'The fact of that division shall be made manifest by an "ictus" [etymologically linked, Prins elsewhere notes, to the verb *to strike*] or "beat," actual or mental, which like a post in a chain railing, shall mark the end of one space, and the commencement of another. This "ictus" is an acknowledged condition of all possible metre' (15). On this account all meter, both ancient and modern, is a function of marking. The ictus marks intervals 'like a post in a chain railing,' simultaneously marking the end of one space and the beginning of another, but without itself taking up time or space. We perceive the spaces between, rather than the mark itself. While the ictus allows meter to materialize, '*it has no material and external existence at all,*' Patmore insists, again in italics (15); it is the process of marking rather than the mark itself. What appears to be a practical lesson in prosody therefore leads Patmore into the more startling insight that meter might be a form of material inscription" (149; Prins quotes from Coventry Patmore, *Essay on English Metrical Law* (1857), ed. Sister Mary Roth [Washington, D.C.: Catholic University Press of America, 1961]). To perceive meter is, in this sense, to perceive the spaces between, to "hear" something that is merely visible, to transmit (it is perhaps not too much of a stretch to suggest) something with no material existence at all. The eroticization of meter in Prins's account is therefore inseparable from the ways in which Swinburne transmits Sappho's poetic corpus, and the ways that his writing is in turn transmitted: hence also, I think, her emphasis on a "memorization" (Hardy's, of Swinburne; or Swinburne's, of Sappho) that can be opposed to "remembering" (171).

4. Queer Atavism and Pater's Aesthetic Sensibility

1. Aristotle, *Metaphysics*, 1047a24–26; quoted in Agamben, "Bartleby," 266.

2. Heller-Roazen, "Editor's Introduction," 1. For a more detailed discussion, see my introduction above.

3. On the queer erotics of Pater's aesthetics and for a detailed account of his model of aesthetic spectatorship, see my "Doomed Creatures of Immature Radiance: Renaissance, Death, and Rapture in Walter Pater," in *Innocence and Rapture,* 13–60. The various coalescences and disjunctions that mark the experience of viewing a work of art in Pater make that experience queer; a similar alternation structures Carolyn Williams's understanding of Pater's "aesthetic historicism" in *Transfigured World*—a book to which my argument here is also indebted in its descriptions of a method that continually recurs to an original context at once irrecuperable and essential to aesthetic meaning. Williams, *Transfigured World: Walter Pater's Aesthetic Historicism* (Ithaca, N.Y.: Cornell University Press, 1989).

For a reading (very congenial to the reading of transmission presented here) of Pater's diaphanous selves that reconsiders the politics of failed subjectivity in queer theory, see Heather Love, "Forced Exile: Walter Pater's Queer Modernism," in *Bad Modernisms,* ed. Rebecca Walkowitz and Douglas Mao (Durham, N.C.: Duke University Press, 2006), 19–43.

4. Carolyn Williams, "Pater's Impressionism," in *Knowing the Past: Victorian Literature and Culture,* ed. Suzy Anger (Ithaca, N.Y.: Cornell University Press, 2001), 77–99, 95.

5. Walter Pater, "Hippolytus Veiled: A Study from Euripides" (from *Imaginary Portraits*), in *Walter Pater: Three Major Texts,* ed. William E. Buckler (New York: New York University Press, 1986), 322–42, 322.

6. For Carolyn Williams, the gap between the present observer and the past—never to be known, therefore, "in itself"—secures the objectification of the past, and its knowability. Mediation is not an obstacle but a condition for knowledge; "subjective" and "objective" relations to the past are not opposed but, rather, form a sort of pincers movement that secures the possibility of knowing the past—of bringing it, in the Paterian metaphor that Williams has so elegantly illuminated, into "relief." See her "Pater's Impressionism" and *Transfigured World.*

7. This is, of course, the same structure as that of the opening sentence of *Marius*: "As, in the triumph of Christianity, the old religion lingered latest in the country, and died out at last as but paganism . . ." so, in an earlier century . . ." Pater, *Marius the Epicurean: His Sensations and Ideas* (New York: Penguin Books, 1985), 37.

8. Theseus himself, we note, is said in this passage to figure "passably, as a kind of mythic shorthand for civilisation" (Pater, "Hippolytus Veiled," 327).

9. See my *Innocence and Rapture,* 27–32, 37–46.

10. In Euripides, for example, it is clear that Phaedra acts on behalf of Aphrodite such that there is in fact only one story: the rivalry of the goddesses and the revenge of Aphrodite. In addition to removing any such narrative clarity, Pater's text renders the relation between the two stories as at once narratively driven (Aphrodite's anger fuels the story) and allegorical.

11. Walter Pater, *The Renaissance: Studies in Art and Poetry* (the 1893 text), ed. Donald Hill (Berkeley: University of California Press, 1980), 38 (on Pico) and, for example, 175 (for one use of "relic" in the essay on Winckelmann). See my *Innocence and Rapture,* esp. 35–46. See also Williams, *Transfigured World* and "Pater's Impressionism"; and Ellis Hanson, "Pater Dolorosa," in *Decadence and Catholicism* (Cambridge, Mass.: Harvard University Press, 1997), 169–228.

12. Edith Hamilton, *Mythology* (Boston: Little, Brown, 1942), 220.

13. "Behold, I will stand before thee there, upon the rocke in Horeb, and thou shalt smite the rocke, and there shall come water out of it, that the people may drinke. And Moses did so, in the sight of the Elders of Israel" (Exod. 17:5); "Hee brought streames also out of the rocke, and caused waters to runne downe like

riuers. . . . Behold, he smote the rocke, that the waters gushed out, and the streames ouerflowed" (Ps. 78:16, 20); "He opened the rocke, and the waters gushed out: they ranne in the dry places like a riuer" (Ps. 105:41).

14. This section on "The Child in the House" is indebted to a discussion with Kristin Imre.

15. Walter Pater, "The Child in the House" (from *Imaginary Portraits*), in *Three Major Texts,* 223–37, 223.

16. For Carolyn Williams, who emphasizes in the text the "brain-building," the process of internalization through which "impressions" (as against the fleeting impressions of the first two paragraphs of Pater's "Conclusion" to *The Renaissance*) are impressed (permanently) on the malleable stuff of consciousness, "accident" is an index of historicity. See Williams, "Pater's Impressionism," 89.

17. "The coming and going of travellers to the town along the way, the shadow of the streets, the sudden breath of the neighbouring gardens, the singular brightness of bright weather there, its singular darkness which linked themselves in his mind to certain engraved illustrations in the old big Bible at home, the coolness of the dark, cavernous shops around the great church, with its giddy winding stair up to the pigeons and the bells—a citadel of peace in the heart of the trouble—all this acted on his childish fancy, so that ever afterwards the like aspects and incidents never failed to throw him into a well-recognised imaginative mood, seeming *actually* to become a part of the texture of his mind" (Pater, "The Child in the House," 225; emphasis added).

18. One might compare this moment in Proust, about the narrator's aunts, who "held that one ought to set before children, and that children showed their own innate good taste in admiring, only such books and pictures as they would continue to admire when their minds were developed and mature. No doubt they regarded aesthetic merits as material objects which an unclouded vision could not fail to discern, without one's needing to nurture equivalents of them and let them slowly ripen in one's heart." Proust, *In Search of Lost Time,* vol. 1, *Swann's Way,* trans. C. K. Scott Moncrieff and Terence Kilmartin; rev. D. J. Enright (New York: Modern Library, 1992), 206.

19. Pater, "Conclusion" to *The Renaissance,* ed. Hill, 186.

20. One might compare the model here to Ruskin's "Two Boyhoods," in *The Genius of John Ruskin: Selections from His Writings,* ed. John D. Rosenberg (Charlottesville and London: University of Virginia Press, 1998), 106–19.

21. For a particularly condensed and explicit version of this argument, see Pater, "Diaphaneitè," which is printed as an appendix to *The Renaissance: Studies in Art and Poetry,* ed. Adam Phillips (Oxford: Oxford University Press, 1986), 154–58.

22. Likewise, we read that the "*old house,* as when Florian talked of it afterwards he always called it (as all children do, who can recollect a change of home,

soon enough but not too soon to mark a period in their lives) really was an old house" (Pater, "The Child in the House," 224).

23. Sigmund Freud, "Mourning and Melancholia," in *On Metapsychology: The Theory of Psychoanalysis,* trans. James Strachey, ed. Angela Richards (New York: Penguin Books, 1991), 245–68. See also Nicolas Abraham and Maria Torok, "Mourning or Melancholia: Introjection versus Incorporation," in *The Shell and the Kernel,* ed. and trans. Nicholas T. Rand, vol. 1 (Chicago: University of Chicago Press, 1994), 125–38.

24. *The Metamorphoses of Ovid,* trans. Allen Mandelbaum (San Diego and New York: Harvest Books, 1993), 534.

5. "That Strange Mimicry of Life by the Living"

1. Bersani, "The Power of Evil and the Power of Love," 81.

2. Oscar Wilde, "The Portrait of Mr. W.H.," in *The Complete Works of Oscar Wilde: Stories, Plays, Poems, and Essays* (New York: Perennial Library of Harper and Row, 1989), 1150–1201, 1198. Citations to "The Portrait of Mr. W.H." hereafter given parenthetically in the text.

3. *Shakespeare's Sonnets,* ed. Booth, 18–19.

4. See Jacques Derrida, *Limited Inc,* trans. Samuel Weber, Jeffrey Mehlman, and Alan Bass (Evanston, Ill.: Northwestern University Press, 1988).

5. Wilde's text makes a complementary point in his fascinating history of boy actors, in which the beauty of those boys moves from Renaissance dramaturgy to Romanticism to the Enlightenment, and the narrator even speculates that Willie could have been among a troupe of boy actors who traveled from England, were slain in Nuremberg, "and [were] secretly buried in a little vineyard outside the city by some young men." ("For was it not from the sorrows of Dionysos that Tragedy sprang?") (Wilde, "The Portrait of Mr. W.H.," 1193).

6. My thinking on this subject is indebted to a conversation with Tyler Thompson.

7. The other effect of Wilde's unmarked quotation, of course, is to allow him to collect in one paragraph, one after another, many of the sonnets' expressions of desire for a boy, and thereby—without protest, but also without concession—to make ineradicable the homoeroticism of these poems.

8. Walter Pater, "The School of Giorgione," in *The Renaissance,* ed. Hill, 102–22, 108–9.

9. One thinks in this regard of the "pure language" that, for Walter Benjamin, is gestured toward by translation, precisely insofar as translation, in its very failures, subtracts the communicable from language and, in this subtraction, bodies forth an unmeaning or a beyond-meaning internal to language. See Benjamin, "The Task of the Translator," trans. Harry Zohn, in *Selected Writings,* vol.

1, *1913–1926*, ed. Marcus Bullock and Michael W. Jennings (Cambridge, Mass.: Belknap Press, 2004), 253–63.

10. Hence, among other reasons, Pater's fascination with the physical quality of aesthetic perception—notably, for instance, in figures (repeated in *Gaston de Latour* and *Plato and Platonism*) of perceptions that modify the perceiving body, as an insect comes to resemble the plant it sits on. Likewise, in the characterization of the "perpetual motion" of the body in the "Conclusion" to *The Renaissance*—"the passage of the blood, the waste and repairing of the lenses of the eye, the modification of the tissues of the brain under every ray of light and sound" (Pater, "Conclusion" to *The Renaissance*, ed. Hill, 186)—the brain is physically modified by beauty. This linking of aesthetic perception to the waxing and waning of the organization of the material world ultimately underlies (in Pater's description of the cultivation of an aesthetic sensibility) the eroticism of aesthetic apprehension in his account. These strands are also linked to Pater's insistence (apparent, we noted, in "The Child in the House") on a situated, embodied form of aesthetic perception: "Such metaphysical speculation did but reinforce what was instinctive in his way of receiving the world, and for him, everywhere, that sensible vehicle or occasion became, perhaps only too surely, the necessary concomitant of any perception of things, real enough to be of any weight or reckoning, in his house of thought. There were times when he could think of the necessity he was under of associating all thoughts to touch and sight, as a sympathetic link between himself and actual, feeling, living objects; a protest in favour of real men and women against mere grey, unreal abstractions; and he remembered gratefully how the Christian religion, hardly less than the religion of the ancient Greeks, translating so much of its spiritual verity into things that may be seen, condescends in part to sanction this infirmity, if so it be, of our human existence, wherein the world of sense is so much with us, and welcomed this thought as a kind of keeper and sentinel over his soul therein. But certainly, he came more and more to be unable to care for, or think of soul but as in an actual body, or of any world but that wherein are water and trees, and where men and women look, so or so, and press actual hands" (Pater, "The Child in the House," 231–32). (The potentially redemptive quality of sense perception is condensed, it is perhaps worth noting in passing, in Pater's rewriting of Wordsworth: "the world is too much with us" to "the world of sense is so much with us." The recovery of the pagan world toward which Wordsworth yearns takes shape in an oblique, highly mediated way.)

11. On Wilde's use of these two meanings of *realise* in *De Profundis*, and for a reading of that text as a complex aesthetic treatise, see chapter 6 below.

12. It is notable in this regard that Jesper Svenbro links the development of silent reading to the theater: once separated from the stage, watching actors speak lines that they had memorized (at a distance, therefore, from the text), it became possible to conceptualize silent reading, to conceptualize texts having "voices"

that one hears in one's head: "The written word simply seeks to 'speak' to him. He is 'listening' to writing—exactly like the spectator in the theater, who listens to the vocal writing of the actors. The text that is 'recognized' visually seems to have the same autonomy as the acting on the stage. The letters, the *grammata*, 'read' themselves—or rather, 'pronounce' themselves. . . . The reading voice is internalized" (Svenbro, *Phrasikleia*, 171). As he remarks, "the written word and the actor are analogous, interchangeable" (178). Later, he notes that the actor's mind is "inscribed" by the writer (180).

13. From *The Picture of Dorian Gray*: "For there would be a real pleasure in watching it. He would be able to follow his mind into its secret places. This portrait would be to him the most magical of mirrors. As it had revealed to him his own body, so it would reveal to him his own soul" (106).

14. Percy Bysshe Shelley: "Poets are the hierophants of an unapprehended inspiration; the mirrors of the gigantic shadows which futurity casts upon the present; the words which express what they understand not; the trumpets which sing to battle, and feel not what they inspire; the influence which is moved not, but moves. Poets are the unacknowledged legislators of the world." Shelley, "A Defense of Poetry," in *Shelley's Poetry and Prose*, ed. Donald H. Reiman and Sharon Powers (New York: W. W. Norton, 1977), 478–508, 508.

15. One thinks in this regard of the kind of exposure Basil Hallward imagines in *The Picture of Dorian Gray* ("Every portrait that is painted with feeling is a portrait of the artist, not of the sitter. The sitter is merely the accident, the occasion. It is not he who is revealed by the painter; it is rather the painter who, on the coloured canvas, reveals himself. The reason I will not exhibit this picture is that I am afraid that I have shown in it the secret of my own soul"), or indeed of Dorian's self-recognition in the painting, whose language echoes the terms here (Wilde, *The Picture of Dorian Gray*, 5).

16. This moment evokes Pater's recurrent fascination in *The Renaissance* with the blank stares of statues. It perhaps also provides a context for understanding why Wilde, in his discussion of acting, links artistry to a becoming-mute and suggests that the actor accedes to the place of the artist when he tears the veil of speech: "But to Shakespeare, the actor was a deliberate and self-conscious fellow worker who gave form and substance to a poet's fancy, and brought into Drama the elements of a noble realism. His silence could be as eloquent as words, and his gestures as expressive, and in those terrible moments of Titan agony or of god-like pain, when thought outstrips utterance, when the soul sick with excess of anguish stammers or is dumb, and the very raiment of speech is rent and torn by passion in its storm, then the actor could become, though it were but for a moment, a creative artist, and touch by his mere presence and personality those springs of terror and of pity to which tragedy appeals" (Wilde, "The Portrait of Mr. W.H.," 1171). As "material," the actor's full expressivity comes not when passion becomes articulate

but when the performance exacerbates the divide between thought and utterance, passion and speech.

17. Giorgio Agamben, "The End of the Poem," in *The End of the Poem: Studies in Poetics,* trans. Daniel Heller-Roazen (Stanford: Stanford University Press, 1999), 109–15.

18. For a more detailed account of this reading, see chapter 1 of my *Innocence and Rapture.*

6. Erotic Bafflement and the Lesson of Oscar Wilde

1. On the history of the letter, see *The Complete Letters of Oscar Wilde,* ed. Merlin Holland and Rupert Hart-Davis (New York: Henry Holt, 2000), 683n1. On Wilde's title, see his letter of April 1, 1897, to Robert Ross: "If the copying is done at Hornton Street the lady type-writer might be fed through a lattice in the door like the Cardinals when they elect a Pope, till she comes out on the balcony and can say to the world '*Habet Mundus Epistolam*'; for indeed it is an Encyclical Letter, and as the Bulls of the Holy Father are named from their opening words, it may be spoken of as the *Epistola: In Carcere et Vinculis*" (782). My citations to Wilde's prison letter will be given parenthetically, and the page numbers refer to *De Profundis* as printed in *The Portable Oscar Wilde,* ed. Richard Aldington and Stanley Weintraub, rev. ed. (New York: Penguin Books, 1981), 508–658. There is an excellent scholarly edition of the letter (in Ross's version and in its later, unexpurgated form) in *The Complete Works of Oscar Wilde,* vol. 2, *De Profundis; 'Epistola: In Carcere et Vinculis,'* ed. Ian Small (Oxford: Oxford University Press, 2004). I have not cited it here because, at $225, it is unlikely to be available to many readers.

2. Richard Ellmann, *Oscar Wilde* (New York: Vintage Books, 1984), 513. Oliver Buckton argues that the staging of confession in the letter "deconstructs the singularity of the autobiographical subject." Buckton, "'Desire without Limit': Dissident Confession in Oscar Wilde's *De Profundis*," in *Victorian Sexual Dissidence,* ed. Richard Dellamora (Chicago: University of Chicago Press, 1999), 171–87, 186. He argues that Wilde plays on the conventions of confession, which dictate a split between the present (narrating, reformed) self and the past, sinful self that is (implicitly) reconciled by the narrating of autobiographical insight. Wilde resists this recuperation by displacing his prior, sinning self onto Bosie; as reader and writer, present and past self, mingle, the letter's autobiographical subject is radically split.

3. Jonathan Dollimore writes, "Wilde repositions himself as the authentic, sincere subject which before he had subverted," suggesting that Wilde's letter represents "the defeat of the marginal and the oppositional of a kind which only ideological domination can effect; a renunciation which is experienced as voluntary and self-confirming but which is in truth a self-defeat and a self-denial massively

coerced through the imposition, by the dominant, of incarceration and suffering and their 'natural' medium, confession." Dollimore, "Different Desires: Subjectivity and Transgression in Wilde and Gide," *Textual Practice* 1 (1987): 48–67, 65–66; quoted by Hanson in *Decadence and Catholicism,* 294. See also Dollimore, *Sexual Dissidence: Augustine to Wilde, Freud to Foucault* (Oxford: Clarendon Press, 1991).

4. Wilde, *The Picture of Dorian Gray,* 18. I offer a more detailed consideration of this confession—and of the dynamics of identification in the novel—in *Innocence and Rapture,* 61–121, esp. 107–10.

5. My discussion here is—inevitably—indebted to the exploration of shame in queer theory. See, among many other texts, David M. Halperin and Valerie Traub, eds., *Gay Shame* (Chicago: University of Chicago Press, 2009); Bersani, "Shame on You," 31–56; Eve Kosofsky Sedgwick, "Shame, Theatricality, and Queer Performativity: Henry James's *The Art of the Novel*" and "Shame in the Cybernetic Fold: Reading Silvan Tomkins," with Adam Frank, both in *Touching Feeling: Affect, Pedagogy, Performativity* (Durham, N.C.: Duke University Press, 2003), 35–65, 93–121; Love, *Feeling Backward*; and Kathryn Bond Stockton, *Beautiful Bottom, Beautiful Shame: Where "Black" Meets Queer* (Durham, N.C.: Duke University Press, 2006). For another compelling account of shame (and one partly critical of queer theory's uses of it), see John Limon, "The Shame of Abu Ghraib," *Critical Inquiry* 33, no. 3 (Spring 2007): 543–72. Bersani is critical of the use of shame by queer theory because, he argues, the concept allows theorists drastically to simplify the relation between the psyche and the social, and, in particular, to make homophobia a purely external effect, and the psyche, a reflex reaction to that external imposition: "Significantly, queer theory expresses great interest in shame—not in guilt, but in shame. Shame is an eminently social emotion; others make me feel it. Consequently, shame is accompanied by innocence; we might even say that it is a sign of innocence. . . . The great appeal of Tomkins's thought is, it seems to me, that it relieves the subject—and in particular the gay subject—from all guilt. . . . Unlike guilt, shame is in perfect symmetry with the external world. Shame has nothing to do with my own drives, with my own secret pleasures; it is entirely what others make me feel. Shame therefore fully justifies an aggressiveness toward a hateful world intent on destroying me, and the only question raised by shame is, as Sedgwick says, how it can be transformed into a sense of the subject's value, or dignity" (Bersani, "Aggression, Shame, and Almodóvar's Art," in *Is the Rectum a Grave?,* 63–82, 68).

6. Thanks to Karen Swann for pointing out to me the cavalier (and self-dramatizing) illogic of Wilde's opening gesture. It is perhaps worth nothing that Merlin Holland and Rupert Hart-Davis tell us that, factually speaking, Wilde exaggerates Douglas's silence; Wilde's indictments, they suggest, should not be taken at face value. Wilde's exaggeration is thus not simply a complaint about a lover's neglect; it also makes explicit that his letter creates, imagines, from the outset, the addressee it needs (Wilde, *Letters,* 684).

7. Wilde, "The Nightingale and the Rose," in *The Complete Works of Oscar Wilde: Stories, Plays, Poems, and Essays,* 292–96.

8. *De Profundis,* 606. "Man of Sorrows," Wilde later notes, is a reference to Isaiah 53:3. *The Complete Letters of Oscar Wilde,* 746n3.

9. Pater, *The Renaissance,* ed. Hill, xix.

10. Society's failure in sending him to jail is for Wilde in large part an aesthetic one: society "has the supreme vice of shallowness, and fails to realise what it has done. . . . I claim on my side that if I realise what I have suffered, Society should realise what it has inflicted on me" (*De Profundis,* 587).

11. For "whatever is, is right," see Alexander Pope, "An Essay on Man," Epistle 1: "All nature is but art, unknown to thee; / All chance, direction, which thou canst not see; / All discord, harmony, not understood; / All partial evil, universal good: / And, spite of pride, in erring reason's spite, / One truth is clear, 'Whatever is, is RIGHT." Pope, *The Major Works,* ed. Pat Rogers (New York: Oxford University Press/World's Classics, 2009), 282. For another source for both Pope and Wilde, see the discussion of evil in book 7 of Augustine's *Confessions:* "So we must conclude that if things are deprived of all good, they cease altogether to be; and this means that as long as they are, they are good. Therefore, whatever is, is good; and evil, the origin of which I was trying to find, is not a substance, because if it were a substance, it would be good." Augustine, *Confessions,* trans. R. S. Pine-Coffin (New York: Penguin Books, 1961), 148.

12. *Occultatio:* "emphasizing something by pointedly seeming to pass over it." Richard A. Lantham, *A Handlist of Rhetorical Terms,* 2nd ed. (Berkeley: University of California Press, 1991), 104.

13. Wilde quotes his own assertion later in *De Profundis* (607), putting this assertion of unity explicitly in quotation marks (and thus undermining its claims at the moment they are reasserted).

14. "The Critic as Artist," in *The Artist as Critic: Critical Writings of Oscar Wilde,* ed. Richard Ellmann (Chicago: University of Chicago Press, 1968), 340–408, 389.

15. For Regenia Gagnier, the timelessness evoked in prison's sorrow reflects the undifferentiated, "timeless isolation" of prison life, which, for her, is in contrast to the imaginative, richly detailed, and differentiated world of Wilde's remembered time with Bosie. Gagnier, "'De Profundis': An Audience of Peers," in *Idylls of the Marketplace: Oscar Wilde and the Victorian Public* (Stanford: Stanford University Press, 1996), 177–95, 180. Autobiography, in her reading, serves to reestablish a referentiality threatened by the monotony and useless labor of prison life. To my mind, the possibilities that emerge in reading Wilde's re-creation of the past as an attempt to reestablish referential certainty—and thus to reconnect to a world whose existence is threatened by prison's monotony—are more compelling than the simpler relation (where Wilde's letter is almost a symptom of its composition's

penal context) that guides other moments of her reading. Thanks to a *Genre* reader for reminding me of the relevance of Gagnier's important argument.

16. On the power of Wilde's post-trial writings to catalyze a distinctively modern gay identity (allowing us to discover, in retrospect, the identity it will have formed), see Wayne Koestenbaum, who understands this condensation of identity as a dynamic of reading. See particularly his comments on *red, read, reading,* and *Reading* in *The Ballad of Reading Gaol,* 186–89. Koestenbaum, "Wilde's Hard Labor and the Birth of Gay Reading," in *Engendering Men: The Question of Male Feminist Criticism,* ed. Joseph Boone and Michael Cadden (New York: Routledge, 1990), 176–89.

17. This "friend" has been traditionally identified as Frank Harris; according to Merlin Holland and Rupert Hart-Davis, however, it is "more likely [Robert] Sherard, who records a similar confession" (in *The Complete Letters of Oscar Wilde,* 769). Thanks to a reader for *Genre* for pointing out the traditional identification and Holland's contesting of it.

18. Ellis Hanson, "Wilde's Exquisite Pain," in *Wilde Writings: Contextual Conditions,* ed. Joseph Bristow (Toronto: University of Toronto Press, with UCLA Center for Seventeenth- and Eighteenth-Century Studies and William Andrews Clark Memorial Library, 2003), 101–23, 116.

19. As Otto Jespersen notes, Wilde often uses *was* instead of *were* in conditional clauses. Jesperson, *A Modern English Grammar on Historical Principles,* vol. 4 (Heidelberg: Carl Winters Universitätsbuchhandlung, 1931), 130–31, 138–39. For instance: "he looks as if he was made of ivory" (*Dorian Gray,* 3); "she behaves as if she was beautiful" (34); "it sounds as if he was having an argument with the furniture" (*The Importance of Being Earnest,* in *The Complete Works: Stories, Plays, Poems, and Essays,* 379). However, he often uses *were*: "if he were not, there would be no battle" (*Dorian Gray,* 198); "I don't think I would go to Harry if I were in trouble" (116); "men treat art as if it were meant to be a form of autobiography" (11); "I have given away my whole soul to some one who treats it as if it were a flower to put in his coat" (12); and, most famously, "If only it were the other way! If it were I who was to be always young, and the picture that was to grow old!" (25). In the instance from *De Profundis,* there are (at least) two other reasons that Wilde might use *was* instead of *were.* First, he may use *was* for emphasis; second, as Jespersen writes, "In the typical examples of the preterit of imagination the reference is to the present or future time, or rather to no time at all, as the reality of the supposition is denied. But sometimes the unreality may refer to some time in the past, and then *was* is preferred to *were*: she spoke as if she was ashamed (not *were*)—but: she speaks as if she were (or *was*) ashamed." Jespersen, *Essentials of English Grammar* (Tuscaloosa: University of Alabama Press, 1964), 256–57. A temporal distinction replays the paradoxical structure I have outlined: such a

distinction might be expected either in a present reporting of past feelings ("she speaks [now] as if she was ashamed [then]") or in "indirect speech" ("I am glad to see you" becomes "He said [thought, etc.] that he was glad to see you"), but Wilde's instance is a direct quotation of an intuition ostensibly present at the time of its (hypothetical) utterance (Jespersen, *Essentials of English Grammar,* 260–63). *Was* for emphasis may be most obvious, but the letter's theorization of paradoxical temporalities of *realization* makes me hesitate: if it is not emphatic but is, rather, a marker of time, then the quoted "if I was saying" would locate the protasis in the past even in relation to the moment at which it was uttered. (In other terms, the temporal separation between quoted and quoting language would become blurred, thus dividing the initial expression, making it different from itself—and thereby rendering the condition's "realization" constitutively impossible.)

20. Plato, *The Symposium,* 7. Thanks to Rob Odom for reminding me of this passage.

21. Strauss, *On Plato's Symposium,* 33.

22. For a discussion of pedagogical erotics and scenarios of shame relevant to my reading of Wilde in this chapter, see Hanson, "Teaching Shame."

7. Lessons of the Master

1. See my "Narrating the Child's Queerness in *What Maisie Knew,*" in *Curiouser: On the Queerness of Children,* ed. Steven Bruhm and Natasha Hurley (Minneapolis: University of Minnesota Press, 2004): 81–106, and "Children," in *Henry James in Context,* ed. David McWhirter (Cambridge: Cambridge University Press, 2010), 115–25.

2. Henry James, "The Lesson of the Master" (text of the *New York Edition*), in *The Figure in the Carpet, and Other Stories,* ed. Frank Kermode (New York: Penguin Books, 1986), 113–88.

3. For example: "She had an air of earnestness. 'Do you think then he's so perfect?' 'Far from it. Some of his later books seem to me of a queerness—!' 'Yes, yes. He knows that.' Paul Overt stared. 'That they seem to me of a queerness—?'" (James, "The Lesson of the Master," 131). "'Well, you know, I don't smoke—my wife doesn't let me,' said St. George, looking for a place to sit down. 'It's very good for me—very good for me. Let us take that sofa.' 'Do you mean smoking's good for you?' 'No no—her not letting me. It's a great thing to have a wife who's so sure of all the things one can do without. One might never find them out one's self. She doesn't allow me to touch a cigarette.' They took possession of a sofa at a distance from the group of smokers, and St. George went on: 'Have you got one yourself?' 'Do you mean a cigarette?' 'Dear no—a wife!'" (138). "'The "one" is of course one's self, one's conscience, one's idea, the singleness of one's aim. I think of that pure

spirit as a man thinks of a woman he has in some detested hour of his youth loved and forsaken. She haunts him with reproachful eyes, she lives for ever before him. As an artist, you know, I've married for money.' Paul stared and even blushed a little, confounded by this avowal; whereupon his host, observing the expression of his face, dropped a quick laugh and pursued: 'You don't follow my figure. I'm not speaking of my dear wife, who had a small fortune—which, however, was not my bribe. I refer to the mercenary muse whom I led to the altar of literature' " (165).

4. Gert Buelens, message to James listserv, jamesf-l@ lists.creighton.edu, January 16, 2010, http://lists.creighton.edu/mailman/private/jamesf-l/.

5. Or, in another passage (with, yet again, multivalent effects of ironization—aimed, it seems, at more than one target): "The lines of her face were those of a woman grown, but the child lingered on in her complexion and in the sweetness of her mouth. Above all she was natural—that was indubitable now; more natural than he had supposed at first, perhaps on account of her aesthetic toggery, which was conventionally unconventional, suggesting what he might have called a torturous spontaneity. He had feared that sort of thing in other cases, and his fears had been justified; for though he was an artist to the essence, the modern reactionary nymph, with the brambles of the woodland caught in her folds and a look as if the satyrs had toyed with her hair, made him shrink not as a man of starch and patent leather, but as a man potentially himself a poet or even a faun" (James, "The Lesson of the Master," 128).

6. See my *Henry James and the Queerness of Style.*

8. The Beast's Storied End

1. Sedgwick, "The Beast in the Closet," and Bersani, "The It in the I." I would add another reading to this (admittedly, highly partial) list of "best" readings of James's tale: Andrew Miller's, in *The Burdens of Perfection,* 211–14.

2. Henry James, *The Beast in the Jungle* (text of the *New York Edition*), in *The Beast in the Jungle, and Other Stories* (New York: Dover Publications, 1993), 33–71, 70.

3. I elsewhere suggest reasons why it is difficult to find the formal characteristics of free-indirect style in late James (and some of the consequences of that for his understanding of character). See chapter 2 of my *Henry James and the Queerness of Style.* See also David Kurnick, "What Does Jamesian Style Want?" *Henry James Review* 28, no. 3 (2007): 213–22.

4. Gavin Alexander, "Prosopopoeia; the Speaking Figure," in *Renaissance Figures of Speech,* ed. Sylvia Adamson, Gavin Alexander, and Katrin Ettenhuber (Cambridge: Cambridge University Press, 2007), 97–112.

5. John Milton, *Paradise Lost,* ed. Gordon Teskey (New York: W. W. Norton,

2005), bk. 9, lines 560–61. Eve here quotes, most immediately, the speaker of *Paradise Lost* (at bk. 9, line 86), whose reference, in turn, is to Genesis: "Now the serpent was more subtill then any beast of the field, which the LORD God had made" (Gen. 3:1).

6. Ann Banfield, *Unspeakable Sentences: Narration and Representation in the Language of Fiction* (Boston: Routledge and Kegan Paul, 1982). See also Banfield, "Describing the Unobserved: Events Grouped around an Empty Centre," in *The Linguistics of Writing: Arguments between Language and Literature,* ed. Nigel Fabb, Derek Attridge, Alan Durant, and Colin MacCabe (Manchester, UK: Manchester University Press, 1987), 265–85.

7. Ann Banfield, "Reflective and Non-Reflective Consciousness in the Language of Fiction," *Poetics Today* 2, no. 2 (1981): 61–76.

8. Barbara Johnson, "Face Value," in *Persons and Things* (Cambridge, Mass.: Harvard University Press, 2008), 179–87, 182; she summarizes Paul de Man, "Autobiography as De-Facement," in *The Rhetoric of Romanticism* (New York: Columbia University Press, 1984), 67–82.

9. Cynthia Chase, "Giving a Face to a Name: De Man's Figures," in *Decomposing Figures: Rhetorical Readings in the Romantic Tradition* (Baltimore: The Johns Hopkins University Press, 1986), 82–112. See also Neil Hertz, "Lurid Figures," in *The Ends of Rhetoric: History, Theory, Practice,* ed. John Bender and David E. Wellbery (Stanford: Stanford University Press, 1990), 100–124; and Hertz, "More Lurid Figures," *Diacritics: A Review of Contemporary Criticism* 20, no. 3 (1990): 2–27.

10. Chase quotes from Paul de Man's "Hypogram and Inscription," in *The Resistance to Theory* (Minneapolis: University of Minnesota Press, 1986), 27–53, 48.

11. As Chase writes, "The most radical of deprivations is implicit in the breaking down of the phenomenology of language into the materiality of inscription and the figurality of figure: with it breaks down the possibility of experience as such, of having such a thing as experience" (Chase, "Giving a Face to a Name," 106).

12. See the final chapter of my *Henry James and the Queerness of Style.* Much of the rest of *Henry James and the Queerness of Style* addresses the "disjunct temporalities of art and life"—see especially chapter 3, on James's late wartime writing.

13. "The definition of *prosopopoeia* links it with apostrophe: like the gesture of address, which assumes the possibility of reply, it confers upon 'an absent, deceased, or voiceless entity' the power of speech. As the only face, in de Man's reading, is the face conferred by catachresis, the only voice is the voice conferred by apostrophe" (Chase, "Giving a Face to a Name," 88; Chase quotes from de Man, "Autobiography as De-Facement," 75).

14. Insofar as thrown voice entails a certain expectation of response: "The poem's opening," Barbara Johnson writes of Baudelaire's "Moesta et Errabunda," "makes explicit the relation between direct address and the desire for the *other*'s

voice: 'Tell me: *you* talk.'" Johnson, "Apostrophe, Animation, Abortion," in *A World of Difference* (Baltimore: The Johns Hopkins University Press, 1987), 184–222, 185.

15. On this withdrawn recognition and shame (by way of Silvan Tomkins), see Sedgwick, "Shame, Theatricality, and Queer Performativity," 35–65.

16. Barbara Johnson suggests that to be given a face is perhaps less to speak than to be addressed; to be given a face may be less personifying than objectifying. Face, she writes, "belongs to the viewer" (Johnson, "Face Value," 184). "A face confers addressability," she continues, "but on condition that it be inanimate. The silence of a thing makes it have no awareness or irony to interfere with the addressee's animation. The human ideal of a person is therefore a thing" (186). Speaking to him, May's tomb enacts a convention of epitaphs, which often, of course, importune the traveler to stop and listen; on epitaphs, see Cynthia Chase, "Reading Epitaphs," in *Deconstruction Is/in America: A New Sense of the Political,* ed. Anselm Haverkamp (New York: New York University Press, 1995), 52–59, and Debra Fried, "Repetition, Refrain, and Epitaph," *ELH* 53, no. 3 (Autumn 1986): 615–32.

17. It would be worthwhile to pursue other echoes here; Marcher's encounter with his younger self evokes James's account in the *New York Edition* prefaces of reading his earlier work, for example. (On this figuration, see Sedgwick, "Shame, Theatricality, and Queer Performativity," esp. 39–44.) Even more striking, perhaps, is the similar choreography of Maggie Verver's famous wandering "round and round" the curious, obscure garden pagoda in *The Golden Bowl.* James, *The Golden Bowl* (text of the *New York Edition*) (Oxford: Oxford University Press/World's Classics, 1991), 299.

18. *Facetious* derives from *facetiae*—"humorous sayings or writings; witticisms," sometimes used (especially in book catalogues) "as a euphemism for pornographic literature" (*Oxford English Dictionary*). "The thing to be, with the one person who knew, was easy and natural—to make the reference rather than seeming to avoid it, to avoid it rather than seeming to make it, and to keep it, in any event, familiar, facetious even, rather than pedantic and portentous" (James, *The Beast in the Jungle,* 44).

19. Adam Verver's proposal to Charlotte Stant, likewise said to be a burning of his ships, leads to this image in *The Golden Bowl*: "Just these things in themselves, however, with all the rest, with his fixed purpose now, his committed deed, the fine pink glow, projected forward, of his ships, behind him, definitely blazing and crackling—this quantity was to push him harder than any word of her own could warn him. All that she was herself, moreover, was so lighted, to its advantage, by the pink glow" (James, *The Golden Bowl,* 163).

20. Eric Savoy's reading of the tale is especially suggestive in its account of what he calls "circling"—which, noting that it is a kind of blocking enacted by

characters in a range of James's texts and noting, too, that it might also be said to characterize typical syntactical structures in James's prose, he links to the future- and narrative-rending movement of the Lacanian drives. See Savoy, "The Feet, Mechanical: Circumscribing 'The Beast in the Jungle.'" in *Conjugating the Subject: Henry James and the Hypothetical* (Columbus: Ohio State University Press, forth- coming); taking up questions similar to those addressed here (dwelling, among other shared concerns, not only on "circling" but on literalization [or the uncer- tain figural status of some of James's figures] and prosopopoeia), Savoy's richly suggestive chapter addresses them in very different ways.

21. Northrop Frye, *Anatomy of Criticism* (Princeton: Princeton University Press, 1957), 249–50, quoted by Jonathan Culler in "Apostrophe," *Diacritics: A Re- view of Contemporary Criticism* 7, no. 4 (1977): 59–69, 60. (One supposes that the appearance of "so to speak" here is no accident.)

22. In "Apostrophe Reconsidered," J. Douglas Kneale insists that what Culler and others call "apostrophe" is in fact prosopopoeia or exclamation, insisting that apostrophe requires a pretext, a situation of address from which the speaker turns away. Apostrophe, he argues, is a "diversion" of speech. In his view, then, the first line of the poem cannot be an apostrophe ("O Wild West Wind . . ."). Whatever the validity of his argument about classical rhetoric, which I am not competent to judge (though it does seem more than possible that he could be right about the trope but not in the conclusions he draws from it in his reading of Culler and others, particularly in the literalization that demands from the lyric an explicit scenario of address, or "pre-text," to turn away *from*: if it is implicit in the forensic context of classical rhetoric, why can it not be in the vocative context of the lyric?), *The Beast in the Jungle* makes manifest how difficult it is to distinguish address from turning away, prosopopoeia from apostrophe, address from ventriloquism. Kneale, "Romantic Aversions: Apostrophe Reconsidered," *ELH* 58, no. 1 (Spring 1991): 141–65.

23. Jonathan Culler, "Reading Lyric," *Yale French Studies* 69 (1985): 98–106, 99.

24. Ruth Bernard Yeazell, "The Imagination of Metaphor," in *Language and Knowledge in the Late Novels of Henry James* (Chicago: University of Chicago Press, 1976), 37–63.

25. Address and belonging are in a sense the subject of David Van Leer's cri- tique of Sedgwick's essay. See Van Leer, "The Beast of the Closet: Homosociality and the Pathology of Manhood," *Critical Inquiry* 15, no. 3 (Spring 1989): 587–605; Eve Kosofsky Sedgwick, "Critical Response I: Tide and Trust," *Critical Inquiry* 15, no. 4 (Summer 1989): 745–57; and Van Leer, "Critical Response II: Trust and Trade," *Critical Inquiry* 15, no. 4 (Summer 1989): 758–63.

26. Henry James, *The Ambassadors* (text of the *New York Edition*) (Oxford: Ox- ford University Press/World's Classics, 1985), 3.

9. "My Spirit's Posthumeity" and the Sleeper's Outflung Hand

First epigraph from "Continuing," in *A Coast of Trees*, by A. R. Ammons. Copyright 1981 by A. R. Ammons. Used by permission of W. W. Norton Company, Inc.

1. On Pater and the queer time of Renaissance, see chapter 4 above and "Doomed Creatures of Immature Radiance," chapter 1 of my *Innocence and Rapture*. On Wilde's *Dorian Gray*, see "Narcissists Anonymous," chapter 2 of *Innocence and Rapture*.

2. William Faulkner, *Absalom, Absalom!* (New York: Vintage Books, 1990), 157. Unless otherwise indicated, all italics are Faulkner's.

3. It is perhaps an overstatement to say that the novel lacks explicit decadent tonalities. For a convincing reading of the relation between Faulkner's novel and Oscar Wilde's works, see Ellen Crowell, "The Picture of Charles Bond: Oscar Wilde's Trip through Faulkner's Yoknapatawpha," *Modern Fiction Studies* 50, no. 3 (Fall 2004): 596–631.

4. It is perhaps also an exaggeration to say that the homoeroticism of the novel has been entirely neglected. See, for example, Norman W. Jones, "Coming Out through History's Hidden Love Letters in *Absalom, Absalom!*," *American Literature* 76, no. 2 (June 2004): 339–66. Jones gives a brief history of readings of the novel attentive to its homoerotic thematics (363n7); he explores, among other things, an "erotics of the gap, of history's lacunae," although his understanding of that gap and of what he calls a "coming-out historiography" differs from the understanding of transmission and history presented here. See also Joseph Allan Boone, *Libidinal Currents: Sexuality and the Shaping of Modernism* (Chicago: University of Chicago Press, 1998), 298–322, and Michael P. Bibler, "Intraracial Homoeroticism and the Loopholes of Taboo in William Faulkner's *Absalom, Absalom!*," in *Cotton's Queer Relations: Same-Sex Intimacy and the Literature of the Southern Plantation, 1936–1968* (Charlottesville: University of Virginia Press, 2009), 63–95.

5. William Faulkner, *The Sound and the Fury: The Corrected Text*, ed. Noel Polk (New York: Vintage International, 1984), 78.

6. For a compelling account of Rosa's desire, and its link to structures of telling in the novel, see John T. Matthews, "The Marriage of Speaking and Hearing in *Absalom, Absalom!*," *ELH* 47, no. 3 (Autumn 1980): 575–94. Matthews's account is in many ways congenial to the one I present here. ("*Absalom*, even more explicitly than *The Sound and the Fury*, encourages the reader to understand the desire of a character for the absent body of his or her beloved as analogous to the desire of the storyteller for his subject's representation and for the achievement of natural sense" [583].)

7. Few things risk the appearance of fatuous self-regard more than commentary on one's own style, but one possibly idiosyncratic element of this chapter's

"technique," namely, its structuring around extended quotations, might need some brief explanation. In my view, Faulkner of all writers especially leads one to prefer extended quotation: it is not merely that the syntax often defies parsing when abstracted in shorter segments, but also that the phrases (as one might say of a musical composition) are so long and, as it were, so far from linear. The prose demands a view extended enough to allow disparate (sometimes overlapping) segments to resonate simultaneously. Viewing the prose in larger units does not only allow one to resolve the elements in an overarching syntactical structure; it also allows one *not* to resolve them, to make evident how they operate, unresolved, in a reticulated syntax that creates multiple effects, simultaneous and nonhierarchical. It would perhaps not be entirely without interest to ask what presumptions about critical activity—what mastery, for example, of its object it is supposed to display, or at least what priority it is supposed to assert—are involved in such academic protocols as those dictating discreet quotation, beyond obscuring, in the service of securing expertise, the simple fact that any writer worth reading, when quoted at length, has the power to make nearly any critic look impoverished. To say no more about that, I would also note that, in a chapter about queer time, the opportunity to intimate concerns and temporalities not assimilable to those pursued by the chapter and, to whatever extent, to layer the chapter's own temporal unfolding made the temptation of extended quotation impossible to resist.

8. Jespersen, *Essentials of English Grammar*, 282–84.

9. One thinks in this regard of the description of Judith as the "blank shape" or "empty vessel" through which Henry and Bon consummate their love for each other (Faulkner, *Absalom, Absalom!*, 95).

10. This structure appears in various registers in the text; Shreve's wry jokes typically give humorous versions of the novel's more fraught ponderings of belatedness and cognitive delay: his comment, for example, that Jones's injunction to "*ride single-handed into Washington and shoot Lincoln*" came "*a year or so too late*" (Faulkner, *Absalom, Absalom!*, 150), and his wry question to Quentin about Sutpen ("How got engaged and then stopped yet still had a wife to repudiate later? He said he didn't remember how he got to Haiti, and he didn't remember how he got into the house with the niggers surrounding it. Now are you going to tell me he didn't even remember getting married?" [205]).

11. "From one point of view," Hortense Spillers writes, "fictional narrative inhabits the only spatio-temporal sequence that is reversible." Spillers, "Topographical Topics: Faulknerian Space," *Mississippi Quarterly: The Journal of Southern Cultures* 57, no. 4 (2004): 535–68, 535.

12. See Agamben, "Bartleby," 1–23. I discuss both in greater detail in the introduction above.

13. One possible source for the word *durance* is book 4 of *Paradise Lost*. Satan, captured after he has been found whispering in Eve's ear, responds to Gabriel's

"Why hast thou, *Satan,* broke the bounds prescrib'd / To thy transgressions": "let him surer barr / His Iron Gates, if he intends our stay / In that dark *durance*" (*Paradise Lost,* bk. 4, lines 878–79 and 897–99).

14. On the lingering, atavistic power of "race" in relation to the conjuring power of the name, see Hortense Spillers, "Mama's Baby, Papa's Maybe: An American Grammar Book," *Diacritics: A Review of Contemporary Criticism* 17, no. 2 (1987): 65–81.

15. On this possibility, see also Spillers, "Faulkner Adds Up: Reading *Absalom, Absalom!* and *The Sound and the Fury,*" in *Black, White, and in Color,* 336–375, 360–61.

16. See Spillers, "Faulkner Adds Up," for a discussion of the difficulties of tracking these various markers of speech and temporal simultaneity; these difficulties are part of what makes the experience of the novel, she writes, like going through "a high-powered car wash *without* your car" (340).

17. Eric Sundquist convincingly suggests that we should hear an echo of "passing" in the strange verb "overpassed." See his "*Absalom, Absalom!* and the House Divided," in *Faulkner: The House Divided* (Baltimore: The Johns Hopkins University Press, 1983), 96–130, 121.

18. In *As I Lay Dying*, Addie Bundren speaks of her students' faulting, seemingly meaning either making a mistake or misbehaving: "I would look forward to the times when they faulted, so I could whip them." William Faulkner, *As I Lay Dying: The Corrected Text* (New York: Modern Library, 2000), 170.

19. The movement outward to another scene occurs at several other moments as well. For instance: "And they—Quentin and Shreve—thinking how after the father spoke and before what he said stopped being shock and began to make sense, the son would recall later how he'd seen through the window beyond his father's head the sister and a lover in the garden, pacing slowly, the sister's head bent with listening, . . . it did not matter to them (Quentin and Shreve) anyway" (Faulkner, *Absalom, Absalom!,* 236).

20. William Faulkner, *Light in August: The Corrected Text* (New York: Modern Library, 2002), 119. (I discuss this passage in detail in chapter 10 below.) In this novel, such a temporal lag likewise marks both the experience of particular characters (Joe Christmas, Hightower, Byron Bunch) and the larger structure of the narrative; the rendering of its Christological narrative as both parody and farce, for example, is, among other things, an effect of a temporal scrambling: a Nativity that is not only tonally deflated ("I have come from Alabama: a fur piece. . . . My, my. A body does get around" [3, 507]), but also coincides with the Crucifixion. The temporal shuffling and compression indexes the story's distance from the redemption whose urgency it at the same time brings into focus.

21. "In the disembodied 'mind' narrating the latter passage, Sutpen, in flat, stale, even lame words, expresses himself: '*He must not marry her, Henry. His*

mother's father told me that her mother had been a Spanish woman. I believed him; it was not until after he was born that I found out that his mother was part negro.' If through such calamity and a narrative witness to it of such unparalleled force, one can *think* (anyone, whoever it is here) so vain a thing, then, yes, indeed, the Civil War ended the right way" (Spillers, "Faulkner Adds Up," 367, quoting *Absalom, Absalom!,* 283).

22. My reading needs—it perhaps cannot go without saying—to confront *that* history. Put another way, there is a content to transmission in *Absalom, Absalom!,* which is America's bloody history of "race," and it does not let me off the hook to note that my topic is something else. It largely disappears here, though, because there is not space to take it up, and to take it up briefly would be worse—implying, as it would, that the relation of queer erotics to "race" in the novel were obvious or easily resolved—than not to take it up at all. The questions left suspended in this chapter are taken up in greater detail in chapter 10 below, in my discussion of *Go Down, Moses.* For an important consideration of Haiti in *Absalom, Absalom!,* see John T. Matthews, "Recalling the West Indies: From Yoknapatawpha to Haiti and Back," *American Literary History* 16, no. 2 (2004): 238–62. Among the crucial historical details Matthews mentions: "As a number of readers have noticed, however, someone seems to be confused about Haitian history in *Absalom,* since by 1804, more than 20 years before Sutpen arrived there, Haiti had overthrown French rule and become the first free black republic in the New World. No white French sugar planters remained in Haiti in 1827, and all slaves had been freed" (250). The temporal scrambling is resonant for my reading of the text, and Matthews points to many ways that this error is more interesting when not taken as mere evidence of Faulkner's own faulty grasp of history.

23. On this passage, see also Spillers, "Who Cuts the Border?," 319–35, esp. 331–34.

24. On miscegenation, see Sundquist, "*Absalom, Absalom!* and the House Divided," 96–130. See also Hortense Spillers, "Notes on an Alternative Model—Neither/Nor," in *Black, White, and in Color,* 301–18.

10. "Vanished but Not Gone, Fixed and Held in the Annealing Dust"

1. See, for example, *The Sound and the Fury,* 78.

2. On the transmission of property in the text, see Thadious M. Davis, *Games of Property: Law, Race, Gender, and Faulkner's "Go Down, Moses"* (Durham, N.C.: Duke University Press, 2003).

3. Spillers, "Mama's Baby, Papa's Maybe," 65–81. "The African-American woman, the mother, the daughter, becomes historically the powerful and shadowy evocation of a cultural synthesis long evaporated—the law of the Mother—only and precisely because legal enslavement removed the African-American male not

so much from sight as from *mimetic* view as a partner in the prevailing social fiction of the Father's name, the Father's law" (80).

4. For a very helpful series of genealogies, see Stephen Railton, "*Go Down, Moses*: The McCaslin Family," http://people.virginia.edu/~sfr/FAULKNER/09gdmgen.html.

5. William Faulkner, *Go Down, Moses* (New York: Vintage International, 1990), 3. Unless otherwise noted, all italics are Faulkner's.

6. The condition of the slave mother was "forever entailed on all her remotest posterity." William Goddell, *The American Slave Code and Theory and Practice Shown by Its Statutes, Judicial Decisions, and Illustrative Facts,* 3rd ed. (New York: American and Foreign Anti-Slavery Society, 1853). See Spillers, "Mama's Baby, Papa's Maybe," 79.

7. This is, of course, Spillers's argument in "Mama's Baby, Papa's Maybe," which, although it never mentions queer theory (or queer desire) is the best essay I know of for thinking about queer theory and race.

8. "It is not immediately clear," writes Eric Sundquist, "what relation the ritual of the hunt has to the stories concerned with racial conflict and intimacy in the old and new South" (Sundquist, *Faulkner,* 134.) More generally, Sundquist's reading of the text brings out some of the ways that *Go Down, Moses* comes apart formally and thematically. "The moments of greatest achievement in *Go Down, Moses*," he writes, "depend on the tensions of this paradox—depend, that is, on Faulkner's attempts to translate into terms of ritual remembrance and celebration acts that resist the translation at every point, as well they might" (139); and later: "*Go Down, Moses* writhes and strains under the moral agony of connecting the spilt blood of the hunt to the spilt blood—and, moreover, the violently disseminated blood—of slavery" (148).

9. See, for example, Sedgwick, "Queer and Now," 1–22.

10. My thinking in this paragraph is indebted to John Limon.

11. Nicholas de Villiers pointed out to me (justly) that I too swiftly dismiss "intersectional" analyses of race and sexuality. A detailed consideration of the vital work done on race in queer theory is beyond the scope of this book. See, for example, E. Patrick Johnson and Mae Henderson, eds., *Black Queer Studies: A Critical Anthology* (Durham, N.C.: Duke University Press, 2005).

12. At one point during the hunt for Old Ben, the boy reflects on the unfathomable endurance of Lion: "Then the dog looked at him. It moved its head and looked at him across the trivial uproar of the hounds, out of the yellow eyes as depthless as Boon's, as free as Boon's of meanness or generosity or gentleness or viciousness. They were just cold and sleepy. Then it blinked, and he knew it was not looking at him and never had been, without even bothering to turn its head away" (Faulkner, *Go Down, Moses,* 227–28). What at first looks like a registering of difference—the boy can see that the animal is no more animated by recognizable human feeling than Boon is—is then deprived even of that as it becomes clear that,

for the dog, too, the boy was not there. As evocative as that blank, unseeing gaze is (and it must surely call to mind the possibility that Ike's epiphanies at the end of "The Bear" could also be called into question, the possibility that they, too, might be unwarranted projections), it is also striking that we are given this two-phase rhythm: "Then the dog looked at him. . . . Then it blinked, and he knew it was not looking at him and never had been." Among other things, this moment—in just one of the text's many registers, the question of discovering human meaning in animal life—seems to allegorize a movement toward and away from a unification of disparate registers or "worlds."

13. Spillers reads this scene in relation to the imagined slave revolt later in the novel ("both episodes share their common source in a weave of related textures— from some secret and invisible posture, a putative subject of an interior generates unspecified, unspecifiable power that Sutpen can only guess"); both scenes, in multivalent ways, are about the equivocal positing of interiors; see Spillers, "Who Cuts the Border?, 319–35, esp. 327–34, quotation 332.

14. William Faulkner, *Intruder in the Dust* (London: Vintage Books, 1996), 15.

15. In *Intruder in the Dust,* this structure appears in repeated moments that suggest that Chick will remember something (or that something unspecified nags at his attention)—moments that precede, often by several pages, the memory or the realization evoked.

16. William Faulkner, *Light in August,* 119.

17. For a concise explanation of these relations (the most important revelations occur in "The Bear" and in "Delta Autumn"), see Stephen Railton's genealogies, cited in note 4 above. Briefly, Ike discovers in "The Bear" that Tomey's Turl is the daughter of Tomey and Lucius Quintus Carothers McCaslin (discovers that Lucius [Ike's grandfather] raped his own daughter). In "Delta Autumn," he finds that the unnamed woman who visits the camp with an infant fathered by Roth Edmonds is the granddaughter of Lucas Beauchamp's brother James (aka "Tennie's Jim"). (Lucas and James are sons of Tomey's Turl and Tennie Beauchamp, whose marriage is one of the unspecified results of the poker game in "Was.") This means, Railton writes, that, like Lucius's rape of Tomey, "her relationship with Roth is technically both incest and miscegenation."

18. See *The Sound and the Fury,* 86–88. Contemplating the different experience of race in the North and the South, Quentin remembers an encounter with a black man who, sitting on a mule, waited for the train Quentin was riding to move. Among other complications presented by this passage is the difficulty of distinguishing his nostalgia for more explicitly marked racial hierarchies from the homesickness of missing particular people: "I didn't know that I really had missed Roskus and Dilsey and them until that morning in Virginia" (86).

19. For a not unrelated argument, see Love, *Feeling Backward.*

20. For another version of this, see Faulkner's "That Evening Sun": "White man

can come in my house, but I cant stop him. When white man want to come in my house, I aint got no house." "That Evening Sun," in *Collected Stories of William Faulkner* (New York: Vintage International, 1995), 292. The assimilation of women to the status of property (and therefore to being dispropriable) has terrible costs for women, as that story makes clear. On the relation between homophobia and this understanding of racism, see Lee Edelman, "The Part for the (W)hole: Baldwin and the Fantasmatics of Race," in *Homographesis*, 42–78.

21. John Limon points out some of the ways naming goes awry in the text, which is part of his larger reading of the many ways communities fail to cohere in (and around) the text. Read as a rite of initiation, for instance, the hunt produces not a name but a nickname. Limon, "The Integration of Faulkner's *Go Down, Moses*," *Critical Inquiry* 12, no. 3 (Winter 1986): 422–38.

22. "What concerns the libido," Deleuze writes, "what the libido invests, presents itself with an indefinite article, or rather is presented by the indefinite article: *an* animal as the qualification of a becoming or the specification of a trajectory (*a* horse, *a* chicken); a body or an organ as the power to affect and to be affected (*a* stomach, *some* eyes . . .); and even the characters that obstruct a pathway and inhibit affects, or on the contrary that further them (*a* father, *some* people . . .). Children express themselves in this manner—a father, a body, a horse. These indefinites often seem to result from a lack of determination due to the defenses of consciousness. For psychoanalysis, it is always a question of *my* father, *me, my* body. [. . .] Yet the indefinite lacks nothing; above all, it does not lack determination. It is the determination of a becoming, its characteristic power, the power of an impersonal that is not a generality but a singularity at its highest point. [. . .] Art also attains this celestial state that no longer retains anything of the personal or rational. It its own way, art says what children say" (Deleuze, "What Children Say," in *Essays Critical and Clinical*, 65; brackets indicate my ellipses; the rest are in the original).

23. See, for example, Deleuze, "Bartleby," 68–90, esp. 84–88.

24. Gilles Deleuze, "Immanence: A Life," in *Pure Immanence: Essays on a Life*, trans. Anne Boyman (New York: Zone Books, 2001), 30, 28, 29. "We will say of pure immanence that it is A LIFE, and nothing else. It is not immanence to life, but the immanent that is in nothing is itself a life. A life is the immanence of immanence, absolute immanence: it is complete power, complete bliss" (27).

25. "What to Read Now. And Why," *Newsweek*, June 27, 2009, http://www.Newsweek.com/ID/204300.

26. Sundquist makes a related point: "What Ike's repudiation most reveals is that it is incapable of translating into a realm of timelessness events that have everywhere the temporally visible and tragic actuality that the text of the ledgers codifies. . . . Both the renunciation of his patrimony and the timeless beauty of the remembered wilderness sacrifice fail to arrest the long agony of racial conflict and,

when it occurs once again more than a century later, the horror of miscegenation" (Sundquist, *Faulkner,* 138–39).

27. See also Ike's epiphany at the end of "The Bear" (whose resolution I will discuss in greater detail): "He only paused, quitting the knoll which was no abode of the dead because there was no death, not Lion and not Sam: not held fast in earth but free in earth and not in earth but of earth" (313).

28. A stereopticon, according to the *Oxford English Dictionary*, is "a double magic lantern arranged to combine two images of the same object or scene upon a screen simultaneously, so as to produce the appearance of solidity; also used to cause the image of one object or scene to pass gradually into that of another with a dissolving effect." Faulkner's use seems to be the inverse: not two views of the same scene, but two scenes made into one view; also striking is his use of *instantaneous* to describe a space. Perhaps not unrelated is the description of Lucas Beauchamp's face as a "composite": "It was not at all the face of their grandfather, Carothers McCaslin. It was the face of the generation which had just preceded them: the composite tintype face of ten thousand undefeated Confederate soldiers almost indistinguishably caricatured, composed, cold, colder than his, more ruthless than his, with more bottom than he had" (Faulkner, "The Fire and the Hearth," 104–5). For an illuminating reading of the stereopticon (in a compelling account, more generally, of race in the text), see also John T. Matthews, "Touching Race in *Go Down, Moses,*" in *New Essays on "Go Down, Moses,"* ed. Linda Wagner-Martin (Cambridge: Cambridge University Press, 1996), 21–47, esp. 26–28.

29. For a reading of the final story in the text (in relation to such questions of coherence)—"Go Down, Moses," which I do not discuss in this chapter—see Matthews, "Touching Race in *Go Down, Moses.*"

30. I was led to think about the relation of these two passages to my larger argument by conversations with Gregory Kenny and Justin Howell.

31. For another reading of Keats's poem (one that brings out the temporal paradoxes of both texts and the importance a foreclosed grief ("yet, do not grieve," he points out, is a line Cass does not read), see Sundquist, *Faulkner,* 136–39. I was led to think about the role of Keats's poem in the text by Barbara Johnson's "Muteness Envy," in *The Feminist Difference* (Cambridge, Mass.: Harvard University Press, 1998), 129–53.

32. John Keats, "Ode on a Grecian Urn," in *John Keats: Selected Poems and Letters,* ed. Douglas Bush (Boston: Houghton Mifflin, 1959), 207–8.

33. The story is in many ways about its illegibility. See, among other examples, Limon's reading of the grave "marked off . . . by shards of pottery and broken bottles and old brick and other objects insignificant to sight but actually of a profound meaning and fatal to touch, which no white man could have read" (Faulkner, *Go Down, Moses,* 131–32; quoted in Limon, "The Integration of Faulkner's *Go Down, Moses,*" 434).

34. Limon phrases the structure in terms of interpretive communities: "But in 'Pantaloon in Black,' Faulkner has formed a text in the image of a Southern Negro and invited us to join an interpretive community on the model of Yoknapatawpha County. Insofar as we take up that invitation, we fail to understand his story; insofar as we reject it, we also fail to understand his story. The paradox is the result of our being forced to join a community which does not cohere; to the degree that that community fails to cohere, so does our reading" (Limon, "The Integration of Faulkner's *Go Down, Moses,*" 423).

35. One effect of this is to make it in a sense impossible not to repeat the deputy's presumption: as Limon writes, "We are no better than the Southerners who cannot understand Rider. It is not difficult to read 'Pantaloon in Black'—it is impossible. Or, rather, it is impossible to read it in Rider's terms, which means that to trust our own interpretive community is to repeat the deputy's stupidity" (Limon, "The Integration of Faulkner's *Go Down, Moses,*" 436).

36. One perhaps also thinks of Keats's epitaph: "Here lies one whose name was writ in water," an allusion, most immediately, to Beaumont and Fletcher, but no doubt also to Plato's *Phaedrus*: "And then when he is in earnest he will not take a pen and write in water or sow his seed in the black fluid called ink, to produce discourses which cannot defend themselves viva voce or give any adequate account of the truth." Plato, *Phaedrus and the Seventh and Eighth Letters,* trans. Walter Hamilton (New York: Penguin Books, 1973), 98–99 [276 in the Greek text]).

Index

252–53, 260; narrative temporality
of, 242–47, 249, 310n27
Epistola: In Carcere et Vinculis (Wilde).
See *De Profundis*
erastés/erómenos, 14, 16, 267n31,
269n34
eros, 2, 17, 18, 278n16; male, 105;
realization and, 19–20, 27; reading
and, 46, 174
Eros the Bittersweet (Carson), 16–19,
46, 72, 270n41, 271n46, 287n11
eternity, 130; of animal life, 248,
250; narrative unfolding of, 238,
242–44, 251
Euripides, 4, 83, 86, 88, 89
Exodus, 90, 289–90n13

face: as aspect, 99–100; erotic legibility
of, 126, 146–47, 151, 178, 188, 190,
198–99, 214, 227, 300n13, 301n16,
310n28; as mask or prosopopoeia,
159–73; recognition of, 125, 138
fascination, 106; erotics of, 121, 145–46,
153; of literary texts, 109–10, 116,
118–19
father(s): belatedness and, 227; community of, 213, 214; curse of, 228;
death of, 49, 59; dispossession and,
241, 242; future with, 63; names
and, 212, 214; overlapping narrative
of, 201; sons and, 20–22; temporality and, 229, 235. See also paternity
Faulkner, William, 4, 8–9, 10, 22,
26, 31, 177, 200, 211, 212, 214–15,
219–60, 265n18, 303nn3–4,
303–4n7, 304n10, 306n22, 310n28.
See also *Absalom, Absalom!*; *Go
Down, Moses*; *Intruder in the Dust*;
Light in August; *Mansion, The*;
Sound and the Fury, The; "That
Evening Sun"; *Town, The*

fault, 197–99; as mistake or misbehav-
ior, 205n18
Fifth Hammer, The (Heller-Roazen),
267–68n33
"Figure in the Carpet, The" (James),
145
finitude, 10, 12, 45
Fix, Stephen, 265nn22–23
focalization. See perspective
forgetfulness: absorption and, 3,
49–54, 57–58, 60–61, 65, 281n4n5,
284n22; erotics of, 113; human
knowledge and, 45–48, 82, 105,
264–65n17; legibility of face and,
170; reader and, 198; realization
and, 135–36; prosopopoeia and, 161;
"unforgettable voice," 69
formalization, 250–55. See also *Bildung*; realization/realize
forms (Plato), 44
Forms of Being (Bersani), 16
fortune, 208, 298–99n3
Foucault, Michel, 15–16, 267nn33–34,
271n50
fragmentation, 1, 3, 17, 31, 69–81,
286n6
freedom, 50, 64, 284n22, 306n22;
internal and external life, 232, 239,
242–45, 310n27
free indirect style, 25, 149, 158–60,
170–73, 195, 250, 299n3; quasi-free-
indirect style, 198
Freud, Sigmund, 21, 99, 271n51, 277n5
friendship (as translation of *philia*),
268n33
futurity (Edelman), 6–7

Gagnier, Regina, 296–97n15
Gaston de Latour (Pater), 91
gay reading, 115, 119, 137
gender, 5; celebration of, 117; question

KEVIN OHI is professor of English at Boston College. He is the author of *Innocence and Rapture: The Erotic Child in Pater, Wilde, James, and Nabokov* and *Henry James and the Queerness of Style* (Minnesota, 2011).